To
Frank

12/16/17

"Nostalgic Blood"

By

J.Crockett

Full Definition of NOSTALGIA

1
: the state of being homesick : homesickness
2
: a wistful or excessively sentimental yearning for return to or of some past period or irrecoverable condition; ALSO : something that evokes nostalgia

---

nostalgic

adjective sentimental, longing, emotional, homesick, wistful, maudlin, regretful I got nostalgic the other night and dug out my old photos.

Blood in this novel represent family

Bloodline definition

Your *bloodline* is your heritage or ancestry. In other words, your *bloodline* includes your parents, grandparents, great-grandparents, and so on.

The Old English root word *blod*, means "blood." By the 13th century, *blood* also meant "family" or "heritage."

Market Monster Publishing, LLC.
Email: marketmonsterpublishing@gmail.com

Ordering Information:
Quantity sales. Special discounts are available on quantity purchases by corporations, associations, and others. For details, contact the publisher at the address above.
Orders by U.S. trade bookstores and wholesalers. Please contact Big Distribution: Tel: 773-563-3947

Acknowledgements

- No one walks alone on the journey of life. Just where do you start to thank those that joined you, walked beside you, and helped you along the way continuously urged me to write a book, to put my thoughts down on over the years, those that I have met and worked with have paper, and to share my insights together with the secrets to my continual, positive approach to life and all that life throws at us. So at last, here it is. So, perhaps this book and its pages will be seen as "thanks" to the tens of thousands of you who have helped make my life what is today. Much of what I have learned over the years will be identified as you read this book. Some of your names had to be changed, but I am sure that you guys would understand. Many of you have inspired me and, subconsciously contributed a tremendous amount to the content of this book. A little bit of each of them will be found here weaving in and out of the pages – in loving memory for those who did not make it out alive. I also have to thank Roseanne Beam for being supportive, motivating and pushed me beyond description, which I can't say. I also need to thank my mom Annie Copeland, wonderful woman who kept me under her wing; any time my mind strayed I thought about how she would feel. My step dad Andy Copeland for being a guide in my life. My dad, Joseph Crockett thank you for being so honest about life in general. You saved me in many ways. Even though you don't think my book will do well, time will tell.

- It's strange to think that I have been working on this book for 20 years. I lost it three times, recovered it somehow through the grace of the higher power; I believe it was meant for me to complete this book and share my story with the world. Valencia Copeland, I can't thank you enough for everything you have done. Vivian Copeland, keep inventing because it's worth it. I also want to thank all of you who took the time out of your day to help with the book cover survey, thanks guys. That helped me.

- I want to thank Custom Plastic and signs, Chris Cuevas for being so patient with me with designing the book cover. I know I can be picky, if not for your expertise, who knows what the book cover would look like. For any printing of signs, plastic moldings, Chris can do it. Call him 209 933 9711

- Lyrell McGee, thanks for everything you did, just did not have enough time, when you ready to publish, I will be there for you.

- Last but not least, I want to thank all of the Stocktonians who took a chance and bought my book. Some of you gave me whatever you had as a donation to help me climb to the level of publishing. It was you, the residents of Stockton, Ca that helped me get into the stores worldwide. Thank you so much. Look forwarded to more great books from me.

North Korea (listen), officially the**Democratic People's Republic of Korea(DPRK**; Chosŏn'gŭl: 조선민주주의인민공화국;hancha: 朝鮮民主主義人民共和國;MR: *Chosŏn Minjujuŭi Inmin Konghwaguk*), is a country in East Asia, in the northern part of the Korean Peninsula. The name *Korea* is derived from the Kingdom of Goryeo, also spelled as *Koryŏ*. The capital and largest city is Pyongyang. North Korea shares a land border with China to the north and north-west, along the Amnok (Yalu) and Tumen rivers, and a small section of the Tumen River also forms a border with Russia to the north-east.[8] The Korean Demilitarized Zone marks the *de facto* boundary between North Korea and South Korea. The legitimacy of this border is not accepted by either side, as both states claim to be the legitimate government of the entire peninsula.

The Empire of Japan annexed Korea in 1910. After the Japanese surrender at the end ofWorld War II in 1945, Korea was divided into two zones by the United States and the Soviet Union, with the north occupied by the Sovietsand the south by the Americans. Negotiations on reunification failed, and in 1948 two separate governments were formed: the Democratic People's Republic of Korea in the north, and the Republic of Korea in the south. These conflicting claims of sovereignty led to the Korean War (1950–53). Although theKorean Armistice Agreement brought about a ceasefire, no official peace treaty was ever signed.[9] Both states were accepted into theUnited Nations in 1991.[10]

The DPRK officially describes itself as a self-reliant socialist state and holds elections.[11]Internationally, however, it is considered atotalitarian dictatorship. Various outlets have called it Stalinist,[20][21][22] particularly noting the elaborate cult of personality around Kim Il-sung and his family. International organizations have also assessed human rights violations in North Korea as belonging to a category of their own, with no parallel in the contemporary world.[23][24][25] TheWorkers' Party of Korea, led by a member of the ruling family,[22] holds power in the state and leads the Democratic Front for the Reunification of the Fatherland of which all political officers are required to be a member.[26]

Over time North Korea has gradually distanced itself from the world communistmovement. *Juche*, an ideology of national self-reliance, was introduced into the constitution as a "creative application ofMarxism–Leninism" in 1972.[27][28] Themeans of production are owned by the state through state-run enterprises andcollectivized farms. Most services such as healthcare, education, housing and food production are subsidized or state-funded.[29]In the late 1990s, North Korea suffered from a famine that resulted in the deaths of hundreds of thousands of civilians; the country continues to struggle with food production.[30]

North Korea follows *Songun,* or "military-first" policy.[31] It is the world's most militarizedsociety, with a total of 9,495,000 active,reserve, and paramilitarypersonnel[*citation needed*]. Its active duty army of 1.21 million is the fourth largest in the world, after China, the U.S., and India.[32] It also possesses nuclear weapons.[33][34]

Nostalgic Blood takes place during the Kim Jong Il dictatorship, from biography.com is his life story.

Kim Jong Il's dominating personality and complete concentration of power has come to define the country North Korea. Born in either 1941 or 1942, much of Kim Jong Il's persona is based on a cult of personality, meaning that legend and official North Korean government accounts describe his life, character, and actions in ways that promote and legitimize his leadership, including his birth. Over the years, Kim's dominating personality and complete concentration of power has come to define the country North Korea.

Early Life

Born February 16, 1941, though official accounts place birth a year later. Some mystery surrounds when and where Kim Jong Il was born. Official North Korean biographies state that his birth occurred on February 16, 1942, in a secret camp on Mount Paekdu along the Chinese border, in Samjiyon County, Ryanggang Province, in the Democratic People's Republic of Korea (North Korea). Other reports indicate he was born a year later in Vyatskoye in the former Soviet Union.

During World War II, his father commanded the 1st Battalion of the Soviet 88th Brigade, composed of Chinese and Korean exiles battling the Japanese Army. Kim Jong Il's mother was Kim Jong Suk, his father's first wife. Official accounts indicate that Kim Jong Il comes from a family of nationalists who actively resisted imperialism from the Japanese in the early 20th century.

His official government biography claims Kim Jong Il completed his general education between September 1950 and August 1960 in Pyongyang, the current capital city of North Korea. But scholars point out that the first few years of this period were during the Korean War and contend his early education took place in the People's Republic of China, where it was safer to live. Official accounts claim that throughout his schooling, Kim was involved in politics. While attending the Namsan Higher Middle School in Pyongyang, he was active in the Children's Union—a youth organization that promotes the concept of Juche, or the spirit of self-reliance—and the Democratic Youth League (DYL), taking part in the study of Marxist political theory. During his youth, Kim Jong Il showed an interest in a wide range of subjects including agriculture, music, and mechanics. In high school, he took classes in automotive repair and participated in trips to farms and factories. Official accounts of his early schooling also point out his leadership capabilities: as vice chairman of his school's DYL branch, he encouraged younger classmates to pursue greater ideological education and organized academic competitions and seminars as well as field trips.

Kim Jong Il graduated from Namsan Higher Middle School in 1960 and enrolled the same year in Kim Il Sung University. He majored in Marxist political economy and minored in philosophy and military science. While at the university, Kim trained as an apprentice in a textile machine factory and took classes in building TV broadcast equipment. During this time, he also accompanied his father on tours of field guidance in several of North Korea's provinces.

Rise to Power

Kim Jong Il joined the Workers' Party, the official ruling party of North Korea, in July 1961. Most political experts believe the party follows the traditions of Stalinist politics even though North Korea began distancing itself from Soviet domination in 1956. The Workers' Party claims to have its own ideology, steeped in the philosophy of Juche. However, in the late 1960s, the party instituted a policy of "burning loyalty" to the "Great Leader" (Kim Il Sung). This practice of personality cult is reminiscent of Stalinist Russia but was taken to new heights with Kim Il Sung and would continue with Kim Jong Il.

Soon after his 1964 graduation from the university, Kim Jong Il began his rise through the ranks of the Korean Workers' Party. The 1960s were a time of high tension between many Communist countries. China and the Soviet Union were clashing over ideological differences that resulted in several border skirmishes, Soviet satellite nations in Eastern Europe were simmering with dissention, and North Korea was pulling away from both Soviet and Chinese influence. Within North Korea, internal forces were attempting to revise the party's revolutionary message. Kim Jong Il was appointed to the Workers' Party Central Committee to lead the offensive against the revisionists and ensure the party did not deviate from the ideological line set by his father. He also led efforts to expose dissidents and deviant policies to ensure strict enforcement of the party's ideological system. In addition, he took on major military reform to strengthen the party's control of the military and expelled disloyal officers.

Kim Jong Il oversaw the Propaganda and Agitation department, the government agency responsible for media control and censorship. Kim gave firm instructions that the party's monolithic ideological message be communicated constantly by writers, artists, and officials in the media. According to official accounts, he revolutionized Korean fine arts by encouraging the production of new works in new media. This included the art of film and cinema. Mixing history, political ideology, and movie-making, Kim encouraged the production of several epic films, which glorified works written by his father. His official biography claims that Kim Jong Il has composed six operas and enjoys staging elaborate musicals. Kim is reported to be an avid film buff who owns more than 20,000 movies, including the entire series of James Bond films, for his personal enjoyment.

Kim Il Sung began preparing his son to lead North Korea in the early 1970s. Between 1971 and 1980, Kim Jong Il was appointed to increasingly important positions in the Korean Workers' Party. During this time, he instituted policies to bring party officials closer to the people by forcing bureaucrats to work among subordinates for one month a year. He launched the Three-Revolution Team Movement, in which teams of political, technical, and scientific technicians traveled around the country to provide training. He was also involved in economic planning to develop certain sectors of the economy.

By the 1980s, preparations were being made for Kim to succeed his father as the leader of North Korea. At this time, the government began building a personality cult around Kim Jong Il patterned after that of his father. Just as Kim Il Sung was known as the "Great Leader," Kim Jong Il was hailed in the North Korean media as the "fearless leader" and "the great successor to the revolutionary cause." His portraits appeared in public buildings along with his father's. He also initiated a series of drop-in inspections of businesses, factories, and government offices. At the Sixth Party Congress in 1980, Kim Jong Il was given senior posts in the Politburo (the policy committee of the Korean Workers' Party), the Military Commission, and the Secretariat (the executive department charged with carrying out policy). Thus, Kim was positioned to control all aspects of the government.

The one area of leadership in which Kim Jong Il might have had a perceived weakness was the military. The army was the foundation of power in North Korea, and Kim had no military service experience. With the assistance of allies in the military, Kim was able to gain acceptance by the army officials as the next leader of North Korea. By 1991, he was designated as the supreme commander of the Korean People's Army, thus giving him the tool he needed to maintain complete control of the government once he took power.

Following the death of Kim Il Sung in July 1994, Kim Jong Il took total control of the country. This transition of power from father to son had never been seen before in a communist regime. In deference to his father, the office of president was abolished, and Kim Jong Il took the titles of general secretary of the Workers' Party and chairman of the National Defense Commission, which was declared the highest office of the state.

Foreign Aid and Nuclear Testing

It is important to understand that much of Kim Jong Il's persona is based on a cult of personality, meaning that legend and official North Korean government accounts describe his life, character, and actions in ways that promote and legitimize his leadership. Examples include his family's nationalist revolutionary roots and claims that his birth was foretold by a swallow, the appearance of a double rainbow over Mount Paekdu, and a new star in the heavens. He is known to personally manage the country's affairs and sets operational guidelines for individual industries. He is said to be arrogant and self-centered in policy decisions, openly rejecting criticism or opinions that differ from his. He is suspicious of nearly all of those who surround him and volatile in his emotions. There are many stories of his eccentricities, his playboy lifestyle, the lifts in his shoes and pompadour hairstyle that make him appear taller, and his fear of flying. Some stories can be verified while others are most likely exaggerated, possibly circulated by foreign operatives from hostile countries.

In the 1990s, North Korea went through a series of devastating and debilitating economic episodes. With the collapse of the Soviet Union in 1991, North Korea lost its main trading partner. Strained relations with China following China's normalization with South Korea in 1992 further limited North Korea's trade options. Record-breaking floods in 1995 and 1996 followed by drought in 1997 crippled North Korea's food production. With only 18 percent of its land suitable for farming in the best of times, North Korea began experiencing a devastating famine. Worried about his position in power, Kim Jong Il instituted the Military First policy, which prioritized national resources to the military. Thus, the military would be pacified and remain in his control. Kim could defend himself from threats domestic and foreign, while economic conditions worsened. The policy did produce some economic growth and along with some socialist-type market practices—characterized as a "flirtation with capitalism"—North Korea has been able to remain operational despite being heavily dependent on foreign aid for food.

In 1994, the Clinton administration and North Korea agreed to a framework designed to freeze and eventually dismantle North Korea's nuclear weapons program. In exchange, the United States would provide assistance in producing two power-generating nuclear reactors and supplying fuel oil and other economic aid. In 2000, the presidents of North Korea and South Korea met for diplomatic talks and agreed to promote reconciliation and economic cooperation between the two countries. The agreement allowed families from both countries to reunite and signaled a move toward increased trade and investment. For a time, it appeared that North Korea was reentering the international community.

Then in 2002, U.S. intelligence agencies suspected North Korea was enriching uranium or building the facilities to do so, presumably for making nuclear weapons. In his 2002 State of the Union address, President George W. Bush identified North Korea as one of the countries in the "axis of evil" (along with Iraq and Iran). The Bush administration soon revoked the 1994 treaty designed to eliminate North Korea's nuclear weapons program. Finally, in 2003, Kim Jong Il's government admitted to having produced nuclear weapons for security purposes, citing tensions with President Bush. Late in 2003, the Central Intelligence Agency issued a report that North Korea possessed one and possibly two nuclear bombs. The Chinese government stepped in to try to mediate a settlement, but President Bush refused to meet with Kim Jong Il one-on-one and instead insisted on multilateral negotiations. China was able to gather Russia, Japan, South Korea, and the United States for negotiations with North Korea. Talks were held in 2003, 2004, and twice in 2005. All through the meetings, the Bush administration demanded North Korea eliminate its nuclear weapons program. It adamantly maintained any normalcy of relations between North Korea and the United States would come about only if North Korea changed its human rights policies, eliminated all chemical and biological weapons programs, and ended missile technology proliferation. North Korea continually rejected the proposal. In 2006, North Korea's Central News Agency announced North Korea had successfully conducted an underground nuclear bomb test.

Failing Health

There have been many reports and claims regarding Kim Jong Il's health and physical condition. In August 2008, a Japanese publication claimed Kim had died in 2003 and had been replaced with a stand-in for public appearances. It was also noted that Kim hadn't made a public appearance for the Olympic torch ceremony in Pyongyang in April 2008. After Kim failed to show up for a military parade celebrating North Korea's 60th anniversary, U.S. intelligence agencies believed Kim to be gravely ill after possibly suffering a stroke. During the fall of 2008, numerous news sources gave conflicting reports on his condition. The North Korean news agency reported Kim participated in national elections in March 2009 and was unanimously elected to a seat in the Supreme People's Assembly, the North Korean parliament. The assembly will vote later to confirm him as chairman of the National Defense Commission. In the report, it was said Kim cast his ballot at the Kim Il Sung University and later toured the facility and talked to a small group of people.

Kim's health was watched closely by other countries because of his volatile nature, the country's possession of nuclear weapons, and its precarious economic condition. Kim also had no apparent successors to his regime, as did his father. His three sons spent most of their lives outside the country and none seemed to be in the favor of the "Dear Leader" to ascend to the top spot. Many international experts believed that when Kim died, there would be mayhem because there seemed to be no apparent method for a transfer of power. But due to the North Korean government's predilection for secrecy, this was too hard to know.

In 2009, however, news reports revealed that Kim planned to name his son, Kim Jong Un as his successor. Very little was known about Kim's heir apparent; until 2010, only one officially confirmed photo of Jong Un existed, and not even his official birthdate had been revealed. The twenty-something was officially confirmed in September 2010.

Kim Jon-Il died December 17, 2011, of a heart attack while traveling on a train. Media reports say the leader was on a work trip for official duties. Upon news of The Dear Leader's death, North Koreans marched on the capital, weeping and mourning.

Kim is said to be survived by three wives, three sons and three daughters. Other reports claim he has fathered 70 children, most of whom are housed in villas throughout North Korea.

His son, Kim Jong Un, is reported to take up leadership, and the military pledged to support Jong Un's succession.

26 Weird and Bizarre Facts about North Korea that reveal the horrifying truth about life there

North Korea remains among the world's most repressive countries. Under the Kim family's rule, basic freedoms and access to needs have been severely restricted and continue to get frighteningly worse. Akin to Hitler's Germany, North Korea operates secret prison camps where people are violently tortured, abused and forced into hard labour. There is no religious freedom, dissent is silenced through nefarious means and society continues to break down. North Korea shuns the idea of collective co-operation to help itself and others, and may just be a literal hell on earth, isolated as it is from the rest of the world. We bring you 26 weird and bizarre facts about North Korea that will make you thankful that you don't live there.

1.North Korea follows a " three generations of punishment" rule, meaning that if one person violated the law or sent to prison, their children, parents AND grandparents are sent to work with them.

Anyone found guilty of committing a crime (which could be as little as trying to escape North Korea), is sent to the Kaechon internment camp along with their entire family. The subsequent two generations would be born *in* the camp and must also live their entire lives in servitude and die there.

2. In the 1990' s, it was made compulsory for all teachers in North Korea to learn how to play the accordion.

The accordion was often called the 'people's instrument' since it was easy to carry along anywhere. There would be accompanied singing to tunes such as 'We Have Nothing to Envy in the World,' which was a rehash of 'Twinkle, Twinkle Little Star'.

3. A fake propaganda village called Kijong-dong was built in the 1950's after the Korean war to put up the front of a peaceful, prosperous place and to encourage people from the South to defect.

In the last 60 years, over 23,000 North Koreans have defected to South Korea whereas only two South Koreans have gone to the North. According to the North Korean government's official story, Kijong-dong is a collection of multistory buildings that house 200 families who spend their days happily engaging in normal, day-to-day activities. In reality, the buildings' windows have no glasses in them and the electric lights (a luxury that is unheard of to rural North Koreans) are operated on an automatic timer. The only people in sight are maintenance workers who sweep the roads once in a while to give the impression of ongoing activity.

4. Kim Jong-il kidnapped prolific South Korean director Shin Sang-ok and forced him to remake famous Hollywood films in propaganda style.

The kidnap plot was masterminded by Kim Jong-il who was in charge of North Korean film industry before he took up office as the country's leader. He had Shing Sang-ok and the actress Choi Eun-hee kidnapped and the both were kept separate from each other in prison for five years until the former relented. Kim Jong-il's aim was to compel them to create movies that would wow the world. They worked together and produced a series of films, the most notable one being *Pulgasari*, a socialist, propaganda-fueled version of Hollywood's *Godzilla*.

5. North Korea's most popular attraction is visiting Kim Jong-il's preserved body.

The North Korean dictator' s embalmed body rests in a state mausoleum and is open for visitation even to foreign tourists. The local guides have a comprehensive knowledge of Kim' s life and eagerly point out details about his great achievements and godlike abilities.

6. Elections are held every 5 years in North Korea, but only one name appears on the ballot list. If a voter wishes to choose someone else, they can do so by crossing the name out, but without any anonymity and privacy.

The candidate has a near-100% turnout and the seats are essentially uncompetitive as all of them are chosen and won by the Democratic Front for the Reunification of the Fatherland. Because of this, North Korean elections are termed as "show elections" since they only double as unofficial censuses.

7. Students in North Korea are required to pay for chairs they sit on, the desks they use and the heating fuel during winters.

Shockingly, some students are even made to work producing goods for the government. Parents often bribe the teachers to exempt their kids from this type of hard labour or just don't send them to school, even though it's an act that violates official policy.

8. Human faeces is used instead of fertiliser in North Korea, due to the severe lack of resources. The supply shortage is so extreme that the citizens are FORCED to provide it.

North Korea has zero to none amounts of chemical fertiliser, so the government ordered every person to produce hundreds of kilogrammes of faeces. The faeces is usually mixed with straw and used as a replacement, but the excrement is harder to procure than expected. Cases of theft of squat toilets have been reported, and people have installed locks on their lavatories to prevent this.

9. Kim Jong-un was once caught with a bondage magazine during his school days in Switzerland.

He attended the expensive Liebefeld School near Berne and according to his classmates, was much more interested in football and computer games than his lessons. Also a big fan of Michael Jordan, Kim Jong-un was a good basketball player and was once caught with a bondage magazine in his school bag.

10. It is the year 105 in North Korea, not 2016 because the country marks years from the birth of Kim Il-sung, not Jesus.

North Korea uses the *Juche* calendar, which was introduced in 1997 and is based on Kim Il-sung's date of birth: 15 April 1912. The year 1912 is used as *Juche 1* and there is no *Juche 0*. However, the calendar does maintain the Gregorian calendar's traditional months and the number of days in a month.

11. Distribution, possession and consumption of cannabis is legal in North Korea, and in fact, is recommended as a healthier alternative to tobacco.

According to Sokeel Park, the director of research and strategy at Liberty In North Korea, cannabis grows wildly in North Korea is even sold abroad by government agencies to earn foreign currency. Marijuana is also as good as legal since there is no stigma attached to it and neither is it fetishized as much as it is in the west.

12. In North Korea, the Internet is limited to a very small circle of the elite (only 1,579 IP addresses exist for a population of 25 million). They also have their own operating system called Red Star and the content is pre-filtered by the state.

Red Star is based on Linux and runs a state-approved search engine. Chats, emails, and forum boards are regularly monitored and Internet access in general is only permitted with special authorization and primarily used for government purposes or by foreigners.

13. North Korea enlists around 2000 attractive women as part of a ' Pleasure Squad' who provide entertainment and sexual services for top officials.

The existence of Kim Jong-il's harems has been known to the South Korean intelligence community. According to the account of a Pleasure Squad defector Mi Hyang, groups of young, attractive women were enlisted regularly to provide entertainment and sexual services to top-level government officials.

14. Border relations between North and South Korea are so tense that when soldiers from the South open the door to the North in the Demilitarized Zone, they hold hands to avoid being physically pulled into the other side.

If that doesn't sound crazy enough, here's something. In 2014, South Korean Christians put up a Christmas tree visible from the North Korean Border. North Korea responded by calling it a "tool for psychological warfare" and threatened to bomb it. Bizarrely, North Korea also uses a fax machine to send threats to South Korea.

15. The North Korean regime has long enforced strict rules on styling one's hair; most of the barber shops in Pyongyang advertise photos of government-sanctioned haircuts.

Since Kim Jong-un took power in 2011, the rules have been relaxed a little. It is still preferred that men and women stick to conservative haircuts. Older women can only wear their hair short, whereas the young ones are allowed to sport loose locks, albeit in a neat and cropped fashion. Long hairstyles are generally frowned upon, especially for men.

16. There are an estimated 34,000 statues of Kim Il Sung in North Korea – one for every 3.5 km, or one for every 750 people. All North Koreans are also required to wear a badge featuring his face as a mark of their loyalty to the founder of the nation.

Wearing the badge on their lapels is a daily ritual for everyone and in a city where people rarely carry expensive or valuable items and credit cards, they are highly prized by pickpockets and thieves. So much so, that each badge can be exchanged on the black market for several hundred NKW.

17. Public transportation connecting the main towns is nearly non-existent as citizens need permits to go from one place to another even within the country. Because of this, the streets in North Korea are so empty that children use them as playgrounds and soldiers can be seen hitchhiking on the highways.

In addition to the massive public transport problem, freedom of movement in North Korea is also extremely limited and citizens are rarely allowed to move around freely inside their own country. Cars are strange, foreign things to children and old people that move around on the deserted streets, and often put their lives in danger while crossing the road without looking for oncoming vehicles.

18. A night image of the Korean Peninsula taken by NASA illustrates the sheer isolation and underlying electricity problems in North Korea. Compared to its neighbours South Korea and China, it is completely dark.

Since the defunct Soviet Union stopped supplying power to North Korea in the early 1990's, the country has become entirely energy-bankrupt. Compared to South Korea, where each person consumes 10,162-kilowatt hours of power, the average North Korean uses just 739. Recently released photos from the International Space Station show how North Korea completely blends into the surrounding blackness, other than a couple of small spots of light.

19. According to data that the government of North Korea provided to the UNESCO, the country' s literacy rate is 100% and it boasts that it is on par with the U.S.

With the supposed 100% literacy rate, North Korea ranks equally with the U.S., U.K., and champions hundreds of other countries on that front. According to Asian scholars like Andrei Lankov, this is accomplished by teaching school children how to write the names of "President for Eternity" Kim, Il-sung and "Dear Leader" Kim, Jong-il before they can write their own name and that of their parents'. Once this is done, the North Korean Government declares the student literate in writing. The authenticity of this information still remains to be proved, however.

20. Kim Jong-il was apparently born under a double rainbow and his birth caused a new star to appear in the sky; he learned to walk and talk before 6 months and has the ability to control the weather by his moods, according to the official government-released biography of his life.

An extreme personality cult around the *Kims* exists in North Korea, which even surpasses that of Stalin or Mao Zedong. As part of its propaganda and brain-washing methods, the government elevates its leaders to a godlike status in the minds of the average citizen. One defector, Kang Chol-hwan writes of his childhood in North Korea:

21. Wearing jeans is banned in North Korea as it is seen as a sign of American imperialism.

In a whole slew of restrictions, Kim Jong-un recently issued a ban on jeans and piercings. Pyongyang, the country's elite-infested capital fears that its citizens are being exposed to western clothing, however, the ban will focus primarily on the North Hamgyong province and Yanggang.

22. North Korea is the world's only necrocracy: a government that still operates under the rules of a former, dead leader.

The incumbent president of North Korea is Kim Il-Sung, even though he's been dead for 18 years. He assumed the office of the Eternal Presidency on July 8, 1994, and continues to hold onto power.

23. In 1974, Kim Il-sung took 1,000 Volvo sedans worth € 300M from Sweden to North Korea and never paid for them. They were never returned and are currently still being used.

Tor Rauden Källstigen, a Swedish photographer and entrepreneur who traveled to North Korea in 2008 says,

"Many of the Volvos were put to serve in the small but very present taxi fleet in Pyongyang.I think I've never been inside such an old car even back home in Sweden. This taxi was very well maintained too, close to mint condition it seemed."

The fact remains that despite the semi-annual reminders of payment by the Swedish risk advisory, North Korea refuses to pay for stealing (rather, scamming) Sweden out of the 1,000 volvos. North Korea now considers Sweden a US pawn that is manipulated by the imperialists.

24. In North Korea, possessing Bibles, watching South Korean movies and distributing pornography may be punishable by death.

In November of 2013, the government executed 80 people in public for watching South Korean movies and owning Bibles. According to one source, women and children were brought into a sports stadium and forced to watch people being shot dead by machine-gun fire. Despite it being illegal, it is estimated that there are 100,000 Christians living in North Korea.

25. North Koreans don't celebrate birthdays on July 8 and December 17, since those are the dates that Kim Il-sung and Kim Jong-il died.

Approximately 100,000 North Koreans celebrate displaced birthdays on July 9 or December 18 due to this reason. There is a provision for people born on these dates before 1994, where they can change their birthday with official recognition.

26. The national animal of North Korea is the Chollima; a mythical winged horse that supposedly symbolizes heroism and the country' s indomitable spirit.

The word Chollima is derived from the Chinese word Qianlima which means talent and ability. This mythical winged horse actually originates from Chinese classics. The national capital Pyongyang hosts a number of Chollima statues, and strangely enough, the North Korean football team is also named the same.

Table of Content

Chapter One

Honolulu, Hawaii

The early morning breeze pushed the lingering fog from the night before through the jogging path. Jamie kept her stride, so Ziggy could keep up. She stopped, "Ziggy, come on boy." She tried to coach him, but he had been intrigued by something. He sniffed until he found a trail through a bush. He came out when he heard his name, looked at her with great concern.

"Boy, if you don't bring your rump here." She wiped her sweat, fanned her face, and went to pick him up, but he ran into the bushes. "Oh my God, are you serious." Frustrated, she went after him, almost having his tail, "When I get my hands on you." She was dirty from the fall to her knees, scratches from the thorny bushes.

He barked, just out of reach of her fingers; it was almost like he was pulling her closer to where he had been. Just on the other side of this huge leaf, she reached in as hard as she could, grabbed him by the tail. "What the hell are you…" she looked up, not far from where she stood, not believing what she was watching. She covered her mouth to prevent her scream from being heard. "No!" she held Ziggy tight, "Please stop!" She wanted to run, but her feet inched closer, her eyes pooled with fear, "Stop! Please don't hurt him."

Before she knew it, she was closer to the men that were beating a man with objects as he hung from a tree, the screams for help quickly went silent when his mouth was stuffed with a white towel. She could not understand how they ignored her plea. From the corner of his eye, he tried to tell her to run. The blood and wounds that puffed his face was unbearable. She woke up from this reoccurring dream, breathing hard, chest pounded like she had been running. She reached over and slammed her palm on the alarm clock that woke her up. She wanted to know why her dreams were so vivid; it was as if she was really there. She sighed, grabbed her cell and noticed three missed calls from her boyfriend, "Damn, I got to get going." She jumped up, tossed her panties and bra on as she made her way to the rest room. Her cell rang, with her toothbrush in her mouth, "Hello."

"Hey gorgeous, were you sleeping?" he waited in line to pass through customs.

"Matter of fact I was, but I'll meet you at your house" They both ended the call.

"Excuse me sir, can you please accompany me to my office?" A soft voice came from behind. His nerves started to bother him. But it wasn't unusual under these circumstances.

"Well..." He stuttered. "Sure, why not." He spoke with a smile, and wiped the perspiration from his forehead and wondered if they would notice his hands. She looked at his airline ticket.

"Mr. Kalargo Choi, do you have your passport?" The customs agent asked. He held all his emotions under control, just like he had practiced.

"Well certainly. It should be in my carry-on bag, the side pocket."

He thought to himself and wondered about the consequences. He looked around and saw himself in the reflection. He sighed. "What did I get myself into?"

He saw a small particle on his shoulder, and immediately removed it with his left hand as if it was illegal. He wore Levi's jeans neatly ironed with a blue polo pull over, and a pair of black ostrich ankle high boots. Mr. Choi stood no more than 5'10, two hundred fifteen pounds. He was a handsome Gambian who is as ebony as jet ink. He was well built physically and mentally due to years of jiujutsu martial arts, that was accompanied with a third degree black belt. At this moment, customs are the only people he feared.

"Mr. Choi, where are you arriving from?"The customs officer asked him.

He responded quickly. "I'm arriving from South Africa." He remembered to not add anything to the conversation between the two.

"Are you a citizen of the United States of America?"

"Yes I am." He breathed lightly to ease his nerves.

"How long have you been in South Africa?"

He looked mystified for a split second. "No more than a month." He plunged his pinky finger in his left ear.

"Are you transporting any illegal drugs, weapons, or any items that would be contraband?" the customs agent placed his hands on top of his bags.

"No I'm not." He spoke with confidence.

"Are you carrying a large amount of cash that you have not declared on your customs sheet?" He looked at the ceiling and quickly returned eye contact.

"No sir."
"Are you bringing back any gifts?"

He shook his head. "No sir." He removed a tear of sweat with his right pinky finger. At the same time the customs officer went through his luggage, and took out the obvious. They searched carefully, one item at a time.

"What is this?" He asked.

"I'm sorry. I made that myself upon arriving in South Africa. Is that considered a gift?" He frowned.

The officer gave him an innocent pout. He looked at him, "Not really, I guess not. It's mighty small."

"Where do you reside in the U.S.?"

He was day dreaming and did not hear him.

"Excuse me sir, I asked you a question. Where do you live in the U.S.?"

He responded, "Honolulu."

"What's your occupation?"

He smiled, "I'm a martial arts instructor, a personal trainer and I own import/export business."

The officer looked him in the eyes with his passport in his hand, "Welcome back to the U.S, be careful of the heavy snow in the mountains at this time of the year. You may proceed. Pack your clothes." He said with a steady stare.

Kalargo returned the stare and finally relaxed to a mood of safety and comfort. He sighed with a password. "Tell the people who are visiting Hawaii about the snow." He packed his bags.

"Why this can't be any easier?" He was still nervous as hell.

He stood in front of a mirror in the airport bathroom and removed all signs of perspiration and guilt. He perfected his gig line up with his belt. Finally he combed his hair with an Afro pick.

He walked toward the exit with his luggage in tow, pulled out his cell phone, from memory he dialed Na Min's number and waited.

"Yes hello." A female voice responded in fluent Korean.

"Yes, Na Min." The phone went silent for a moment.

"Yes, He'll be right with you."

He walked toward the limo stand. The Hawaiian heat embraced his face like an old friend who had not seen him in years. He could see the afternoon sun hovering over the horizon. He smiled. "Damn, I'm glad to be back."

A voice interrupted him. "Kalargo, how was your trip?"

He laughed with a joyful voice. "Just great, could not be better.

Na Min had a Korean accent when he spoke English. "Where are you now?"

"Waiting for my driver, I should be home in about forty five minutes."

"Well I'm glad to know you are back and safe, call me later." after a couple more words, they both terminated the line and he placed the phone in his top left pocket.

The driver pulled up alongside him, he tossed his bags in the car, and departed Honolulu International airport to get on the Queen Liliuokalani freeway, he pondered his first day he came to Hawaii and most of all, and how he got to South Korea.

At the age of nine, he lived in The Gambia. Unknown to his knowledge, he was in hiding. He and his uncle lived in a shack under a tin roof. They barely ate four complete meals a week. Mugumbi, his uncle has been taking care of him for the past five years. After he was laid off from the diamond mine, they struggled for weeks until he found work at the docks. He loved ships and saw them as the beast of the sea. Later he found a way out of Africa, a way to riches. As usual Kalargo was in the streets while his uncle continued to work hard and planed their great escape.

After three years, his plan came to him in the middle of the night. The next morning he woke up with a smile.

"Good morning little one, it's time to open your eyes and smell the sunshine." He literally meant the humidity including the outstanding stench that floated among them like a friend, a dirty friend or worst a flatulent ghost with murderous intentions. They lived in a small-cemented center block efficiency, half kitchen with an outside bathroom. There was one thing that they had in common and it only occurred in the middle of the night, their dreams, and they ended when their eyelids opened and allowed reality to piss in their face.

"Tipi, it's time to eat, so go ahead and wash your face, he would've added brushing his teeth to the list of things to do but neither owned one." This time he spoke with a little more authority in his voice. The nickname Tipi stuck to Kalargo every since he was younger. Most of his family had been killed and leaving to get away from the genocide was the last option. But somehow and a mysterious reason, it was like they followed them. The house bombing nearly killed him. A huge gash on the side of his neck was a reminder.

He lay on the floor between a dirty sheet and blanket. Surprisingly, his eyes flickered to keep out the early morning sunlight. He yawned to get himself started.

"It's early." Neither of them spoke English nor read or write their own language.

"This week…" He said with a smile. "I have big plans for the both of us. But you have to promise me…" He bent down beside him on the floor. He lifted his chin to look him directly in his eyes. He licked his thumb to wet it real good, wiped the dried saliva and eye snot from the corners of his face. Hardly awake he sat up right and looked into his uncle's eyes.

"What's the happiness for?" Before he could finish, his uncle spoke.

"Promise me you'll never say a word! One day you and I will be out of here, just wait you'll see."

Kalargo couldn't believe the words that suddenly became melodic.

"Do you promise not to say a word to no one?"

He was so hungry, he would promise anything at this moment, "I promise, but what are you talking about?" He looked like he was begging for food and lost.

"When the time come, I'll let you know. From this day on, just be happy and don't ask or mention this conversation again." He knew it would be hard to be happy under these conditions, if he had a plan, it must be a good one.

After six months of waiting, He started to wonder. "Uncle…" He began to say with an inquisitive voice. He stood between the door way of their shack. He leaned with his left hand on his hip. The humidity made him melt like ice cream and his upper lip tasted salty, sticky sweat that wet his shirt. His uncle stared out and down the street admiring what he hoped to never see again.

The next-door neighbor exited her house. "Hello, how is it going?"

"Fabulous, just like a garden of roses." he said as she walked across the street carrying a pot on top of her head filled with clothes. She mumbled under her breath.

"Yep, He's getting crazier and crazier. Just look at him." She smiled at him. They used to date. But everything had changed. He hadn't been with a woman in six months. But no one could tell from his gestures.

Tipi approached him with a sad pout. He took up the space between the door and his uncle. Nothing had changed, not even the scuba tight pants. It drove him insane. People in the neighborhood began to call his uncle crazy behind his back.

"Tipi…" He paused for a second that felt like a lifetime. He held his face in his palms to hide his pain.

"Tipi…" He put his hands on his right shoulder. "…how would you like to come with me to work tonight? At least you won't be bored." He sighed, "You know Tipi, tonight is that night." He whispered.

Kalargo's head lifted slowly. These were the best words he had ever heard. Before he replied, his uncle interrupted him.

"We are leaving tonight. I've been waiting six months, six damn months!" A tear fell out of joy.

"Tipi, say good bye to Africa. You may never return."

His heartbeat began to race. He wanted to dream, scream and celebrate at the same time. He also remembered to keep calm.

Mugumbi's plan was to travel to the United States by ship as a stowaway. Only if the ship they had boarded was going to America. Due to his inability to read, they boarded a ship with an American flag that ended up in South Korea. After months of working under the table for slave wages, Mugumbi finally got a break. He met his future Korean American wife that introduced him to a prestigious individual, her stepfather, double agent Na Min Choi.

Kalargo's driver was steady talking, not realizing that his mind was far away until they pulled up to the gate of his house.

He retrieved his PDA cell phone and used it to open the remote controlled gate. She drove up the driveway in the Hawaiikai section of Honolulu.

"Home sweet home…" He dialed Na Min's number. He walked in to his home with the cell phone to his ear. "Good after noon. Mr. Choi, please."

He tossed his bags on the bed and pulled off his shirt and threw it in the basket of dirty clothes.

"Kalargo, are you feeling pretty good?"

He lay on the bed, tired. "I was wondering if we could meet later tonight and…"

Kalargo interrupted him "Well, hold on for a moment. I have to check my schedule", he came back. "Of course I have time."

He stood up, unclothed himself and prepared his bath water.

"I say after ten pm." The sound of bath water can be heard in the back ground.

"You want to meet at Nicolis Nicolis?"

"Sure,why not. So ten it is." They ended the conversation.

The huge bathroom covered with ivory pearl tile displayed a checkerboard design, ivory white sink and brass facets handles. The lit watermelon candles and bubble bath was exactly what he needed, relaxation. The Jacuzzi's pumps massaged his back while he closed his eyes under dim lights. He thought of how successful he wanted to be. He already owned one of the most popular martial arts and fitness spas on the island. But the bulk of his money came from international arms trade and distribution, sound fancy. In reality, he supplied war torn countries weapons to fight. On his list was his native country The Gambia that was in need of his service.

The phone rang several times. "Who is bothering me now?" He opened his eyes and reached for the phone. "Yes who's calling?"

His thick African accent could not be mistaken for anything other than a Gambian. He splashed water that can be heard in the background. He paused for a second or two.

"Hello." He said just before he pushed the button to end the call. He heard a female voice. It sounded like Jamie.

"I heard you playing with your rubber ducky." She said in a seductive voice that purred in his ear. He laughed and blew off her comment, in one ear and out the other.

"I thought you were my rubber ducky? Having fun?" With her lips she made this sound that always excited him. He raised himself forward to pull the plug to the drain.

"Jamie, Could you call me back or I'll call you." He asked her. He hopped out of the deep Jacuzzi to dry off. She hesitated before she responded.

"You promise?"

"Well I tell you what; you call me in fifteen minutes. I should be dry by then." She agreed and they terminated the line.

The Hawaiian nights are what people enjoy, but the sun and beaches are what they come for. The weather attracted tourist from all parts of the globe. He rarely left the island. He was glad to be home. He lounged in his four-bedroom house surrounded by a seven-foot wall in one of the exclusive neighborhoods in Hawaii.

He entered the kitchen to prepare a snack. He wore his favorite white cotton robe, blue pajamas and slippers that matched. His house was built to look and have an Oriental appeal. His admiration for the Korean was evident. He ate with chopsticks like they were born in his hand.

There was nothing he did not know. He cooked their food more and better than Gambian. But he had a slightly different taste bud when it came to women. He had grown to be this debonair that he had dreamed of. He lived in Hawaii for ten years. He was lonely and missed his only family, Mugumbi.

He opened the fridge. "Well now…" He looked at baked chicken, noodles and a plate jeon. He grabbed a little of everything just to satisfy all his taste buds. He spoke out loud. "I guess a little red wine…" He tuned out loud. "…should not hurt the mind, at least not this time."

He grabbed a flute shaped glass walked into the living room under dim lights. He picked up the remote control.

"Hmm…" With one touch, the wall unit rose from the floor and the entertainment center appeared.

"Do I want to watch T.V., listen to jazz?" He hit the music button, "may be some Jazz." He flopped in to the colossal circular black sofa.

"Spanish Jazz, I 'm in the mood for." He looked at his watch and noticed it was nearly eight thirty. He picked up the phone to call Jamie. The ring tone buzzed his ear and his eyes watched the EQ on the stereo, jazz filtered the entire house.

"Hello this is Jamie…" Kalargo sighed. "Hey what's up? You are kind of late calling." He was interrupted with a rueful voice.

"Can you hold?" It caught him off guard and he had to wait a moment. She finally came back with this cheerful voice.

"I am so sorry, who is this?" Like a dummy he spoke in to the machine.

"This is Kalargo."

"I am not in at the moment. Please leave a short to the point message. I'll get a hold of you verbally, mentally, physically, or joyfully. Thank you." He grinned.

"She gets me every time. Yeah Jamie, I call to say hello and to return your call…" A buzzer interrupted him. He stood up to check his monitor.

"Anyway just call me" He slid the phone in his robe pocket.

"Are you going to let me in?" Jamie stood at the gate camera. She hopped in to her car.

"Of course, park your car next to the Lexus. Make sure to be careful, I just had the roses planted."

Jamie stood 5'7, long curly blonde hair with a pecan like tan with crystal sky blue eyes. Jamie was born in San Diego and lived on the island ever since her parents separated. Upon meeting him, she worked at a fruit market for three years on the side of the road in an unpopulated section of the island.

After she parked her car, she double-checked to make certain there was space between the Lexus.

"How's it?" She said and embraced him and pushed her tongue down his throat.

"Well, you know as usual."

"Come on in, I'm having a glass of wine. She made herself comfortable. She sat her black purse on the sofa and sighed like she had never been there before.

"So how was your flight?" She chose a champagne glass.

"You want champagne or wine?" He held a bottle of each in both hands.

"I'll have whatever you are having." She held her glass up and watched the wine pour. She looked at him with cunning gesture and sipped a little before she took her glass to the sofa and sat down like a lady.

"My day was boring. I arrived on the afternoon flight; actually it was delayed due to a layover in the Philippines. Other than that I was listening to some Jazz."

"So how is your dad?" She crossed her legs.

"Actually He's doing fine. I am meeting him tonight. What are you doing later? He would love to see you." He sat next to her. She watched T.V. with her glass touching her lips. "Nothing really, I wanted to spend some time with you."

He stood up and looked at his watch. "I guess you wouldn't mind coming with me to meet him?" He headed toward the master suite but can be heard. "Then we can go to the beach afterwards."

"Should I change my clothes?" She sat the glass on the table, stood from the sofa and entered the kitchen.

"You know I like to go to the beach, especially at night." He came from the master suite "Yati yati yati, we both know why you like the beach."

She was in front of the open fridge picking grapes from the bag. She tossed a couple of them in her mouth. Suddenly he came from behind with a loving embrace. He put his lips on the back of her neck. His body pressed against hers. She wore a pair of skintight jeans that made her look luscious. She grinds her buttocks into his mid section.

"Now you know you like to tease and keep me hungry for you." She looked over her shoulder.

"Why would I…" The ringing of his cellular phone interrupted her.

"What time is it?" He asked looking down at his watch.

"Nine fifteen." He sighed.

"Yes hello." He walked away from Jamie. The voice on the phone quickly put a smile on his voluptuous lips. He moved far enough to talk in private.

"So how is it going on your end?" The voice asked him.

"Very well, I sent the package. It should arrive in less than four hours. The commander is part of the flight crew. He should be contacting you one hour after they land to inform you where to meet him." he walked into an unoccupied part of the house and then entered his office.

"Everything is cool but what about the other crew members?"

"Like I said, everything is under control. Nobody else knows a thing. It's what they call TOP SERCET. We are taking this seriously."

"Well, until then I'll wait on the call and I'll be near the base in a couple of hours. I'll talk to you later, out." They both ended the phone call.

Chapter 2

The blazing sun glared on the ocean that made a mirror reflection. It was amazing how beautiful and calm a huge body of water could be. The Indian Ocean can be lonely at times but once in a while the calm and peaceful waters are disturbed by an U.S.S. aircraft carrier.

The U.S.S. Carl Vinson operated a hundred miles off the island of Diego Garcia, population six hundred; the island was three miles wide and twenty-eight miles long. One of the beautiful islands that Great Britain owned and not known to many. It was used as a military installation.

The battle group cruised towards the North Arabian Sea. It carried a crew of five thousand and over fifty aircraft of various squadrons. Squadron VRC-50 was the most love and expected aircraft to land. The twin turbo prop C-2 better known as the GREYHOUND delivered passengers, parts, and most important, mail. Its day or night, long range capabilities and any weather were perfect for Naval Logistics. The squadron was stationed out of Cubi Point Naval Air station, Philippines. The squadron detached personnel aboard the carrier to assist in logistics. The sound of a C-2 was like x-mas every time.

"Good morning, how does the flight deck look?" The leading Petty Officer entered the small cramped workspace crowded with toolboxes and six sailors waiting to recover an aircraft.

"Well, the ETA says fourteen hundred hours but we got to have it ready for the next flight cycle."

A voice mumbled out. "Ok it's thirteen thirty now. In about ten minutes. I want to be up on the flight deck and ready. I don't want the air boss breathing down my neck and chewing my ass out for not recovering are own bird. He took a seat on the edge of the desk.

"Airman Crockett, do a quick turnaround. It doesn't have to be too thorough, just look for the obvious and write it down. I know it's your first time out at sea. And you are the plane captain but out here we are one team, one family. We pitch in. Basically, we don't do major maintenance out here unless we absolutely have to. If you find something, let me know, write it down. We'll let the crew back on land handle it. Oh by the way, make sure you put your order in for whatever you need from base." He sat there like a big shot with goggles on the top of his cranial like a tank commander.

"The other squadrons don't mind helping us out with supplies only because we do them favors. So stock supplies for the minor problems."

His dingy olive green fatigues were tucked in his unpolished boots. A crew of six included an aviation mechanic, structural/hydraulic, electrician, avionics, plane captain, and a Q/A quality and assurance, just enough to get the job done.

"Did they say what they were carrying?" Airman Crockett asked while sitting on top of a toolbox holding a pair of gloves in his hand. He looked like he was expecting his Japanese girlfriend to jump out of a birthday cake.

"Well I'm not sure but I do know they have about ten passengers and two weeks of backed up mail." The leading Petty Officer said.

Airman Crockett stood 5'9, twenty years old with a military haircut, a hundred seventy pounds, an African American from Miami Florida. He just arrived to the squadron eight months ago.

"Well it's about that time." The leading Petty Officer headed out the iron integrity door of the ship. The workspace was located just below the flight deck, starboard aft section. There is a sixty-foot drop into the ocean if anyone wanted to free dive. Not like it has not been done before by lonely sailors who are in desperate need to go home. The catwalk was made of iron and it lead to the flight deck. You could hear and see the waves that splashed against the side of the ship through the iron that was beneath your feet.

The catapult can be felt as it launches the fighter jets and bombers. Even with ear protection you can barely hear the person next to you screaming in your ear. The use of hand signals told everyone when, what, and where to go on the flight deck. The fumes that hovered the mini airport from more than fifteen planes at any given time are just as dangerous. The exhaust from any one of them could blow you off the flight deck into the ocean, worst-case scenario, to be blown into the engine of another plane.

Petty Officer, E-7, the quality assurance officer and leader of the detachment, the career type was born in Paris, Texas, a country fellow that spoke with a deep drawl. His is a dishwater blonde red head that stood 5'11, two hundred thirty pounds. The Petty Officer walked over to Airman Crockett.

"Now look, the air boss want the C-2 parked next to the island of the aircraft carrier, just below the flight control center. You won't be shutting the engines down. They will unload and take off. Ok?" He screamed in his direction of his earmuff. He spoke over the loud engines that were at high power six feet away.

"There she is." The C-2 was pointed out circling the ship in between the high clouds; it looked like a flying dot. It did donuts around the carrier waiting for its chance to land. There is no other aircraft that looked as dangerous as the wide fat big nose short C-2 landing on the flight deck. You have to imagine the ship shifting left to right and up and down according to motion of the ocean. Then the C-2 Greyhound trying to land, believe me, it is a sight to see. And do not forget about the wind that drifts the plane as it tries to land.

As the plane approached for landing, the flight deck firemen and other crew members were on standby. Not more than one mile out, it took the last fly by before it descended. The C-2 lined up with lighting that guided the plane in. A long trail of exhaust smoke lingered behind the turbo prop as it struggled to line itself for landing. It looked like it would crash into the ocean or the ship.

"On deck! On deck!" The flight deck loud speaker said. The plane quickly full throttled in case they missed four of the landing cables they have in place to catch them. The tail hook lifted, and they taxied to the island. Not more than two minutes later an F-14 landed and the process continued.

After unloading passengers and mail the leading Petty Officer sent a crew member to the workspace with two unbelievable flat boxes two and a half by fifteen inches.

"What! Pizza Hut! Hot damn, Pizza Hut in the middle of the ocean! Where did that come from?" Airman Crockett yelled.

"It came from where we are going next..." Petty Officer Ramsey yelled back, "...North Arabian Sea?" The guy smiled and walked off, "War baby."

The C-2 was directed to the catapult and ready for takeoff. Like a slingshot it was thrown off the front of the ship at a minimum of one hundred fifty miles per hour.

Moments later, the phone rang in the VRC-50 workspace. They had slices of pizza in their mouths and gobbling like wild turkeys.

"VRC-50 this is a non secure line how can I help you sir or maim?" P.O. Ramsey had licked his lips and fingers while holding the phone with shoulder.

"This is the air boss, did they deliver the pizza?"

"Yes sir, it should be there. It's already in route."

"Tell your crew, job well done..." he added a couple of more words and ended the call.

Several hours had passed and the sun was swallowed by the horizon that made a cloudless night filled with stars. At any given time you could make a wish to a fallen star. Airman Crockett looked out into the pitch darkness knowing that only the battle group was near. Flight operations went on until 2200 hours.

"Well, it's about that time to hit the rack." He looked at his watch and sighed. "We don't have to be up until what, 1330 hours?" He looked at the POD the plan of the day to verify when the next C-2 will arrive.

The voice of the Captain of the ship bellowed the speaker of the 1-M-C that the entire ship can hear. "This is the Captain, I would like to have everyone's attention for a moment. Today was a fine working day. Currently I would like to give an AT a Boy to squadron VF-120 and VA-140 for doing an excellent job on their bomb runs. It carried out expeditiously without injuries. However we all know that we all work as a team, a ship is nothing without its crew. I also know that it is a little hard on some of us being away from family and love ones for such a long period of time. In three days it'll be Christmas and…" The captain paused. "Yes it's a difficult time. But we are out here making sure the international sea lanes are open and not controlled by countries whom wish to do harm or take over countries that can't take up for themselves. So yes, as the most powerful country in the world, we have a job to do, an obligation to protect international waters." He cleared his throat and continued.

"I just got word today that our mission has changed. The chief of Naval Operations has given us the orders to be on standby due to Saddam Hussein's Army attacking Kuwait. At this very moment we are full speed ahead to the Persian Gulf in which is now called the Arabian Sea." As the Captain spoke Airman Crockett could feel mood change among his crew. It humbles some; it got serious all of a sudden. He wondered, will this be war? He had noticed weeks earlier that they had replenished the carrier with bombs and the practice flights had increased dramatically. He also remembered that another group of his squadron was detached to Manama, Bahrain, fifty miles from Saudi Arabia and three hundred miles from Kuwait. He knew that was within scud missile range. He thought about the threat of gas attacks and chemical suits. He shook his head and sighed. The buildup of more battle groups were being positioned and there were two battle groups already there, U.S.S. Midway, U.S.S. Enterprise. He thought about what the President of the United States said, "War is eminent."

*   *   *

Two weeks later, under an unforgiving blistering sun that made sweat feel like boiling water on the flight deck with high powered exhaust hot enough to melt your skin beneath a brown turtle neck sweater. Airman Crockett carried a set of three chains to secure the C-2 to the flight deck to prevent the plane from shifting when the ship rocks and roll. The leading Petty Officer walked over to him.

"Hey after you secure the C-2 we have a meeting, so don't disappear.

"What's the meeting about?"

"We have to go over our tools and get ready to take off. We are flying to Bahrain first thing in the morning. The bird is spending the night. So after we go over some details as a group, be ready for a catapult take off."

"Damn flying off the ship." he sighed.

Later that night he barely slept because he could not stop thinking about this catapult take off. He had seen it many times and now, he has to experience it. He felt like the C-2 Greyhound now looked like a flying coffin instead of looking like a friendly snoopy. He slept in a coffin rack that was the size of a real coffin, may be seven feet long by three feet wide. The berthing quarters stacked the coffin like beds three up and three in front of him, very small space where he have to lift his bed to put all of his belongings. If it doesn't fit, you don't need it.

The 0430 wakeup call was a tapping noise on the edge of the rack. "It is that time." A fellow crew member gave him a wakeup call.

"Do I have time to eat?" He asked with a war ending breath that he covered with the sheet.

"We have box lunches ready for us on the plane. The in flight plane captain has already pick those up, by the way have you ever taken off from an aircraft carrier?"

"No." He peeked through the sheets that had covered his head.

"Well there is a first time for everything." He walked away with a grin.

The C-2 had to be the slowest aircraft the Navy has. The flight was like riding a snail with wings. It would take a fighter thirty minutes to fly from where the ship was located. The C-2 took two hours and thirty minutes to arrive in Bahrain. Airman Crockett closed his eyes and thought about the very first time he landed in a foreign country.

Eight months ago

The night was hot, humid, and beautiful at the same time. He knew he was in a whole new world. The people were different by culture, language, habit, and much more. The Philippine women, you could not ask for any more exotic. The short, dark skin almond eyes with jet-black hair and their accent, was mind blowing. He was dropped into heaven without a white flag.

"Have you heard about the game called QUARTERS?" A passenger asked him.

"This guy knows where all the good spots to go to, you coming?"

He frowned, "Naa, You guys go without me. I already know about QUARTERS."

His dream was interrupted when the in flight plane captain shook his shoulder.

"We are landing in five minutes." He went around waking up everyone who was sleeping.

He sighed and opened his eyes. He looked out the window and saw dessert for miles. "Wow! Now this is a whole new world."

*   *   *

Honolulu, Hawaii

Jamie slept through the night having the same horrific dream. She mumbled words that Kalargo ignored until she almost gagged. In her dream she was jogging on a trail like she usually does.

"I'm going jogging along the trail. I'll be back within the hour." She spoke into her answering machine. She exited the house wearing her red tights and white t-shirt with a pouch around her waist. She went back in to the house to change her batteries for her walk man head set. She also grabbed her best cassette tape, Phil Collins.

"Where are you?" she called and whistled for her cute annoying black chiwawa with a little bit of brown on its belly. Ziggy ran from the pet entrance of the door that swung both directions.

"Come on Ziggy. It's time for our morning run. He wagged his tail and moved around like he had been waiting on her the whole time. He jumped in to the grass from the porch and took his ritual pump and morning dump. After he finished he turn around to smell it, licked it, and backed away from it.

It was a perfect morning to jog under a cloudless sky with pockets of fog that looked like they floated just above the ground along the green grassy trail. Some people referred to Jamie as a health addict and others just labeled her as drop dead gorgeous.

After a mile and a half her heartbeat was at a normal joggers beat on a trail that she jogged at least three times a week. She arrived at her turn around point and noticed that Ziggy was not behind her. She stopped and removed her headphones. She began to trace backwards.

"Ziggy!" She yelled out his name. She listened. Suddenly Ziggy came from the bushes.

"There you are!" She was relieved. But Ziggy stood there and looked into the bushes. He wagged his tail and barked two times. The closer she got, the further he would go into the bushes. She sighed.

"I don't have time for this. Come on boy." She begged him.

Ziggy peaked out of a small hole between the bushes like he was calling her, as soon as she got closer. He took off behind the bushes again. It was like a game he played.

When she walked through the bushes and pulled huge leaves aside to make her way. She saw a black man hanging upside down from a tree. His blood dripped like a faucet, and his face was swollen like water balloons. She grabbed her chest with her right hand and covered her mouth with her left. It was as if the two guys that beat him mercilessly could not see her standing there. The body moved on every strike until they stop beating him. She walked closer with tears in her eyes, "Stop! What are you doing?" She asked them.

They ignored her like she was invisible. The closer she got, the more she realized that she was like a ghost.

She dropped to her knees and pleaded the two soldiers to stop beating him. "You are going to kill him!" She screamed from the bottom of her lungs and pulling on her shirt like she was going to rip it off.

"What are you doing?!" She reached for his hand.

His eyes opened as blood spilled from his mouth like a gutted pig. She crawled over to him and grabbed his bloody hand that barely touched the dirt that had mixed together. She squeezed his hand tight.

"Wake up Jamie! Hey, you must be having a bad dream." He held her hand. Her eyes opened wide and she jumped away from him like he was the attacker.

"Are you going to be ok?" He sighed and got her a glass of water.

She looked around with sweat on her forehead. She scratched her chest and rubbed her nose. Her blood shot wet eyes made her realized that she was safe, but her scratches on her chest and the tears from the corner of her eyes said otherwise.

"My God," She swallowed a dry throat of saliva, "was I talking in my sleep?" She asked him.

"What! You were mumbling and moaning something, looked like you were having a…" He was interrupted. "…A nightmare on Elm Street." He laughed and gave her some water.

"What were you dreaming about?"

"I…" She sighed. "I can't remember." She paused and cuddled with him.

"I can't believe I do not know what I was dreaming about. I'm pretty sure it will come to me sooner or later." She lay there with his favorite white robe on with nothing else beneath. Her beautiful lips and facial features gave her a VIP passed to anywhere.

"Hold me." He kissed her on the neck and embraced her.

"Are you hungry? I cooked breakfast while you were sleeping."

She inhaled and smelt fresh eggs and bacon.

"Yes, love to eat" She stood up and tightened the robe around her. His beeper went off. He looked down and picked up the phone.

"I tell you what..." She walked into the kitchen. "...I'll fix my plate, you answer your beeper." She grabbed two plates for them both.

Chapter 3

"Na Min, what's going on? I am surprise to hear from you this early."

"Good morning to you too, I think we have a problem. The shipment we got several weeks ago."

Kalargo is outside opening his car door. "What about it?"

He heard him sigh, "All of that has to be shipped out. There is another shipment coming in tomorrow. From what I understand, it needs to go ASAP." He became quiet.

He was caught by surprise. He pondered while he sat in his car. "Does it have to be done tonight?" He sounded like a kid on punishment. "My contact is not able to move anything right now. I have no way to get trucks." He rubbed his left pinky finger on his left collarbone below where his scar was.

"The ship will be docked in the harbor. The name is "RUSH" Captain Tomzach will be expecting your arrival three hours prior to their departure. If you have to rent the trucks, do it. We have people counting on this."

Kalargo spoke and thought at the same time, "Tell them handyman is on the move." They ended the call.

He looked in the rear view mirror to pick a fight with a painful nose hair. Then he quickly dialed a number from memory.

"Bennett, yeah good morning, wake up. Hey I know you can hear me."

A voice responded. "What are you doing calling me so early?" He coughed and spat in to the trash.

"We got work to do tonight." He explained.

"What time is it?" He laid his head in to the pillow.

"It's Ten am but by ten tonight, we need to have everything loaded on the dock."

Bennett stopped him, "Tonight! I thought…"

"I know what you thought, I said the same thing. Grab ten of your guys, don't worry they will be paid well as usual. Because of the short notice, I will rent the trucks."

He sighed with his head under the pillow with the phone to his mouth. "I guess I could be ready in a couple of hours." He tried to hang up the phone but Kalargo got a couple of last words in.

"I'll call you at six o'clock on the dot. Have them ready." The line went dead.

Jamie tiptoed towards the car like she was modeling on top of hot stones for a pageant with no shoes on.

"Your breakfast is getting cold. Did you want milk or orange juice?" She leaned forward with her hands on her knees still in his robe.

"Orange juice." They both walked hand in hand in to the house.

*   *   *

"Yes I would like to speak to Zang please."

Na Min stood 5'6 with a receding hairline and gray streaks that blended among his straight hair that touched his shoulder. He was an expert in computer programming, and the gathering of Tactical Intelligence. He spoke four languages and held a black belt in martial arts. He trained Kalargo in his younger days. Because he was a Korean American and spoke Korean it gave him an ability to be a good spook until he turned. He was born in Korea raised in Seattle. At the age of thirty he became a leading Agent and a double Agent for the North Koreans. He had moved so far up the ladder. He had frequent meetings with the President of the United States to personally inform him of the North Koreans nuclear technology advancement, troop movement, and activities. But what Agent Na Min did not inform him on was their activities outside the borders of the North Korean peninsula.

"Yes Na Min, How is it going in Hawaii?" Zang spoke in Korean.

"I am calling to inform you that the equipment should be on the move tonight. Now you said the next load should be in tomorrow. But nothing changes, right?" he waited for his response.

"That will be right. I know this is premature; however I am sorry for the short notice. Everything's going well…" Agent Na Min was interrupted.

"How's the weather?" Zang asked. They both grinned.

*   *   *

Kalargo's house

The whole house smelt like fried eggs, bacon and sausages that floated pass their noses.

"Tell me when too much." She put eggs on the plate until he held his hand up to signal that's enough. He tossed a couple of strips of bacon, and sausages on the plate and parked his rear end on the sofa. They watched T.V. and enjoyed each other's company.

"Is there any more apple juice?" He spoke with a piece of bacon between his teeth and talking at the same time.

"Actually I had the last glass of apple juice last night. Only thing left is orange juice, grapefruit, and milk." She looked in the fridge with a half of sausage in her right hand and the other half in her mouth.

"Mix orange juice and fruit punch." he requested. She frowned like that was a nasty combination.

"I never mix my drinks." She carefully gave it to him and sat next to him. She leaned over and sucked his lips with a wet kiss.

"I love you." She said.

"I love you too." Kalargo responded.

"What are you watching?" she reached for the remote.

"Nothing really, you can change it if you want" he told her with his plate on his lap just behind his knees.

In the past couple of months their relationship had grown to a more serious than a physical attraction. They bonded so well until they knew mentally that they were meant for each other. But at times she felt like he was too busy for her with work, travel, and the fitness spa. He never thought he was ready to settle down for something as serious as this. He never pressured her in to bed and gave her the utmost respect. At one point she thought he was gay because he had held out for so long. She was convinced, all that had changed when she was allowed to spend the night. For all the time she had waited was so worth that one night of a Jacuzzi bath filled with French vanilla milk and rose peddles floating all around them. The lit candles dripped and filled the bathroom with a cotton candy smell. He picked her up in his arms and let the milk drip dry with rose peddles sticking to her wet body. She knew she would never receive treatment like this from anyone remotely close. He had her when he first poured warm milk on the back of her neck, chest, and hair. The red and white colors were mind blowing; she knew that he knew how to treat a woman to the fullest.

He took his plate in to the kitchen "You know what today's date is?"

"I think it's the twenty second of Dec." She responded.

"Do you have to work tomorrow?" he asked.

"Why?" she asked.

"I just wanted to know if you wanted to work out anytime soon." The faucet water can be heard as he put his plate in the sink.

"Matter of fact, I need to start getting ready, order the rental trucks, oh yeah let me double check on Bennett." He walked in to the bedroom to change clothes.

"Knowing him he went back to sleep..." He thought about it and put the phone down, "...actually, he's pretty reliable." He mumbled to himself.

Due to short notice he was only able to rent six trucks and they had to be picked up by seven pm.

"Jamie, I might have to leave early. What are your plans?"

She walked out of the bathroom flossing her teeth and talking at the same time. "I should be ready..." She pulled the floss through her back molars "...as soon as I wash up."

He walked across a gray Persian rug as he entered his office and tapped on the key board of his computer to secure the perimeter of his home at three pm. He stood up and retrieved a hand full of fish food from the shelf behind him to feed his piranhas that looked hungry.

His office looked like a corporate space but the size of a bedroom. The thick glass table that held his computer was neatly organized. The blue light in the fish tank exposed the coral reef that he handpicked from Central America. The two marble chiseled tribesman that stood 5 feet with spears and a shield in their hands with twenty-four karat gold eyes. He walked over to his safe and dabbled with the keypad. It beeped and opened on its own.

"Ok, three clips." He grabbed his custom made Chinese Mauser chrome .45 caliber nickel plated, pearl handle with gold screws and aim sight that he got from his dad as a gift. It was engraved, "Life or Death, You choose." It was last produced in the 1920's or 1930's, the Chinese markings on the side meant "Type One". He shoved it in his shoulder holster and slid his arms through. Before he walked out he activated the security alarm.

"Are you ready?" He yelled as he threw on his windbreaker to hide his armor. When he looked into the room she was sliding into her pink thongs with purple butterfly prints. He went to the car. She came out and kissed him on the cheek.

"Hey call me later." They closed their doors and drove off.

The overcast had passed making the sky partly cloudy with slight wind from the east off the beautiful glittering ocean. He could see cargo ships out on the horizon and he knew one of them was a cargo ship named "RUSH". He looked at his car clock and notice that traffic wasn't heavy as usual. For it to be two forty five, that was good he thought, less time he'll have to deal with stupid drivers. His thoughts were interrupted by his cellular.

"Bennett, I knew I could count on you."

"Don't do your counting yet, I was only able to get four men." he can hear Kalargo spitting up cuss words in Korean that he couldn't understand.

"Where is everyone?" he vehemently asked

"Two guys are on the big island and..."

Kalargo's vehemence would have blown a radiator cap, "Bennett! " He paused to calm down. He let out a sigh from deep down.

"Beeeenneeet, listen. Do whatever you need to do to bring the original crew together. Or else tonight will be a long night." He paused to make a right turn to get on the Queen Liliuokalani freeway.

"Have four of the guys meet at your place at five o'clock. I'm on my way, should be there in forty-five minutes. That way we could have the trucks in position." They both agreed and ended the phone call.

Chapter 4

Waikiki beach was crowded with tourist trying to get the ultimate super tan. On a partly cloudy day with showers that had just passed would not stop them from waiting on the beach for the sun to come out. Kalargo drove down Kalakaua Ave and pulled into Kuhio Beach Park parking meter on the beachfront. He sat there just watching the kids play in the sand, and diving off the concrete wall into the waves that rushed the shoreline. He noticed the different cultures that walked and tanned on the beach. A gay couple passed his car holding hands. The volleyball was being chased and kept above ground. Through all of this was like watching a silent scream movie from the interior of his car. He realized that he pulled into the parking lot to get a burger from Jack in the Box. Suddenly he opened his door and beach life was in full swing.

He returned to his car from Kapahulu Ave with a combo meal. He noticed how dirty his car was. He opened the car door and sat his food on the passenger seat. It was this moment he thought about a friend of his that was killed fifteen years ago in Seoul, South Korea.

On a cold night with snow flurries falling like ash from a distant fire. He was on his way to meet Yhong, a nice fellow, bright and handsome dark tanned Korean. He was supposed to deliver documents that were classified. He found him shot in the head and one bullet in the chest. Did he betray Na Min? Did the Chinese kill him? All these unanswered questions routinely tip toed back into his mind. It was something Yhong wanted to tell him. But by the time he reached him his lungs were drowning him in his own blood. There was nothing he could do but run and avoid questioning. If he had not have been late. He could have helped him, or got a bullet.

By the time he reached Mugumbi's house he was nervous and paced around trying to explain. "Yhong is dead!" he sat down with his palms shielding his face.

He could remember how limp his body was, he was trying to tell him something before he pulled and tugged with his bloody hands on his gray and white button down shirt. He died with Kalargo's ear to his lips.

Mugumbi had just walked in to the house thirty minutes before he did. He was not surprised of this news. Did he know about this already? Kalargo did not know what kind of work he was doing for Na Min so he would have not suspected his own uncle to be the killer.

Mugumbi's first executive party put ten thousand U.S. dollars in his hands. It was his secret between him and Na Min. He was a tall Gambian with a three-inch Afro, faded on the side, with deep sunken eyes that looked like he was on a hunger strike. His lips were a distinctive and very much African that was under a neatly trimmed thick mustache. He always maintained a successful appearance that hid his addiction to heroin.

The drug relaxed him as he listened to Kalargo and thought about his first executive party. The mood, weather, atmosphere, location and the face that he had never forgotten, he was so nervous and scared. The key to the judge's house, and the security code was in Mugumbi's possession. The family was on vacation and he stood in all black in his closet of the master bedroom suite. He remembered the small bubbles of sweat that slowly rolled one by one down the curved valley that followed his spine of his back. The masked that revealed the blood shot red eyes that gave death no chance to run or hide. The heavy steal revolver that was heavier with a silencer. His hands shook and the feeling of moving earthworms crawled on the bottom of his stomach.

The sound of the brakes came to a halt when the judge pulled in front of his house. He took a deep breath, gripped his revolver and tightens the silencer. He held the weapon three inches in front of his face. He held a picture of the judge in his left hand and waited.

Suddenly, Mugumbi had realized his day dream was over and was back in the kitchen, listening to Kalargo babble on about Yhong.

"I can't believe someone would want to kill him." Mugumbi said to comfort him.

Mugumbi's drug addiction started two months after the death of the judge. His now wife Yuki a beautiful exotic Asian lured him in with love and a habit that paid a price. The drug helped him cope with his feelings. The two things he had never forgotten, his first kill and first hit of heroin.

She came in from getting her daily dosage of heroin. The sound of church bells can be heard on this Sunday afternoon under a blue sky with warm intentions. He had wished like hell he could shoot who ever pulling the damn rope to that bell. The traffic of churchgoers passed slowly.

Yuki was no more than 5'5, hundred fifteen pounds, and pale complexion with the most gorgeous eyes. She desired for a bigger rack on her chest, but her buttocks compensated her for that. Her denim jeans, two inch heels and blue leather double breasted coat that was knotted with her belt. Her new hair cut gave her a younger look.

"Hey baby…" he said as she walked in the room. She put her purse on the bed. "How are you feeling?" she asked him. She kicked off her heels and pushed them under the foot of the bed.

"Did you come back with…" she interrupted him. "Are you sure you want to try this?" she held the small baggy in between her right thumb and index fingers.

He put his hands on top of hers.

"Yuki…" he paused. "If… it helps me to forget my past and my pain. If it numbs me and makes me feel good like you say it does…" he nodded his head. "I got to have it."

He never told her the real reason just some made up tale about The Gambian police beatings, hangings of his family and friends that haunted him. She also would have never guessed that he was a hit man. He was good at keeping her out of his business.

"Now my love…" she spoke with a syringe horizontally between her lips. She wrapped the belt around his right arm just above his elbow and tightens it to expose his veins. She was teary eyed as a falling tear landed on the crease of his inner elbow; it was like hot acid that boiled into his dark black skin. It slowly made its way down and crossed his up rooted like veins. She sighed as she pulled the cap off the syringe and squirted a little. She used her forearm to wipe her runny eyes to clear her vision for a better aim. She wanted to explain what he should expect but she was interrupted.

"Please, just do it." He begged to get it over with as the needle pinched his skin. His blood mixed with the heroin in the syringe. When she pulled the handle to make sure she had a vein. Then she slowly and carefully pushed the handle of the syringe to insert the brownish liquid monster that will love, neglect, disappoint, numb, and embrace him like no other. His marriage and love affair will be a rocky boundless one that will only give him a temporary escape and a dream that he will only make him more vulnerable.

He realized that he had drifted into a day dream and Kalargo was standing over the kitchen sink trying to clean his shirt of Yhong's blood.

"Uncle, what do you think is going on?"

*   *   *

Honolulu Beach
Back at the beach

The sound of kids passed Kalargo's car as he chewed on a cold French fry with his half empty cup. All this was going through his mind while sitting at the beach. He tossed a French fry in his mouth and took a good chunky bite of his burger.

He wondered what his uncle was up to these days. He picked up his cellular phone and licked his fingers of ketchup and dialed a number.

"Hello Bennett, are you ready? Do you have everything?" he asked. He replied with an assuring voice.

"Of course, we are waiting on you." Bennett said.

He cranks his car. "Ok I'm on my way." And ended the call, he opened his door and tossed the remaining food towards the trash can and missed. He rushed to meet Bennett.

He entered Bennett's house and was immediately approached by him, "Listen, I was only able to round up six trucks. It may take awhile but we'll get it done on time."

Moments later they were on their way to the warehouse.

Kalargo opened the last rusty metal door. "Yes…" he walked over to a stock pile of wooden crates. He repositioned his holster inside his jacket. He stood over a crate that he was about to open. The sound of forklifts and motors revved up, and the loading had begun.

"Ok let me see what I'm sending to my homeland?" he pulled out a RPG-7. The crate contained ten of them. The forklifts continued to load the other crates. In total the shipment manifested Mauser C96's, assault rifles(AK's), light machineguns RPK's and RPD's), M-37's,M-38's, anti armor(RPG-16's), B-10's, M-42's, F-1 anti personnel hand grenades, DS-39's, SG-43 Godunov's, AVS-36's, M1911A1's, Russian M1938's, PPSH41's, DP Ruchnoy Pulemyot light machine guns, RG-42 grenades, and Nambu pistols type 14.

He rolled up his manifest list and tucked it in his back pocket and jumped on a forklift to help loaded the crates.

His cellular rung as he maneuvered the forklift, "Hello."

"Hey what's going on?" the voice sounded familiar. He looked at the screen and realized that it was a Philippine country code. It had to be Jenko.

"Hey where were you? I was just in the Philippines, I tried to get a hold of you." He was excited to hear from his childhood friend.

"I changed my number not long ago. I've been so busy with my new business, man it's crazy. But I finally settled in and this is my new number." Jenko said.

"Jenko…"

"Yeah?" Jenko said.

"I am so in the middle of something." He put the phone down and yelled at his workers, "Come on people, let's stay on schedule." He returned to his conversation. "Are you going to be up later?" Kalargo asked.

"Hey finish what you're doing and give me a call. Any time, Oh before I forget, you think you'll be able to come here for the martial arts competition in July?"

"Wow now that is a good question…" he stopped the forklift to wait to load the next load. He leaned on the wheel, "…I can't really say. I have not missed one yet, but if I can't I will give you a call. Hey, keep in touch and stop being a stranger." The line was dead after they said their goodbyes.

The two of them had been friends since teenagers. They competed against each other in martial arts and Jenko felt second to him to this very day.

"Hey Bennett, how many crates are left to be loaded?" He climbed down from the forklift and pulled himself up on the truck to tie down the cargo.

"Thirty more, we should be done in fifteen minutes."

"Ok listen, meet me at the dock. I'll take three drivers with me so I can start unloading on the ship. The RUSH is at pier 89." He looked at his watch.

"I need three of you to drive!" he yelled over Bennett's shoulder.

"I'll see you there in no more than thirty minutes." He quickly walked away and returned to his supervisory mode.

He pulled out his cellular and noticed that he had four missed calls from Jamie. He decided not to call.

Then he noticed a missed call from Na Min.

"Good morning…" he always spoke to him in Korean to keep him in practice. "How is it going, on schedule?"

"Of course, the first three trucks are on the way. I'm in the first truck."

"I'll call Tomzach." They both ended the line.

*   *   *

The shipping docks were quiet with an occasional ships horn that echoed through the harbor of darkness. The thick fog draped the bay like wet curtains that allowed the low flying screaming seagulls that flew over the choppy water searching for floating trash. The smell of matured exposed fruit with a mixture of caged animals lingered.

Among the ships are two cruise ships that frequently traveled from Waikiki to Los Angeles and three super cargo ships down there was a small beat up two hundred yard rust can known as the "RUSH".

Captain Tomzach peered through his binoculars. He stood in a crimson trench coat with a white lapel and gold metallic buttons with two huge anchors on both sides. He was 5'11, 230 lbs Russian that spoke fluent Korean and horrible English. He looked like a fifty year old who just graduated from boot camp.

His Russian accent rolled off his tongue.

"Get that crane ready and put this load aft of the ship on the starboard."

"Yes, they are on time." He said and looked down at his wrist watch. He picked up the ship's phone to inform his crew to prepare for loading.

Kalargo stepped out of the truck before it came to a complete stop. He directed the following trucks to wait in line. He waved to Captain Tomzach and approached the ramp of the ship.

"Welcome aboard." The captain greeted him with a firm hand shake.

"Is everything going accordingly?"

He sighed, "As planned, are they ready to load them?"

The captain held up his left index finger, "My men are always ready." He looked him in his eyes. He picked up the ships phone and gave a command in horrible English to start loading.

After two hours, the eastern morning sky commenced to brighten and the herd of ship yard employees slowly dragged their feet like they were forced to go to a funeral.

Kalargo's crew had finished just in time before shift changed and he stopped by the security gate to drop off a brown paper bag to the guard. They shook hands as the last truck passed. "Now you don't spend all that in one place."

"Oh don't worry Mr. Choi, I have a special place for it." He smiled and tucked it away in behind his security belt until he got home.

Chapter 5

Gambia, West Africa

The African country of the Gambia is located on the northern west coast of Africa and bordered Senegal. For many years it was not known for having any significant natural resources. Seventy percent depends on crop and live stock for its livelihood. A small-scale manufacturing activity features the process of peanuts, fish, and hide.

In a small village of Farafenni, Gambia, a Korean team of prospectors discovered that north of the Gambian river had an abundance of diamonds, gold, and oil. The civil war that lasted for more than twenty five years had prevented the successes and growth. The North Koreans were supplying the rebels with weapons to overthrow King Shabonee with the help of double agent Na Min.

King Shabonee had two wives, three daughters and two sons that died in a genocide blood bath. The village that spoke his native tongue had been burned to the ground, and to make sure that no one could claim the throne. Everyone in the village was beheaded. The rebels gutted the pregnant women like fish to make sure there were no surviving sons.

But the King had one brother that did survive and gave him the position of General of the Gambian army. It would be thirty years later when he would find out that he had one son who escaped the genocide.

The civil war had replaced this beautiful country of green mountains, waterfalls, and culture friendly into a divided population.

Attaining control of this government would bring prosperity to those outside of this country. It's a new frontier that has not been touched. The most fascinating question is who would control these natural resources?

The United Nations has hesitated; neighboring countries has no desire to get involved. The country of Senegal closed their borders to over two hundred fifty thousand refugees that now live along their border. These innocent people are dying by the hundreds. The King ordered all men, women, boys and girls as young as twelve to bear arms. He would not allow the Gambian Islamic republic Army who are being funded with weapons by a communist country to over throw his government.

King Shabonee sat in front of his bedroom window overlooking the city of Gunjur. His beautiful view of the North Atlantic Ocean was breath taking. He held his oxygen mask to his face and fogged it with his breath. He had grown old, ill, but most importantly, still alive. A servant knocked on his door.

"Your majesty…" Paul slowly twisted the knob and peeked in. "…I hope I am not disturbing you, do you mind?"

The King looked over his shoulder and twisted himself to see him. "Paul?"

"Yes, it is me."

The King turned to his view watching the small fishermen coming in from the Ocean. He put his oxygen mask on his lap. "Come on in Paul, how is your day?"

Paul entered humbled with his hands along his side. "I have good news to report, the General has taken control of the northern side of the river. The war is turning in our favor. He is doing an excellent job."

He offered the King a cup of tea, "Morning tea?" he held the empty cup up before he poured the tea.

The King sighed as a relief that he has finally gained control of half of his country. He smiled and rubbed his chin.

"Paul…" The King slowly stood and dragged his green oxygen tank to where he stood.

"Do you need…" before he could ask if he needed help walking. The King had refused.

"I think I will pour my own cup of tea today" he smiled at him and patted him on the shoulder. They celebrated with tea.

*   *   *

Honolulu, Hi

The sun slowly made its way through Kalargo's room. His right eye slowly opened with eye snot in the corners, lucky his uncle was not around.

"Oh my god," He looked at the clock "damn, three o'clock already." He batted his eyes to adjust his vision. He quickly covered his face in the pillow and grunted. He felt hungry. But stood up, walked and stretched his way towards the bathroom. The phone rang.

"Oh great timing, whoever it is can wait." He mumbled.

A message was not left. "I guess it wasn't that important." A few moments later, it rang again. He leaned over the toilet and urinated. He sighed. After the third, he answered. "Hello."

There was silence for a moment, "Good afternoon." Her voice was erotic as always. "I was trying to get a hold of you last night." She said. Before he could respond, "How would you like to meet a friend of mine? She's coming in from San Diego." She waited for his response.

He paused, "Well..." He tried to quickly think of what he had to do later on that day, "...hmmm, well I don't have anything planned, yeah why not." His face was two inches away from the bathroom mirror softly touching a zit. He frowned.

"I've told her about you..." she was interrupted.

"What time does her flight arrive?"

"She is going to call me when she arrive to her hotel. That should be around four o'clock. I'll call you, how that sounds?"

He sighed with a yawn that followed. "Good, I am just waking up. Make sure you call first." They ended the call.

After a quick shower he splashed his favorite cologne on his abdominal and neck. He noticed the time and wondered how long he can live like this. He picked up his cell phone and dialed a long distance number. He waited patiently for an answer. Finally he terminated the call. He walked into the kitchen, but thought about where his uncle Mugumbi could be. For years he thought his uncle lived a modest life with his girlfriend.

He opened the refrigerator and grabbed a bowl of green seedless grapes, walked over to the French doors that over looked the pool. He thought about his first murder. Though it was in self defense, his true colors came out. He found out that his uncle was a hit man for the North Koreans.

His thought took him back ten years, it was Perth, Australia.
"Do you know these people?!"

"Make a left off the highway exit!" Mugumbi said before he could inquire for more information there were more directions to follow.

It was three o'clock in the morning with patches of fog that creped slowly across the highway from a soiled field along side. The nearest town outside of Perth was miles away. He drove at speeds up to a hundred twenty miles per hour. Their hearts were pumping like generators. The sweat that soaked their backs was uncomfortable and the last thing they wanted to think about. The rental car fish tailed as they ran a yellow light changed to red. Mugumbi looked back to see if they were still in chase.

"What is the hell going on?!" he desperately wanted to know. Mugumbi opened the glove compartment and pulled out two desert eagles chrome pistols. He shoved the clips into them both.

"Damn…" He swallowed and sighed

Mugumbi could not, by all means tell him about the assassinations of this list of wealthy and powerful people. They both frequently looked into the mirrors. But Mugumbi sighed, and decided not to tell him.

"Make a left!"

"Ok, I'll tell you, but you can't tell anybody. I mean, not a sole." He hesitated and looked back and noticed the head lights right on their tail. Damn near kissing their bumper, "I am a hit man."

"What! Get out of here!"

"Listen earlier I just killed a man. That's what I do. I kill for a living. Now take this gun, because tonight will be your first kill, so man up." He handed the pistol to him with the handle in his hand. He grabbed it by the handle and looked in the rear view mirror.

"Make a right! Make a right!" he told him. The sound of gun fire erupted, but the early morning dew had dampened the road. The car lost control and hit a ditch. It did not take long before all hell broke loose. The car landed in a muddy cow pasture.

"We got to get out of here, now! Let's go!" Mugumbi took the lead, despite the minor injuries; he grabbed him by the shirt, they made their way across the field to a barn. Kalargo was scared and he felt his legs weaken as he ran for his life. The ankle deep mud slowed them but they used the cows as cover until they got to the barn.

"Hey stand here, I'll be over there. When I start shooting, I want you to hold your fire until I whistle. Then you let them have it." He walked away to the other side of the barn.

Kalargo stood in between a group of cows. He still remembered that stench and how his shoes were ruined. He remembered the cold chrome barrel that he rubbed against his forehead. How his hands shook because his mind told him he was going to die in a barn with cow shit on his damn shoes, before he could say a prayer, gun shots were fired from an automatic. The cows began to run. It was now or never. He started shooting after he heard the whistle. He shot two of the guys and Mugumbi shot and killed the other.

Kalargo ran over and kicked the mac-10 away from the hands from one of them. The other guy laid face up gagging and holding his throat. The bullet went through his neck. He stood there in shock.

"Well, what are you waiting on?"

The other survivor looked up at them with a bullet in his upper torso. The full moon lit the cloudless sky and provided enough light to see the eyes of this older man.

"Well, it's your kill. You shot him. You finish him."

Mugumbi walked over to the guy he shot and put another bullet in his head.

Kalargo looked at him.

"Well, I thought I heard him breathe..." He frowned at him, "...just a little bit." His accent was stronger than his because he learned English later in life.

Mugumbi walked over to him and stood behind him. "Listen..." he held Kalargo's arm up and aimed the pistol. "...Just." He spoke with a calm and relaxed voice, "...aim, and just pulled the trigger. Trust me, the last thing you need is to see this ass hole again one day." He whispered in his ear. He looked at his uncle and sighed. He quickly pulled the trigger four times. His nerves in his stomach were jumping like they were attached to a jack hammer.

He patted him on his back, "Welcome to a world that not many people have a chance to experience. Hey, it was self-defense. You can always tell your innersoul that, if that'll make you comfortable, at least I won't tell anyone."

He looked at his uncle, and shoved the pistol into his gut.

"Look at it this way; you never have to kill him twice."

" Now I can live with that" Kalargo told him.

He thought to himself, "Ten years went fast." The taste of a bad grape reminded him that he was in his living room overlooking the pool through the French doors.

*   *   *

Later that evening

"Hello." Kalargo spoke into his cellular.

Jamie spoke over the music in the background. "Are you busy?"

"Of course not..." Kalargo said.

"We are going out to dinner at Nicholis Nicholis. Do you think you can meet us there?" Jamie asked.

He was looking through his closet. "Sure I can. What time?"

"Ten thirty, I made reservations already. We'll see you there." They ended the call.

He entered his office and called Na Min. He sat at his desk with his feet propped on the edge of the two-inch thick glass.

"Annyong-haseyo…" Kalargo said.

Na Min was happy to hear from him, "Kalargo, I've been expecting your call. I've already transferred those funds. How did last night go? No problems?"

Kalargo slightly twisted his neck and spoke with confidence. "Of course not, you know how those last minute decisions are handled."

They both grinned a little. "How's Jamie doing?"

"Just fine, matter of fact her and I are meeting tonight for dinner."

"She's a beautiful woman. I can see you and her being together for a very long time…" he quickly changed the subject, "…when was the last time you spoke to your uncle?"

He was surprised to be asked. "Actually I tried to call him today. But I got the answering machine."

"Have you heard about the store they opened?"

"What! He didn't tell me about that. That son of a gun, he's moving up in the world." He sighed.

"So that's the second store. The first one is in Osan. Where is the…" before he could finish.

"Yes, and the other store is in Pusan. Him and his wife…" he was interrupted.

"What, he tied the knot? After all these years…" he rubbed his left index finger across his eyebrow, "…he could have invited me." He sighed.

"Hey I don't mean to be rude but I'm a little busy. However I wanted to tell you about the transfer, and to keep up the good work." Before he could end the call Kalargo asked him about the civil war in The Gambia.

"Everything's going accordingly, sometime this week we'll have to sit down and discuss an important issue." he spoke with a more serious tone.

"If you are flying in from South Korea, it has to be important." He told him.

"Anyway, I'll give you a call. Until then, make sure you call your uncle." He agreed and they ended the call.

Kalargo flipped the switch on the computer and within minutes he was looking at his bank account. He transferred the funds to his business account, "Southern Pacific Martial Arts and Fitness" and most to a Swiss account. He smiled at the screen and decided to give his employees a bonus.

Moments later, the phone rang. "Hello."

The voice on the other end sounded muffled and echoed. "Hey Kalargo..."

"Yeah, who is this?" Kalargo said.

He looked down at the caller id and did not recognize the area code or country code. "This is Crockett!"

"Heeey Crockett. Long times no hear, what's going on?" Kalargo asked, before he could respond, "Where are you?"

He barely understood him. "I just arrived in Bahrain, a small island in the Persian Gulf."

"Wow that big ship pulled into port?"

Crockett wiped his forehead of sweat. "No actually we flew in from the carrier."

Kalargo leaned back and relaxed. "It's kind of hectic over in the Persian Gulf with Sadam acting a fool. You boys will be at war soon. What is it called, Desert Storm?"

"Yep, but I'm lucky I'll be in Bahrain, fifty miles from Saudi Arabia and three hundred miles from Kuwait." He stood in a small red phone booth.

"I know you wish you were back in Hawaii or at the least the Philippines?" Kalargo asked. "You have no idea how long you'll be over there?"

"It's no telling, may be six months."

"Well..." he was interrupted.

"I might see you when I pass through for the martial arts competition in the Philippines."

"Well I'm not sure if I will fly back or go back by ship. I would hate to miss a port of call in Australia." The phone booth was like a lava pit. "I've been here five days and haven't seen a woman yet. They are all wrapped up"

They both laughed. "Hey be happy you're not in Afghanistan where they are covered from head to toe, and if caught starring to long is considered stalking." They laughed hard.

"Well I am guilty as hell. Listen I have to go, I am running out of minutes." he quickly said. "When I get out I was thinking about working for you. You know once I get out of the military. It's time to make some real money. But we…" The female voice interrupted his conversation to advise him of his remaining seconds.

"Hey, you just keep your head low. The most important thing is making it back. I'll always have a place for you ok, but next time call me collect." They both agreed and ended the call.

Chapter 6

Kalargo grabbed his keys and walked out the door. He wore a black Giovanni Versace suit with a white button up shirt. He looked his Lexus over for dirt. He sat in the driver seat and pushed the number three for his theme song, "Pay Back" by James Brown. He looked in the rear view mirror to make sure his face was clear of shameful objects. He opened the arm rest and lifted a bottle of Available by All Means cologne. He turned up the music and drove to the Nicholis Nicholis.

It was a Tuesday night with a slight breeze from the east with clear skies. He arrived at the hotel that hosted the restaurant on the thirty-second floor.

He pulled up to valet and the attendant gave him a ticket, exited and casually walked into the hotel. Before he could push the button, a couple entered the elevator, obviously drunk and having a good time.

"What floor?"

"Fifteen please." She said.

Her breast was literally falling out of her non-supportive dress. He looked away and pushed fifteen on the panel.

"Sorry." The female said as they stumbled out on the fifteenth floor. Her dark brunette hair with a small amount of gray strings gave her a Spanish look. He guessed that she had to be at least forty-five. Her earrings were studded with diamonds that matched her bracelet. He sighed with a smile and pushed the button.

He rubbed his mustache and eyebrows as he looked in the elevator mirror. As each floor passed the sound of the bell would ding, twenty-one, twenty two, and etc.

Finally, the elevator opened on the thirty-second floor and the skyline of Waikiki was beautiful. The live band can be heard. The candles that lit each table gave a welcoming feeling.

The host welcomed him. "Mr. Choi, your party awaits you. How is everything?"

He was known here like it was a second home, "Just fine and you Steve?"

Jamie walked over and gave him hug and a kiss.

"We have a table by the window" she told him as they approached this white and burgundy clothed table.

Her friend was a gorgeous knock out blonde. She stood and greeted him. The waiter spoke to him, "I just started my shift. You enjoy. Your waiter will be with you shortly, drinks?"

He pulled his seat out and slowly sat down. "Give me a wine cooler, with the lemon flavor."

"Ladies and you're having?" Steve asked.

"I'll have a glass of your house wine." Jamie ordered, Stacy requested the same.

"So, this is Stacy the world has been talking about." He reached over to shake her hand, "...and I am Kalargo. I hope Jamie has told you all the good things about me." He smiled; his African accent can be heard a little on certain words.

"I've heard so much about you." She said.

He grunted, "I'm an ok type of guy."

She leaned forward. Her long hair was pinned up in a bun, but a small portion was in her face, using her thumbs to separate and push it behind her ears. Her lips were lined with a pencil. She was like a Barbie that had walked out of the Barbie doll factory. Her deep cleavage allowed her breast to rest on the table, not that he was starring, but, hey they were actually starting to talk to him.

"I..." She paused.

"And here are your drinks." The waiter placed them on the table, "Would you like to order or you need more time?"

They looked at each other and agreed for more time. The waiter quickly walked away.

"Listen she was trying to tell me how you, how can I say it. Came here from Africa, is it true?" she looked him in his eyes.

Jamie interrupted, "Girl he doesn't want to talk about that stuff. Those were painful memories."

"Were they? I mean if you choose not to talk about it I would totally understand." Stacy said with a humbled voice.

He leaned forward and held Jamie's hand, "Well..." He looked her in the eyes. "There is something that I have not told anyone." He sighed and swallowed air.

"I tell you what. Lets order and then I'll tell you how I and my uncle made our journey." He said as he looked over the menu. They agreed.

Stacy had to be no more than 5'8, hundred thirty five pounds, straight blonde hair that came to the middle of her back, thirty eight double d and her lips were glossy, and kissable. She wore a satin dress that came two inches above her knees. Her tan was perfect. All of Stacy's gestures said to come home with me, not next week, or next month but right now.

"Is this your first time in Hawaii?" Kalargo looked at Stacy.

"Yes, she has been trying to have me visit her for years." She looked out of the huge picture window at the sky line. "It's so beautiful and scenic. I should have come a long time ago." She sighed.

"Girl, it took this long to get you here, now I hope it won't take the same amount of time to convince you to stay." Jamie grabbed her hand and they both smiled.

He thought that they were mighty touchy and clingy, but that's how females are in America he told himself.

"What do you think about her staying in Hawaii?" Jamie asked him.

He had to quickly pull his tongue out of Stacy's panties. He frowned. "Why not... I." He paused. "I'll leave it up to you guys. It is kind of expensive to live here." He sighed. "But..." He frowned and touched his mustache. "...I 'm sure she'll find work..." He was interrupted.

The waiter accosted the table. "Hello..." He stood with his hands behind his back. "Are you guys ready to order yet?" He asked with a patient but feminine voice and gesture.

Kalargo rubbed his stomach.

"Hmm, yes I would say we are ready. I'll have whatever the special is." He looked at them to confirm.

They ordered their food while he patiently wrote everything down. He repeated their order and asked. "Anything else you would like to add?"

They were sure they had everything. He sighed and closed his eyes, rubbed the back of his neck. He took a swallow of his wine. Jamie and Stacy waited for this amazing story of survival.

"Ok, Africa, well I was born in a small village and from my understanding. My whole family was killed. The village was burned to the ground. My uncle took me from The Gambia, Africa to South Africa and worked in a diamond mine. He was later laid off and found work at the port loading cargo."Thinking of these events had his eyes pinkish red, tearful and increased his heart beat. He sighed and continued.

"Well…" He decided to skip a portion; "It was so many years ago, I had to be, what, nine?" He put his hands together in front of his face, rested his chin between his thumb and the bottom of his index finger. He told an intriguing story.

It was the early 70's

"Kalargo, you see that crate…" Mugumbi asked, "…You have to get inside, it's the only way we can go to America."

"I stood on the pier behind six foot crates stacked on top of each other. A small amount of people working at three o'clock in the morning but the crowd had not arrived." He swallowed a good portion of his wine to remove the itchy sand paper feeling that lay at the bottom of his throat.

"I'm scared." I told him, "He grabbed me by my shirt and yanked me towards him." He paused.

"You listen to me. This is not the time to be scared! This is our only chance to get out of here!" He spoke with passion. His gestures were almost vivid. His hands were in front of him just as if he had taken the place of his uncle.

"If we get caught trying to go away as stowaway. We will regret it for the rest of our lives!" Mugumbi's hard whisper vibrated his ears.

"For six months I've been planning this trip. There is no time to horse around. Now crawl in!" He demanded.

He gently placed his hands on the table. Stacy and Jamie were totally blown away. The music by the band was tuned out. He had them by their ears like kids that were in trouble. Their eyes were fixed on his lips. He took a moment to look them in their wet eyes. He had noticed that they both were in shock and scared for his ordeal, but could not wait for what would happen next.

"Duck down! Shhh…" They quickly hid behind a wall of crates. A worker walked by, "Listen Tipi, These crates are next to be loaded, we have to do this now!" The look on Mugumbi's face was like the eyes of a lion, a mad pissed off lion.

"I crawled in and he told me, now listen, whatever you do. Don't panic! You see these holes. Use them for breathing. I will come looking for you in four hours. He knew the order of loading. My crate will be on top. I'll come and get you out." He told me.

He gave me my travel bag that had food. He closed the crate. It was dark and scary. The heat was unbearable. The stench made me vomit so much I gave up on trying to hold it in. I was in this motionless position that had paralyzed me."

"I cried when I felt the crane lift the crate into the air. I felt like a caged animal. I held on to my bag and closed my eyes. For the first time I told God that I was scared and I asked him to watch over me. I went to sleep."

Jamie and Stacy were so into his story. They forgot all about their drinks.

"I mean, of course I trusted him with my life, besides he did most of the loading on the pier. So I had no reason not to believe what he was telling me." He rubbed his face with his hands and shook his head. He scratched the back of his neck and leaned back into the chair. He was exhausted. The story brought back memories; the kind that would make a kid wet his pants.

His voice was lowered. "It, we were in those crates for three days!" He whispered like a kitten. He held his hands together in a praying form. His humbled voice could reach out and touch any ones heart. He sighed.

"I was sea sick two different times. The Indian Ocean truly has no mercy on a weak stomach." He rubbed his stomach.

"I heard a voice calling me. Tipi, are you OK?" I was weak. My lips were dry, too weak to respond, my uncle opened the crate. He threw water on my face. I was so thirsty; I tried to lick my forehead." He smiled but he was serious. "I almost died. He lifted my hand, and told me we made it. We are here." He told me. He gave me some food that he had gotten out of the garbage. Damn it was good to have something, anything. I can't tell you what it was. It was all mixed up with other food that was tossed out. But I know it was fresh, because it warmed my palms as I ate it out of my hands." He folded his lips inward and continued his story.

"When the ship docked in South Korea…" their eyes and mouth open wider, "… yes, I said South Korea." He gasped for air and the girls swallowed his pain.

"Because my uncle couldn't read, he assumed that the ship was going to America…" He leaned forward and looked them directly in their eyes, "…and we damn sure didn't speak Korean!"

"What the hell happened?" Somehow Stacy asked without moving her lips.

"Well the ship had an American flag on it, but it went to…" He had this look of surprise. "South Korea."

Their mouths were literally on the table. "No way!" they looked at each other.

"My legs were numb. I was wet from urine and defecation. The smell of just me was enough to commit suicide. I was out of food after my third day. As far as being thirsty, I drank whatever I had to drink, and yes my own urine." He frowned, "Somehow my uncle thought it took four days to get to America." He laughed.

They both slithered their tongues out in disgust. Jamie wiped her eyes with the back of her hand. She carefully tried not to smear her makeup.

"I couldn't do it..." Stacy said.

He interrupted her. "Trust me; never say what you won't do." He waved his left index finger in front of them.

"I thank God my uncle made me drink water for three days straight before our trip. I just can't imagine..." He paused. He was going to continue but the waiter had delivered their food.

"OK, you ordered the house special, all three of you. " His female like voice was distinctive. He also thought Kalargo was handsome. He placed the plates on the table. The steam from the food can be seen.

Jamie looked at her plate and said, "Excuse me, hmm. What in the world is this?" She looked cute and timid as her curiosity gave suspicion. The waiter smiled and batted his lightly lined eyes.

"That is squid covered with a lightly marinated peanut butter, a splash of lemon, and on the side. You have garlic bread and pasta with a squid sauce that's buttered." He stood with his hands behind his back.

"Have you tried this? "Stacy asked him.

"No, but I heard it's good and very healthy." He paused. "If you have found it not what you want, I'll be more than happy to replace it. No problem." They agreed.

Kalargo quickly mixed his squid into his pasta and commenced to chow down on his food. "Now this is good."

He added more seasoning and squeezed a tab bit of lemon, with his mouth filled to his gills, he said, "I remember the first time I had this." He used the table napkin to wipe his lips. "I had to be... what ten years old. It's a Korean dish that is usually served as a celebration, but now a day, it's more or less a regular meal."

He held the fork in his right hand and pointed it at their plate. "But, you do have to acquire a taste for it." He smiled.

It was at this moment Stacy was overwhelmed by this burning desire to have sex with him. She liked how his broken English rolled off his lips, and how intelligent he is. He knew so much about other places. He was so intriguing. Her eyes were wet, but her panties were wetter, she cried and wiped her eyes. She knew it would never happen. He just didn't seem like that type of guy, someone that would understand her.

At the end of their dinner they rubbed their bellies and declared themselves full.

"Not bad, for a plate of, whatever it was." She smiled and pushed her plate away. Stacy looked at Jamie.

"You still wanted to see his house?" she asked her, before she could respond he raised his hand like a child in grade school that had an answer to a question,

"Check please. Oh yeah, you wanted to see my house? It's OK." He said as he pushed his shoulders up.

"I have to return for something anyway." He thought about her and how she's been playing footsy under the table with him.

In his mind he had to ask himself 'what kind of a friend is she? She just met me and flirting with me?' He thought all of it was strange.

Later, they arrived at his house, the touch of a button, his double iron gates opened. Stacy's eyes open wide.

"Wow…" she looked out the window like a kid's first time at Disney World and all the cartoon characters were lined to meet her.

This is gorgeous and wondered how he can afford such a luxurious place. Like a tour guide, Jamie explained the designs and culture behind the architecture.

"As you can see how fond he is of the Oriental culture…" she pointed out the native plants from South Korea, arches, and Buddha.

"Now whatever you do…" they closed the doors to the car. "Don't step on his rose garden." Stacy carefully made sure not to.

After showing Stacy around Jamie pulled him into the bathroom.

"I know what you are thinking and she's not your type." She smiled as she unzipped his pants and pulled out his penis. He chuckled and looked directly in her eyes. His thumb slowly and lightly touched her forehead. She sat on the toilet and put his python in her mouth.

Suddenly, there was a knock at the door. "Jamie, where is the T.V. and entertainment you told me about, from behind the door his soft voice said, "She's busy. But the remote that's on the coffee table, push the second red, button." A brief pause before he could catch his breath. He combed his fingers through her hair, "Yeah, just push the red button and aim it at the wall across from the couch.

Stacy put her ear to the bathroom door, giggled with her hands over her mouth and tiptoed away. The red button produced an entertainment center from the floor and she was entertained.

Moments later, Jamie entered the living room with a smile, "Girl…" Stacy put her hands over her mouth. "Shhh… I don't want to hear it." They both laughed.

"Jamie, where did you find this man?" Stacy looked at her with this curious look. Her lips tooted up as she tilted her head.

Jamie flopped on to the couch, crossed her legs and signed.

"You could have at least tried to brush your hair and wiped a little lipstick on or something." They both giggled like teens. Stacy leaned over, "What does he do?" She asked with curiosity.

The phone rang. "Do you want me to get that?" Jamie asked.

Kalargo's voice came from behind the bedroom door. "I got it! Hello."

The voice on the receiver was deep and troubled.

"Kalargo, the warehouse was raided!" Bennett said.

"What! Who all was arrested?" Kalargo asked.

He sounded like he was almost out of breath. "Pat, Damion, and big Mike. I had just left and I'll be damn…" He paused.

"Do you know who raided?"

"Honolulu police, it looked like they were looking for drugs. You need to call the dock!" He said.

"Who is the weakest link of them all?"

Bennett paused, "Damion."

"Well, get the lawyer and bail them all out, make sure you bail Damion out first. Was anything left behind?"

"No."

"But if they interrogate Damion long enough. They might find out that it's on the dock and the answer to your question, everything was already taken to the dock."

"I'll call you back. I got to call the dock." The phone call ended.

He slammed his fist down on the desk, "Shit." He dialed captain Tomzack's number nervously.

After the phone call he sat on the edge of the desk with his head in his palms. His buzz from the alcohol slowly drifted away. He heard the music coming from the living room. He thought of Stacy tits and ass.

"Hey." He rose up and threw on a pair of jeans. He applied green apple lotion and a small amount of Hugo Boss cologne on his chocolicious body.

"Sorry for being a horrible host." He walked out bare footed. Stacy legs were slightly open.

"Jamie, you didn't offer her anything?"

"We were just sitting here thumbing through the music and talking about old times."

He walked over to the wet bar. "Let me see… I have Cognac, white wine or Vodka."

Jamie immediately said, "I'll have some white wine. Do you have any strawberries or grapes?"

Stacy boldly requested, "I'll have the bottle of cognac." She let out a strong sigh that lifted her small strands of hair from the front of her face.

He thought if she drinks this bottle, it's over. The freak will for sure come out tonight, he spoke beneath his breathe. I'll have her stripping and eating Jamie's crotch and sucking me like a drunken vacuum." He continued to speak to himself.

"My God, it's going to be a fabulous night and Jamie, she'll be too drunk to remember anything." He smiled.

"Ladies…" He gave them a glass and begins pouring Jamie's drink first. Stacy quickly grabbed the cognac bottle, popped the cork and slammed the mouth of the bottle like she had deep throated before. His eyes opened wide.

"Oh my…" He looked at Jamie. "You might need to keep an eye on her." He said with a sarcastic voice. He turned up the music and told them he'll be back. He slipped into his office. He sighed and used his palms to push the stress from his eyes to his ears and to the back of his neck.

"I got to call Na Min…" He held the phone in his left hand and sighed.

"This is going to be harder than I thought" He pushed the first number. "If I do it now, I won't be interrupted later."

"Good evening." he answered the phone. They spoke in Korean. He let him know that it was a small matter and it was nothing to worry about. Their conversation ended.

He returned to the living room. "Surprise, I am back." He stopped dead in his tracks. The bottle of cognac that was full was now half full. He pretended like he didn't see it.

"They were laughing from the top of their gills. They had tears rolling down their faces. The wild life channel showed a rare monkey encounters with a female monkey. The Japanese monkeys were in a cage. When the monkeys are having sex, the jealous male monkeys attack the male while he's having sex, knowing that he won't stop having sex until he has an orgasm. They immediately run when they are finish. The zoo doctors said that this is the only time they have an advantage in fighting this male monkey. He flopped down between them and laughed like he had never seen it before. Jamie leaned on him putting her right hand on his stomach. Stacy laughed so hard at the monkeys facial expressions until tears fell. Her legs were open and rubbing against his.

The monkeys yanked on his tail, punched and vigorously pulled his facial hair. He looked so pissed off, but like usual he didn't stop.

Stacy grabbed the bottle of cognac and took a huge gulp. At the same time Jamie looked at him, "Don't pay her any attention."

She held her stomach to reduce the pain that her laughter gave her. She stood and laughed her way to the kitchen, obviously drunk.

"Why is your kitchen moving so much?" She asked.

Jamie looked at him, "Nope… don't think about it."

For some reason no matter how idiotic she looked. She looked hot as hell. Suddenly the phone rang, "Thank God." Jamie said.

After three rings he had not moved, "Go ahead and get the phone… tell them I'm not here."

She picked up the phone, "Hello…" She looked at him. "It sounds very important." She handed him the receiver.

"I'll take it in the office." He grunted like a kid.

Jamie walked over to her, "Why are trying to lead him on?"

Her eyes blood shot red and a fresh smell of cognac on her breath. She slowly and carefully leaned forward. "You told me..." Jamie was interrupted. Stacy softly placed her index over her lips.

"I am just having fun." She held on to Jamie for support.

"I really don't mean any harm." She struggled to return to the coach. Her words drooled off her lips, "Jamie..." her eyes filled with tears.

"Why can't I find me a man like you?" She slowly shook her head and scratched her neck. Jamie laid her down on the couch.

"No harm intended, you know everyone tell me that I am so beautiful, but I can't keep a man." She reached for the bottle. Jamie pulled her hand.

"No... I think you've had enough of that. Have you spoken to anyone about this?" Jamie asked her.

She looked her in the eyes; she softly bit her bottom lip. "Girl, it's been an ongoing nightmare." She used her left pinky finger to dig into her right ear.

"Did I ever tell you how jealous I was of you? Every since we were kids... I think I was cursed." She pushed her tears back and buried her face into the pillow. Jamie began to emotionally break down. Her best friend in the world is deeply depressed. She gave her a hug. They both burst into tears. She grabbed her hands and brought them to her face. "Stacy, you have to stay strong!"

"I know, but it's so hard!" Stacy whispered. "And one understands." She looked Jamie in her eyes and grunted.

"I am fucked up." She said.

Jamie stopped her. "No, you are my friend. You are Stacy." They both laughed and kissed each other on the lips.

Kalargo came from the room partially dressed, "Ladies... I'll be right back."

Jamie rose from the couch and walked over to him. "Is everything OK?"

"Yeah..."

She looked over her shoulder as she walked him to the door.

"I just have to take care of something. I'll be back." He gave her a passionate kiss on her lips and held her tight.

"I apologize for Stacy." She said.

He wedged his lips between hers and French kissed her. He inhaled her breath with his eyes closed.

"If I ever wanted a best friend, it would be you." He held her hand as he walked to the door. She leaned her head in his upper arm. It was this moment that he had realized how he truly felt for her.

"Put Stacy in the guest room." He opened the door. "When I get back, I want you in your birthday suit." They giggled and kissed each other good-bye.

Chapter 7

Seoul, South Korea

Agent Na Min Choi sat at his desk. His diamond channel set pinky ring sparkled when he reached for the phone. He dialed his step daughter's home and waited for someone to answer. His old fashion reading glasses sat at the lower tip of his nose, his beige robe with gold initials, "NC". It was early in the morning, but this call was important. His step daughter answered in Korean. "Annyong-haseyo"

"Hello Yuki, don't mean to call you so late…" he was interrupted.

"Daddy, I was thinking of you earlier today. How is everything?"

He sighed, "Well…" He never discusses his business with her and she totally understood.

"Let's say a little hectic." He paused like he had a lot on his mind.

"Your work is going to kill you; it's time for you to retire." Her words melted the wax in his ears. "Yeah in another five years."

But she knew he could afford to retire now but he was in too deep. She looked over at Mugumbi, "Well I am sure if you are calling this late, you must be calling for Mugumbi."

She heard his sigh, "I love you my dear."

"Yes I know." She gave the phone to her husband. "Honey, it's my dad."

Na Min tapped the tip of his fingers on the calendar that covered his desk. It was seconds before Mugumbi cleared his throat with his face half buried into the pillow. His Korean was horrible in the morning hours, day hours, and whenever he tried to speak Korean, "Annyong-haseyo."

Whenever he called for business their dialogue was always coded to their understanding. "I am inviting you to the next executive party." His voice was calm.

He looked at the clock, "OK."

"I know this is bad timing, but I need you on the next flight to Hawaii. You will have more details once you get there." He circled a date on his calendar, "Next flight?" He sighed.

"Not a problem." Mugumbi closed his eyes.

A the age of forty seven he felt like a thirty year old, fit, healthy, but his down fall is his addiction. So far it has not yet interfered with his work. He used his left thumb to snatch an annoying nose hair. He looked at it.

"Is everything else OK?" Na Min asked.

"Oh yeah, can't compliant. Listen, I will call you when I touch down on the island." The line ended.

Na Min removed his glasses, grabbed his bottle of Gin and thought about the first time he met Ginifer. He looked at the glass and asked, "I no longer wonder how you have become my best friend?"

Of course she did not respond. He liked that about her. She gave him no lip, no limit to her love, and most of all, she had given him plenty of nights of satisfaction, and someone to talk to. She relieved him of bad dreams of those unspeakable acts to humans for the name of national security. Some times their faces haunted him in his sleep. He knew he could tell her his deepest secrets without her going around blabbing his business and getting him in trouble. He also knew that Ginifer was slowly killing him. His liver was not functioning properly. He picked up his glass of Gin and slowly touched his lips. He kissed edge of the shot glass and licked the rim. It was cold, he tilted it just enough to sip her wetness. She was warm and soaking wet, the no longer burning of his throat made their bond stronger. He looked at the glass.

"Am I an alcoholic, nope? Not I say Ginifer." Na Min grinned.

He twisted the shot glass and poured it in to his mouth like he was doing something super special. His tongue was relieved, his throat burned just enough to remind him of their bond, but not like it used to. Her strength was no longer potent.

"Am I losing my love for her?" He asked himself, "Ginifer?" He tilted his head to the left, raised his voice and looked at the glass and then the bottle.

"Now you know, you and I go way back. We can talk about anything." He tilted his head like she was naughtier than he.

"You are not satisfying me like you used to. Is there anything that you would like to tell me?" He examined the bottle to make sure he had not substituted her for a cheaper whore in a bottle form. He knew she would not have liked that.

"Never." He poured another shot.

Suddenly his wife knocked at the door. "Is everything OK?" She peeked in on him trying to make love to Ginifer. He was caught in the act. She once told him that she was no good for him. He looked at her.

"Just finishing my dear, I'll be to bed soon, just cleansing my breath." He quickly downed Ginifer one last time for the night and tucked the Gin bottle in his cabinet behind him.

"You know what?" He whispered to the bottle of Gin, "She has been jealous for years." And finally cut the desk light off. "Good night, see you next time."

*   *   *

Honolulu, Hawaii

Kalargo's car cruised smoothly on the highway at eighty miles per hour. He was tempted to go faster, but he was the only driver on the road at two forty five in the morning. He slowed down to fifty five; he received a call from an old friend that suggested that he meet him at the cafe off the highway. Even though he had not seen him in awhile, he felt like he had always been trustworthy, so why not?

The cafe practically empty and spooky under the circumstances he parked and entered. He sighed as he sat at the counter. The waitress asked, "Need a menu?" She reached for the menu.

He stopped her, "No, just a cup of coffee please." He looked around while he waited. He stretched.

"Sugar?"

"Ummm, yeah and milk."
The waitress gave him a spoon and a napkin and went to get cream. He used the napkin to clean up, but he noticed some writing on the other side. He flipped it over. He thought it was very strange, he found it to be strange because it was in Chinese. He quickly looked around. He read it, "Someone is dirty among you, clean house immediately!"

His eyes opened wide. He stood up and tossed two dollars on the counter and stormed out the café, "Too spooky." He felt as he jumped in the car and sped off.

On the way home he thought about each and every guy that worked for him in the past and to this date. He smiled because Stacy kept popping up on his mind, but he knew he had to focus.

Moments later, he arrived to his house. He tiptoed through the living room. The TV on, he cut it off. The guest room door was open, he closed it. He quietly crawled in bed like a sneaky snake. Jamie was sound asleep, naked, beautiful, and desirable. She was awakening by his wet tongue on her ankle and up her calf. She smiled and played like she was so sleepy. He knew how to wake her up and he did it very well. They made love through bout the night.

The next morning sun slowly moved between the shades and across Stacy's face.

"Ahhh..." She moaned.

"My head," it pounded like a bass drum as she lay in bed on her back holding her head, "I must have had way too much to drink." She lifted the sheets. She never got out of her clothes.

"I can't handle anymore of these wild nights." She mumbled, looked around and realized that she was still at Kalargo's house. She was in the bathroom when she overheard Jamie and him making love. She leaned over the sink and sighed.

She was sad deep down inside. She couldn't have a relationship that lasted more than two or three weeks. The relationship would end the first night of copulation. She buried her face in her palms and sucked up her depression, let out an aggravating sigh of relief. She had learned to ignore her feelings and move on with life.

Kalargo sat behind Jamie in the Jacuzzi bubbled with strawberry suds. He slowly washed, massage, and combed through her hair with his fingers. The shampoo lathered as he used more of it to wash and massage her back. He kissed her on the back of her neck. She leaned back and rested on his chest. She turned around and kissed him on the lips.

"I wish I could lie here all day." She put one leg out of the Jacuzzi. Suddenly she submerged herself and stood up, "but I know I can't." Her glossy body stood before him. She tiptoed into the shower to wash her hair of shampoo.

Moments later he remembered the napkin. He raised himself from the water and nakedly walked into the bedroom. His wet foot prints trailed his every move. The soap suds slowly slid down his shiny wet body. He grabbed his pants from the dirty clothes hamper.

"Damn." He read it again, "Someone is dirty among your crew. Clean up the coffee spill, he has priors." He stood there thinking, naked as a j bird. His wet hands soaked the napkin. He looked up at the ceiling.

"Need a towel?" He looked around as the towel landed on his shoulder. He wrapped it around his neck. He walked over to the night stand grabbed a lighter and thought about burning the napkin.

He pulled his pants up his legs and grabbed a white t-shirt. With the receiver in his hand, he dialed Bennett's number.

"Yeah, hello."

"Hey Bennett, wake up!" He commanded.

"I am, awake."

"What happened last night?" He walked into the bathroom to brush his teeth.

"I did exactly what you told me. I bailed Damion out, and I am going to bail the others out right now." He paused, "What time is it?"

"Twelve thirty." He spoke with a mouth full of toothpaste and toothbrush in his hand.

"Hold on." He could hear him coughing and clearing his throat and chest. "Babe, get up and get breakfast going. It's going to be another long day." Bennett told his wife in the back ground, "Yeah I'm back, now Damion, seem to be cool. He didn't say anything and they didn't ask him much either." He took a drag from his cigarette, "You know Kalargo, I think they knew he was a new guy, a truck driver that picked up and delivered. You know what I mean?"

"Hmmm, yeah." He gargled and spat out tooth paste and mouth wash. He thought about telling him about the napkin.

"How did they know about the warehouse?" There was silence.

"No idea, only reason I got away. I was standing by the escape tunnel." There was a pause and a question.

"So what's next Kalargo?"

He walked out the bathroom, "Hmmm, go bail out the other two; after wards make sure you bring them both to me. At the same time, I got some checking around to do.", before he ended the call, "oh yeah, Bennett! Make sure." He repeated himself, "make sure that you are not followed. They may put a tail on them." They both agreed.

"Bring them to Burger King on Nue Nue st." The call ended.

As he placed the phone down, He could hear the TV and stereo on from the living room. He knew Jamie was in the closet getting dressed.

"Jamie, go and ask Stacy if she's going to eat breakfast. If not…" He reached for his shoes. "Are you hungry?" He asked her.

She exited the closet with a pair of jean shorts, "We are going to get a bite to eat, how these look?"

He looked over his shoulder as he dug into the drawer for socks, "Absolutely stunning."

She walked over and kissed him.

"Well I guess I'll get something on the go." He said.

She grabbed her keys and purse, "I'll call you later."

She left with Stacy.

*   *   *

The sun beamed through Kalargo's windshield as he kept a paranoid eye on the inmate release at the Honolulu jail. He parked a half a block away to make sure Bennett was not followed. The first thirty minutes was crucial. He blast the air condition hoping it would stop the trail of sweat that crawl down his back. He debated in his mind if he should take a chance of going to use the bathroom.

"Damn, I knew I should have used it before I left." He pushed down on his mid section and looked in his driver side mirror. He grabbed a piece of gum and tossed it in his mouth and mumbled as he chewed his gum.

He reclined his seat and adjusted his mirror. He sighed and nervously looked in all his mirrors and looked at his watch.

"Five more minutes." He looked around and spotted a cafe that he could duck into to use the bathroom. He tapped his left foot against the bottom of the driver door.

"What the hell. I can run in and be out." He mumbled and opened the door. The sound of traffic and the smell of the downtown came to life. The exhaust of a cement truck slapped him as he dipped across the street and into the cafe. He weaved his way through the line.

"Excuse me, bathroom?" he pointed his finger.

"It's out of order." The employee said.

He rolled his eyes and turned around for the door. He step outside and immediately looked towards the jail. He walked funny, desperate and noticed an alley across the street.

"Thank God!" He quickly held his hand up at the moving traffic to jay walk, "Hey sorry." He waved at the driver. In the middle of the street was when he saw a patrolman watching him.

"Great, ahh no." he saw Bennett, Steve, and Pat shaking hands with the bondsman. He quickly turned around and rushed back to his car. He sighed.

"Damn it! About time they come out!" He jumped in and cranks the car, blew a bubble as he looked in the driver mirror.

"Come on!" he inclined his seat.

He put his car in drive and just before he could drive off. The patrolman tapped on his window. He looked at him and signaled to roll down the window. He nearly pissed on himself.

"Shit. Shit. Shit." He slowly rested his head on the head rest.

"How can I help you Mr. Police officer?" He looked like he had piss up to his eyes.

The officer stepped back from the car.

He looked Samoan, big and well tanned with curly short hair. He was very big, perhaps closer to fat and fighting to stay in his little brother's uniform. He looked very cultural. He smiled. He held his frown tightly.He held his pad in his hand and pulled his pen from his shirt.

Kalargo was tapping his foot nonstop.

"This is a fine automobile. Is this one of those new Lexus's LS400?"

He was in shock and a little pissed, "Yeah."

"Bro I like this car. I was thinking of getting my daughter one of these. You know for her graduation. How does it ride, pretty fast?"

Kalargo looked in his mirror, "Hmmm, Super fast" He anxiously said.

"I saw you earlier. You looked kind of lost."

"Well, I am a little lost. Do I make a left or right to get to the hospital?" He looked at Bennett's car drive by. He quickly answered his own question, "Now I remember a left and two blocks on the right." He looked up at the officer.

"You got it right." He noticed a car parking in front of a fire hydrant, "You have a nice day." He went from a fan to an officer of the law.

He followed Bennett trying to notice a tailing undercover car, nothing. "So far so good." he mumbled.

It took thirty minutes to get to the Burger King. He dialed Bennett's number.

"Bennett, what's going on?" He parked several blocks away after carefully driving around, "It's cool baby, just here waiting for you to call. I didn't think you would show." He sighed and sipped on a vanilla milk shake.

"Well what's going on?" He closed his car door and walked towards the Burger King.

"They have a court date."

"Who's the judge?" He waited for a response. He could hear him asking them in the back ground.

"Judge Kalauani, does he ring a bell?"

"Well, let's just say thank God it's him." He laughed and sat down across the street from the Burger King and looked for anything out of the normal.

"Let's say him and my father are golfing buddies. We can take care of him." He pulled a seat and thought about how crooked he is.

"I'll handle it from here. Everybody go home and wait for my call. I'll have the lawyers drop some names and get this thrown out."

*   *   *

Under clear blue western skies that were being chased by darkness from the east. The sun descended slowly. The purple and yellowish red eye danced on the horizon. The brightest stars can be seen as the flight from South Korea circle the island of Oahu.

"Ding ding." The fasten seat belt light illuminated. The captain's voice was calm over the intercom.

"Ladies and Gentlemen, I would like to welcome you to Honolulu, Hawaii. The weather is currently 89 degrees with a slight breeze out of the north. I hope you have enjoyed your flight to the southern pacific islands of paradise. We should be landing in twenty five minutes." The captain pointed out the different islands of Hawaii and a little bit of history about them.

Mugumbi stretched and lifted his blind to his window. He reached for the air plane's phone. He slid his credit card through the slot and started dialing. His Korean was warm to hear and his wife was excited to talk to him.

"Hello. " She was still in bed.

"Just letting you know that the plane will be touching down soon."
She loved his accent in Korean, but she never knew it was a voice of a hit man.

"I love you." She said.

"I love you. I'll be back in a week, may be sooner." He put his seat belt on.

"I'll be waiting." She gave him a kiss over the phone and they ended the call.

Chapter 8

The sweat dripped from Kalargo's body as he strained to push 270 lbs off his chest. His veins were like roots from a three hundred year old tree. He trembled as he slowly pushed the bar. He didn't have a spotter to help him. He found the inner strength and concentration to clear the stand. His heavy breathing pushed small amounts of sweat from around his lips, as he sat up and hung his head between his chests, resting his elbows on his upper thigh. He deeply planted his thumbs on his temples and massaged his headache, looked around his weight room and sighed. He used his fore arm to wipe his face. He was stunned.

"What the hell…" His forearm was smeared with blood. He ran over to the mirror. "Damn." He grabbed a towel. Lately his nose bleeds and headaches started to reoccur. He relaxed and held his head back with the towel on his nose. Before leaving he noticed CNN news was talking about the Persian Gulf and Iraq invasion of Kuwait.

"It's shameful how they focus on all of this oil. When there are many countries at war. But because they have nothing to truly contribute to the world…" He shook his head in a disappointed way. "…they are over looked, thousands die without help, but then again this is sadly my way of making money." He walked into the living room.

He checked the towel for blood. "Someone has to help the poorest people in the world." He claimed.

"They are sending five hundred thousand troops. For what, oil?" He sucked air between his beautiful white teeth. "I've sent ammo to over thirty countries that have been at war for more than five years, but no one jumped in to stop the mass killings in none of those countries." He checked his nose and grabbed a bottle of water.

"Yep, let them keep worrying about the powerful countries. I'll keep making my money." He said as he nodded his head at a shameful game the world plays. As he passed through the living room he pushed play to hear Anita Baker while he took a long hot bath. He lit the candles, ran the water and plucked nose hairs. He applied his shaving cream.

*   *   *

"Room four fifty five please." Mugumbi checked into his hotel. The receptionist gave him a key without question.

"Enjoy your vacation." She smiled. She didn't know it, but she had just ruined his moment. He hated people that displayed a fake smile.

He nodded his head, "Thank you."

He found his room, slid his key, and opened the door. He looked in the bathroom, closets, and under the bed. Finally he looked under the mattress and pulled a small black case that contained a .380 caliber revolver and silencer. He looked at his watch and walked over to the T.V. and turned it on. He scans the channels for his favorite South Korean program.

The United States seemed so different to him. He had grown accustom to the South Korean way of life. However, Hawaii catered to the Japanese tourist.

"Found it." He always amazed Americans when he spoke Korean better than he spoke English. He entered the bathroom and looked in the mirror. He rubbed his fingers across his mustache, pushed his lip up to inspect his gums. He licked his lips to moisturize them. He looked down at his arm and touched his needle tracks. One by one he touched them like his temple had been destroyed. For the first time he realized how ugly and embarrassing they were. He wore long sleeve shirts to hide them.

He spent some time in the bathroom. The hotel phone rang; he walked over to answer it. His beloved dope in his right hand and picked up the receiver. He sat down on the bed and listened. Finally he hung the receiver on the phone. He walked over to open the door. There was no one; he saw an exit door down the hall. He quickly grabbed his .380, loaded it and slid it in his front right pocket. He ran towards the exit and hid.

Behind the exit door, he peeped through the crack of the door. "Hmm…" he raised his eye brows out of curiosity. He saw a twenty five year old, short curly black hair, Polynesian decent.

He stopped in front of Mugumbi's hotel room door, without hesitation he pulled an eight by twelve mustard envelope from beneath his shirt and slid it beneath the door. He quickly ran down the hall and disappeared. For the first time he actually saw who the messenger was. He made sure it was clear before coming from behind the exit door. In his room he retrieved the envelope that contained a map, itinerary, photo, and directions to the location of his victim.

He pulled the picture out and sat down at the desk. The light from the window entered that side of the room. He leaned forward, resting his elbows and studied the picture. He wanted to remember as much as possible, like the scar beneath the bridge of his nose.

After an hour of preparation, he grabbed the receiver, and dialed 0, "Yes, this the front desk of the Marriott Waikiki how can I help you?"

"Yes I would like to have a rental car to go sightseeing."

"Are you interested in a small, compact or economy?"

He thought about it. "Do you have a four door sedan?"

"I can check, give me one moment please. Can you hold?"

"Yes." He held the photo in his hand.

"Yes we do, we have the Chrysler cirrus." There was a silence. He had no idea what the Chrysler cirrus was, but it sounded good.

"Yeah I'll be down to pick it up in thirty minutes." They both agreed and ended the call. He quickly primped, and left the room.

He wanted to be as familiar with the area as much as possible and with the victim's daily movement. The target lived in a high rise condo on Ala Wai blvd, a busy one way that becomes quiet after one thirty in the morning. The canal that separated Waikiki from Honolulu had a golf course that stretched the length of the canal. He is nocturnal creature of the night. His favorite place on the weekend is a popular club by the name of Candy Paint. He was known to be heavily drunk, and flamboyant.

He drove down the Blvd checking every alley, garbage dumpster, nook and cranny. He looked for cameras, smoke areas and parking garages. He looked at his watch. The hour hand was on the nine and the minute hand was slightly on the six. He pulled over to the right and grabbed his bag of bread to feed the ducks. He wanted to walk and learn the area. He may have to jump in the canal and run across the golf course to get away. He wore a pair of lose fitted cotton shorts, golfer's wide brim hat, with sandals that buckled around his ankle. His gun was tucked between his belt in the back of his pants. He walked for two hours before he decided to walk to the club.

*   *   *

The next morning the sun rose between the mountains and played peak-a- boo with the clouds. Some parts of Honolulu were damped from passing showers. Mugumbi lay in bed tossing and turning from a dream. He spoke in his native tongue. He woke up reaching for his right thigh and realized there were knocking at the door. He sighed.

His eyes opened as he heard the lock on the door opening.

"Room service."

"Good morning…" He quickly slid the gun in the pocket of his Marriott robe.

"Room service?" She asked.

"Hmm…" He stood and slowly asked for her to come in.

"It's not a problem, I could come back later if you prefer?" her timid manner and voice was cute. He walked over to the window and sat down holding his leg. He rubbed the scars that had not healed properly.

"You need ice on that?" The maid said as she entered the bathroom.

"No, it's not as bad as it looks." He walked over to remove his travel bag from the edge of the bed.

"Lesson learned." he said to the maid.

She peaked from the bathroom. "Excuse me."

He felt like talking since she had seen him touching his leg.

"The scar, I said that it was a lesson learned." He opened the travel bag.

"And what was that?" She said and returned to cleaning the bathroom.

"The lesson learned was to always be careful with your enemies." He laughed and she didn't get it. He stuffed the eight by twelve envelope under his arm and walked out the room.

When he returned, the room was cold, cleaned and scented. He tossed his news paper on the bed, unbuckled his belt and pulled it from around his waist. He opened his needle kit and sat on the edge of the bed next to the night stand. He put a small amount of water on his crooked shaped spoon. Like a scientist, he carefully added his heroin to the water and heated the spoon with a lighter. The flamed darken it black as the substance bubbled. From the spoon to the syringe he put it, quickly grabbed the belt and tightens it around his upper bicep. He put the end of the belt in between his teeth to hold it. He pulled harder until his veins looked like a batch of muddy earth worms.

He sighed as the rush of dope made its way through his body. He sat there thinking about the feeling, the warmth and love that followed.

*   *   *

Seoul, South Korea

In the eyes of a fifteen inch gold fish that swam toward the glass of a beautiful fish tank. It looked forward to being fed. Na Min stood with food in his hand, "Here Topi, I don't know if I'm feeding you too much or too little." He tossed food in the tank; Topi swam to the top to gobble the crumbs.

He turned his back to the huge exotic fish tank that held some of the world's rarest fish. "Damn what's taking him so long to call me?" He looked at his watch. "He's late."

He walked over to his desk to make a decision. He decided to wait for Zang's phone call. "Honey if the phone ring, take a message, I'll be ..." He was interrupted by the phone, without hesitation. "Hello."

"Yeah, Na Min, I hope I did not have you waiting?"Zang sighed. "We have a small problem," he paused.

"What kind of a problem?" Na Min's asked.

There were silence and then a huge sigh that warmed his earpiece. "Well as you know we have invested a lot of money in this country. Our people are not, how can I say it? They don't quite fit in. They stand out like pink tigers."

Na Min sat down and tapped his eraser of his pencil on the desk top calendar. He broke the silence. "Other words, you would like to have, perhaps a black..." He swallowed his fear of his request. "...person." The tapping stopped and the pencil fell from his hand. He rubbed his thumb across his eyebrows and slowly pushed his hand to the back of his neck and massaged it.

"Zang, I don't have anyone who is qualified with the military experience." He leaned back into the seat. "That is a lot to be asking for Zang. Do you know people are watching me? They are suspicious. Do you think I have people that I can just pluck from my hand for this kind of stuff?" He closed his eyes.

"Listen, we trust you and it's the only reason we are asking you. We trust your decisions and we are willing to make it worth your while." Zang said.

"Zang, you think you guys have all the answers. This year is supposed to be our final operation. But now you call me with all this. I don't know what to make of it. I mean, come on. What do you think this is Zang?" He threw the pencil across the desk with anger, "I just can't believe this." He poured a glass of Gennifer and slammed it down his throat.

"Na Min, I swear we are planning to make this our final request of you. You have delivered throughout the years and you have had some close calls and hairy situations. We are willing to compensate you for everything you have done for us."

His breathing can slightly be heard; before he could speak he was interrupted.

"How would you like to mysteriously inherit a two million dollar apt building?" He waited for him to respond.

"How important is this so call, black person? What do you need him to do?"

84

"Well, we need someone who could go in undetected, speak the native language good enough to pass as one of their own, and we are willing to train him if we need to." He paused.

"And the mission of this person?" he knew he preferred not to talk about it.

"We need to give an executive party to the General Kakambo Twigani."

He realized how heavy this was and the difference it would make to the war. The North Koreans were no longer trying to just make money from the diamonds and oil. They were trying to perhaps colonize and control this small African country.

The sound of the Gin came from the bottle as he poured another glass. "Zang, Zang, my God what are you trying to…" He held the receiver from his ear and choked it with his hands and gritted his teeth. He calmly put the receiver back to his ear. He sighed. He leaned forward and planted his elbows on the desk.

"How long before the drilling will begin for oil and diamonds?" He asked him.

"Well, that is a part of the problem. A lot of things can't get done unless the war is over, but, if we don't have control over the situation. One of the NATO countries will eventually step in and gain control and discover the natural resources."

"How many apt buildings do you have?"

Zang grunted, "Plenty in the United States and in other countries."

"I tell you what. I want three apt buildings at ten million inherited to me." He said.

"So, this means you can deliver?" His desperate voice of urgency was slowly relieved.

"Listen, we will go over everything in greater detail." Na Min said.

"Hmm… We need someone soon, like in the next three weeks." He said with concern.

"Zang, relax and wait for my phone call." He ended the call.

*   *   *

It was nine thirty and Mugumbi's mind was made up to where the hit will take place. He figured he would follow him and park down the street from the club.

He looked in his rear view mirror, finally he saw the black Benz pull out from the condominium.

"OK." He waited until he passed him, looked to verify license plate number. "That is it."

After two hours, he was frustrated. The prospector stopped four different places before arriving to the club, he knew if allowed his frustration to get involved something could go wrong. It was one thirty in the morning when they arrived at the club, now came the wait.

Chapter 9

The parking garage of the club was located among a plaza of stores, three stories high and very spacious.

"Ding, ding." The elevator door opened and the club customers giggled as they looked for their cars.

"I hope this is the right floor." She was obviously drunk and leaned on the shoulder of her girlfriend. Their voices echoed as the clacking of their hills tapped and scratched the concrete. The voices silenced as they walked further away from him. The sound of keys dangled and the laughter can barely be heard.

He looked at his watch, and sighed. "It's almost about that time." He wiped a bead of sweat from his nose. His black golf gloves were skin tight. He also thought the garage could be a bad place to make this happened. The crowd continued to exit the elevator and walk to their cars. He ducked, a couple walked from the floor below searching for their car. The keys are heard opening the car door. Their lips locked with a French kiss. One thing lead to another, it did not take long for the windows to fog. She moaned softly but the movement of the car was inevitable.

"Ding ding." A group of people walked off the elevator. "Look!" They were in shock. "God, Oh my." They giggled as they stared at the couple and rushed toward their cars.

More people passed them and finally they cranked their car up and left. Not many cars remained on this floor, and again the prospector took forever. Suddenly the elevator door opened and the man on the photo exited. He whistled, as he retrieved his keys from his pocket.

"Good nobody is around." faced down in front of the victims car. He pulled out his gun and twisted the silencer on tightly. The echoes of his whistling stopped. Mugumbi's heart pounded his chest so hard it felt like it was in slow motion. He did not know if he had been seen or not, but it was an uncomfortable feeling. The victim stopped to where only his shoes could be seen. He appeared to be looking around. Finally, he slowly walked cautiously as if he was suspicious.

Just before he pulled the trigger, suddenly a car horn blasted the parking garage.

"Oh my God!" it startled him. A loud voice came from a far.

"Long time no see."

"Wow, Mr. Kobalulu. How long has it been? At the least, what? Five years."
They hugged and spoke for awhile. Their conversation was unintelligible. They
laughed as they said their goodbyes.

"Come on." He waited for his friend to drive off, wet his lips, gripped the
handled on his gun.

He inhaled deeply, closed his eyes and listened to his footsteps. The sound of
the car keys dangled. It was so quiet, peaceful, and sudden. The sound of the
silencer was so vacuumed like and just powerful. The victim fell over in his car.

"Perfect." He walked by and quickly closed the door with his hip. He looked
around the garage and shook his head. He looked into the car and shot him two
more times in the head to make sure he was dead, and walked away unnoticed.

*   *   *

Kalargo covered his head with his pillow. The phone rang; he tried to ignore it
by pushing a button on the night stand to shut off the ringers on all the phones in
the house. Ten minutes later, his cellular phone was ringing. He also turns it off as
he mumbled and cussed, "It's probably Jamie."

Fifteen minutes later, his pager goes off, "God damn it!" he snatched his pager
and looked at it. "No way..." he turns the phones on and dialed Mugumbi's
number. They spoke in their native tongue, "...hey uncle. It has been awhile. You
picked a good time to call."

"Well I was in town for a couple of days, so I decided to visit my nephew."

He pulled the pillow over his face and looked at the clock. "Hmmm, it's ten in
the morning." He swallowed a dry throat. "I needed to get up anyway." He gave
him directions to where he lived.

Later that day

As Mugumbi walked out of Kalargo's house, Bennett walked up the driveway.

"Uncle this is my number one guy, Bennett. This is my Uncle I always tell you
about." They shook hands.

"South Korea, right yeah he speaks of you. It's a pleasure to meet you. Hey I'll
be inside." Bennett made his way in the house.

"Yeah go ahead."

After ten minutes Kalargo came in. "I got some information."

"What you got?" Bennett ask.

He pulled out a photo of Saul. "Do you recognize him?"

"Yeah, he used to work for me. Where did you..." before he could say another word, he showed him a note, "I found this on my windshield." He gave him the note.

"Wow." He gave him the note back and told him to wait a moment. He told him about the napkin from the café.

"What does it mean, you have a spill?" Bennett ask.

"Clean up the dirty spill, someone is dirty among you." They both looked at each other and shook their heads. Bennett rubbed his bottom lip with his left thumb and sighed.

"And he left out of the blue, no reason at all; you know what we have to do?" Kalargo looked at him. "This is the rat that had the warehouse raided." He grunted.

"How do you know?" Bennett wanted to be for sure.

Kalargo sat down to explain, "Check this out the same night the warehouse was raided. I received a phone call from an old friend of mine. He told me to meet him at the cafe. It was important. But when I got there, I waited, ordered coffee. Somehow, this note manages to come with my coffee. The waitress had no idea how it got there."

"So who is the old friend?" Bennett ask.

Kalargo's right index finger pointed toward the ceiling, "I can't say. If he went through this much trouble to let me know this. It would be best to keep him anonymous." They both agreed.

That was one of the good qualities that he liked about Bennett, If he did not try to know more than what he needed to know.

"So this is the guy?"

"Got to be." Kalargo assured him.

"Are we sure?" Bennett looked at him.

"All of this can't be a coincidence."

"I guess he got it coming." Bennett sat down and sighed. "Just say when boss."

"Go ahead and go home, I'll call you later to night when I get the address on this guy." Bennett stood and walked himself out.

Later that night

Bennett opened the door of the Kalargo's old mustard green 1970 impala. The interior was dated, the rust on the outside made its way to the inside. The motor sounded like a sewing machine, but the overall appearance was downright ugly.

"Wow, you are really trying to be low key, aren't you?" he laughed. "Where in the hell did you get this from?"

He smiled, "A guy at a junk yard. They were giving it away." before he could respond, "Hey, you have everything? I don't want to have to return for anything."

"Yep." He looked at his disguise, fake tattoo on his neck, curly hair wig and paste on beard. They both looked like they were flash back disco seventy kids.

"So where does he live?" Bennett ask.

"The other side of the island there is a small house in the middle of nowhere." He made a left turn as the sound of the blinker ended. "He lives by himself."

"So how you want to do this?" Bennett scratched the back of neck.

"I don't know but it depends on my feelings." He cracked the window to allow the highway wind to cool his scalp. He looked at the dash board clock, and down between his legs were his black gloves. He grabbed one and used his right knee to steer the car at seventy miles an hour. He pulled the glove over his right hand and then the left.

"Go ahead and put your gloves on, I got this." He pointed at a bottle of general purpose cleaning spray," Go ahead and wipe down everything, that way if we have to run, our finger prints won't be in the car."

That was one of the qualities he like about Kalargo, he was smart, and on top of his shit.

"If you have to sneeze, don't. But if you have to, do it on your sleeve, better yet, in your shirt." As he was talking Bennett pulled out a pack of cigarette, "And if you have to smoke…" he paused and looked at him. "…swallow the butt of the cigarette."

"Yeah right…" He pulled out a cigarette and put it between his lips. He looked at him.

"That cigarette will get you one or the other, prison time, or killed."

Bennett slowly and unwillingly pulled the cigarette from his lips like a lollypop had been snatch from a kid. He looked out the window and looked at all the palms trees that started to look like long haired cigarettes. He placed the cigarette above his ear. He sighed.

"Are you serious?" He asked him as the cigarette palm trees passed his window.

"DNA, it has sent more people to prison than any witness. Hey we'll be there in five minutes."

The entry from the highway down this dark road was perfect. They parked the car and retrieved a bat, two pistols, and rope.

The lights up stairs had just turned off. The television was the only thing that was visible. They both stood outside and planned how they would gain entry into the house.

"Are you sure that there isn't anyone home?" Bennett asked him as he slid the pistol into his right back pocket.

He sighed, "Well..." He scratched his head. "...if it is." He rubbed his nose with his left hand, "We can't leave any witnesses."

"But, it shouldn't be." He led the way towards the front door. Their voices were at a whisper.

"On three, we kick the door in and run up stairs." They both nodded.

"One, two..." Before they counted to three, a person came down the stairs. It was him. They looked at each other. They started the count over.

The huge noise of the door crashing down, glass shattered everywhere scared Saul. He dropped his glass and before he could reach for a weapon. A pistol was on top of his upper lip.

"Don't move." Bennett said with a crooked smile. His mask covered his face, but his eyes stared him down.

"You snitch ass mother fucker."

Saul tried to explain. "What!" His fat jiggled like an ornament on a windy day. His white shorts sagged, the sleeveless shirt revealed his hairy armpits, his chest hairs protruded out the v cut shirt. His huge feet looked stressed from the three hundred and ninety pound body weight that gave him hard time breathing.

"Sit your ass down!" Kalargo said.

The table was behind him. A fresh cup of hazel nut coffee and plate of ginger cookies sat untouched. He had returned to get his night snack.

"Man, what is this. What you want, money? Look I got money!" He pushed his shoulders upward like money was no problem.

Kalargo held his head back and let out a huge sigh of relief. From the bottom of his throat he pulled off the mask.

Saul fell from the chair as he tried to crawl away from him. "Kalargo! What are you doing here?"

He walked around the table. Saul eyes followed his every move. He tried to read his mind.

"Are these fresh?" He picked up the plate of cookies.

"Yeah, go ahead have some." He was so scared.

"I still can't think of a reason." Bennett stood between them both until Kalargo walked completely around and leaned on the out dated kitchen counter. He looked around and noticed how he was living. He took a bite into one of the cookies, and tossed the rest in his mouth.

"Oh my God, Did you bake these?" He tried to catch a fallen crumb.

"Bennett, you can take off the mask now. I know it's uncomfortable."

"Yeah" he pulled it off, "it's hot as hell in here." His sweat ran down his neck, fanning himself to cool off.

"Listen, this is not what you think it is. I can explain." He was interrupted.

"How long have you had this house?"

He looked puzzled. "Little over three years."

"Hey, Bennett you want a cookie?" He turned it down, "They don't make cookies like these in my home country, are you sure you baked these? You mean to tell me that there is no other person here?" Kalargo wiped his mouth with his forearm.

"I swear I baked them." Saul breathing was in between his words.

Kalargo turned his back, "Now it's a shame that I had to come out here on this occasion." However, he turned around with his mouth filled with cookies, "Damn, I think I am addicted to these cookies." He held one cookie in his hand. He walked over to Saul.

"I know you didn't think I was going to hog all of the cookies did you?" He walked over to him.

"I got two choices for you. Deed me the property and we could act as if this never happened."

Before he could finish, "Yeah anything Kalargo, whatever you want!" He begged him. His fat face gave him a sad clown look.

"Or you could give me the recipe for these cookies and maybe." He paused a minute. "Just maybe, we could work something out." Before he could finish, Saul fell to the floor like a struggling whale begging to go back out to sea. From his knees he started yelling out the recipe.

"Shhhh, hey it's no way I could remember that, come on man." Kalargo was smiling.

"Hey sit back in the chair." It took him two minutes to climb his ass back into the chair that creaked and moaned that it may break into pieces any moment. He looked back at the counter at the plate. One cookie left. He reached for it, just before he bit it. He asked him if he wanted it. He hesitated, but he said yeah nervously. In the palm of the black glove was the last cookie.

"Milk?" he asked him. He nodded his head.

"Now I really did not come here to hear all these excuses. You understand me?" he cleared his nostril, "Now you have two choices right?"

"But out of those two, which one you think I want?" He looked him dead in his eyes. The shape of the cookie can damn near be seen going down his throat.

"The house?" he looked at him.

He stood back and open his eyes and hands as if he guessed the right answer. He pulled out some documents and told him to sign them.

"So for what you have done. And you know…" He threw up his hands like it was obvious. I am going to punish you forever to be poor." He scratched his head.

Bennett looked at him like he was crazy.

Saul looked relieved. "So if I sign them, everything would be forgotten about?"

"Did you, drink some milk?" He pointed at the milk.

Saul quickly grabbed the cup and drank it empty; milk spilled from his bottom lip and ran into the valley and creeks of his fat flaky rolls of caked up dirt around his neck.

"Oh yeah, how much money you have?" Kalargo paced the kitchen floor. He pulled down on the bottom of his gloves to tighten them.

"I have six hundred thousand under the stair case." He pointed to the key on the wall. "That's the key, the brown one."

He gave him the ink pen. "You did well, especially with the cookies."

"Bennett, keep an eye on him. I'll go check the stair case out."

It took him five minute to pull out the huge duffel bags of money out from the staircase. He walked back into the kitchen sweating like he had run a marathon.

"Jesus Christ, you were not lying." He looked at his watch. He knew he only had about five more minutes before the cyanide pill would kick in.

"Bennett, give me a hand with these bags."

"What about..." He started to ask.

He peeked into the kitchen, looked at Bennett and then at Saul. He waved his hand and looked at his watch.

"He'll be fine." He returned to the stare case.

They carried the two duffel bags to the car. They were breathing hard, sweating through their clothes. "Come on lets go." He told him.

The ride back was peaceful; Bennett reached over and turned the radio on. He sighed and pulled out a cigarette. He kept his mouth shut and waited for him to say something.

Kalargo looked in the mirror for any followers. "Bennett, when we get to where we are going, take one of the bags for yourself. But whatever you do. Don't let anyone know you got it." He looked at him. He agreed to it.

"Do me another favor, let the window down?" Bennett responded, "Not a problem."

Chapter 10

"Listen!" Na Min vehemently said. "Your Honor, this warehouse is owned by the U.S. Navy, which is two miles down the road. Everything inside of it belongs to training exercise that is top secret. The FBI had been given a bad lead. Yes! I do appreciate their duties and professionalism. However a bad lead does not give them the right to confiscate, interfere with a government training exercise." He looked the federal judge directly into his eyes. "I really need you to look the other way, drop the case."

As they sat over a dinner that had not been touched, He slid an envelope that held an undisclosed amount of cash.

"Done?" He held his hand on top of it.

The judge sighed; He quickly pulled the envelope from the table. He shook his head, "Consider it done."

He had learned a long time ago to always cover his own ass. As he walked out the restaurant, he pulled from his coat pocket a digital voice recorder and turned it off.

As he walked towards the street, he reached for his phone and dialed Kalargo's cell.

"Yes hello."

"Hold on, let me get off the other line." He clicked over to Jamie.

"Hey Jamie it's my father. I will call you after I talk to him." She pouted and he clicked over.

"Kalargo."

"Yes I am here." He sighed and wondered what he wanted to talk to him about. He hoped that it had nothing to do with Saul's murder.

"Listen, I wanted to talk to you about a project that requires your caliber of expertise." Na Min paused.

Kalargo stood up and walked into his master suite. "Hmm, hold on. Is it anything like Jakarta?"

"Oh no, no, no nothing like Jakarta." He grinned.

"But it does, hey listen. I'm in Hawaii. Most of what I need to tell you. I prefer to speak to you in person. What are you doing in one hour?"

He looked at his watch, "That will be, ten thirty." He sighed. "Where would you like to meet? You know you are always welcome to come over to my place." Kalargo suggested.

"You live to far, and it is late. I have a flight in the morning." He sighed. "Meet me at the bar that we always meet at. Say no later than ten forty five." They agreed and the line ended.

He quickly called Jamie. "Hey…"

She was excited. "Wow that was fast."

"We have a change in plans. My father is in Hawaii and he says he needs to speak to me in person. Hmmm, maybe I can meet you after I finish talking to him."

"Or maybe you could pick me up on your way to meet him. I'm sure he would be happy to see us together." She could hear it in his voice that it might not be a good idea.

"No, how about we meet at eleven thirty at the bar. You know the same bar we met at before."

She remembered, "OK eleven thirty. I'll be there." They ended the line.

*   *   *

The club Le Femme was partly crowded, it was eleven o'clock, and from a distance it looked like the conversation that they were having was secretive, and they appeared to not agree on what they talked about.

The dancers were nude as they fondled one another. The fog smoke from the stage spilled over. The lights flashed with different colors, and the music blared loud enough to drown people's conversations into secrecy. In a corner booth a waitress walked over with their third round of drinks. She placed them down and expected her tip. She was topless, heavy set rack that looked fake, but perfect. Kalargo gave her a two dollar tip so she could leave.

"No! You mean to tell me that," He raised his shoulders and opened his eyes to amazement. "You… out of all people can't find someone to go over and do this?" He pushed his diet coke away from him. He sighed and took notice to the dancers.

"Listen, it's not that I or we can't find someone else. The matter is." He took a drink from his gin and orange juice. "We want or prefer someone whom we can trust."

He sat back with his drink in his hand, "Mugumbi, what about him?"

"Too old, we need someone young, which can easily fit into the population. I mean, you are exactly what we need."

He sipped from the glass of diet coke, "You know… this is worse than Jakarta. This is insane." He leaned back and rested his head, let out a huge sigh. He rubbed his face with his left hand vigorously.

"How long is this supposed to take?" Kalargo looked at him.

"No more than two weeks, you'll be in and out." Na Min told him.

He smiled and laughed at an inside joke, "That sound like what I told Jamie when I first met her." They both grinned.

He threw up his hands, "What am I suppose to tell Jamie? Oh my God, you know this is not something I was expecting to hear. Jamie is going to flip. How am I suppose to get in The Gambia?" before he could say another word. "This sounds like a bad idea to me."

Na Min slammed the rest of his drink down his throat and flagged for the waitress. "Well…" He raised his palms to try to calm him down. "First of all, you will have to fly down to the Philippines for training. That will be at least a week, or two." He hoped he was not counting the weeks as he spoke.

"Then we have special transportation that will deliver you to where ever you need to go. From there you will have to parachute into the Gambia under the night sky." Na Min paused.

Kalargo's eyes opened wide, "Parachute?"

"Hold on, you will have everything you would need." He was interrupted.

"Will there be like helpers that I can meet with while I am there?"

He looked him in his eyes, "Unfortunately, once you are there. You will be completely on your own." The waitress delivered more drinks.

"This…" he waited for her to leave. "…thank you, this sounds like a suicide mission. A no return deal." He sucked air through his pearly white teeth.

"Listen, if I thought that this was something you could not do, or the slightest chance that you would not return. I would not have brought this to you. You are my son, like a son. I gave you my last name. I raised you as if you were my own. This is coming from my heart. I am not saying that this will be a walk in the park. It won't be. This might be one of the most difficult things you will ever do." He was interrupted.

"How much am I going to be paid?" he sipped on his diet coke.

"Two million."

"Two million!" He looked at him with a surprising facial expression. He sighed and downed his drink. "Make it four million, and I'll go."

Na Min put his Genifer back down on the table. "You have a deal, but before I forget..." He held his right hand up to stop him. "...whatever you do, under no circumstance should you ever speak your native language. Never, never, and again never speak your native tongue."

"Is there a reason why?"

"You have two languages that you were born speaking. One of them is the one that you and Mugumbi speak. And then it is the other one that you hardly ever speak and only because you have no one to speak it with. However if someone speaks to you in this native tongue, you must. I cannot stress this enough. You must act like you have no idea what they are talking about. Do you hear me?" he grabbed his hand and looked him in the eyes.

"OK, I hear you. I have not spoken that tongue since I was a kid." He sighed.

He drum rolled his palms on the table, "So the General it is."

Suddenly Jamie walked over to the table, "Hello Na Min." She gave him a kiss on the cheek.

"He was surprised to see her. "Wow, isn't she beautiful." He looked at him. "No wonder you were crying earlier." He smiled at them both and looked at his watch.

"Wow, he looks at the time..." He stood from the table and slammed his drink. "...well, it was a pleasure to see you again, Jamie." She stood and gave him a hug. He cleared his throat, "Kalargo..." They hugged like father and son, "...you will be hearing from me very soon." He nodded his head as he walked towards the exit.

* * *

The next morning

Jamie walked out of the room half asleep. "Good morning." She wore a night gown that barely came to her pubic hair. Her nipples were hard and she sighed because she was horny.

"Good morning." Kalargo replied without taking his eyes off the morning paper. The front page read, "Parking Garage Murder"

She grabbed a plastic cup and poured a glass of orange juice. "You want some?"

"Hmm, what are you having, orange juice?"

"Yes." She said.

"Why not, are you cooking breakfast?" She poured him a glass of orange juice and took it to him. "Well I could but I wanted to get some more sleep." She put the glass on the glass coffee table and headed back to the room. He tilted the paper and watched her ass cheeks bounce as she walked on her toes across the floor.

"I can wait till you wake up." He continued to read, looking for an article about Saul Kaapuluu's murder.

"Hmmm, nothing." he put the paper down, and drunk his orange juice. He stood up and paused. He noticed how horrible he felt. This nauseous feeling, headaches, and loose bowels that was uncontrollable. He let out a huge sigh and walked into his office. He fed the fish and talked to them.

"Hey big fella." he flopped into his corporate office chair and thought about Jamie, the trip to Africa, the circumstances, and the what if. He wondered how to tell Jamie. He thought it would be easier to some way include her, like having her manage the gym while he was gone. It sounded good. Perhaps watch over the house, check the mail, and make sure the lawn was cut, stuff like that.

"Yeah, ok." He turned around in the chair. "And don't forget, feed the fish."

He sat there thinking for three hours. He tapped his feet the entire time. But he was convinced, this is something he could do, and get away with it. He cracked his knuckles and the bones in his neck. He leaned forward and twisted his back to crack his bones along his vertebrae. He placed his elbows on his knees and placed his face in his palms.

"Damn it." He grabbed his bottom lip with his upper teeth and slowly let it slide away.

He stood up and walked out of his office. Moments later he slowly crawled into bed. Her warm body was soft, and desirable. He kissed her shoulder and she turned around and pulled him closer. They made passionate love and fell asleep in each other arms.

"Stop!" she screamed. She was having another bad dream. "Please." she cried.

He shook her until she was awake. "Jamie, wake up. You are having a bad dream."

She looked around with the sheets close to her face. She grabbed him and held him tightly.

"It's OK. You are safe."

"I keep having this dream of this black man hanging from this tree." She buried her face into the pillow. She wiped her tears, sighed and was happy it was just a dream.

"It just, seems so real." She shook her head. "So real, like before, last time I had the same exact dream. This guy was hanging upside down from this huge tree." She swallowed her saliva to continue.

She sat up to face him. She looked him in his eyes. "Two men were beating him." Her facial expression was like she was really there. Her eyes widen as she told the dream. She turned around and sat with her legs crossed in the Indian position, "Why do I have these silly dreams?"

It was very obvious that she was frustrated. "Pass me…" She pointed at the orange juice.

"May be you seen a movie, perhaps awhile ago and somehow you are having these nightmares."

"No…" She shook her head, "…and then it's like I always have this dog that, somehow leads me to where this is happening." She explained.

He smiled, "You know what, not trying to be funny, but maybe you should just kill the dog." He nodded his head and they both laughed it off.

He comforted her, kissed her and made her laugh. He locked his lips with hers. She grabbed his mighty python and directed it into the passage of warmth that would lead to another round of passionate love.

Later that night, the phone rang and he answered it, " Hello."

"Sound like you're sleeping."

"Well…" before he could finish, "…I'm calling to tell that by morning you'll know when you will fly out to the Philippines. But go ahead and get your sleep,

I'll let you know if the date is official."

He cleared his throat and said, "Ok." The line ended.

He looked over his shoulder and knew he would have to tell Jamie. But he let her sleep for now.

*   *   *

The next morning

Kalargo's office at the gym was filled with laughter. He told a funny story about Bennett. They held their sides, wiped their eyes of tears. He slammed his fist on his desk, "Stop! Stop!" They begged.

Kalargo laughed uncontrollably. His back ached, abdominal were tight. Bennett had not walked in yet. He had the office on their knees begging for him to stop.

"Just wait till he gets here, he'll tell you." He wipes his eyes with his shirt. "I swear he will tell you the same story. Trust me, I'm not lying." Two of his workers rolled off the couch, they held their sides and tears.

"No more..." they begged. "...you are killing me!" he choked and tried to catch his breath.

Suddenly, Bennett entered the office, and then there was silence, but he could hear the moans of them trying to hold back their laughter. Their faces were filled with this balloon expression of being under pressure.

He looked around the office, and he looked at Kalargo. He shook his head because he couldn't hold water. He knew the joke had to be on him. The office exploded with laughter.

"Ahhh..." he pointed at him, "...you were telling them about my fat girlfriend?" He shook his head.

A voice from behind, "It's true!" and curled over to the floor.

"Hey, hey..." He raised his hand to defend himself, "...I can't help that I like big bitches, fat girls, if she's not over two hundred fifty pounds of good loving, she is too small." He tried to explain his desire for big gals.

"Man, one day one of them whales is going to hurt your tall skinny ass!" Steve said.

He shook his head and pointed his finger at him, "This one already did." They fell out with laughter.

He walked over and put his diet coke on the desk. "Wait. Let me tell you how it really happened." He began to tell his side of the story.

"Oh shiiit…" Kevin said.

"It'll be my pleasure; God knows what he told you guys." He looked at Kalargo.

"One day I was riding, minding my own business, my mind was not thinking about any fat bitches, low and behold, I needed some smokes. So, I pulled into the convenient store, you know the one on Taano ave and Wawa." He took a sip of his diet coke.

"Now on my way out, I see a crowd of people looking down the street." He pointed in the direction with his hand.

"At first I didn't pay it any mind, but after cranking the car and pulling out of the parking lot." He shook his head in disgust.

"I'll be God damn if I didn't see this huge fat bitch, just ah running down the street, right. Now…" His eyes open wide; he used his hands to form the shape of this huge whale, and his hands were not close together either.

"She passed me. Till this day, I never heard of a…" he was lost for words. "Something as big…I mean elephants don't run this fast." The office begged him to stop.

"Now she already caught my eye with her size, right? But she had the God damn nerve to have a hot pink mini skirt on, legs and all that ass…" his lips curled up bent crooked. "…bounced around, shit no lie. I got excited as hell." He jumped up and down as they burst into laughter. His eyes became tearful.

"Now this bitch running down the street with a jar of damn pickles!" he shook his head wildly, "and it had no top on it! The juice was going everywhere, all on her face, and her clothes." He started to laugh, "Imagine Carl Lewis running the fifty yard dash, now put him in a hippo outfit with a jar of pickles underneath his arms." He tried to hold his composure. He leaned forward.

"And not one pickle came out that jar, not one!" He held his index finger up, took a deep breath and continued.

"She crossed the street going towards that run down gas station. Man… she fell down, bruised her knees, and elbows, but she didn't lose a pickle!" He took another sip of his diet coke. He stood there biting his bottom lip. He was really into telling his version of the story.

"I paused for a moment…I said to myself." He held his left hand across his heart and right hand over his mouth. "Look, just look at my bitch run! Go girl, go!

That's my bitch right there…" He pointed at the wall. He was so excited. "Man I got to have her!"

"So she ran into the men's room, it was dirty, nasty, floor was wet, and the smell was like no other…" before he finished.

Kalargo's cell phone rang; he walked out of the office to avoid the loud laughter.

Bennett continued, "…now this bathroom had me holding my breath…" he deepens his voice, "…but I entered anyway!"

"This bathroom had writing on the walls, mirrors, like call Candy for free blow jobs, and Kitty Kat Pat has no pussy lips." His entire body shook like he was disgusted.

"But…" he held a hand up and changed his voice to this deep Lion King, "I entered anyway!" he lowered his head like he really meant business.

"So I finally saw her, breathing hard as she sat on the wet floor. God knows what was down there before she got there. I looked at this sexy wounded whale." He raised his eyebrows, "Well, I am the eyes of the beholder. I asked her, What the hell are you doing?!" he held his hands over his mouth as if he was really in the bathroom. He spoke threw his mouth due to his thumb and index closing off his nose.

"We looked at each other with this frantic look on our faces. Now, she had these beautiful Asian eyes, soft smooth skin, not one pimple, her hair was long and wavy. She had blonde streaks. Now her breast had to be in the triple D's. I saw that she was nervous, but it was a moment of love at first sight. Do you guys believe in love at first sight?"

They grinned, wiped their tears, and held their abdominals.

"She sat there in the corner behind the toilet with her hand in the pickle jar. Her wide back spread out like heavy wings on a fat angel. Her knees were pulled inward touching her chest. I will not…" the following words he stressed. "…I will not." He twisted his neck and pointed his finger.

"Tell you how turned on I was when I couldn't see her panties due to all of that fat." He smiled and they laughed.

"I…" he held his right hand up to God. "…I love fat bitches. I am a sucker for them." He paused. "I could not see her panties because her fat was just… everywhere. I just knew that she was for me." He licked his chops.

"Guess what she asked me?" he looked around the room.

"What!" Steve boldly asked.

"She bit down on a pickle, and said…" He looked sad when he got to this part of the story. "…did anybody else see me come in here? It's my third strike, I can't get caught."

She had her mouth filled with pickle and talking at the same time. He tossed the empty soda can in the trash like he was talking about the world coming to an end.

"Fellas…I have had at least five beautiful slim women in my life." He cleared his chest of phlegm and swallowed. "Now, don't look at me like I'm sick, but there is nothing like licking that sweaty salty taste that only sit between the fat of a big woman." He held his tongue out with his eyes closed like a sick Lion that have not eating in forty five days. He gave everyone in the office chills and creeps. He made their skin crawl as they fell back with disgusting looks on their faces.

"And you know what? That was five years ago." He pulled out a resent picture of her.

"What!" Steve yelled out.

"No way, can't be her?" Damion said.

For the first time, Bennett looked disgusted, sad; he shook his head, "Yep, that's her."

A voice said, "She is gorgeous. What the hell happened?"

Bennett snatched his photo and shoved it back into his wallet with anger. "What happened? Shit… this bitch started exercising, going on this…" he made this strange facial expression. "Damn diet!"

He slammed his fist into his left hand, "Can you believe the audacity, now she wanted to go on a fucken diet." He shook his head.

Steve stood up, "What a damn minute. You are saying that you are pissed that she lost the weight?"

He grunted and sighed, he rigorously rubbed his hands through his hair. "Guys…" he looked like a poor wounded hyena. "…I pray, I pray to five different Gods…" he started counting with his thumb to his pinky finger, "…to please bring my fat bitch back home." The office filled with laughter.

"No, I am serious, I want my…" He held his hands up in front of him, "…everything about her, the roundness, gone! Big BREAST, GONE! Her ass, GONE! You could just say my dream bitch, GONE!" he tossed his right hand over his shoulder.

"So why haven't you left her yet?" a new guy asked.

"We've been through so much together, most of all, I love her." He walked over to the shelf behind Kalargo's desk and pulled out a magazine. She was on the cover. "I am so proud of her. I..." He was interrupted.

The door opened. "Bennett... I need to talk to you." Kalargo nodded his head to talk with him in private.

*   *   *

Later that night he called Jamie.

"Jamie, what are you doing?"

She was happy to hear from him.

"I need to talk to you. Are you able to come over?" He could not find an easy way to tell her.

"Of course... you sound a little down. Are you ok?" her voice was concerned.

He pulled the cellular away from his ear and sighed with a frustrated expression. "Oh no I am good, just wanted to talk to you, spend a little time together. I'll be here when you arrive; just drive on in, the gate will be open."

After she arrived, he told her he was going on a business trip that will last two months. He explained how he wanted her to run the gym while he was gone. He had already told his staff that she would be in charge with the help of one of his employees. He also wanted her to check the mail box, make sure the landscapers cut the grass and most importantly to feed the fish. She sat there on the edge of the bed like she had seen a ghost.

"But, when do you have to leave?" she asked with a childish look, reached for his hand and held it tight. She kissed his hand and rubbed it across her face to wipe her tears.

"In six hours." He rubbed his hands through her hair,

Her eyes filled with tears. "You have to... so soon?"She looked in the corner of the room and saw that his carryon bag filled, ready and waiting.

"Oh my God Kalargo, I did not know you would have to go so soon." She stood up on her tip toes and locked her lips on his like a kissing fish. He slowly moved his lips to her eye brows. He held her face in his palms and placed his forehead on hers, "I will miss you."

"Are you going to call me?" she asked.

"Of course I will, every chance I get, I will call you…" he whispered to her ear.

"So that means I can call you?" she waited for him to say yes.

"Yes…" He wrapped his arms around her enter locked his fingers. "…I will have a global phone with me." He sighed. Their French kiss followed with a round of passionate love.

Chapter 11

Seoul, South Korea

Na Min sat at the dinner table resting his left elbow, and holding his reading glasses to his mouth. His wife cooked, and prepared their food. The house smelt like rice and chicken, the Puerto Rican dish that they loved. He had returned from Hawaii the day before and the pressure from the North Koreans to send Kalargo to kill the General, weighed heavy on his mind. He knew that he was more than capable of this mission, but anything can happen and that's what concerned him. He also thought about the damage he has done over the years by giving the North Koreans Top Secret information, it looked like his retirement was his only way out.

He never thought he would ever betray his country, but greed took him under at a time when he was vulnerable, weak, and hurt. In Thailand, he saw how fellow service men smuggled heroin on military planes, not I he had told himself. But this was no different, he felt. May be if he had said something, perhaps all of this could have turned out differently. He shook his head and thought if he had a chance to do it all over again.

He would do it all different. All the money in the world could not replace the pride he had. He rubbed his right hand across his heart. He remembered when he used to pledge to the allegiance when he was in high school in Seattle, Washington. Now his heart felt like an over matured rotten mango that had been stepped on, and remained beneath someone's shoe.

His plate was placed in front of him, cranberry juice to the left. She returned with hers and sat down. She grabbed his hand and they closed their eyes to pray. He had to ask God to forgive him. He could hear his wife's voice as she prayed out loud, beneath his breath he thanked him for every day he had breathed and to forgive him for taking the breath of others. He slowly opened his eyes and realized that she was waiting on him to open his.

"Are you ok?" she sipped her cranberry juice.

He drove the fork into the yellow rice, "Yeah of course, este es bien." He closed his eyes and chewed on his food.

"Oh you are practicing your Spanish?" They laughed, held hands and kissed.

"One of these months we should fly over to Puerto Rico." He said.

She looked at him and smiled. "Now that sounds like a good idea."

"How is the weather in two months?" he asked her.

"Are you serious?" she was happy. "It's gorgeous…" she tried to continue.

"Now don't quote me, it's just a thought." He put another fork full in his mouth and they enjoyed their dinner as they talked about the Caribbean Islands.

Later that night they cuddle in bed, and watched American TV. He slowly closed his eyes and daydreamed.

It was 1979 Osan, South Korea, in the middle of winter. The door opened and the sound of the blistering wind that blew snowflakes behind Agent Bradley was silenced when the door slammed shut. He stomped his feet, and brushed off the snowflakes that covered his walnut mink trench coat. He snatched off his gloves and looked Na Min dead in his eyes. The sound of the burning wood in the fire place, the smell of it lingered the safe house that was fifteen miles outside the city, and three hours from North Korea.

He sat at the dinner table lighting his tobacco pipe. He wore a caramel thick wool turtle neck sweater, a pair of blue jeans with three pair of long johns beneath them. His beard was a six months of not shaving.

"I thought we were partners?" Bradley threw his gloves on the table and walked over to him in a disturbing manner. He planted the palm of his hands on the dinner table.

Na Min expressed no emotions, and took a drag from his cigar and allowed his smoke to rise in his face.

"What are you talking about?" NaMin looked at him.

"Na Min, what's going on man? We have known each for a long time, and I know when things are not right." Bradley said.

He stood up from the table and grabbed his coat, gloves, and hat that covered his ears. "I told you last week that the drop spot had changed. Did you follow the signs?" Na Min said.

"What signs? You did not tell me about any signs!" Bradley looked confused.

Na Min sighed and knew it was time to get this over with. His pain of broken trust was up to his throat. No matter how he tried to forgive and forget, his voice had begun to gnaw at him like maggots. He kept his furious temper in control.

"Let's go, grabbed your belongings, I guess I have to show you these signs in person." Na Min exhaled his smoke through his nostrils like a mad bull.

They left the house and drove forty five minutes north of the safe house. The weather had worsened; the ground was covered with four feet of snow. The heat in the car was on full blast.

"No wonder you can't see the signs, they are covered by the snow." The chit chat continued, "You make a left turn here." He parked the car and they both got out. There was an old farm house that had not been lived in for five years or more. They walked behind the barn to search for documents. Bradley stopped; he saw a hole that was six feet deep with a small amount of snow in it. He turned around and Na Min had his .45 caliber in his face.

"What the hell are you doing? Are you crazy?" The look on his face was of shock.

Na Min waved the gun at him. "I trusted you." He looked at him. He just had to say these final words. He sighed deeply. "I've been trying to hold this deep anger in for too long."

"But…" Bradley tried to speak.

"Shut up! I don't want to hear it. You destroyed everything I had planned. I was happy. You took away the one thing that I had pride in. Do you know how important family is?" He backed away from him. The wind had reduced their body temperatures. Their faces and toes were going numb, and the feeling of being in the middle of nowhere worried him. He let out visible thick breath from his nose and mouth.

"Na Min…" He held up his hands, and swallowed his saliva, "…relax ok, we can talk this out. We… don't have to do this." He begged him.

He raised his voice, "You think I did not know!?" He gritted his teeth with frustration. He tried to walk away from the grave. The sound of the gun went off.

"Don't move! You really think I don't know? Who you think requested for you to get transferred for duty. Me! I wanted you here. I wanted you! I have tried to get you here for six months. You were denied duty in South America because of me!" he talked and Bradley looked down at the grave.

"Listen, what are you talking about? Are you losing your mind?" The gun went off again, he fell. "Ouch, ahh…" he grabbed his left leg and screamed, "…ass hole…"

He shot him again in the other leg.

"You still want to pretend you don't know what this is about! She told me everything. Na Min tears fell from his eyes. He had been hurting for so long. He had asked God to forgive him for sleeping with his wife Kandance. He had forgiven his wife, but just could not forgive him. Deep down inside he was so torn apart; his anger of the thoughts was eating him alive.

The sound of his cries, he begged for his life. "Na Min, please. Don't do it."

He put the gun to his own head, but he could not do it.

"Why..." Na Min asked.

"You were never home. She needed someone to be there." He applied pressure to his wounds,

"Get me to a hospital, I am going to die out here."

"Die piss ant. I want you to feel what I have been feeling. I have been holding this shit in for way to long. You will die... slow!"

"You want to know something that has been, well a little TOP SECRET mother fucker?" He cracked a smile, a sarcastic one that did not last long.

"Justin was your..." he pointed the pistol at him. "...son, that's right ass hole." He was starting to feel the chill of winter crawl down his back, numb his ears, and fingers.

Bradley looked at him and before he pulled the trigger he asked him for one favor. He begged him to listen. "What about my daughter? Can you look out for Yuki?" he wanted to be told that he would look out for her. He wanted to hear it from his mouth. "And let her know that her father loved her."

Before he squeezed the trigger, "I'll grant you that. I will take her in as my own and I'll always let her know that you loved her." The three gun shots silenced the farm, the cries, the anger, and the hate.

Na Min opened his eyes, and looked at his wife. She was sound asleep. He crawled out of bed in need of a sleeping pill that had been prescribed to him. He shook his head and swallowed them and fell asleep.

*   *   *

Philippine training camp

The heat and humidity was like wearing a plastic bag with a hundred insects crawling over him. Kalargo was exhausted, sleepy, hungry, and thirsty. The jungle training was intense. He crawled through muddy wet rain forest where everything imaginable lived. He had crawled for three miles, swim across rivers, swamps, peeled leeches from his back, neck, and stomach like relentless duck tape. He carried a small container of water that he could drink every five hours. He was on very strict water consumption for the entire thirty days he had been there. His urine had to be as pure as possible. This was a three day exercise that required him to survive off of the jungle. He didn't mind taste of snakes, frog, and grass hoppers. They were everywhere and easy to catch, and cook. The grass hoppers were a lot easier to catch and swallow so he would grab them as he made his way through the dense jungle.

He looked up at the night sky and saw how beautiful it was. The stars were so bright. It was his final night of training and he was so close to finishing in a record time. So he pushed on to the finish.

He came from a grassy area on to a road that led him to a waiting jeep. The early morning sun crawled out like it was tired of rising. The fellow waiting for him was sound asleep.

"Good morning." Kalargo said.

The Pilipino rebel was startled that he had arrived so soon. He looked at the stop watch, and pushed the button. He spoke in his dialect and tried to speak English but manage to communicate. "You are past." He said with a smile that had missing, rotten, decayed teeth.

"It's fast, with an f. Fast." He tried to correct him. In the Philippine dialects they pronounce their p's like f's and their f's like p's.

"I am starving." he rubbed his stomach to show him what he was saying.

"Yes." he pointed. "Let go." He cranked the jeep and drove off into the sunrise. He tried talking to the driver, but his English was so horrible. It was like trying to talk to six monkeys that studied Rosetta Stone course. So he gave up the conversation and let the driver talk to himself. He inhaled his arm pit of his shirt and frowned, in need of a shower, and a good night sleep.

After breakfast he did his final urine test. He was pissing water by now. He held it up, "Now that is clean." He smiled and handed it to the doctor, Now I can have a diet coke?" He asked the doctor.

The short Pilipino doctor tightens the lid on the cap and said, "No your urine has to maintain clarity for drinking, you can't drink the water there. You will have to drink your own urine if clean water is not available."

He turned around and gave him a plastic bag. "These are your furipiers." They looked like small tubular sugar packages. He opened the plastic bag noticed the different flavors.

"These are to kill the taste in your urine. These…" He pulled one from the bag and to show him. "…I recommend that you start with the lemon flavor first." The doctor said.

Kalargo stood up and walked towards the door. "Doctor... I don't think I could actually drink my own urine." He looked at him.

The doctor smiled, "What do you mean? Your urine has been clean for the last fifteen days, what you think you have been drinking from your canteen? The only difference, the water in your canteen was half and half water, unflavored." He looked him in his eyes like it was no surprise. He pushed up his shoulders like. "I thought you knew already."

Kalargo's jaw dropped and he sighed. "No way..."

"No one told you? Well hey now you know, but make sure..." He held his right index finger up. "...do not lose these. Keep them in this plastic bag. Believe me you will use them sooner or later."

He walked out of the make shift medical office and sighed as he looked up at the sky. A voice came from behind him, "Kalargo... we finally meet." Zang spoke in Korean.

"And who are you?" he asked him in Korean.

He bowed and he did the same. "I am Zang. I came a long way to meet you." They shook hands.

"I wanted to personally meet you." He directed him to his waiting car. He opened the back door for him and they both chatted as the driver drove around the small terrorist camp.

He had noticed Zang's throat had been slashed and left side of his face had third degree burns from years ago. His hair did a poor job of covering his ear that was reduced to a hole on the side of his head. His voice was hard to understand due to his throat being damaged. That made his Korean harder to comprehend.

"I have to apologize for my Korean. I am lacking the practice. Do you speak English?" Zang laughed as his skin tighten. He blushed.

He tried not to stare at his wounds and that hole on the side of his head.

"Kalrago..." He looked at him. "I speak perfect English." He laughed.

"So... in the morning you will be flying out at four am." He reached in his coat pocket and gave him all the documents that he would need. "Airline tickets, new passport from Canada...driver can you lower the air condition?"

"Yes Mr. Zang." The driver replied.

"When you arrive to Afghanistan, you will change planes to a noncommercial plane to a humanitarian flight to a country in Africa and then you parachute into the Gambia. All of your equipment will be parachuted along with you. Do you have any questions?"

He held the documents in his hand. He read the name on the Canadian driver license. He sighed. He noticed that the airline tickets were purchase through WORLDBRIDGETAVEL.COM.

"Well I guess I don't have any questions. Phone… Can I use your phone?" Kalargo asked.

Zang hesitated. "Well due to security reasons…" He sighed.
He spoke before he did.

"I understand. Everything is a security reason." Kalargo tapped the documents on his thigh. Moments later they pulled up in front of his living quarters.

"Kalargo, I want to wish you good luck and a safe return." They shook hands and he exited the car.

* * *

Gambia, Africa

General Kakambo Twigani stood 5'8, hundred eighty pounds, dark complexion and short Afro. His hair looked pushed back like an unwanted hat. At the age of forty two, he became the General of the Gambian Army while his older brother sat on the throne as King.

Their family has ruled the Gambia for more than eighty years. The General smoked Cuban cigars back to back. He always released his smoke through his wide nose like a bull, wore pressed olive green camouflage, and maintained spit shined boots.

He had lost a lot of soldiers and desperately wanted to know who was behind the supplying of the enemy troops. He gave orders to kill any rebel fighter, and take no prisoners. Gambia was in chaos. He chopped a father's head off because his son did not know his name. He felt that if his son did not know who he was. His father had to be a rebel.

"General!" an officer entered his office standing at attention with good news to report. He saluted the General. After returning his salute, he approached his desk.

The General converted an abandoned church that was riddled with bullet holes into his headquarters. His office was located in the basement. The paint on the walls had pealed and distorted the faces of the painted angels. His photo of him in his younger days hung behind him. The dust blanked the cracked concrete floor;

Cuban cigar smoke lingered and found its way out every time the door opened.

"We have gained control of the cities of Kaba, Gubio, and Mostiwa." the officer said. The entire church vibrated after a bomb exploded, dust floated from the ceiling.

General Twigani removed his cigar from his mouth with his right hand. He stood with excitement. "Yes!" He walked around the small four legged table and stood in front of the map that hung on the wall. He exhaled smoke from his nose and pointed to the map with his cigar between his fingers.

"We have to have this town back." He said with his back facing the officer. He spoke about his home town.

"What town is that?" the officer walked over and stood next to him.

"The town of Magbigan." He took a long drag as the cherry brighten on the cigar.

Officer Baggihk closed his eyes as the smoke irritated them.

"How's your family doing?" The General asked him.

"Sir its war, they are either dead or relocated to refugee camps."

The General turned around and looked up at the ceiling. "I would consider yourself lucky. The King and I are the only survivors in our family. For our family sake, we must win this war. Don't you agree?" He looked at him. He placed red flag thumb tacks on the cities of Kaba, Gubio, and Mostiwa.

"Of course."

Dust floated from the ceiling again. "How hard can it be to find the bastards that's bombing the runway?" before the officer could respond.

"Yes, we have control of the airport, but what good is it if we can't land on the damn thing." His cigar was short and midget like compared to a new one.

"I have a question for you, do you know who's supplying these rebels?" the General walked over to his desk and put the cigar out in the ash tray.

"You will be the first to know." He said.

"Coffee?" He offered the officer as he poured his own.

"No sir. I have work to do. Thanks anyway." He saluted the General, "Permission to leave sir?"

The General returned his salute and the officer walked out the office, dust floated from the ceiling, he looked up and sighed.

Chapter 12

Seoul, South Korea

Yuki lay next to Mugumbi with tears slowly falling sideways towards her ear. His right leg crossed her legs as he lay asleep. They both snuggle under a purple silk comforter that had small designs of gold umbrellas. She opened her blurry wet eyes to see the white carpeted bedroom.

She saw herself in the mirrored wall across from the bed. The sound of the water bed occasionally rippled. She turned over to her left side and looked at the clock. She closed her eyes and tried not to think of her biological father, CIA agent Bradley.

Yuki's mother died when she was born. Her father was the best thing she ever had. She frequently dreamed of her father's funeral, and how Na Min walked her up to his casket. He held her hand and picked her up as they got closer. She slowly fell back to sleep under Mugumbi's arms.

*   *   *

The smell of blueberry candle danced Na Min's newly decorated office. The leather cream sofa against the far wall with an oil based painting of him. He sat there with a picture in his left hand of his family, wife, and children.

He removed his reading glasses to wipe a falling tear. Beneath his eyes were puffy and his face had grown wrinkle over the years. He rubbed his forehead with his right hand. He had a receding hair line with a substantial amount of gray hair. But for an old man, he was in good health.

He went into deep thought that took him back thirty years. He was twenty five years old on his first assignment for the CIA in Central America. As an Intelligence officer, it was his duty to train the rebels and interrogate prisoners; all information was directly reported to his senior officer in D.C.

San Salvador was a beautiful country with some of the most gorgeous people of the region. However, it was also a place of many horrors and theses horrors eventually consumed him. Na Min had become a viscous cold blooded killer, blood thirsty was a better way of describing him. His methods of interrogating went from the norm to the extreme, even torture, and death. He had grown accustomed to witnessing, and participating in some of the most horrific tortures to mankind. He was highly recommended for leading all interrogations. He no longer followed the rules of Geneva. He was known to be out of control.

The morning of June 8, four am, he crawled and inched his way between two bushes, with his binoculars to his eyes, the muddy dirt painted his face. He focused in on a communist rebel army camp.

"Let me see what we have here." He whispered out to a San Salvadorian platoon leader.

"Now, if I could find out who is supplying them their weapons?" He sighed and passed the binoculars to the platoon leader. "Look, tell me what you see just passed the tent."

Na Min rolled over to his left. He wore green fatigues and black soldier boots. His uniform had no insignia or country of origin. It took ten days of crossing the jungle. The platoon of novice soldiers were exhausted but under good leadership.

The small camp consisted of approximately forty rebels and lots of supplies. It was imperative that he find out the supply route and supplier.

"Juan, in that tent I believe there are at least twelve soldiers." he reached for the binoculars with his left hand. He slowly pulls a leaf down to get a better view.

"In one hour, we will be able to see better with early morning sunrise." He whispered.

"Na Min, I think it would be better if we call in for an air strike." Juan said.

Na Min sighed, "Just make sure we don't blow everything to pieces, I would like to be able to interrogate someone this time."

"Hey don't blame that last one on me. I had a new radioman. He gave the coordinates." Juan explained.

"Well either the radioman could not read your writing or you gave him the wrong coordinates. Either way, we can't afford to not get a lead on this supply trail. I mean just imagine how far we have come. If we blow this, I can truly say your country will be at civil war for many years to come." he looked at him, and patted him on the shoulder.

"It would be big news if the Russians are supplying but even worse, Fidel." Carlos said and slapped the back of his neck to kill a mosquito.

"It's all the same, If the Cubans or the Russians. Everybody knows who backs Cuba, but to have someone to point the finger would make it a lot easier." Na Min said.

Juan approached three of his soldiers, "Listen, in one hour, Jose take seven men and set up a perimeter on the left flank." He said as he reached deep into his shirt to pull out a map.

"Gomez, take six of your guys just on the right flank." He pulled his flash light out and held it between his teeth to keep a steady aim on the map. He closely examined the map to coordinate the air strike. "Now Gomez, take these, you see the tent right there?"

"Si senor." he peered through the binoculars, "Na Min believes the most important people in the camp are there, so you know what that mean?"

Gomez used his arm sleeve to wipe his sweat from his forehead and nose. "Si yo se que debo de hacer." He tried to speak his English, "Shoot for legs, no kill." He pointed at Carlos's legs.

Na Min sat beneath a tree thinking his plan through. He hoped to have at least five prisoners to interrogate. Juan came from behind; "Smokes?" he pulled one from the pack and Juan lit them both.

"In fifteen minutes..." He looked at his watch and let out a huge puff of smoke. "Gomez and Jose will have their teams in position."

After the air strike the smell of burning flesh, rubber, and debris filled the air. The injured can be heard, but slowly and quietly dying off. His special team of four waited for the green light that everything was secured. The crackle sound that came over the radio said, "Todo bien, todo bien, operacion exito."

"OK boys and girls let's see what we have here to work with." Na Min said to his team.

They used their machetes to cut through the three hundred feet of dense jungle and down the slope that led them to the camp. He patiently walked through the camp using his feet and occasionally his hands to turn bodies over.

"Hmmm..." he mumbled with the tip of the cigarette but barely hanging between his lips. Juan came over with excitement, jumping over debris and bodies.

"Senor, we have fifteen prisoners for interrogation." He sighed and wiped his sweat from his forehead. His armpits were wet and his American m-16 was strapped around his back.

"Well, let's get this party started." he said with confidence, "If anyone knows anything, we'll get it out of them." He took a deep drag from his cigarette.

"Juan, set up a make shift tent here and I want you to put the prisoners..." he pointed. "... there."

He immediately started snapping his fingers and yelling in Spanish.

"Na Min, one of my soldiers found some documents-you might be interested in." He told him as he pulled out his box of cigarettes from his top left pocket.

The young soldier gave the documents to him. He looked no older than sixteen years old. He looked over the papers.

"Now this…" he waved the papers above his right shoulder. "…is interesting." He stuffed the papers in his right side pants pocket. "Where are these so call prisoners?"

They brought fifteen guys, some were tied, and others too wounded to tie up. They all looked like they wished they were dead. Na Min slowly walked through them, looking at each one. He finally made his decision.

"Him!" he pointed.

The prisoner eyes opened wide and the fear on his face closed his mouth with a wrinkle pout. A soldier picked him up by the back of his shirt collar and practically dragged him to the front of the group.

"Juan, I want you to translate for me. Tell the rest of them that I am here for information only. They can make it easy or hard. I have all day, but I won't spend all day asking the same questions. I personally don't…" He kind of waved his hands in the air with a sarcastic grin, "…have that kind of all day patients. However, there will be an award for cooperating."

Juan could be heard translating every word like a bilingual parrot. He continued, and the prisoners paid close attention as Na Min walked towards his first prisoner. He used his right thumb to close off right nostril, blew mucous from his nose, and wiped his hand on the back of his pants.

"Are you a talker?" He waited for a response, "Tommy, bring me that can of gas."

He was cold hearted, by now he had over forty two murders under his belt. In a normal world he would be considered a serial killer, but in this situation, location, circumstances, he is the God of information extraction, but an example always had to set, and unfortunately. Any many miny moe either way somebody will have to die first.

The soldier started speaking Spanish. As far as he was concerned, he had no real use for him. He knew this poor peasant was worthless. He had chosen him just to kill. He was no more than an insect to him, someone to torture to get the others ready to talk. He knew they'll be begging to talk first.

He looked in the eyes of the others and saw the fear in their eyes, but it was the same fear that he had seen before, not fearful enough. Some mumbled Spanish reiterate of some sort, others began crying with those senseless crocodiles tears that won't save them. The sound of the match grew the cries wider. Their death was eminent by the hands of a monster. Some looked up like they had an unforgiving God.

"Na Min, I think we can interrogate a different way! This is insane!" Juan spoke out loud.

"You think so!" like a monster on steroids; "I don't have any more patients to dick around with these dirt farmers!" he walked over to him. He put the match to his cigarette and inhaled. He looked at him directly in his eyes.

"These are the same farmers who are resisting and fighting against democracy." With a calm and mellow voice, Na Min blows smoke over his shoulder. He takes a visual survey of Juan's soldiers watching the scene.

He leaned in closer and whispered in his left ear, "Juan don't ever interrupt my God damn interrogation, ever, under any circumstances, claro?" He patted him on the shoulder and smiled at everyone else.

"Si Senor." Juan felt threaten.

Na Min turned around and slowly walked over to the prisoner that was soaked in gasoline. "Juan! Tell these bastards they have two minutes to tell me where and who are supplying them ammo, weapons, and bla bla bla" He pointed his index finger at each of them, with his right boot he pushed a small pile of dirt back and forward.

The early morning sun gave light to the damage to the camp. Most of his soldiers were gathering what they could. His team surrounded the prisoners with an additional soldiers from the platoon watched.

"Translate, if you dirt farmers want to save this poor comrade of yours from burning a painful death…" he inhaled on his cigarette. Juan's voice can be heard translating in the background. Three of the prisoners started saying, "Padre Nuestro que esta en el cielo, santificado sea tu nombre…"

Those that did not have a higher power chose other final words to comfort them.

"Speak your mind to forever hold your peace." he put the cigarette close to the wet prisoner.

The prisoner closed his eyes and screamed, quickly saying the Lord's Prayer, "Padre Nuestro, que esta en el cielo, santificado sea tu nombre…"

Just before he flicked the cigarette, a brave soul yelled out, "Te hablare!"

Na Min quickly pointed him out like God gave him this power to torture human beings. "Take him! Translate! If you lie to me, any of you, I will know!"

The prisoner was dragged across the early morning dark wet dirt with his hands tied in front of him. He begged to spare his life.

"Ask him! Where and who is supplying them?" His voice echoed throughout the camp.

The nearby birds flew away to safety. The sound of a grown men cried, the prisoner was covered in blood, and dirt. He looked malnourished and pitiful. He bowed back and forward, begging and pleading for forgiveness in Spanish.

Juan translated, "He said, 'Please don't kill his brother. He is the last brother that he has." He paused to see how he would respond.

"What does he know about the supplies?!" Na Min demanded.

The prisoner's hands were up to his face begging him like a helpless peon. He crawled towards Carlos. He held on to his left leg like a child that is happy to see their father. Carlos kicked him in the face.

He proceeded towards Na Min like an animal begging for food. He praised and kissed his boots. He snatched his left foot and then his right boot away from his lips. "This is pathetic and depressing. What is he saying? Did he answer my question?"

Juan sighed heavily, with his mouth filled with air. He slowly let it out and shook his head. His five o'clock shadow beard gave him this exhausted look on his face. He didn't want to tell him what he had said.

"What did he say?!" Na Min asked.

"He said he does not know anything about where and how…" He combs his right hand through his hair, "…he is begging you not to kill his brother. They are the last men in their family." He looked up at the sky and rubbed his five o'clock shadow beard.

"Well I can see for myself that he is begging Juan!" Na Min paused. "So nobody knows anything." He walked around the prisoners to come in between the brothers. "I am not here for family counseling, family matters, or any other crap they will try to throw at me. I want facts, info, and what the hell are two brothers doing fighting." He pointed his finger at them both.

"You knew you two were not going to make it…" He cracked an ugly smile at them. He sighed and cleared his throat and tried to spit but it hung from his mouth like a long spaghetti noodle that would not break away. He used his left hand to break it off.

"Juan, tell him for his brother's sake… I won't kill his only brother…" he played with a small pile of dirt with his left boot.

The prisoner became joyful. He crawled over to his brother and put his tied hands around him and cried.

Na Min walked over to them both and pulled out his .45 caliber and shot him. "But, I did not say I would spare you." He said as he stood over them both. The smoke lingered from the barrel. One shot to the chest, and he watched him struggled for his final breathe for four minutes. The brother screamed as his older brother bled to death with his arms around him.

The silence among the prisoners was like they had died, speechless, the fear kept them quiet. Suddenly, three soldiers tried to get away. "Shoot them in the legs! Now I have who I am looking for." He smiled and put his .45 in his holster and fastened the leather strap.

"I want these three separated from each other. Have the rest start digging holes. If they are too injured to dig, kill them!" he yelled out loud, "It was about time we got down to the bottom of this mess. After they dig the holes…" He whispered to Carlos. "… Kill them all."

*   *   *

Six months later
Washington D.C.

"Today is promotion day." Na Min embraced his wife and locked his lips with hers. He rubbed her back and soothed her muscles.

"I am so glad you invited the family to join you. You have no idea how much we have missed you." She told him with her Eskimo kisses.

Kandance remained a stunning blonde for having two kids. She stood 5'9 at a hundred twenty five pounds. She was not bad for an ex model. She thought about going back into the modeling business just to keep her busy. She ran five miles a day and dieted to remain in shape. They met in college in a fitness gym. She was attracted to Asian men as he was attracted to blondes. She set aside her career goals to be with him.

She wore a white blouse and blue jean shorts, her hair pinned up in a bun. She walked across the hotel room, stepped over Cynthia and called for Justin.

"Are you hiding again?" She asked with a smile as she entered the bathroom. From the bathroom her voice can be heard "Honey, maybe we could do this more often…" she looked out from the bathroom door, so happy to be with him. "…you know, travel and meeting you in different locations. That would be nice, right?" She ducked back into the bathroom, grabbed her toothbrush and toothpaste. She walked out with the toothbrush in her mouth.

He knew that would be a security risk. Before he could disappoint her, she said "I know everyone has a job to do…" she stood in front of him, cheerful, and talking with a mouth full of toothpaste, smoothly brushing her teeth.

"But I know the agency, perhaps that would be a risk of security, right?" she asked.

He stood up, "Damn, you are right, but if I could get around it, you bet we all would be in some of the places that I go to."

She returned to rinse her mouth, "And then we could visit all the beautiful cities that you go to."

"Daddy, what time are we leaving?" Cynthia asked. She had been asking to go to the Washington D.C. Zoo every since she saw the hotel pamphlet.

Justin, her younger brother came from under the bed. "Yeah, don't forget parrot jungle."

Cynthia pinched him and said "Parrot Jungle is in Florida."

Justin rubbed his arm with a frown, and begins to cry. She walked over to apologize, but he balled into a fetal position and hid beneath the bed.

"Justin boy, stop crying and be a big boy." Na Min changed his voice to soothe his pain, "Stop letting these girls see you cry." He stood in front of the bed and picked him up, tickled him until he heard him laugh. "You aren't hurt, boy stop playing."

His head peeked through with a big smile. "I love you daddy."

"I love you too." He held him high and bounced him onto the bed.

Then Cynthia jumped on the bed. "Look mommy look."

Kandance smiled, looked at the hotel clock. "OK kids, it's time to go to bed. We have an early wake up call." The laughter that smeared the room settled down.

"Did you put in for the 7 o'clock wakeup call?" Na Min asked.

"No, actually 8 am, did you want 7 am?" she looked at him.

"Hmmm, 8 am is good, ok kids settle down and get ready for bed." He said.

The hotel phone rang. "Yes hello this is Marriott guess services. We are confirming your wake up call for 8 am correct?" before she could respond, "We also would like to offer a full breakfast delivered to your room, free of charge, are you interested?"

"One moment please." She put them on hold.

"Yes we would be interested."

"What time would you want breakfast to be delivered?"

"9 am sharp." She looked at him, he didn't disagree.

"It will be the continental breakfast for a party of four; it comes with a jug of orange juice, milk, and croissants."

"Thank you." Moments later she softly placed the receiver on the phone.

Na Min tossed and turned throughout the night. His sleeping medication kept the nightmares to a minimum. He finally opened his eyes to look at the clock.

"Damn…" he sighed, "…still too early." He rubbed his eyes and cleared his throat. The clock said four thirty am. He twisted his back until his bones crack one after another. He twisted his head to his left and right to crack his neck bones. He stood up and bent down to touch his toes, and forced his forehead to touch his knees.

The room was dark with only the television on. The broadcast had ended and the sound of static echoed the family suite. He paused and looked at how uncomfortable his son looks as he lay on the bed. He walked over and tucked him neatly, and kissed him on the forehead and thought of all the freedom that they have. He walked over to the window and pulled the curtain to look from the sixth floor. An inch of snow had fallen over night, and the remaining flurries floated softly. In the distance he could see the white house and Capitol Hill. He closed the curtain and walked into the bathroom and pissed. The sound of falling liquid echoed, until it dripped. He grabbed a small amount of tissue to wipe the toilet seat, and flushed. He looked into the mirror as he washed his hands. He looked at his tattoo of a lion head with torn arm in his mouth. He rubbed it and thought of the day he had it done. He quickly hit the light switch, it brought back to many memories.

He crawled back into bed and held his wife tight, "Honey…" She spoke in a low voice and turned on to her right side. She felt his breath on the back of her neck. His lips nibbled her ear. Her left hand reached behind her buttocks to caress his mighty python. She stroked him until his erection was powerful. His left hand found its way between her legs. Her breathing became heavy as his middle finger

124

groped her lips, pushed her clit to the left, right, and finally snorkeled its way deep in to her wet pawn. She held him as his breathing increased with his heart beat. Suddenly, they stopped and looked across the room.

"They still sleep?" she asked.

"Hmm, yeah." he moved his middle finger faster. She put her left hand to her mouth and licked her palm twice to lubricate her palm.

"Oh my." he said. He penetrated deep and she stroked him faster. He stopped to look at the children. "Still sleep?"

She squeezed his monster tight, gritted her teeth and threatened him with a horny agitated whispering voice, "If you stop again when I'm ready to cum. I will snatch it off!"

He quickly rotated his index finger across her clit, her back arched. She grabbed the sheets into a bundle. He spoke softly in her ear. "Let's finish this in the bathroom."

She stopped and looked at the kids. They were sound asleep. With a smile she French kissed him and tossed the bed sheets to the floor.

He held his head back and slowly caressed her head. They made passionate love until they could no longer stand. The print of her back smeared the mirror. Their bodies were weak and sweaty. He placed her on the edge of the sink and vacuumed her love pawn dry; her knees trembled as she moaned beneath her breath.

"Quack Quack!" he stepped on a rubber duck as he picked her up and carried her to the bedroom. She held him tight with her arms around his neck; she licked his sweat from his face, and shoved her tongue down his throat. He placed her on the bed and lay next to her naked underneath the sheets. Their heart beats slowly came to a normal strong thump. Their over worked bodies felt heavy, it didn't take them long to fall asleep.

The sunrise eased its way between the curtains and the early wakeup call tortured them. "My God, please answer that."

She picked up the receiver and placed it back down. "Honey, it's time to get up." She said with her thumb and index finger closing his nose. His eyes opened with a moan, and turned over. His right leg hung off the edge of the bed. His right arm lay beneath his body. She embraced him.

"I love you." She said.

He moaned, lifted his head and looked over at the kids. His head fell like a bowling ball into the pillow. "Yeah yeah..." he said in Korean.

Kandance lay across from him. She looked at the kids and turned to him. "Are you ready for round two?"

"Hell no." He mumbled in Korean.

"Oh what does that mean?" She smiled with her right hand beneath the sheets and holding his Johnson. "Look like somebody is ready for round two." She smiled.

"Well in Korean, that means hell no, but you can run my shower for me." He smiled.

She smiled, licked her beautiful lips, and tossed her hair from her face, "Anything for my Emperor."

He watched her sexy ass walk across the room; he smiled and knew that he was the luckiest man alive.

She wakes the kids as he showered; his 1:30 pm meeting with the director of the CIA will be in Langley, Virginia. He had murdered a lot of people to get this information and it has finally paid off. He discovered the North Koreans were supplying the rebels; he had photos, and document to prove it.

"Honey, did you pack my republican tie… you know my favorite red tie with the gold leaves on it?" he asked while he was drying off. He could hear her mumbling, it took her a moment to search the luggage. She sighed in disappointment and knew this was his favorite tie that his father gave him. He always felt like it was his good luck charm. It made him feel confident, and gave him a sense of empowerment.

"Damn, how could I have forgotten it?" She questioned herself, "Honey." She spoke sadly. It didn't sound like she had found it. "I completely forgot it. I swear I took it out of the closet…" She tries to explain before he gets upset. She remembered how he responded the last time he got upset over wasted tooth paste awhile back. She stopped and said no more. It was silent for a moment, she thought quickly, "Hey I'll run down and get another tie."

He walked out of the bathroom, "Don't worry about it. You go ahead get the kids ready and I'll run down to the gift shop to get something." He held the towel around his neck and put his lips on hers. She smiled and sighed.

He arrived to the gift shop in tennis shoes without socks, a thin sweater, and damped hair. He looked desperate to find something. He looked around before asking the salesman.

"Are these the only ties you have?" He asked impatiently.

The salesman frowned "Unfortunately, that's all we have."

He rolled his eyes and headed out the door.

"For your information, there is a store on the corner." He twisted his lips in a girlish manner, and moved his hands like he had a broken wrist. His well manicured glossy nails were moving in every direction. When they finally stopped in the direction of the store, he bolted out of the gift shop saying, "Thanks!"

He found the store to be closed, "No! No! No!" He stood there as the cold air gave him a chill. He danced a little to keep warm. He held his hands in front of his mouth to warm them. He looked up at the sky as the snowflakes fall. Suddenly he saw a sales woman pass, "Hey!" He tapped on the glass door and frantically pointed at his watch.

"What time you open?" He could feel his toes starting to get cold.

She walked over to the door and smiled; one of those pseudo retail smiles. "Fifteen minutes!" she yelled through the glass doors and pointed at the clock on the wall.

He shivered and lowered his head, "I... do I look like I can wait fifteen more minutes?"

She thought he was cute, and desperate to get inside from the elements. She looked at her watch and the clock on the wall, "You have to wait fifteen more minutes." She walked away.

He pulled his badge and tapped it hard on the glass. He was frustrated. She turned around, but the badge changed her attitude. She looked at him and felt sorry for him. She threw up both of her hands and said, "The key."

She returned a couple of seconds later, bent down like a lady with her knees together and upper body twisted to accommodate her position.

Before she turned the key she asked, "Let me see that badge again... I know a fake one when I see one." The sound of the key unlocked the door. The cold air rushed in and the sound of the early morning commute filtered into the store.

"Oh thank you so much." He stood there to brush off the snow flakes, and tried to get comfortable in the heated store.

"What are you doing without a coat?" the saleswoman asked.

He interrupted her, "I need a tie...prefer red." He said with a gesture of urgency. He still held his hands to his mouth.

She felt ignored. "Yes we have some blue ties."

"You have no idea how important this is to me. I thank you from the bottom of my heart." He followed her toward the suites and ties.

The saleswoman was a beautiful 5'6, dark eyed, curly haired Puerto Rican, shape was to die for and her accent was a sniper in the bush and she admired him for some reason.

"I take it you have an important meeting you have to go to?" she asked cunningly as she flirted.

He was so into finding the perfect tie. He hadn't noticed her gestures. "What about these ties?"

"Is that... well that's not the only tie you have... is it?" He impatiently searched for another suitable tie.

He frantically looked at his watch, "Damn! You..."

"Listen..." she interrupted him. "Hey I have more ties in the back that I guarantee you would not walk out of here without."

Moments later she returned with an arm filled with some of the most beautiful ties in the world. "Now here are..." she was interrupted.

"You have to help me. My wife shop for my ties..." he said carefully holding two ties in the air for comparison.

She smirked and picked out the most expensive tie. Her attitude changed from a flirting to a disappointed one, voice became tolerating than a helping one.

"Well..." she picked out a blue tie, "...this is your tie that you have to buy. It goes with all suits. The colors that twine in between..."

He stopped her. "Excuse me, I am so sorry, but I have to really be somewhere. Just charge it to my credit card." He put his credit card on the glass counter.

"Do you have I.D.?" she asked.

He showed her his C.I.A. badge and identification. "Do you have state I.D.?"

He impatiently reached for his wallet, "Here!" He rudely put it on the glass instead of her hand and sighed with frustration.

She look at it, compared the two.

He combed his fingers through his jet black hair and rolled his eyes.

"Aah…how much is it?"

She pulled the tag from the back of the tie and cleared her throat, "Eight hundred dollars and forty three cents." She frowned and he almost past out.

"What! Eight hundred dollars and forty three cents." he looked at the clock. "This is not the cheapest tie you have!" He panicked as he almost pulled his hair out.

"Well… you did ask for red…" she pushed her lips upward and forced herself to smile. "And this is the last tie that we have.", before she could say another word.

"Just charge it." He told himself that he would most definitely bring it back. He shook his head as the machine made all kind of noise as it printed the receipt. He wanted to reach over and choke this bitch, but it was not her fault, beside he had just noticed how cute her accent was. She was beautiful, make up was flawless, teeth were pearly white; she used her right index to specifically scratch in one spot of her scalp.

She held his credit card closer to her face to read his name, "Mr. Choi." He nodded his head.

"Not many people can pronounce it." He looked at her name tag and said her name with the proper Spanish accent.

She was shocked, "wow…"

He stopped her before she could ask. "It's a good chance that I speak Spanish better than you."

She handed him his credit card and I.D. with his bag with the tie in it. He quickly said his good bye and dashed out of the store with his credit card and receipt between his lips. A snow flake touched his eyebrow, the cold winter elements rushed him as he hurried back to the hotel, being occupied with putting everything back in his wallet and the sound of the snow crunched after every step. Thinking it was dumb of him to leave without a jacket. He wanted to make it back to eat breakfast with his family, something he had not done in three years.

Kandance heard a knock at the door, "Who is it?"
She walked towards the door.

"It's room service."

The kids got excited, "Ok kids, it's time to eat breakfast."

"Where is daddy? Cynthia asked.

"He should be back soon."

Kandance opened the door, "Good morning."

The waiter pushed the cart in to the room, "You have to sign here Ma'am." He gave her the bill.

"Is that it?"she asked.

"Yes Ma'am, enjoy." She gave him a tip and closed the door behind him.

"OK Justin!" she arranged the table, "Come have a sit at the table." She pushed the cart and the table closer to the window as they gathered around as she opened the curtains.

"Mommy can I have extra bacon?" Cynthia asked.

Down below, Na Min was a hundred feet from the entrance to the Marriott. Suddenly, the explosion vibrated the surrounding buildings, shattered windows across the street. He fell to his knees as debris of glass and brick hit him. The people on the street panicked; nearby car alarms sounded, people ran for their lives.

He stood and wiped his eyes and noticed he was bleeding. He looked up at the hotel and saw that it was his hotel room that had exploded. He screamed.

"Noooo!" he looked on the ground and saw one of his son's shoes. He folded. "Nooooo!" he cried. The smoke from the hotel burned. He looked around and ran to his daughter. He was having a difficult time swallowing his pain. He held her, and cried. She was dead. She was missing an arm and a leg.

"Cynthia! Cynthia!" he held her close. He tried mouth to mouth resuscitation. She was gone. He screamed to the top of his lungs, "Why!" He yelled in Korean.

"Kandance! Justin!" He stood up and frantically searched. He was covered in his daughter's blood.

His tears fell and choked him. His wife lay on top of the hood of a taxi. He ran over to her with a loss for words. He touched her, her eyes opened. "Help is on the way!"

She cried and held him while she went into shock. He was so nervous; he couldn't think straight. Her legs were gone and blood pumped out. He carried her from the hood of the taxi to the sidewalk.

She grabbed him, "Justin!" She tried to scream. Her voice was cracked and low. She grabbed her chest and frowned. She had a puncture wound to her lungs. "Justin... save my boy!" she pointed.

He looked in the direction that she pointed. He ran over, but it was too late. "Justin! Don't you die on me! No!" he picked him up and carried him to his mother. He looked fine, but he had a puncture wound to his heart.

"Cynthia!?" she asked.

He cried as the sirens got closer. She took her last breath. Justin died moments later, no longer bothered by the cold winter morning. His anger heated him. He slammed his fist on to the sidewalk until his knuckles bled. He rested on his knees; he slowly forced his hands to come to his face.

"Our father …" he prayed for the first time in five years. He fell forward as he mumbled the Lord's Prayer out of his mouth. He collapsed to the side walk, curled like an infant; the love of his life was snatched from him. He had wished he had died. He never recovered mentally from this lost.

He sat there at his desk holding a family photo. His wet eyes were evidence that he could not hide from his current wife; she walked into his office.

"Honey, are you ok?" She stood at the door.

"Yeah." He picked up his glass of Genifer and took a sip and sighed. She knew there were times he would go through a moment of depression, especially, when he thought about his kids, and she was unable to bare any. She walked over and kissed him on the lips. He looked at the photo of Kalargo when he was fourteen in his martial art class. He was so proud of him, and most of all, that he had adopted him.

They cut the lights out and walked out of the office.

Chapter 13

Seoul, South Korea

One year had passed after the hotel bombing, "Did you meet your contact? He asked.

Bradley sighed, scratched his eyebrow, he exhaled the visible hot breath from his mouth and nose. His scarf was wrapped around his neck. He stomped his feet and rubbed his hands. It was very cold; they both looked like Michelin men under their clothes. He blew on his hands to keep them warm. He opened the back door of the fish market and Agent Bradley followed.

Agent Bradley was born Korean American working deep cover in South Korea and North Korea as a C.I.A. operative. He looked one hundred percent Korean and spoke their language with no foreign accent. Both of his parents were born in South Korea and he had lived in Seoul, South Korea until the age of fourteen.

He was very comfortable being in his home country, among his family helped blend him in very well. But he and his daughter lived in the United States. He was older than Na Min, but he looked up to him like a hero. He had heard of the Central America interrogations. He felt like he was working with a legend.

The 10 degree below zero weather chilled them to their bones. They sighed after the door was closed and stood there and let the heat absorb their faces before they stomped the ice from their boots.

He looked at him with this stupid look on his face before he smiled. "Yes!" he said with an excited but low tone of voice.

"I have…" he pulled him aside and reached in his pocket. "He showed him a roll of film. "Launch pads, bases, missile storage, and…" they quickly changed the subject as a worker walked passed them. He slowly slid the roll of film back into his pocket. They took their coats off and hung them on the coat hooks.

"Are you guys working or chatting for a pay check?" the supervisor asked them both.

They remained in character, "We work for our checks boss!"

"I'll believe it when I see it."

"You are on table one and Na Min take table three, Kim can't make it today." Their supervisor walked away.

Before they separated Bradley pulled him by his shirt and whispered, "Our tunnels are complete; we can go in to the north whenever we want now."

A loud voice in Korean came over the loud speaker, "Hey we need more eel head, and octopus heart!"

"Right on it!" He yelled back, smiled and sighed at his flawless Korean.

"Yeah and guess what..." he leaned towards him, looked away a moment. Na Min's butcher knife cut open a baby octopus in half. He frowned and could not stand his deep cover assignment.

"They are making a submarine that carry nukes." They both chopped up eels and octopus. The smell of the sea no longer bothered them.

"We need to get over there and take photos." Na Min said.

Bradley pulled out a small folded paper with his finger tips, carefully to not get blood on it. "Check this out." he raised his eyebrows. "Wow, tell me this is not what I think it is?" he quickly shoved it in his back pocket."Six months, it will be completed."

"How did you get this?" Na Min looked at him strangely. He always tried to impress him; he knew it would do exactly that and also bring him closer to his death.

"Another thing, this job has to go!" he pointed his long pointy knife at him. He laughed, "This is where I get all of my drops."

"Eel, octopus ready!" Na Min said.

"If it's not broke, don't fix it." Bradley looked at him.

"Whale eyes, ready!" Bradley said.

The sound of their stainless steel knives can be heard chopping away.

"This needs to be cut in smaller portions!" the head fisherman said. They looked at each other, and then at the packaged fish.

"This is it." they both reached for it. Bradley grabbed it first. They looked around the kitchen suspiciously. He ran his hand in between the guts of this huge eel. He felt something.

"Yes, this is it." he pulled out a roll of film that had been wrapped in plastic. Bradley had this nervous feeling that he had never felt before.

Na Min wiped his forehead with the inside of his sweaty forearm. He held his butcher knife in his left hand. They smiled.

"Good work. Damn good work, but I could have done it without..." he kind of nodded his head to the left. "…may be hurting someone." They both smiled.

Six months later

"This is good, look at this." Na Min looked at the negative at an angle above his head; holding it between his finger tips.

"Beautiful. They are going to slobber all over these." Bradley said.

Their safe house was close to the DMZ (demilitarize zone).

The Korean War never really ended between the south and the north. For almost twenty years they have been at war. But not a bullet has been fired. The American and South Koreans stand guard all day, every day. It is so intense around the DMZ, no one is allowed to smile, show fear, or help the enemy.

The white paint that separates the south from the north is twelve inches in width. The soldiers are always at attention or in the ready position.

"Yep, this is definitely what they are looking for." he said as he held another negative towards the ceiling.

"OK tomorrow would be a good time to go to Seoul." Bradley said.

"You want me to make reservations?" Na Min asked.

"Yes." He holds a negative in each hand up to the light.

The following day
Seoul, South Korea

"Yes, how can I help you?" a beautiful Korean asked.

"Hmm, yes we have two rooms reserved for five nights." the sound of the computer keys tapped away.

"Do you have identification?" she smiled, her straight black hair passed her elbows, no cleavage, but her blue suit fitted her well.

She turned away to code their room keys. Her calves were thick, and hips flat.

"OK gentlemen, your rooms are across from one another. If you need any assistance dial seven, for room service dial eight, and for emergencies dial nine." she pushed the keys across the counter. She ripped the receipt from the printer.

"And you must sign... here, and here." she pointed at both of the receipts.

Bradley looked at his watch, "Still early, first thing first, I'll run over to the base..." he touched his watch.

"I'll find Mr. Bonjivich to develop these negs."

"We'll meet back here at nineteen hundred hour." they both agreed and separated to their rooms.

1830 hundred hours

Na Min returned early, slowly slid in his key, the light blinked, the sound of the lock unlocked. He struggled to retrieve his key for a moment. The door opened. The beige carpet matched the bed spread and the contrast of wallpaper said a lot about the interior designer. He had to be drunk or blind, but the hotel was super clean, and dated.

He rushed toward the bathroom as he begin to remove some of his clothes, unbuckle his pants; he passed the television, queen size bed, office desk, and the old rusty iron heater. He thought he would have gotten down to the third layer of clothes by now.

"God damn it!" He danced, wiggled his way around the bathroom floor, still not ready, he held his legs together. He unzipped, pulled four sweaters upward, finally he stood still long enough to urinate everywhere but in the toilet.

"Jesus Christ!" his aim was just a little off. He cleaned the mess that he made and sighed as he walked out the bathroom.

"Hmmm... Bradley must have left something for me." the brown paper bag was wrapped tightly with yellow rubber bands around it. No note. He sniffed it for bomb materials. He grabbed one of his shoes and stood halfway in the bathroom, aimed, and threw the shoe at it. "Nothing." he thought.

He scratched his ear, forehead, and stomach before approaching the bed. Before he picked the package up, he scratched again. He did this scratching thing every time he got nervous. Slowly, one rubber band at a time he removed them. After the fourth rubber band the sound of the paper bag begin to unravel. He peeked; looked, put his right hand in the bag that would change the rest of his life. It will cause him to lye, spy, and do what he never thought he would do in a life time.

This would be the beginning of crossing the line of integrity. He had two chances to turn back. He didn't.

His bottom jaw dropped. What he held in his hand caused his fingers to tremble. He ran to the door and peeped through the peephole for fifty nine seconds.

"What the hell is going on?" he asked himself as he peeped through the peephole. He walked over to the bed and shoved it in the pillow case. He sweated heavily; he took off his layer of clothing. With just his light blue boxers on he tiptoed to the door again.

"Nobody!" he acted like a drug addict. He looked through the peephole for a hundred thirty two seconds. He felt like someone was watching him. He took his eye from the peephole, looked at his watch.

"Where is he? It's eighteen thirty five..." He saw Bradley walk up to his door. His heart pounded his chest like wild apes.

Bradley dropped his key, but he finally got into his room.

Na Min watched for awhile to make sure he was not followed, thinking the phone would ring in his hotel; he hoped he would call him soon.

He stood dumb founded with his back against the door. He curled his toes into the carpet. His palms itched and his arm pits perspired. He closed his eyes and waited.

"This has to be a joke, a test, but why?" he asked himself. He dug his nails into his palms trying to cure the itch. The knock at the door startled him. He peeped through the peephole. He opened the door and the room lit up from the hallway light.

Bradley entered the room with just the bathroom light on. "Na Min... well damn it's dark in here." He walked over to the dresser and flicked on the night stand light.

He stood there in his light blue boxers with the Winnie the Pooh printed on them. "So how was your day?" he asked with a little curiosity.

Bradley took a load off of his feet."I talked to what's his name... and it's a go." he put out his cigarette in the ash tray. "I got everything lined up for Tuesday. The u-2 should be able to get some better photos to confirm this submarine facility." he said as he cleared his throat.

Na Min slid into his pants, right leg first. He hoped he would ask about the package on the bed. Maybe he had one on his bed that he was curious about.

Years later, he will wish he had asked about it.

"Well my end should be good to go. I dropped off the negs." Suddenly he yawned. "Boy, I am getting tired. What time in the morning?" Na Minasked him.

"It'll be a late start... go ahead and get some rest." Bradley stood up and headed towards the door.

"Hey just call me." Na Min said.

"Will do." the door closed behind him.

Five days later

Bradley and Na Min stood in the lobby of their hotel talking to a couple of Army officers.

"That gets me every time..." An officer said. They spoke about Vietnam. Their bodies were tipsy of liquor as they leaned on each other.

"So you boys are headed back to the DMZ in the morning?" Bradley asked them.

"Well unfortunately we are. Shit, to be honest, I can't wait to go back State side." He expressed with hands of a flying airplane landing on his palm. Their Rum had kicked in a while ago.

"Well..." looking at his watch, "…this old fart must head in." Na Min shook hands and said his good byes.

Later he entered his hotel room nervously. He quickly closed the door. He looked at the bed and felt like falling to the floor, another package on his bed.

"Damn, damn, damn..." he sighed. He used both of his hands to cover his face and slowly dragged them down his chin. He no longer looked through the peephole. His alcohol slowly reduced its affect. The party was over. Reality was smacking him in the face. This was the fourth package. He was pretty sure that the content is the same as before, fifteen thousand dollars American. It made him more nervous that he had not said anything. He opened it. He sighed. He felt like any moment there would be agents rushing into his room to arrest him, including Agent Bradley.

"Oh my God, what am I getting myself into" he looked up at the ceiling. He grabbed the package and threw it against the wall, knocking over a flower pot.

There was a note, and photos that lay on the floor among the money. He felt like throwing up. This is the classic case of black mail. He looked at the picture of him passing a newspaper to a known foreign national. It looked like he was doing nothing wrong. The next picture was of him counting a huge amount of money in the hotel room. He felt like he was trapped, cornered.

He read the note, "Hello... there is no way out. We have you counting your money, exchanging documents, which contained secrets. Meet me at the coffee shop across the street in the morning eight am."

He bald the note up into his palm, and gritted his teeth. His left eye lid twitched when his blood pressure rose, and it twitched none stop. He sighed deeply as he just let his body fall backwards on to the bed. He grabbed the bed spread with his hands and covered his face. He knew he had not betrayed his country, but he felt guilty, looked guilty, and if it got out that he is a trader. He would die without the honor of a true American hero.

*   *   *

Pyongyang, North Korea
Two years later

"I can't do this!" Na Min sat in an old mildew smelling apartment. The fire wood crackles every once in awhile as the snow fell outside. He sat in a chair surrounded by four North Koreans secret service men. Their sweaters came up to their chins; their heavy duty snow boots were still wet from the melted snow.

"I just can't no more. I rather die, I've giving you enough!" Na Min said.

The room was silent. The ruby red curtains missed links at the top where it hung horribly.

"Listen, you must not understand your position?" One of them walked over to him. "Smoke?" He was short, but cocky.

"No!" he stood up to leave, snatching his coat from the back of his chair.

"We own you..." his voice had a lot of respect when he spoke. He walked forward and the others stepped back. He came from the darkest part of the room, like a ghost, "…for treason, you will get the death penalty!" he pulled the chair and repositioned it.

Na Min's hand was on the door knob.

"Relax, so far so good, no one knows anything about your treason." He smiled.

With his head down, he wished he could commit suicide, just get it over with."And who are you?" he let go of the door knob.

"No one has to know." he spoke with an assuring voice."You are one of our highest ranking agents that we have on our payroll. Is it the money? OK we'll give you more of it, but..." He pushed the chair towards him and pointed at it, "...sit the fuck down!" For that one split second, he sounded like an American.

"I will never! Never allow you to walk free!" He spoke with this calm and collective voice."You have moved up in rank. We want secrets, and shipments going to The Gambia."

He stood in front of him with his fingers inner locked. He placed his hands on his face and looked him in his eyes.

"We are going to colonize The Gambia, Africa. We have knowledge that there are minerals and if we can take over the country, it would bring more revenue..." he pointed his index finger at him. "...with your ability, you would be able to help ship weapons to help over throw this country."

"Your ass belongs to me wherever you are in the world!" his voice was bone chilling. The vibration of his words melted his spirits. He felt like a trader.

"Who are you?" Na Min bravely asked.

"My name is Agent Zang." he stood up and walked over to the window with his hands behind his back. The hole on the side of his head, ear burned off, and his skin tight on his face, making him frown.

"Now, let us continue this beautiful relationship." he looked over his shoulder to look at this powerless man that had once killed, tortured, spat on others, and abused his enemy. He held his head up, but his dignity, and shame was like a first time abused dog with his tail between his legs. He sighed.

"Can I have something to drink?" Make it strong, no ice, straight." he whispered like a scary bitch that had been down in a pit of darkness and begged to be pulled out. He felt like he had to behave, cooperate or face the consequences.

For two hours he paid close attention to their plans for Africa, nick name, "The Program" Finally the meeting was over; he had his new mission of being a double agent for the North Koreans. One by one they walked out of the apartment. In came two transporters to take him back to South Korea. They walked him down the stairs to the parking garage. The driver was ready. He got in the back seat as the two transporters sat to his left and right. As this small dusty red four door car pulled out into the street.

"Here." the driver reached around and tossed him a blue eye less hood so he would not see the way to and from there underground tunnel that they use to travel from North Korea to South Korea. It took years to build this twenty mile tunnel to

South Korea to a house in a small farm town.

Back at the safe house in South Korea, Na Min stood at the window overlooking the street as Bradley walked across the street for the second time to mail a letter off to his sister that lived in Chicago. May be it was strange, but not unusual. He often mailed letters to his daughter, Yuki. So it didn't cross his mind to ask him about it.

*   *   *

Present day

He came back to reality from a daydream that wet the corner of his eyes. In front of him sat a bottle of Gin and a glass half full. The blueberry candles scented the room. He sighed as he put his family picture back in its place, near the far corner of his desk in front of him. He always wished that he could turn back the clock. He would have never invited his wife and kids to Washington D.C.

He looked at his glorious painting of himself. He frowned in disgust to how he became. But the money was so plentiful; it made him comfortable, and led him into the mind frame that it was OK.

He reached for his glass and slowly put it to his lips. The taste soothed his pain, heeled his inner scars instantly. It justified his past. He nodded his head and agreed; "It's going to be OK." he looked at the entrance to his office. His current wife walked in looking just as beautiful as the day he bought the tie. He was excited by her presence. He stood up and paused. He stumbled forward.

She came to his aid."Baby, you are drunk again." she put her shoulder underneath his left arm for support.

"Well, it's time for bed. They staggered step by step. He twisted his fingers in her shiny black curly hair. Her Spanish accent thundered his left ear.

"Come on." she said.

With his lips he made the sound of a vacuum,"Vroooom vrooom."

She laughed and grinned. He rubbed her breast softly."Just a little further..." they stumbled a little, "...and you are in no shape to do that." She pushed him on to the bed. Took off his shoes, socks, pants, and noticed that he had a violent hard on, "Yeah, you go to sleep."

He rubbed her thigh and tried to kiss her weak spot, the back of her ear. She whacks his hard on hard, he fell on to the bed.

"Not fare! That hurt!" he slurred his drunken words. Finally, she rolled him on to his stomach, and covers him with the bed sheet.

*   *   *

The phone rings several times, before Zang could hang up, "Hello, Jenko how is the Phillipines?" his voice filled the ear piece.

"Just fine, can't complaint, doing some paper work." Jenko said.

"Did you get a chance to talk to Kalargo?" Zang asked, there was a pause in the conversation.

"Why!" he asked.

"Well I thought he would have contacted you. I mean he has been in the Philippines for a month already."

"What!"

"He was down in southern islands of the Philippines for training. He was busy, but he did come through Manila International airport."

Jenko sighed, not really caring that much about it. He never really got along with him. But put up a front to do business with him. He could not stand Kalargo and no one knew this deep animosity. "Well, you know how that Bruce Lee wanna be is." Jenko had to throw that comment into the conversation.

Zang thought back when Kalargo had defeated him so many times in their Karate competition. He never could defeat him. For years he hated him, but their friendship grew despite the browns, yellows, and blue belts of martial arts. Their leadership capability that they exhibited was proof that secured their future with Zang and Na Min.

Between the two of them, they divided the Asian Pacific, Kalargo supplied weapons to Africa and South America. Jenko supplied weapons to Thailand, Burma, Vietnam, Philippines, Laos, Singapore, and Indonesia. For many years, first place or second, they remain friends and shared information between the two of them.

However, as teens the bitter taste that he had for him remained at the bottom of his throat. He learned to deal with his issues and grew out of it, but it left a dark side to him.

Jenko stood 5'8, hundred eighty five pounds with a caramel chocolate complexion, and almond eyes from his dad, who was a Korean American. His clean shaven model physique gave him a boost among the Philippine community, but his status in martial arts gave him an ultimate high.

His premiere opening to his martial arts training facility was a huge success.

Deep down inside he did not really want to listen to all this crap, but he did anyway since they had been associates for many years.

"Well basically I am calling to congratulate you on your business venture. I wish you all well."

"Thank you, will there be any other shipments?" Jenko asked.

"No, but if anything pop up I will definitely let you know. I'll keep in touch." And they both said their good byes.

He was so happy to get off the phone. He gritted his teeth until his veins and muscles showed through his neck and face. He slammed the receiver down, and felt like he owed him something. The money was good, war has always been a booming business and so far, there was no looking back.

Jenko stood in his office holding a picture of him and his mother. He tossed it a side rather than hanging it up. He wanted his mother to witness his success, not hear about it. He grabbed it again and walked towards a file cabinet along the back wall that had over twenty trophies, another fifteen were placed in the front of the training facility for display of experience. He bent down to pull the bottom drawer. He stopped before tossing it, with his left hand he picked up an unframed photo. He looked at it, and sighed. He was sixteen years old and stood next to a trophy that was taller than him. The photo also had Kalargo standing next to him with a first place trophy that stood taller than his trophy. That was the last competition they participated in. He placed it back in the drawer, and decided to hang the photo of him and his mom on the wall.

"Right here…" held the nail and tapped it with a small hammer. He proudly hung the photo and made sure that it was perfect.

*   *   *

Seoul, South Korea 1970's
Mugumbi meets Na Min

"Listen, my stepfather is a reputable man in South Korea, if anyone can help you, he can." Yuki said to Mugumbi in his native language Jola.

Mugumbi and Tipi had been in South Korea for several months. He looked for work, but the language barrier got in the way. They both sat in a small bar about ten blocks away from a military base. He slowly sipped his cocktail. There was hand full of Koreans and mostly Americans that frequented the bar. An occasional regular would walk in and take a seat. His dark complexion and features gave him a non American look. So he couldn't really blend in as an American. Some of

them who had been stationed there long enough had the privilege of speaking Korean. The music blared of Micheal Jackson,"
"ABC".

The darkness of the bar would spook a stranger, but normalize a regular customer.

"Mugumbi, listen to me." The bar door opened and the day light illuminated the bar briefly. They looked to see who was entering. The voices of the bar welcomed a regular, "Bill!" They raised their glasses to him.

He walked over to his favorite part of the bar and lifted his wrist at everyone. His hand was blown off during the Korean War by a grenade.

"Yuki..." he leaned back on the stool. His jet black African features highly defined his culture, nose, lips, Afro, and being in South Korea was as strange as a snake wearing a jean jacket to keep warm. He felt like a main attraction, a freak at times. People would literally want and often touched his skin out of curiosity. They want to see if the makeup would rub off.

"Yuki, how are you able to speak my native language Jola? I felt so lost before I met you." He held her hand. "Now, it's almost like I am dependent on you. Can you teach me your language?"

She lit a cigarette and puffed, blew the smoke away from his face, leaned over and locked her lips on to his, "Of course I will. You want to learned English also?" she smiled and puffed until the cherry of her cigarette couldn't get any brighter.

"As far as how I speak your native tongue..." she paused and looked down at his hands, "...my biological father moved to Africa and I lived there for four years. I had a nanny that taught me to read and write." She took a sip of her drink, and played with the ends of her hair.

"Let's just say that..." she looked him in his eyes, "...someone else was more serious about me learning the language than I was ever interested." They both laughed.

"Well I can truly say she did a good job" he sips on his drink. He slowly looked at his half empty glass and slowly put it down. He sighed. "What happen to your father?"

She turned her head and pushed her hair out of her face.

"If you prefer not to talk about it, I would totally understand." He held her hand.

"No, no, I mean it's not that. Just thinking of him and the memories that I do have of him..." she downed her drink, "...he was everything; my father gave me the security that I looked for. You know.That protection that nothing would happen to me."

"Well he's an American hero." She smiled. "He died in a gun fight in Osan. He tried to save my stepfather in a shootout. Just before he died he told his partner…"

"Another drink?" the bartender was ready to refill their glass.

"Yes, two." Mugumbi agreed with two fingers. "Yeah, I don't want to be nervous when your step father gets here."

"Tequila, coming up."

"Yes" he looked at her. "That means yes?" he asked her. "I will learn Korean, just give me some time."

She waved her hands in front of her face as if she forgets where she had ended the story about her father.

"What kind of work your father did" he asked her. "Logistics business?"

She looked at his dried lower lip. She placed her index finger on his chin and played with his clit tickler, the small patch of hair below his lower lip curled outward.

Just before she spoke, she sneezed.

"God bless." He gave her a napkin.

"Well he traveled a lot." She wiped her nose and moved in closer to his face with her slanted eyes, high cheek bone, and pale face. Her thin lips touched his lips, even though he was not attractive, but she liked him. Finally she found something to say. She ignored his question.

"So anyway, long story short…" she interrupted him, but before she could get a word out. The door opened and the burst of outside light entered the bar. She looked over her shoulder and it was Na Min standing there searching with his eyes. There was no huge welcome for him. He wasn't a regular.

"Oh no…" Yuki said.

"What?" Mugumbi looked at the door.

She stood from her stool. It was obvious that he had arrived. The alcohol was not working like he had thought it would. He quickly slammed his drink down his throat and pounded his fist on his chest. He frowned, gagged, and exhaled the burning sensation of the Tequila from his throat.

She waved him towards them. Their smiles were mutual. She stood and bowed slightly. He felt obliged to do the same.

Na Min reached out and gave her a hug.

"Daddy this is Mugumbi." She pointed her hands towards Mugumbi.

He looked at him and nodded his head, "So you are the lucky man I have been hearing about." He reached his right hand out and shook his hand. "I have heard about your journey from Africa, amazing." He spoke to them in English. Yuki translated every word to him.

"I am a very busy man, but whatever I can do to help on behalf of my daughter." He took a seat and waved his hand to the bartender, "Gin please."

"He needs work. He doesn't speak Korean, but he speaks some English." She looked at her stepfather.

He let out a huge sigh and sipped from his glass. "He needs a miracle."

"But you make miracles happen all the time." She grabbed Mugumbi by the arm.

"Most of my miracles start with the same language. This is different. This is South Korea."

"Oh yeah, he also has a nephew that came along." She said with a hesitant smile.

Na Min looked at her, "Damn, what did you do, inherit these people?" he sighed and rubbed his eyes with both hands. He looked at Mugumbi. There were questions he wanted to ask, but not in front of Yuki.

He looked at them both, and mentally asked "Can this guy be trusted? There is only one way to find out."

"I tell you what; I may be able to get him some work as a dishwasher." He looked at him. "I know some people that might hire him." He picked up his drink and held up to toast. Their glasses cling as they touched.

He licked his dry lips and smiled. He extended his hand, and they shook on it. Out of respect, Mugumbi bowed. "Thank you, thank you."

"Mugumbi, I am an American. So shaking my hand is apart my culture." They laughed.

"I will call you in the morning." They agreed.

He reached into his faded blue jeans and pulled out money to pay the tab for them both. "Bartender, keep the change!" he said out loud. He kissed Yuki on the cheek and rubbed her on her back. He said his goodbyes and walked away into the darkness of the bar.

The burst of light filled the bar as the door opened, darkness resumed as the door closed.

Chapter 14

"Yuki, listen I have a translator for him. He'll be there to pick him up. Tell him to be ready in an hour" he slowly put the phone on the receiver.

The blue sky carried a breeze from the east at 10 mph. periodically the smell of the bread bakery not far away from her small apartment lingered. The mixture of eggs, bacon, and grits clashed with the sweet bakery bread.

"Mugumbi!" her child like voice from the kitchen.

"Yeah." he responded from the bedroom.

"Your ride will be here in an hour." She stirred the eggs.

Kalargo slept on the floor beneath the blanket. The sound of voices awakens him. He opened his eyes to the smell of food, stretched his little body and rubbed his eyes. "I am hungry."

Mugumbi entered the living room, "I have an interview for a job."

Kalargo rolled over.

"Are you hungry?" she asked. Just like a kid, his head popped through the blanket.

"Breakfast is served." She put the plates on the table.

The translator knocked on the door.

"One moment…" Yuki peeped through the peep hole.

"Well he's here." She kissed him on his lips, with her teeth; she held his lower lip in a romantic vice grip. A small amount of saliva oozed from their mouths for a sloppy kiss good bye.

"Hey." The translator extended his hand out. "Good morning…" with a smile, "…my name is Bogig for short, Bo. Na Min wants me to teach you Korean, show you around town."

Bo had an earring of a cross with diamonds around it, small but cute, a super thick mustache, with a failed attempt to dye his gray hairs.

"I am not sure what job you will have, but whatever it is, do your best, because there are better positions." He led the way to his car.

Mugumbi walked towards the left side of the car and opened the door. "First I have to learn Korean." The sound of the engine roared.

"This is a nice ride." He complimented his five year old '74 Isuzu.

"Seat belts… well believe me, if they like you, they will send you to school for whatever you need to learn. When I first came here fifteen years ago, I spoke no Korean and I got a break washing dishes. Everything went up hill from that point on. Hopefully…" he was interrupted by his cell phone.

His Korean was almost flawless. He was amazed how well he spoke. After three minutes on the phone, Bo flipped his left traffic signal. "Well I have a pit stop to make." Their conversation continued.

The store fronts and street signs were all foreign to him; traffic drove on the right side of the street. It appeared that every Korean in the country had a bicycle.

Driving through small narrow roads, squeezing along side park cars, they arrived at the back of an apartment building and parked.

"Now what?" Mugumbi asked.

Bo pulled out a box of cigarettes, "Smoke?"

"Why not." he leaned over to use his flame from his match that had burned half way down its stem.

"In about five minutes…" Bo inhaled his smoke. He turned the radio down a little, "…a white guy will drop off an envelope. The alarm lights will flash on that brown Toyota to let us know the package is ready for pick up. Even though we may not see this guy, I know he's an American, and military. But what matters is that we get the package and deliver it." The front two windows were rolled down.

They both exhaled a cloud of smoke. He paid close attention to his surroundings. Bo blood shot eyes; rough black skin tone gave him a sinister look. He stood 5'7, 215 pounds, mostly around his waist, and buttocks.

"So I guess we are like a carrier service, pick up and deliver?" Mugumbi asked.

Bo flicked the ashes out the window and laughed. "If that's how you see it. Yeah I guess, in a way."

The alarm sounded on the Toyota and Bo opens his car door. "I'll be right back."

Moments later, the interior lights came on and Bo was back with an envelope. "Now we can go." He tossed it on the back seat. "Now I can take you where you need to be." He started the car and drove off.

The rest of the day went smooth, eventually coming to an end. "Mugumbi! Wake up!" he nudged his shoulder, "Get yourself together." Bo shifted the gear to park.

He exhaled hard. "I'm up…" he opened his eyes and looked around, "…damn where are we?"

"We are here. Listen, if this guy likes you. You'll have a job." Bo pointed his finger at him.

Mugumbi turned and leaned to the left, quickly licked the back of his index finger to check for bad breathe. "Damn…" he frowned. "…doing what?"

Bo took the keys out of the ignition. "Just be happy to have a job, this is Korea, the job choose us."

He sighed and crossed his fingers. They parked in a parking garage two blocks away.

"Wow, this is downtown?" Mugumbi looked amazed.

They approached one of the tallest buildings in the downtown area.
The streets were pack with pedestrians and bicycles. He just could not get over how many bicycles that neatly lined the street.

He looked up at the clock read 12pm.

"Right here." Bo said.

He paused and looked upward. "Wow."

"Well here goes everything." He pulled one of the quadruple glass doors. The emblem of an eye that covered the marble floor, above it was Net Rem Grat Services. He stood still as people bumped into him.

"Come on." Bo said.

"The elevators are over here." He pointed into the direction. Upon entering the building, two Korean women bowed at them. They bowed back.

"Ding ding." The elevator doors closed as the last person squeezed his way in. "Hey, pressed the eighteenth floor." Bo said.

The elevators were not sparred from top notch decorating, oak wood, and velvet. Coming from Africa, this was definitely first class.

The crowd looked shy but whispered among themselves. They giggled.

"What are they saying?" Mugumbi asked.

Bo smiled, "You don't want to know."

"Hey… you are supposed to teach me."

Bo grinned and looked at him, "Let's just say that they admire how dark we are." He rubbed the back of his hand.

"Are lips are so big." He closed his mouth and exhaled hard enough so his lips would purposely vibrate. Three of the women burst into giggles behind the palms of their hands that covered their mouths.

"Ding ding." The women walked off on the eleventh floor.

"Seven more floors to go." Bo said.

They exited the elevator and the vanilla fragrance tickled their nose. The receptionist stood and bowed, "Good afternoon"

In huge gold platted letters, "Net Rem Grat services inc." on a reddish orange wall that said, "We deliver when they say it's impossible."

The wall to wall gray carpet felt like cotton beneath their feet. The marble and oak gave an affluent atmosphere.

"Yes we have an appointment." Bo leaned on the counter that was up to his chest.

After she bowed again she pushed two bottoms on the computer, and one on the phone. The voice on the loud speaker was cut short when she picked the receiver up.

"Yes…" as she spoke on the phone.

Mugumbi walked over to the miniature statues and paintings, one by one. The oldest one of them all, he felt obliged to touch.

It was a South Korean miniature forest with a water fall that fogged at the bottom of the mini pawn. The sound of falling water echoed the pawn as it fell. He looked at the bottom of the pool of water and saw some strange objects that appeared to be dirty stones. Just before he dipped his hand, he noticed a sign in Korean.

"Bo, what does this say?" his finger pointed.

Bo strolled over with his hands behind his back. His lips mumbled. "Well, it says high voltage. Try at your own risk."

"Excuse me sir." The receptionist called. "He will be with you in a moment."

They took their seat in the waiting area. They looked at the magazines. Clients entered and left for four hours. Mugumbi dosed off, tried to fight off sand man, but he looked as if he was being kicked around, his head bobbed back and forward. He tried to rest his head to the left and trying to find a good position every twenty minutes. The magazine he held had fallen between his legs and woke him up. He opened his eyes to look around to see if anyone was watching. He saw Bo standing and flirting with the receptionist.

"Damn..." he stood up and stretched. He was frustrated.

The phone rang and a moment of silence, she pointed toward the double glass doors framed in brass. Upon entering, there was another receptionist.

"Oh my..." before he could sigh.

"He is expecting you. The door on the left, she directed them. The doors automatically opened as they approached. The American voice filled the huge office; the English speaking man faced the bay window that over looked Seoul.

Mugumbi had never seen a city line from this view. They stood and waited as this big office consumed their little bodies. The fish tank appeared to be a section out of the Pacific Ocean. The ugliest deep water fish man has ever seen. Their teeth looked mangled outside of their mouths. They looked dangerous and exotic at the same time.

The voice spoke from behind the chair. "I caught twenty of them myself. The others were flown in from different parts of the world. He continued his conversation on the phone.

"Yes, not a problem, how about I fly into D.C. next month, say the 15th of April, at the pentagon 8:30 sharp." He paused. His chair turned around. It was Na Min, Mugumbi stopped sweating immediately, but he kept his composure.

His cotton and rayon shirt was neatly pressed. The cuff links sparkled. The skinny knotted cream colored tie was neatly pressed up to his Adams apple. The gray pin stripped suit looked expensive. The desk had a calendar that sat in the middle, neatly arranged papers, and a miniature golf bag that was an ink pen holder. The miniature bar was to the left and a small conference table to the right, in the far corner stood a coat rack that hung one coat.

He held the phone away from his mouth. He gestured with his finger, "One moment." He turned the chair back towards the sky line. "See you then sir." The conversation ended.

He turned back around to face them both. He leaned forward resting his elbows on the desk. He looked Mugumbi up and down, placed his hands beneath his chin. He sighed.

"Please have a seat." He told them. Bo translated.

He twisted his head with his left hand. He showed a doubtful look on his face. Finally he held his hands in front of him.

"OK listen, you are not hired yet. However, you have six months to learn enough Korean to be able to communicate with me." Bo can be heard translating.

"Second, you will have classes to help you. I will get you a passport, and work visa. That's if you are hired. For right now, you are considered help, and only help."

He stood and walked over to the window. He turned around on the back of his left hill of his shoe. The late 70's designed pants flared at the bottom. A neatly trimmed beard and a shaggy hair style, "Drinks?"

They both looked at each other, Bo translated.

"Yes."

The atmosphere of the office was calm with the jazz tunes in the background. The ice chattered the glass, the Gin poured smoothly.

"Yes." He sipped. "Now at all times, you will have contact with me through Bo. The faster you learn the language." He paused. "Matter of fact, English also, the faster the better."

He placed his drink down on the desk next to the Rolodex and ink pen holder. "What we discuss is never, never to be spoken outside of us." He folded his arms, "Never." He repeated.

Mugumbi looked at Bo as he pointed his index finger, and translating word for word. He nodded his head with a hundred percent comprehension.

"You will be paid bi weekly in cash for learning the two languages; however, you will work for free." he sipped his Gin.

He pulled a scrap sheet of paper and wrote down what he would pay him bi weekly.

"In thirty days, I will be going to D.C. You have thirty days to learn these manuals, if so; I will have your passport ready for you." He looked at them both and scratched his nose.

"But for right now, take him to Baru restaurant and put him to work."

He sat back in his leather chair and reached for his drink. "Bo, teach him everything he needs to know."

"Yes, I will." He responded with a nod.

Mugumbi's armpits were sweaty. He was nervous, and in need of a job right away, finally, he has one.

"One more thing..." he stood up and walked over to the painting on the wall of a Hwarang. His left index finger pushed a button in the right corner of the frame that made the painting slid to the left. The knob on the safe clicked with every turn to the left... to the right... and then the left.

"Damn!" he paused. "Oh I remember it." He started over. Every two months he felt the need to change his combination. As he gets older and trying to remember it, gets harder.

The safe opened, he reached in and pulled out a small bundle of won. He counted eight hundred thousand won.

"Here, this is for your pocket." He tossed the remaining back into the safe.

Mugumbi held his arms close to his side, wiped his palms on his pants leg before he reached for the won, and without counting it he shoved it deep into his right pocket. "Gamsahabnida."

He was surprised. "Now you see..." he pointed his index finger at him, "...that's what I'm talking about. No matter what, practice a language and eventually, you will speak the language."

Bo translated and they all smiled.

"On your way out, the receptionist will take a photo of you for your passport; from there you will go to the restaurant."

They bowed; Na Min waved his hand in disapproval. He extended his right hand to shake theirs, and said their goodbyes.

One year later

The hot steam soaked Mugumbi's clothes. The red tiled floor with a drain hole was slippery wet. His forehead had a glossy shine from working hard, up to his elbows in a deep sink filled with dishes. The half filled garbage smelt horrible. The sleeves of his dingy white t shirt were dark brown from the wiping his forehead and nose of sweat.

A cook pushed open the door and yelled, "More plates!"

Mugumbi responded back in Korean, "Plates are ready! I got them right here!" he pulled both hands out of the water and slid the soapsuds off each arm one at a time. He carefully walked across the wet floor as he held his balance. Behind him was a wall of clean pots and plates on the stainless steel counter. He grabbed ten plates and took them out to the kitchen. He felt like a peasant.

"Mugumbi!" the cook yelled for him.

His frustration grew every time he heard his name.

The cook peeked through the door, "You have a visitor."

He snatched a towel to dry his hands, and tossed it over his left shoulder, took a whiff of his armpits, "Not bad."

He walked out the back door of the restaurant into the potholed alley of garbage bens. The stench of old thrown away food blanketed his face under early morning dew. He looked at his wristwatch and noticed the sun rising.

"Damn, it's 5:30." He spoke under his breath.

Bo stepped out from behind a trash bend smoking a cigarette. The red cherry lit up as he inhaled. The scene spooked him. Before he spoke he looked down the alley to make sure he was alone.

"What's going on?" Mugumbi asked. He removed the towel to dry his sweaty palms and whipped his face and neck.

Bo flicked the cigarette butt to the ground, with the toe of his left shoe, stepped forward and twisted to put it out. His burnt orange double breasted suit that cuffed at the bottom.

"Aren't you looking stylish?" Mugumbi said.

Bo's mood remained calm. "Hey, it's time." he paused, looked around. He pulled out a new pack of cigarettes, unwrapped the plastic cellophane that slowly drifted to the ground, "Cigarette?"

Mugumbi used his thumb and index to make sure that he only touched one cigarette.

The cherry blazed as the flamed brighten the dark alley, with smoke in his lungs, he placed the lighter in his coat pocket.

"Na Min wants you to deliver a package. My car is around the corner." He started to walk toward the end of the alley.

"Wait...I left my bag." he ran back into the kitchen. A Filipino had taken his placed washing dishes. It startled him at first. He traded his work boots for his own. He grabbed his bag, and headed out the back door.

"Listen, these are the directions, this is the package, and some pocket money." Bo pulled out of the alley on to the one way. "I'm taking you to the subway. Under no circumstances, will you let this package out of your site." He made a right turn, and looked in his rearview mirror.

"This is a photo of your contact. Call me once you have dropped the package off, any questions?"Bo looked in his rearview to make sure they were not being followed.

He frowned and shook his head, "No."

"Take this with you..." he reached behind the passenger seat and grabbed a brown paper bag. "...it's a .38 snug nose revolver, go ahead open it up and take it out. Here are the bullets."

Mugumbi began to load the bullets with his towel to make sure his fingerprints weren't on them. He sighed. They pulled over at the corner store. He reached for the gun, "I'll load it, go in and get some cigarettes." He pulled the car around the side of the store to load the gun.

When he returned to the car he looked nervous.

"Hey... this is nothing, just a little easy work. Just don't let the package out of your site." He pulled up to the subway, "Call me if you have any questions." They shook hands.

He took two steps at a time down to the subway platform. He stopped to read the directions. He looked to his left and then his right. All the signs were written in Korean. He compared it to his directions and figured out what train to take.

"This way." he paid for his train ticket.

The early morning crowd carried their coffee, tea and briefcases. They bundled together as the train approached. The streaking sound of the train came to a stop. The crowd pushed and shoved their way on. He kept the package under his left armpit.

He noticed some people read novels, and newspapers. Several people had their face mask on to keep from spreading germs. He sighed deeply as the train rocked and wobbled its way along the track.

He periodically thought of the gun in his back pocket. He looked at the directions. He counted ten more stops. The closer he got. The more nervous he became. He began to pop his bones throughout his body.

"Ding ding." He exited the train and took a deep breath. The platform over looked the city. The sun was in full bloom.

"Taxi…" His Korean was not perfect but he said, "…take me to this address." The taxi driver nodded his head and waves his hand to indicate to get in.

Forty five minutes had passed and he was awoken by a pot hole in the road. He quickly reached for the package and gun.

"Where are we?" He looked around and read his directions. He licked his lips and stretched.

"You will be there in five minutes." He held his hand up to show five fingers. He figured his Korean was not that great by his accent.

The apartment building was seven floors, clean, decent neighborhood. He noticed the kids yelling and playing in the first apartment. He looked down at his directions.

"Apt 505." he sighed and knocked four times, and paused. Then two more times.

A voice oozed from beneath the door before the door slowly opened.

The guy had a short military style hair cut, blonde, deep sunken blue eyes. He stared at him from head to toe. He looked European, perhaps German or Russian. His mustache was bushy and smelt like expensive aftershave.

"Are you alone?" his Korean was almost perfect to him but he knew he was not born in this part of the world.

Mugumbi looked around, "Yes I'm alone."

"Quickly come in." he stood aside and let him pass. He checked the hallway to make sure. "Did anyone see you come in to the building?" he closed the door, before he could respond, "Have a seat, relax."

The sound of the locks on the door clicked, snapped, one by one, three of them. He sighed. This guy does some type of drugs he thought.

The apartment had three bedrooms and two bathrooms and looked pretty much unlived in. The wooden floors moaned and cried as he walked to the mini bar. The smell of food lingered from the kitchen.

"Is that it?" the European asked.

"I'm Tony, they call me the Dutchman." He gave him a drink.

He gave him the package and thought about the photo of the guy he had in his pocket.

"I have something to give you, hold on." He went into the kitchen and opened the package. He looked around into the living room. "So, where are you from?" The Dutchman asked.

"Africa." Mugumbi said.

Tony came out from the kitchen, "I'm from Holland, but I grew up in Pusan."

Mugumbi sized him up. He looked like a muscular fighter, couldn't tell from the lose clothes he had on.

"I'll be right back. I got to get some things from the car that I have to give you." Tony left the apartment.

Mugumbi sighed, he felt uncomfortable. He stood to walk around to get rid of the butterflies. He cracked the door to one of the bedrooms. It was small, clean for a guy he thought. He quickly looked in the second bedroom. His eyes opened wide. It was covered in plastic, even the ceiling. He quickly closed the door. That room gave him the chills. He walked across the painful sounding wooden floor to the kitchen.

The opened package on the counter had a note. His eyes opened, it was in Korean, but it didn't make sense. He heard a door close in the hallway of the apartment building. He read the note one more time, and figured it out. His heart pounded his chest as he headed to exit the apartment.

Tony opened the door, "Hey sorry it took me awhile." He gave him an envelope with some money, and asked him to help him move something from the darkroom covered in plastic.

He sighed and felt like maybe he was just jittery. Tony walked in first and opened the door to the closet. "Yeah, I have to take this to my friend. He was relieved when he found out he was moving photography equipment. He sighed, but the note.

"Wait…" he told him as he held up one end of a heavy generator. Tony walked behind him to clear their path.

The razor sharp piano string was tossed around Mugumbi's neck. They struggled hard and violently. He flipped him over his shoulder and slammed his body to the floor. The sound of plastic raddled loudly. He punched him and kicked him in the ribs. Tony pulled the piano wire tighter, and pulled him to the floor. He broke loose and kicked him again in the head.

Tony pulled a knife and cut him across the chest that left a bleeding wound. Another slice on his upper arm, blood fell on the plastic as he charges him with the knife over his head.

He tried to reason with him, but he only responded with rage in his face. They both fell backwards as he reached for the .38 and shot him in the chest. He slumped on top of him. He pushed him to the side and rolled on to his back. He couldn't believe all of this. He cleaned the gun and dropped it. He pocketed the money and ran into the kitchen to read the note again.

"Damn!" he first read the note, it did not make sense, it read to kill him and get rid of his body. He sighed and knew he had to quickly get out of the building. He grabbed a shirt from the other room to cover the wounds and blood. He opened the door just enough. He walked calmly but not unnoticed, but he escaped.

He was angry as he looked for a taxi. "What the hell is going on?"

The taxi door opened and got in. His wounds weren't as bad as he thought, surface wounds. He told the driver where he wanted to go, and couldn't wait to catch up with Bo.

Chapter 15

Seoul, South Korea
Several years later

"Ha! Ha!" Kalargo gestured as he round housed a karate kick. The martial arts competition finals began with eighty competitors. The final six remained with high expectations of winning.

"Kalargo listen, you can do it. Just practice what I taught you. You have an advantage over these other kids. You're mentally stronger, and confident. You trained harder than all of them." Na Min told him.

In front of a crowd of eighteen hundred chanting fans, "All you have to do is win this next round, beat Jenko. He is the only true competition that you have." he encouraged him.

As a kid, Kalargo had been winning for the last four years, being the only African; he was a sight to see. That's until Jenko came on to the scene. For the last two years his best friend has not spoken to him, and he now faces him again for the championship title. The wedge deepens between the two.

Kalargo has all the trophies and notoriety. Jenko won one title due to him falling ill, but that trophy didn't count unless he was defeated. The deep ambition to win boiled over. He just had to face him with all the skills he had.

Jenko's chest was pushed in from a kick that made him stagger. He shook it off and hooked Kalargo with a left. He head butted him as he threw him to the ground, twisted his right leg and the crowd heard a moan. His facial expression said it was painful, but broke out of it quickly, and they both were back on their feet. His nose dripped of blood.

Jenko ran in to attack, but a round house kick slammed into his left rib cage. He held his chest tight as he fell to one knee. His breathing appeared shallow. He fought the pain and stood up in the ready position, but his opponent was quicker, smarter, and well trained.

Kalargo rushed him with a kick to the head, but by surprise his leg was swept from the ground. He fell hard, and a quick kick to the rib cage was very painful. He moaned and held his upper armpit area. He rolled on to his side and he felt his jaw buckle from a left punch. He grabbed him by the waist and picked him up into the air and slammed him sideways.

Kalargo's head was in a tight arm lock that cut off circulation. The fear of not breathing made him attack his rib cage with devastating blows. He broke loose and upper cut him to the face. Jenko backed off in a painful daze that gave him an opportunity. Kalargo took it by dropping him with another kick to the head that knocked him down.

Before he could attack, the ref jumped in between to stop the fight. He saw that Jenko was in no shape to defend himself.

Jenko jumped up in anger, "I can fight. I can fight." His right eye was swollen, nose bled, and he held his rib cage.

"No it's over!" he walked over to the winner and raised Kalargo's hand and declared him as the winner by KO.

Kalargo walked over to him to embrace him. He raised his left hand and leaned over to his ear. "Good fight, damn good fight."

Jenko was infuriated. The medic walked over to attend him.

Kalargo held a towel to his nose as he sat. "Damn you kicked his ass. I told you that round house is a knockout punch in disguise." Na Min said as he congratulated him on his victory, embraced him like a son that he once had.

"We have to celebrate, how about we go to the theme park?" Kalargo asked with excitement.

"Yes!" Na Min said with enthusiasm. They grabbed their belongings. He looked Kalargo in his eyes, "Son, its one important thing about sportsmanship..." he began to teach him.

Kalargo stood there with his towel across his shoulder. He used it to wipe his sweat, and check his nose for blood.

"I think it would be a good idea to invite Jenko. No matter how you look at it, he is a good fighter, and he is your friend. It should be an honor to invite him." Na Min said.

He looked over at Jenko. The medic had his head back with a towel on his face. He wondered how he could ask him without insulting him. Kalargo sighed.

"Well he is my friend." He slowly walked across the wide and long royal blue mat. He subdued his arrogance. He sat next to him and his trainer.

"Is he going to be ok?" he felt like that was the wrong thing to ask at a time like this.

Of course the trainer had to say, "He'll be fine, just a nose bleed, and a small cut above his eye."

"So how you feel?" Kalargo looked at him.

"Well I can start with a headache, and ear ache… can you fix it?" Jenko asked with a smile.

Kalargo lifted the towel to look at his nose. The blood slowed down but the towel needed to be changed.

"Here, let me change the towel." He quickly gave him a new one.

"Hey I was wondering if you wanted to come with me to theme park?" he waited for his response.

Jenko leaned forward and looked out of surprise, "Ouch, dude it hurts. Can the doctor come?" he smiled. "You kicked my ass and now you invite me to a theme park?" He replaced his hand to hold the towel to his nose.

"Well I will have to ask for permission, but I don't see why they would say no." He looked at the towel. The bleeding had stopped. He moaned when he stood up. "I hope not too soon. I feel like crap right now."

Kalargo held his rib cage as he stood. "Cool, I'll call you in three weeks…hey sorry about the nose."

He smiled, "Don't be, I'm not sorry for anything I did."

He walked across the mat. The crowd slowly dispersed.

Several years later, Kalargo stood looking at himself in the mirror. With his right thumb, he pushed his upper lip up then his bottom lip down to examine his gums. He wore his yellow and white graduation gown with a yellow graduation hat. He checked his breath. He danced to a song and patted himself on the back. In the mirror, he could see the wall of trophies that stood tall, ribbons hung proudly, and realized how big of a deal this was.

One of his karate uniforms hung across a chair in the corner of his room. The framed pictures of his powerful roundhouse kick hung in two places. The perfect captures of his opponents were of pain with their sweat in mid flight off of their faces. His room was fairly clean for an eighteen year old who was on his way to further his education. But then again, he was very disciplined. He finally felt like dreams can really come true. Suddenly, he slammed his head back to slow the flow of a nosebleed.

"Damn! I hate this!" he rushed towards the bathroom and pulled a couple of sheets of toilet paper. He was happy not to mess up his gown.

"Kalargo!"

"Yeah, here I come!"

"Mugumbi and Yuki is here, it's about that time!" Na Min peeked in on him.

"Where is the camera? I want to video this." By then their English, Korean, and Chinese had remarkably improved. The Korean culture was second nature to him. He took it seriously because as a kid he wanted to fit in. His eating habits, how he cooked his food, but he later found out learning the language earned you the most respect in a foreign country. It showed how dedicated a person is to learn another culture, especially how he embraced it, but no matter how he felt he was being treated, there were always those who admired him, and acknowledged through his popularity from the martial arts world. He loved Korea, and he liked being the different one.

The excitement filled the auditorium as the grad caps were tossed into the air. The students kissed and hung one another as they said their goodbyes. They took pictures that would last a lifetime.

As the family walked towards their car, a voice from a distance bellowed out. "Kalargo!"

It was Jenko, "Hey let's take a picture."

"Wait I got you a gift." Kalargo pulled out a wrapped box and gave it to him.

"No, I didn't bring you anything!" Jenko said as they posed for the camera. The first picture was good, "Go ahead open it..."

The gift-wrap fell to the ground; the box was thrown after the excitement of the gift. "No way dude, this is beautiful, he read the engraving. "I wish you good health, my friendship, and success." It was hand crafted English on one side and Korean on the other. Their picture was perfect.

*   *   *

Gambia, Africa

"Kalargo!" the loadmaster woke him. The loud roar of the c-130 aircraft engines hummed in sync, the turbulence vibrated the plane every so often. The interior of the cargo plane cleared his mind and reality was in place of a trip down memory lane. He sighed and rubbed his hands of sweat on his knees. He closed his eyes and wiped the corners of them. He stood up and stretched, and moaned. The clouds floated by the window in the early morning darkness. The stars above flickered spontaneously. At twenty thousand feet and descending into cloudier sky, he looked around the cargo plane; it was his equipment and pallets of rice to be parachuted into a country of starving people. It was stamped "Feed Africa"

"How long before I jump?" Kalargo asked.

The loadmaster checked his watch "Forty five minutes." The short Filipino said.

He picked up his parachute and tossed it on to his back. The loadmaster helped him tighten his straps. He checks his knife, flashlight, compass, photos of the General, .45 caliber, and pulled out his map to verify the drop zone, the roads to which he would travel.

He sighed, closed his eyes and prayed. The red rotating lights warned that he had twenty minutes. He grabbed his helmet and put it on. The butterflies in his stomach were intensive.

The feeling of the decent increased with the vibration. The engines roared to an equal hum. The dense clouds fogged the circular windows. Suddenly, the ex American cargo plane leveled out, calmed itself and cruise at ten thousand feet. A warning buzzer sounded and a yellow light flashed as the cargo ramp lowered slowly. The loadmaster held a black cord that he carried in his left hand, pushed a button on his helmet to talk to the pilots. He held his hand up at Kalargo to signal that he had five minutes.

He tightens his chinstrap and pulled down his goggles. He stood in the ready position. His hands, legs, teeth, fearfully shook. His breathing increased. The green light flashed. The two containers of equipment were pushed out. He waved for him to come forward. He wobbled his way to stand behind a painted yellow line. The loadmaster gave him a thumb up as they maintained their balance.

"Go!Go!Go!" the loadmaster yelled.

He nodded and wobbled his way to the edge of the ramp and leaned forward into the pitch-black sky, before he realized it, his chute was deployed. The sound of the c-130 slowly faded away. It was the most peaceful moment he had ever experienced. The smell of jp-5 aircraft fuel slowly became pure clean air. The c-130 made a sharp right and climb toward the full moon that made it look like a slow moving horsefly, crawling, and struggling for its last flight.

The two containers can be seen floating to earth. He pulled his guide strings to land near them. The wind gusted strong from the west and the smell of earth tickled his nose. He pulled down his night goggles. The smell of plants trees increased. In a matter of seconds, earth swallowed him. The open patch of land was a perfect landing zone.

He quickly rolled his parachute and ran into the tree line. The dense jungle created a pulse that he only felt out of fear, from a beautiful, peaceful float out of the heavens above, has now become survival.

"Damn. What did I get myself into?" he asked himself, he cut his parachute lines and began searching for the containers. He found one of them. Suddenly, he stopped to listen. He was motionless, only his eyes moved to lurk the darkness through his night goggles. He very slowly rotated his head to his right, chin touched his right collarbone. He tried to calculate how far away the gunfire was from him. He turned focus back to his search. He found the second container and dragged it near the first one. He sighed and pulled out his flashlight, map and took off his night goggles.

"Hmm, I am here somewhere…" he pointed to the city of Nabin chi. He wiped sweat from his nose. "This has to be at least eight miles." He sucked air between his teeth. He coughed and spat over his left shoulder. It was no way he could get there with two containers.

He focused back to the map, "Ok, let me see, show me away." He drove his index finger to the south to a village. He swatted away mosquitoes, "Fifteen miles, what time is it?" he mumbled as he looked at his watch. The sun will be up in two hours." He pushed his finger across the map. "This road leads me there, and this is less than a third away from it."

He looked at his compass to make sure he was headed in the right direction. He folded the map neatly to replace it with the remaining papers in a plastic bag and stuffed it in his flight suit. He walked due south.

After fifteen minutes of walking through dense jungle, he knew the road was not much further ahead. He pushed himself until he reached an opening and rested. He closed his eyes.

The sky started to change from dark to lavender, with early morning dew that damped the leaves, exotic birds chirped freely, and the monkeys watched over him like curious knights. They moved in a small heard in search of food. The sound of them laughing woke him. They were skinny bright yellowish, gray with black specs. They scattered when he moved. He looked around and the monkeys kept their distance in the bush. They swung from tree branch to the next.

"Damn." He took off his flight suit and dismantled his gear. He put whatever he needed in his backpack. The two containers were not far away, so he dragged them closer to the road.

He opened the first container and pulled out an envelope. He stuffed it inside his backpack. He grabbed a couple of other things, closed the container and pushed them in between the bushes.

He paused for a second to make sure no one was around. The monkeys curiously watched him.

He walked south on the road to town. The smell of food lingered the air. The sound of kids playing, and cows mooing with bells that dangled from their necks.

Across the field a family plowed a small patch of land with three bovines with horns the size of Texas. He walked into a small village, and immediately felt out of place. The small narrow clayish road separated the straw huts. Some of the kids played naked. They looked like they were thrown into a box of baby powder. A young mother of two carried her infants in her arms.

His body scent was different, clean and foreign. The kids ran up to him begging as they pulled on his pants leg for gum or something sweet.

"Hey little ones, I don't have any candy today…" before he could finish speaking in his native tongue. They scattered away. He made eye contact with an older man that sat on a broken chair that was flipped on his side. The guy never took his eyes off of him. From head to toe, with a bush tongue accent he asked, "Where are you from, the city?"

Kalargo felt relieved that someone spoke to him first. "Yes, just passing through. I am going to…" he paused and realized not say too much, "…is there a way that I can get a horse or a donkey? I have a couple of things to carry." Kalargo bent his knees and put his buttocks a few inches away from the burnt orange clayish ground.

The old man's dingy white button up shirt, his blue pinstriped dusty slacks were dusty of that natural clay. His sandals were throw away second hand that he recovered from some burning trash pile. His pupils were grayish brown with a circular ring of blue that appeared blood shot of an alcoholic.

He looked around in search of a more helpful individual. His focus returned to the old man. He sighed. The old man legs were crossed and appeared very comfortable with his left index finger and thumb he toyed with his cotton strands of hair that harvest his ear. He chuckled with laughter. The soft wrinkled layers of skin shifted and made its own faces with every chuckle. The salt and pepper poorly twisted four-inch beard bounced in the same rhythm. His eyes open wide, leaned back and patted his chest. His cough, looked like he was having a heart attack. He gagged, moaned to clear his lungs, coughed up a teaspoon of yellow green and brownish phlegm that he pearled in the middle of his tongue. Finally, he leaned to his right and held one nostril closed to clear his nose, but he swallowed the phlegm.

He thought to himself, "Lord, have mercy on me! Oohh, when I see Bennett, I'm going to kick his ass. He was supposed to be here with me to help me with this type of crap." He closed his eyes with disappointment.

The old man used his entire left sleeve to wipe his face. He reached to shake his hand. He noticed the dark yellow and brown finger nails that were in need of manicure. He thought he may transfer a disease if he touched him. So he faked a cramp and grabbed his stomach.

"Where is the bathroom?" Kalargo looked around with a desperate look on his face. The old man stood to assist him.

"No! You, you just stay there." Have a seat, before he walked away. He turned around and asked, "Where is the chief of this village?"

The old man laughed and coughed horribly. He raised his hands to the sky and smiled. His cloudy black gums were filmed with a white slime; a quick count of eight crooked teeth, stained of only God knows what.

"You are looking at him." He placed his hands on his chest. "I am he, the Chief."

Before he could react, the old man was shaking his hand. He desperately tried to pull his hand away, but the old man was old, not weak.

Kalargo stared at their hands.

"Wajongi…" The Chief said.

 He imagined ten thousand, five hundred and twenty three yellow, green, brownish phlegm critters charging full speed ahead, yelling, "New body, new body!"

After two hours of negotiating, he finally walked away with a mule, two huge worn out luggage bags, in exchange for his clothes and shoes. The old man played hardball. He would not accept American money because he had never seen it before, it was worthless in his eyes.

The partly cloudy sky, with humidity that made the sun feels as if it was four inches above his head. He pulled his stubborn mule that looked like it suffered malnutrition, just the thought that he had to literally negotiate the clothes off his back, his clothes for the old man's clothes. He really wished they were the same size. Now that he blended in with the locals, he can travel unnoticed.

Chapter 16

The long rocky narrow road through the hillside came to an end. The mule was stubborn, heat and humidity was merciless. The sandals that protected his feet were holding up better than he thought they would, but the hunger became more evident on his stomach. In a distance, he could hear traffic along a highway, and further away the sound of sporadic gunfire. The area had a foul odor that danced between the northern breezes. The closer he pushed towards the city the less wild life he noticed. He sighed and stopped to rest and read his map.

"Hmmm…" He slid his finger across and calculated how many miles he had to walk. He looked at his watch.

"At least five miles… damn another night, by morning." He folded the map and stuffed it back in the back pack. He looked up at the eastern sky that claimed a grayish purple lavender sunset. The first sign that day light was being jeopardized by the fallen sun. It was risky to travel by night, he set up camp as close to the road as possible. He thought about Jamie and knew she would be alright. He had left her a sizeable amount of money for any unexpected emergencies. He looked at the mule as it slowly came to his knees, then his belly and starred at him. He lived his life carrying people belongings. His eyes sagged, long ears wiggled eriodically to shake off the fleas and insects that nagged him. The flies followed him like he was a source of food. He thought of the years that it went without a bath. The mule looked at him as if he was reading his mind. His long fat nozzle was shared by the grayish white hair around his mouth. His rib cage was defined with curves of hunger. The mule looked over his left shoulder. He was startled by an explosion in the distance.

"Yes I know. We are headed in the opposite direction." He said and slowly dosed off.

Alongside the road, traffic kicked up dust as they passed. He entered the city of Nabin Chi. His map took him exactly where to go and set up shop. The outskirts of town, a small shack that made sleeping outside a healthier choice.

After he paid for his room a teenage bell boy took his bags to his room. As the key turned the rust in the door hinges cried. The ray of sun light raced the hallways, mildew reddish carpet with a dash of tearful pink roses that was in need of a deep shampoo.

"Go ahead, put them in the corner." He told the kid. The sound of coins jingled as he reached deep into his pocket to pay him. He was a dusty little kid with good work habits. He gave him just enough that he wouldn't spread the word that someone with a lot of money is town.

As the door closed and reality sunk in, he closed his eyes, sighed, with his right index finger; he pushed the sweat off his eyebrow into his hair line. He opened his eyes and walked over to the window. He pulled the curtains open to view the busy street. He couldn't believe he was in Gambia. He decided to get out of the room to learn the area as quick as possible. He took his map and grabbed a small pistol and silencer from his suitcase. He paused.

"Hmmm, I don't think I need this right now. I'll just learn my way around first, get comfortable with the area." He tossed it back into his suitcase.

The city of Nabin Chi was far from the city of dreams, but the best to offer in the region. The women were good at balancing pots and bundles of their belongings on their head. Their babies were strapped to their chest.

By two pm the heat took over the city and passed out heat exhaustion like bottled water. The rare use of deodorant did not go unnoticed. So to blend in, he went without it.

He observed a life so different from what he had lived, but not so that he could not remember where he was born. He noticed that he would be noticed if he smelt different. But, he imagined how a white man would be looked upon. He smiled, and twisted his neck a little, just enough to hear the sound of his bones in his neck pop. It was like coming home as a new person, it felt overwhelmed. The thoughts came to an end. The horn of the blue bus broke the silence of thought, and reality of the city rubbed his nose, exhaust from traffic scratched his lungs. He sighed as he noticed the soldiers exiting the blue school bus.

"Hmmm..." he walked over to the Sapga bar to have a drink and observe the area. He knew anywhere there were soldiers, there had to be activity of some kind.

"I'll have a beer." He rested his elbows on the bar. The bartender didn't hesitate. The sound of the beer sizzled as the cap was twisted off, bounced on the floor and the bottle slid towards him on the counter of the bar.

"One dalasi!" The bartender said as if he couldn't afford it.

The unshaven bartender had dreadlocks that started in the middle of his head that gave him a moon roof. His pupils were brown with a yellowish eyeballs, and the scars on his neck were visible.

He thought about asking him what was his problem, but he had no time to get into a since less conversation. He pulled out one dalasi that was equal to seventy five cent U.S. dollars and slid it across the bar. The small bar had six customers that talked between each other. He decided to keep his conversation to a minimum. His training taught him to observe and be patient.

After the third beer and four hours of observation, the bartender could not stop talking. His patience paid off, without asking questions about the soldiers. The bartender gave him information he would not have gotten if he had asked for it. He also decided to use him as an ally, but not until he knew that he could trust him.

He looked at his watch and sighed out loud, opened his eyes with a look of surprise.

"Well, I have had enough for today." He rubbed his stomach and slid off his bar stool as he pushed away from the bar.

"Are you leaving so soon?"

"The crowd will start showing up in two or three hours. Hot bush babes from the north. They come every week."

He saluted the bartender and waved to everyone on his way out.

Two weeks had passed and waiting to find the General was getting dreadful. It was taking longer than he thought to find him. Out of the ten possible locations that he has been known to frequent, there was no sign of him.

The sound of a knock at the hotel room door woke him. The keys jingled and the door opened.

"Excuse me, room service. Ooops. I'm sorry, did you want your room cleaned?" she spoke from behind the door.

He rolled to his left and smothered his face into the pillow that he wrapped a t-shirt around to guard his face. The mattress was triple wrapped in three bed sheets and a bed spread.

"No, come tomorrow morning." He muffled out from the pillow. She closed the door.

He forced himself onto his back and finally opens his eyes. The cracks and mildewed water stains covered the ceiling. Every day had been routine, so he decided to visit the locations starting at the bottom of the list. He knew the General could not be that hard to find.

He removed both of his hands from his boxers and sighed. He was hungry and felt the heat in the room. The bed was damped from night sweats. He looked at the clock and begged for the time to go back two hours. He mumbled and covered his face with the pillow. He slowly dosed off.

Six hours later, the clock read 7:30 pm, daylight faded to darkness.

"Damn…" He looked at the clock, and forced himself out of bed. He sat up on the bed disappointed.

"What the hell is wrong with me?" he quickly dressed himself and bolted out of the room. He walked along the sidewalk and his watch read 8:05pm.

"What the hell is wrong with me?"

"It's no use. It's too late, may be the bartender can help in some way," He felt lost in thought, "calm down, calm down." He spoke under his breath.

He didn't want to rush in to anything too quickly. He snapped his finger to an idea that came to him as he stood at the corner of a busy intersection, but first he had to eat.

"That's it. I have not eaten all day." He started to doubt himself about killing the General. "None sense." He told himself.

The street had several stores, restaurants, parlors, and shoeshine stands. The streetlights slowly lit the city and the nightlife slowly oozed to life. He randomly chose a restaurant. Not by smell, or by name, just out of pure hunger.

"Yes, would you like to see a menu?" the hostess asked. Her dark skin glowed with a sparkle glitter like shine. Her braids neatly braided in a circle design. He noticed her full lips, breast and extra wide body. He smiled and thought of Bennett.

"Yes, I would like to also have a table by the window."

She held the menu in her hand, "Follow me please."

"Your waitress will be here shortly, anything to drink while you wait?"

"Orange juice." He said.

She quickly maneuvered through the surrounding tables. He calculated each bounce as her hips slammed from side to side in her loosely fitted brown dress.

After ten minutes, he had a half a glass of orange juice. He noticed how quiet the restaurant had become. A fleet of cars parked in front of the restaurant. They were very unnoticeable old cars. All the doors opened at the same time, soldiers secured the restaurant, and suddenly the General gets out.

He couldn't swallow his orange juice. The General stood there on the other side of the glass. His uniform neatly pressed, his medals dangled, his hat was decorative, the mirror like shades, his lips held an inch long cigar in the left corner of his mouth. He looked around the streets before he entered.

Kalargo's eyes widen and the orange juice went down the wrong way. He coughed and couldn't believe his eyes. The General himself was not only eating in the same restaurant, but five tables away from him in the corner.

"Oh my God, this can't be true." He thought. He scratched his head and made no eye contact. The reflection of the General can be seen in the window of the restaurant. His heartbeat pounded his chess. His food finally arrived.

The waitress whispered in his ear, "Enjoy."

He decided to eat slow and use this time to think out his next move. He observed, slowly ate and asked for more orange juice. The General was surrounded with his bodyguards and few soldiers waited outside. Their laughter was loud, and the smoke was choking.

Suddenly, an idea came to his mind, but he had to return to the hotel before the General left the restaurant. He flagged for the waitress.

"Yes, how can I help you?"

He kept his head towards the window. "I would like to pay for my meal."

"Not a problem, I'll return with your bill"

The sound of plates and silverware chattered, and the hum of conversation absorbed the restaurant. The plastic tablecloth draped three inches from the floor. The wooden chairs were old and worn. He saw the double doors to the kitchen opened in the reflection. He rested his hands beneath his chin with his elbows on the table.

"This is your bill."

Before she could walk away, "I'm ready to pay now." He pulled out his money, "Keep the change."

He tried not to be noticed as he walked out the restaurant. The fresh air kissed his face, but he had no time to waste. He knew this may be the only chance to somehow; some way to kill the General and get away, that was the important part.

"Taxi!" the taxi stop and reversed.

The cars behind him blew their horns and the driver gave them the middle finger. "Go to hell, this is my customer!"

"Where are you going brother?"

He hesitated before entering. At the last minute, he changed his mind. "I can walk. My hotel is in walking distance."

The taxi driver was pissed. He jumped out of his car, yelling how he had stopped him, and now he owed him for the inconvenience.

"You must pay!"

He quickly crossed the street to avoid the confrontation.

"You owe me a fee!" the driver walk away from his car further congesting the traffic. The taxi driver insisted that he pay him.

"Stop him!" He yelled toward a soldier.

Kalargo turned around, "What is your problem?" he tried to defuse the situation. "How much do I owe you" he looked at the driver like this just could not be happening. It would be a lot easier to pay the driver, but it was too late.

"Officer! " The driver jetted across the street to a soldier, "He snatched my money from my hand." His index finger pointed at him.

The sound of a whistle blew, "Halt!"

They pointed their guns at him. A soldier stepped in front of him. The first thing came to his mind, be calm, and pay the guy. He repeated it in his head.

"What's this nonsense?" the soldier asked.

"Listen, it's just a misunderstanding, I'll pay him what I owe him." He tried to explain, three more soldiers arrived.

"You see. He has no respect." The taxi driver pointed out to the soldiers. The situation was getting tense.

"Listen, I apologize. How much do I owe you?"

The driver looked at him, and waved his hand. "You snatched my money and now you want to offer me some of my own money? Are you drunk?" The driver threw his hands up dramatizing the situation, and he was good. It was obvious this was not his first time at this.

The soldier interrupted them both, "So you are guilty?"

Before Kalargo could explain, the soldier grabbed his right hand to put him under arrest.

"No, no I am not guilty of anything."

The taxi driver screamed, "I will see you in court."

He tried to talk his way out to no avail. He reversed his right hand and slammed the soldier to the ground. A second soldier aimed his gun at his chest. He quickly grabbed the gun and pushed it to his left just before the gun went off, "Bang!"

He kicked him in the chest, and chopped him behind his ear and a punch to his nose. Two soldiers jumped from behind, one began to choke him.

He broke his finger and elbowed him in the stomach. One by one they came and he defended himself.

"Bang!" Kalargo was shot. The hot metal stung him like nothing he has ever felt before. He fell to his knees.

A lieutenant pulled his pistol and cocked the hammer, just before he pulled the trigger. The sound of grown men moaned about their broken bones.

"Bang!" The smoke from the General's pistol lingered from the barrel as a lifesaver. "Halt!" He walked over to Kalargo as the barrel of the lieutenant's pistol pressed the back of his head. For the first time he felt helpless so far away from home.

The hot lead took him to his knees, and finally on to his left side. His right lower leg oozed blood as he grabbed it. He gritted his teeth in pain. He couldn't believe he had been shot. He moaned as he tried to raise himself to his feet.

The lieutenant walked over to him and pointed his gun at his head. Suddenly, a second gun was fired. Everything came to a silence.

"I said Halt!" The General said.

The crowd of soldiers that surrounded him made a passage for the General. The man himself stood over him.

"Who are you?" the General asked. He slowly slid his gun in his holster and chewed on his cigar.

"Where are you from?!" the General demanded an answer.

The fear that pounding Kalargo's chest was indescribable, he knew not to speak a word, but that would piss him off even more, especially after saving his life.

"I'm Kalargo." He looked down at his leg. His nerves shook uncontrollably.

"Take him to the hospital!" the General said as he waved his hand in the air.

Three soldiers tossed him in the back of a white Toyota pickup. He was accompanied with the same soldiers he gave a beat down.

The twenty-minute ride was the longest ride ever. Five minutes into the ride the lieutenant slapped him on the left side of his face with the butt of his .45 caliber pistol. The ride went from a bumpy painful one to the worst day of his life.

"You see what you did to me?" the first soldier asked.

"I tried to tell you..." Kalargo tried to explain.

"Shut up!" the second soldier demanded.

"You kicked my teeth out, asshole!" he had pulled his upper lip to his nose.

The lieutenant reached back to pistol whip him. He raised his arm to block the angry frustrated man. The other soldiers kicked him in the face, and ribs. He maintained his grip on the nozzle of the lieutenant pistol. The violent struggle proved to be a challenge. He tussled for his life on this lonely dark road. His grip on the nozzle slipped from his powerful hands. The lieutenant forcefully pulled backwards and loses his balance. The look in the lieutenant's eyes showed his last expression before his head slammed on to the unpaved road. His body was lifeless as he fumbled, tossed, and turned. He came to a stop in the bushes. The sound of the soldier's hands slammed the top of the cabin to stop the truck.

"Stop, stop the truck!"

"He killed the lieutenant!"

"Now look at what you have done." They flipped his body on to his back. His face was torn apart, flesh was to his bone, neck was broken, and his eyes opened. His breathing was very shallow. He tried to speak just before he died.

"He's dead asshole!" the soldier with no upper teeth screamed. They hogged tied Kalargo, dragged him a hundred yards from the road and hung him by his feet in a tree.

Two hours later, upside down from a tree, barely breathing. The broken ribs, collarbone, nose, three teeth missing, and bubbles of blood came from his mouth.

"Take him down! We will kill him tomorrow after the General ok's it. The soldier with the broken nose climbed the tree and cut him loose. He landed face first. They dragged him by his feet and tossed him wildly on the flatbed of the truck. He wished this was all a dream and he would wake up.

"Let's take them both to the General and explain what happened." The voice of one of the soldiers said.

"The General will have his head cut off by noon." The sound of the truck sped off into the darkness with a trail of dust that eventually helped the truck vanish.

Early the next morning, the news spread that he had killed the lieutenant. The atmosphere was creamy thick of hate. Death for him was minutes away. The news had not reached the General. The bedroom of the General was semi-plush, a notch of above the best second hand store.

"General, everyone is seated and waiting for you." The soldier told him. The General stood in front of his four vanity mirrors and looked over his shoulder of is uniform.

"Is Kalargo still in the Hospital?" the flame from his Zippo lighter lit his cigar as he puffed and licked the tip of his cigar.

The soldier was speechless. He hesitated, "I will find out the status Sir."

The room went silent when the General entered the room. "I want to see Kalargo!"

"Sir, there is something we have to tell you…" another soldier took over where he had left off.

"Well sir, there has been a murder last night…" before he could finish, the General eyebrows lifted, smoke came from his ears.

"The lieutenant was killed last night." The double doors opened and Kalargo slumped body was wheeled in on a wheelchair. His face badly disfigured, missing teeth, collarbone broken, ribs fractured, and barely breathing.

"What the hell happened to him?" he walked over to him.

"Sir, he killed the lieutenant and he has been worked over pretty badly."

The General was furious, who is responsible for this?" his voice rumbled the office like an earthquake.

They told him what happened. He looked at Kalargo. He walked over to him and lifted his chin. "Is it true?"

Kalargo tried to explain, but to no avail.

"Tell me more." The General said.

He nodded his head in disbelief as he sucked air between his teeth. He shook his head as if he was the judge and the jury.

The General raised his hand, "Enough, you…" he picked the soldier that had his teeth kicked out. He pulled him to the side and whispered in his ear in a low calm, angry voice. So angry, the fear began to grow his teeth back.

"You have one last chance to get this right. If not… you and your entire family will be burned alive. Now, get him to the hospital. If he needs blood, give it to him. If he needs your heart, give it to him, whatever he needs to stay alive. You will sacrifice your body." He lifted his chin and looked him in his eyes. "The lives of your entire family are on your shoulders. Now make it happened."

The soldier stood tall, and shocked by the words that rolled off his lips. The decision overwhelmed everyone.

Kalargo was immediately removed from the room on his way to the best hospital for a speedy recovery. Everyone was stunned as they mumbled their way out of the office.

Moments later, the General walked over to his office window like a sneaky serpent with a trick up his sleeve. The cherry tip of his cigar brightens as he inhaled.

Down below, Kalargo was carefully positioned into the pickup with his hands handcuffed. The stain of his blood smeared his face as he rested his head on the flatbed. The unbearable pain pooled his eyes to tears. He slowly raised his head in an attempt to remember this location.

Upstairs in the window he looked below, behind a royal blue curtain. He stood with his cigar hanging between his lips. The General had plans for him, just as he had plans for the General.

Not more than an hour had passed and the General received a frantic call from the hospital. "Sir, we have a problem…" the soldier paused.

His voice trembled as he tried to deliver the bad news. He let out a huge sigh, "Sir." He leaned against the wall and grabbed his chest. "Sir, I am not his blood type." He burst into tears. It was a death sentence to not be able to save Kalargo with a blood transfusion.

"He is AB blood type. What do I do?"

The General asked for the highest-ranking soldier to be put on the phone.

"Yes Sir this sergeant Jadkham."

"Take him out back and shoot him in the head. I am on my way and I want to see his body as I walk into the hospital. If any doctor tries to save him, shoot them also." The line terminated.

The convoy of six vehicles sped towards the hospital. The long trail of dust lingered the road. The General wanted him alive. As he walked into the hospital, blood was being cleaned from the floor.

"Where is he?"

The sergeant led him to Kalargo's bedside. The doctor looked at the General. "He's not going to survive."

The General removed his jacket and rolled up his sleeve. "I am his blood type."

Everyone moved quickly to prepare for a blood transfusion.

"Thank God, so you will be the one to save his life." They walked over to the bed next to Kalargo.

"Lay here Sir, just relax, this won't take long." The doctor looked over his shoulder.

"Someone bring the General a pillow."

Chapter 17

Honolulu, Hawaii

"Yes hello, hello…" Jamie's cellular rang twice in the last four hours and no one spoke a word. "My lord, why hasn't he called?"She asked herself.

Stacy sat next to her on the bed to comfort her. "Listen, hang in there. How long did he say he would be gone?"

Jamie looked and frowned with a huge sigh of relief that melted her beautiful face. She lay back on to the bed and covered her face with the pillow. "I just don't understand. It's driving me crazy not knowing what's going on." She muffled through the pillow.

They lay in Kalargo's bed. His scent lingered as if he was near. Her lonely heart had been broken with a promise of returning in thirty days. He never called. She frequently stopped by to check the mail and to make sure everything was ok. He explained to her how to manage the gym, pay the bills, and if she had questions, she could always call Stoky, the gym assistant manager.

Jamie tossed the pillow up and over her head. The cream and Hennessey colored bed sheets were disturbed, unlike how he would have had them. The window shades had been opened to ventilate the house and to bring life into the dark room. She house sat three days out of the week and made sure the mail didn't stack up.

"Well, I mean, what would you think Stacy? Because I am going bonkers and I believe something horrible has happened." She rose up and leaned forward with both hands. She combed her manicured fingers through her blond hair, carefully wiped her tears.

Stacy hugged her and leaned her head on her shoulder as she pulled her close. "Girlfriend…" she sighed profoundly. "…I hope to God nothing has happened, he has to call, a letter or something." Stacy said.

Jamie stood up and walked over to the mirror. She looked carefully, as she checked her makeup and lipstick. "I just don't understand." She twisted her hair into a bun and pulled out a strand or two to hang into her face.

"What about his dad?" Stacy said.

Jamie turned around and leaned on the dresser. "Nothing, I only have a company number." She responded.

"I am pretty sure he has a good reason why he has not written or called." Stacy assured her.

"And when he call, he has a lot of explaining to do." she said with tears in her eyes.

Stacy made eye contact, and silence chilled the room.

Two weeks later

The heat from the sun warmed the air. The footprints in the sand followed Jamie along the beach like a treasure map. Her bronze caramel tan glazed with tropical tanning lotion. Her long blonde high lights curled and waved perfectly as she lay on her back. The tranquility of the ocean allowed the seagulls screams to be heard between the crashing waves. The palm trees barely moved when the gust of wind blew. The partly cloudy sky gave breaks of shade from the sun. Her eyes were closed underneath her Gucci shades. Moments later, a cloud that the wind could not blow stood above her, giving a cool breeze when the wind blew. She gave it no thought until a voice from the sandy beach had her attention.

"Hello Jamie." the voice paused.

She slowly opened her eyes and removed her shades. Her thoughtful cloud became a human figure. The face was not seeable; she held her right hand above her eyebrows to consume the sunlight.

"Hello..." she said with hesitation and curiosity, "...who are you?"

The tall handsome figure could not have been more than 5'10, and well built with a heavy foreign accent. His skin tone looked perfectly melted on his body. He bent down to her level on the sand. Her bottom lip hung heavy as the sun resumed its shine in her face.

"You look as if you don't remember me."

She smiled and blushed with confusion. She tilted her head to the left and finally agreed, "No, I can't remember your face, or your voice." She said as she admired his muscles while he positioned himself in the sand. "Give me a hint." She was enjoying this game.

He laughed.

She had tickled him with her facial expression. She studied his face and short faded haircut, blue and white shorts and designer sandals. She held her bottom lip with her upper teeth and finally, she shook her head.

"No, if I had met you before, I would be able to remember you." she proclaimed.

"I have a question." He said.

"Well maybe not a question, but this has been something I've always wanted to do." He paused.

She waited for him to continue.

"I hope you don't take this the wrong way." he sighed with a little hesitation.

She looked at him and assumed her tanning position.

"I have always wanted to give a female a back massage on the beach with tanning lotion." He waved her bottle of tanning lotion in the air.

She was taken by surprise, but the chance for a back rub by a handsome muscular man was irresistible.

"May be this was a bad idea." He said, as he doubted his confidence. "I knew this was an embarrassing idea."

"Actually, that would be excellent, but first, you have to tell me where we have met and…" she was interrupted by her cell phone. "One moment." She held her finger up.

"Hello." She listened and shook her head up and down.

"Yes I understand." She shook her head to a negative respond.

"Absolutely." she sighed sadly. After a moment of listening, "Thanks Na Min, please let me know the moment you hear something ok, bye."

"Hmmm, that feels good, what are you doing tonight?" she asked.

He smiled.

*   *   *

Seoul, South Korea

Na Min sighed and looked at his red phone on his desk. He wished that it would ring and Karlago's voice would tell him the code phrase. It's the only phone that he would call. He unscrewed the cap on the bottle of Genifer and poured himself a shot. He starred at the shot glass and pondered. His lips mumbled, "Tell me what's going on! Are you ok, do you need help, show me a sign." he picked up the shot glass and put it to his bottom lip, "Damn!" without sipping it, he put it down and held the shot glass in his hand.

"I have faith. I know he is alright." He spoke towards the glass as he raised it to drink it. He paused; the gin barely touched his tongue. He shook his head with disgust, and disbelief.

He sighed, "Did I send the…" He frowned, "He's alive. I know he is."

He slammed Genifer down his throat. His wife walked in to the office. She was just as beautiful as the day they had met in the store. He remembered being outside the glass door in the cold snowy morning in desperate need of a special red tie. She later told him how she over charged him after she found out he was married. It was years later when he visited Washington D.C. for a business meeting and walked into the store to buy a suit. She looked the same as he had remembered her. Her long curly hair bounced as she smoothly walked the floor. Her chilling smile gave him the warmth that he had missed from a woman. Her Spanish accent flowed like a French horn on the French Riviera. He felt comfortable for the first time since his family was murdered. His heartbeat increased and his words began to stutter. But that was years ago, and she walked around his home office with the same grace. She leaned and kissed him.

"Still no word?" she asked.

The silence of them both allowed the Jazz music to filter the office.

He slowly closed his eyes and shook his head with an emotional sigh. "It's been over a month and a half. He is way passed his day of contact."

"What's the chance of him being alive?" she asked.

He leaned forward, places his forehead in his palms, and slowly raised his head to make eye contact with her. "Truthfully, I would say thirty percent. Anything could have gone wrong." He pressed his bottom teeth against his top lip and scratched his bald spot.

"You know, I never went two months without checking in when I was in the jungle." He slammed his fist down with anger. "He's in the city for God sake. He has access to phones." He tried to calm himself.

*   *   *

Honolulu, Hawaii

The phone startled her out of her sleep. It took her a moment to realize that the phone had awakened her. She covered her head with the pillow and moaned to comfort herself back to sleep.

Moments later, again the phone rang, "Hello." With her sleepy voice as she lay across Kalargo's bed. The weeping, crying voice on the phone couldn't have been anyone but Stacy. She was going through an emotional period in her life.

"Hmm…" Jamie moaned and sighed. She spoke from beneath the sheets and pillow, "Stacy, Stacy, not so loud girl, and slow down, now tell me what happened."

Her voice was filled with distress. She cried like a kid that lost their pet. She paused before speaking. "Girl, Tony left me. I tried to be honest with him, and he kicked me out of the car like I was a tramp…" she cleared her throat, "I'm sick of this. Every guy leaves me, and I can't hang on to a good man. What do I need to do?" she blew her nose like an elephant through the phone. Before Jamie could reply, she spoke again.

"I don't understand. I thought being honest was the right thing to do?" she said under heavy tears.

"Girl, how many times have I told you? How long did you wait before telling Tony?" The moment of silence was like killing snails on a hot summer day, long and pitiful. "Stacy, you can't play with these guys. Most of these guys don't understand you. I told you over and over about this."

Jamie sighed with her eyes closed.

"Stacy, you keep hurting yourself when you date these guys and don't warn them, at least say something."

"Where are you?" Jamie's voice thundered through the phone like a caring mother.

"I am back at my apartment." Stacy pulled her hair hard enough to break a couple of strands. Her tears fell like heavy rain. "Why was I born like this? I didn't ask for this…"

Jamie tried to calm her with a soothing voice. "Listen, let me get dressed. I am at Kalargo's house." She peeked from beneath the cover to look at the clock, "Give me an hour and a half…" She paused and looked over her shoulder, "…make it two hours." She had other plans in mind. She hung up the phone, stretched her arms and curled her naked body into a comfortable position. She looked at the other side of the bed. "Hey stranger…" with a smile, "…It's time for round three." As she pushed her fingers across his chest and pushed her hand towards his mid-section.

They both smiled.

"You are such a freak." He grabbed her left nipple, sucked it hard enough to make her squirm, with his right arm he lifted her body to position her back against the head board. At the right angle, he walked his tongue down to her navel, then allowing her pubic hairs to brush his chin.

She closed her eyes and moaned just enough to say, "Don't stop."

When his fingers entered, she gripped the pillows and tighten her legs around his shoulders. He pulled her closer and took total control.

She opened her eyes and realized that he had lifted her up and away from the back board, mid air. His face was wedged between her thighs like a cookie monster gobbling up everything she had to offer. He gave her no chance to recover, after four intense minutes; he sucked her clit hard one last time before letting her free fall onto the bed. Out of breathe, weak at the knees, as if she had stepped off the jogging path. She looked at him with hungry eyes and ready to attack.

He smiled and whipped his face, "Now, round three can begin."

*   *   *

Seoul, South Korea

Na Min shuffled through some papers that he received from Langley in reference to his retirement. He grew old. His chin doubled, ear lobe hung, dark brown spots covered his body, and some occasional pain would punish him for the crimes that he had committed. He covered his mouth with his right hand and coughed horribly. He sounded like a car that choked off a bad fuel. Finally, he sighed before lifting the phone receiver. With a smooth dance of his finger tips to dial the number, he placed the call to the intercom. After several rings, Mugumbi's voice filtered his office.

"Hello."

"Mugumbi, we have not heard anything and the North Koreans are getting impatient." Na Min's voice sounded uncomfortable.

"Nothing at all, but he has a satellite phone, something just not adding up." Mugumbi said.

"We fear…" Na Min could barely say it. "…that he may be dead."

The silence that followed was long and painful. He explains that the North Koreans were ready to send a second man to finish the job.

"Yes, no doubt I am ready whenever you need me." Mugumbi quickly volunteered.

"Mugumbi, you were not our first choice, some people think you're too old for the job. It's very physical."

He was interrupted, "I have been preparing physically for this for sixty days. I am more than ready."

"Listen do you remember Jenko?"

"Who!"

"They never were friends like that."

Na Min's voice quickly dominated the conversation, "Yes, but he's the North Koreans choice."

Mugumbi sighed and sipped on his steaming hot tea. He rubbed his old soft elastic skin beneath his chin, touched his gray hairs, "I just don't trust that guy, Na Min I hope this kid is ok."

"Don't we all, but I will keep in touch. If we hear anything, you will be first to know." They ended the call.

*   *   *

Honolulu, Hawaii

Jamie buzzed 9b for the third time.

"Come on up girl."

The door to the apartment building buzzed to unlock the door. When Jamie exited the elevator, Stacy stood in her apartment door. She looked a hot mess.

"Look at you, you look horrible." They hugged and walked into the apartment.

"When the last time you cleaned this place?" Jamie asked.

"Yesterday." she looked around with confusion, but quickly let her know how she destroyed the place last night looking for her medicine.

"Stacy, you have to get a hold of yourself." She opened the fridge.

"Jamie, do you know how hard it is to tell a guy that I am big down here?" she pointed towards crotch area.

Stacy covered her face. "How can I explain that I have this over size clit between my legs, and oh by the way I am really a female?" Her eyes were wet, and her face was smeared of last night's make up.

"Stacy, you need therapy. Someone to talk to that understands you. I am afraid that you will hurt yourself." She held Stacy's hand and pulled her chin closer with her left hand.

"Promise me you will seek help." Jamie wrapped her arms around her, with an outburst of tears.

"Everyone thinks that I am a boy." The bear hug tightened and her tears soaked her shirt.

*   *   *

Gambia, Africa

Kalargo's eyes opened as he lay in the hospital bed. The pain blanketed his body with every breath. His nose itched, but he found himself handcuffed to the bed rails. The tube down his throat made it difficult to swallow. The cold empty room was like a psychiatric ward of a mental hospital. He sighed profoundly and wondered if there was a chance of escape.

Moments later, a nurse walked in, "Good morning Kalargo. How are you feeling?"

He looked at her like she had come to save his life. He tried to talk. She looked at his medical chart, "Don't worry, later today, we will remove the tube and you will be able to speak and eat on your own." She smiled at him; her white uniform fitted her firmly as her figure bounce gracefully. Her slight limp was noticeable due to a land mine that took her left foot.

With his eyes he tried to get her attention. He knew he had to make contact with Na Min, but this situation was daring, especially when he had two soldiers outside his door that really didn't care for him. As the nurse moved about the room, the soldiers peeked in to make sure everything was all right.

Chapter 18

The medical equipment beeped as it monitored his heart. The handcuffs were uncomfortable. The bright lights behind his closed eyes lids were reddish. He had noticed that the NG tube was taken out, but left his throat sore. The smell of his soiled bedding pinched his nose sharply. His unshaved face calculated the days he had been sleeping. He sighed and opened his eyes. The sound of voices was heard from the other side of the curtain. Just before he could call for the nurse, he yanked his hands with anger. The inhumane conditions were getting to him.

"I need a nurse! Hello, I need to be clean up here!"

He lifted his head and gritted his painful remaining teeth. His ribs had not yet healed, and his face was wrapped. His lips were dry and peeling. He pushed his tongue across his mouth and the taste of blood from his jagged teeth oozed his dry throat. His medicine had worn off and pain was introducing itself.

"Ok Kalargo, just calm down. I am going to bathe you, and take good care of you." She spoke with a soft voice, almost medicine like, but it didn't last. She leaned over and looked him in his eyes. She smiled.

He looked around and thought it would be a good time for an escape plan. He could over power the guards and shoot his way out the front door. He waited for the right moment. The nurse returned with a pushcart and no soldiers.

"Perfect." He closed his eyes and prayed. "It's now or never. When she takes the handcuffs off and take me to the bathroom." He convinced himself.

"Kalargo, it's time for your bath." She pushed a button and the mechanical straps lifted his body. She removed his garments and dipped the rag in the steamy hot water.

He couldn't believe she was going to bathe him while he was handcuffed. He let out a huge sigh of disappointment as she pulled the surgical gloves tighter and the sound of them snapping tighten his eyes with anger.

"Listen, what's your name?" He asking her with his jagged but cunning smile.

"My name is Biquimi." The nurse continued to prepare his bath.

"Ok Biquimi, I am in a situation that requires your help and only your help…" He lifted his head to look towards the door for the soldiers. "I need you to make contact with someone. This is very important…" She interrupted him.

"Kalargo relax, don't talk much." She told him.

"You have to listen to me." He sighed and swallowed. He looked over and looked at the jug of water. She gave him some in a cup.

"Right down this number and call a friend of mine." His eyes looked serious as he tried to explain.

She placed a plastic sheet beneath him and begins to bathe him. He was spread eagle, handcuffed to the bed rail by hand and feet, not to mention naked.

"Are you listening?" He yanked harder on the rails. He looked at his wrist, "Can you help me? My life is in danger."

"How much, tell me how much? I have money, American money!" Kalargo raised his voice a little.

She smiled and poured the warm water on his body. She ignored him throughout the bathing. He was further anguished, but finally, she gave in to his plea for help.

*   *   *

Two weeks later

The voices of the doctors are heard. He thought that this had to be good news. The doctor entered his room with his medical chart in hand.

"Kalargo." He said with a distinguished voice, "We have some excellent news. As you know, you are being released from the hospital today." He slowly read his medical chart.

He was tall, dark, with an eruptible pimple on the left side of his nose. His badge read Dr. Tigo. His dingy white coat needed a good wash.

Suddenly, a short fellow walked in, clean white coat, neatly pressed and well groomed. He was chubby, balding from the back of his head, and smelt of foreign expensive cologne. His badge read Dr. Willogy. "Ok, go ahead and perform a final exam, and then he could be released to the jail. He will be out of our hair."

Kalargo felt probed and fondled. His eyelids were pushed open and a fancy little light was waving across his eyes. He felt his knees being tapped by something that made his reflexes jerk. He felt a warm uncomfortable huge hand fondling his genitals.

"Cough." Dr. Tigo said.

He coughed.

"Cough again." The hand repositioned and squeezed. "One more cough."

He felt violated and hoped this dude hand would fall off, by now he felt assaulted.

"Open your mouth." Before he knew it, that same hand plunged into his mouth. The taste of surgical gloves was probing his lips and gums. He tried to spit out the strands of little hairs that were left to linger his tongue.

"Move your tongue, to the left, up and to the right. Say ahhh." At the same time his blood pressure was being checked.

"Well, Kalargo. You are good enough to be cleared." They both signed their names.

"Now, be careful with your ribs. I give it another thirty days before they will completely heel." Dr. Willogy smiled.

Dr. Tigo raised his right hand that held a prescription, "You will have medicine for the pain." He placed a signed prescription paper.

They exited the room and the soldiers escorted him to the jail.

*   *   *

The overcrowded local jail was old, and filthy. The smell of musky underarm was strong. The portable fans help circulate the stench, but to no avail. The ten-man cell held at least twenty inmates. The walls were wet and sweaty. The floors were in need of a good mopping. There were two toilets, one for defecation, and the other for urination. He read an old sign above the shower curtain that said, "Shower days, Sundays only." He slowly walked in the cell. He stepped over people that slept on stained mattresses on the floor. The dark dungeon like walls was smeared of graffiti.

"Make room!" the guard yelled. All eyes were on him. He felt like new meat. He could feel his perspiration run from his armpit, and the valley of his spine. He sighed profoundly as his cheeks deflated like a balloon. He tried to make no eye contact as he focus on how he will handle this situation. Finally, the silence had been broken.

"Hey, take this..." a man said. He looked as if he had been living here longer than anyone else. "I am the house mouse. Anything you need, let me know, besides one roll of toilet paper, you should already have in your kit. Breakfast is served at one am, lunch is eight am, and dinner is at four pm..." he sighed and looked around.

"As you can see, It's not much room here." He stepped over several sleeping bodies. "What's your name?"

He stood with his pillow, bedspread, and dinghy white sheets hung across his left arm. "My name is Kalargo."

"Well my name is Henry, Henry Davis better known as house mouse…" He interrupted himself. "…look, just get situated and stay out of trouble. Oh yeah, don't nag me about toilet paper." He looked at him as if he was on his own.

The sound of a dialect language can be heard throughout the cell, as he lay four feet from the toilet bowl. The loud echo of voices bounces off the wet walls as he drifted into an uncomfortable sleep.

The four hours of sleep was like hibernation, but the constant noise of the metal cell doors slamming shut, flushing of the toilet was disturbing. He looked over his shoulder in discuss of his surroundings.

"I knew you wouldn't sleep for long, not with all of this house ruckus." His English had an American accent. He was black and Asian, with long wavy hair that he had in a ponytail. He looked no more than thirty-two years old, 5'8, and one hundred seventy pounds. His beard made him look older. He looked stressed and worn. His eyes had bags beneath them. No one wanted to associate with a dead man walking. He was sentenced to death by gelatin.

Kalargo sat up, looked around and noticed that the cell was not as hot. The sun had descended behind a mountain. But the fan that cooled the living space had the odor equal to biting into a raw onion. He sat up with his knees towards his chest with his arms wrapped around them. His hands interlocked to secure his balance.

"What time is it? I am starving." Kalargo asked.

"It's near dinner time, hey if it's anything you don't want, I'll trade with you."

"What's your name?" Kalargo asked.

"Tim actually Timothy, but everyone calls me Tim."

Kalargo was amazed to how good his English was. He looked at Tim with a bit of confusion.

"How do you speak good English…" before he responded to his question, "…where are you from?" Kalargo asked.

Tim tilted his head back with a smirk on his lips. Finally his laugh came to a grin, then subdued to a sad frown. He sighed. "Well, originally." He paused, "I was born in the United States. I lived there until I was twelve. My father is black and my mother was Korean, from there we moved to South Korea.

That raised Kalargo's eyebrows. "So you lived in Korea?"

Tim frowned a little and cleared his nostrils and throat; with his left thumb he rigorously rubbed his nose.

His hazel almond eyes became tearful. He placed a magazine beneath his pillow and laid his body across his bottom bunk.

"Osan, Osan, South Korea, I have lived there for some time, eight years." He let out a profound sigh.

"I moved back to the States after my father died." He grabbed his roll of toilet paper, unraveled enough to blow his nose. He looked at the wet tissue and tossed it in the trash.

He looked at Kalargo and asked. "So how do you speak English so well?"

Kalargo let out a huge sigh of disappointment. "It's a long story; you want to know what's crazier."

"What..."

"When you are innocent and don't belong here." Kalargo let out a huge sigh.

Tim laughed and sat upward to rest his hands above his head on the metal frame of the upper bunk bed.

Kalargo didn't laugh or smile. He decided to speak Korean to him to see what his response would be. In his mind he wanted to know 'what the chances of two Black guys in jail, thousands of miles away from home and able to speak Korean.'

He did look like an afro-tiger, but Korean? He really felt like something is not right. He decided not to speak Korean and kept the conversation to English.

"Osan, South Korea, now imagine that." These words mumbled from Kalargo's lips.

Tim looked at him. "So how the hell you ended up here?"

"I. Well, I got into it with a couple of soldiers. They got the best of me, but I showed them." He threw some punches, and smiled.

"And what about you?" he asked Tim as he looked over his left shoulder and shook his head with a calm, contextual, peaceful attitude. He grunted from the bottom of his stomach. "Believe it or not, for attempting to assassinate the General"

Kalargo's heart pounded his chest, and throat hard enough to quiver his voice. This was a heavy blow to his gut.

"The General!"

Tim nodded his head as he slowly lowered his arms down to rest them.

"Get out of here!" this news was mind blowing.

"Why would you want to kill the General?" He couldn't wait for this response.

"I just went crazy, just don't know why." He proclaimed, but looked like he was holding something back.

Kalargo's thought about it and noted 'yeah right.'

"And I swam from Hawaii to Africa." He licked his gums where his teeth once were.

"So what brings you here?" He stood up to use the bathroom.

"Nostalgia, I felt like I was missing the mother land…" he was interrupted.

"Yeah, the same here." Tim looked to his left and looked at him.

"Well that's the sound of chow." The sound of the cart of food can be heard strolling down the tier. The voices of guards and inmates increase. Those who were sleep are now awake. It became more like an animal shelter around feeding time, everyone want to bark, even though knowing food was on the way.

"What's for dinner?"

"You never know until you see it, believe me it's nothing that will get you fat or taste good. So don't get your panties in a bunch." He looked dreadful, most of the time he had to pinch his nose to swallow the food.

Just before the food came Tim asked him for a favor. "Listen, you are going home soon. Am I right?" he confirmed with his eye contact, "You are getting out of here?" He stood from his bunk.

"I've been here four months and not made any contact with my wife. She has no idea that I won't be coming home, is there a way you could deliver or send her a message?"

He looked him directly in his eyes. The sad look of a dying lonely, concerned man weighed his shoulders.

"Of course, it's almost like fate that we met each other." He looked at Tim's wet eyes. The sadness made him age thirty years over night.

"You have no idea how much I would appreciate this. Tonight, I will write a letter, including my information…" he interrupted him.

"Do you know when you are to be…" before he could finish the sentence.

"Anytime soon… they don't tell you when the public execution will be, they just open the door, and call your name. You could be going to see a doctor, to the yard or the executioner. I have seen four beheadings since I've been here. You see those windows along the top of the ceiling?"

He looked up behind him, "Yeah."

"Well, out there is where they have the executions." Tim said.

He frowned, but contained his emotional response for the sake of Tim.
"Thank God chow is here."

"Come on, get in line!" The voice of the house mouse was heard over everyone.

Later that night, Kalargo lay on his floor mattress. He stared at the mildewed ceiling, glossy walls. The dingy, dirty looking sheet was not so dirty any more. He wrapped himself in it. He covered his mouth and nose of that raw onion, musky smell that had somehow soften the pinch to his nose. The smoky cell vibrated. The echoes of others on the cellblock can still be heard.

Twenty days had passed and their conversations had come to a standstill, but he knew that his name will be called sooner now than later. His demeanor had drastically changed. Some nights he could hear this grown man cry beneath his pillow like a baby. He now understands why none of the other inmates spoke to him. He felt sick to his stomach. Tim gave away most of his food, just couldn't stomach it, causing him to lose weight.

Tim whispered. "Kalargo!"

After several attempts he removed the sheet from his face. He raised his head and opened his left eye. He had just fallen asleep, "Yeah…" His voice was slow to respond.

"I hope I didn't awake you." Tim's head hung off the edge of the bed.

"No, just thinking about a lot." Kalargo sighed.

"I have a bad feeling." He tried to talk under a broken, fearful voice that he had to force off his lips. The harder he tried. The more he felt like throwing up. He tried to talk without shedding a tear, but the butterflies bounce around his insides like fighter jets.

"Kalargo, I feel the need to give you my letter." The papers shook like a leaf in a windstorm. He walked back to his bunk with his left hand across his stomach.

"I have this bad feeling." He rested his head on the bunk.

Kalargo sat upward, speechless.

"Listen, I have been doing some thinking…"

He made eye contact with Tim, scratched his nose and rubbed his tongue across his gums. He coughed to clear his chest and swallowed a cotton ball of saliva.

"Today is Sunday; usually every third Monday is execution day."

He looked at Kalargo as if he said nothing. He had that look in his eyes, his legs wobbled constantly. He looked around, but most people were sleeping.

"What time is it?" Kalargo asked.

"It's early Monday morning, the third Monday, two hours before breakfast." Tim rolled over on his bunk.

The sound of the metal keys opened the heavy metal door. Three guards walked in with their flashlights, waking inmates with their boots, "Make room! Make room!"

"Tim!" one of them had a picture with his information, "It's time."

Tim played sleep, as if he heard nothing. They grabbed him by his arms and lifted him to his feet. He could barely move his legs. He tried as hard as he could, but the strength was not there. Two of the guards placed his arms over their shoulders, and assisted him. His feet dragged the floor on the way out the door.

"I can walk! I can walk!" Tim said.

They allowed him to stand on his own. He collapsed. They helped him to his feet, held him by his arms and assisted him the rest of the way.

The first thing Kalargo wanted to do is read the letter, but he didn't.

Seven days later

The keys were loud as they jingled in the guard's hands. Once again the burning desire to read Tim's ten-page letter made his palms sweaty, and the curiosity was overwhelming. He knew in the back of his mind that the same people hired Tim had hired him.

Finally, he decided to read the letter. "Well, if I am going to deliver something. I have the right to know what I am delivering half way around the world."

He justified to himself. The sounds of the keys were closing in. He reached beneath his mattress for the letter. He paused, his heartbeat increased, his palms were clammy. He lifted the mattress with his right hand and held the letter in his left hand. He sighed and thought about himself. The privacy he would want if he had wrote a letter to Jamie.

"It's not right." He slowly talked himself out of reading it. He slowly lowered the mattress. His gut was telling him to read the damn letter. It had to be something mentioned in it that may be useful for his mission. He opened it and began to read.

"Dear Sara, I wrote this letter in advance just in case the inevitable was to come true…" He was interrupted.

"Kalargo!" the keys opened the cell door. The guard had his picture and information in his hand.

"Pack your belongings, you are being transferred." The guard stood at the door. He looked over his shoulder and sighed. "Transferred?"

"Where am I going?" he slowly moved.

"Pack it up and stop asking questions!" he raised his voice with some authority.

He folded the letter and rolled up his bedding. He tossed the letter with other papers in his pants. He looked confused as he mumbled. "Hmmm, transferred?"

He walked up to the door as if he didn't want to leave the cell. He was nervous.

"Throw your mattress over here and stand on the wall. They patted him down for weapons and escorted him to a room where he sat unattended. His palms were itchy, sweat bubbled on his forehead, and his left foot wagged liked a hungry dog's tail. The sweat from his armpit became visible. He laid his head down and slowly dosed off.

Two hours later, the door opened. His face was wedged between his right pit of his elbow. He lifted his head and opened his unfocused eyes. There were four officers in front of him that made room for another. He smelt the smoke of a rich cigar. When his eyes focused, the General stared him down behind his mirror reflective shades. He exhaled his smoke towards him as he slowly passed in front of him. He sadly frowned his lips.

"How are you doing, your ribs, and bullet wound?" He stopped dead center of the table with his hands behind his back, with his cigar on the tip of his lips.

He sat dumb founded and shocked. He thought about the thirty days of searching for his ass, and now he stands in front of him. His mind also told him that now is not the time. He swallowed his ambition.

"I, I guess I am doing better." He spoke nervously.

The General looked at the guards behind him. "Well, I am starving. How about you?" before he could respond. The General waved his hands and smashed the tip of his cigar. He was happy for that, it just looked like it was ready to fall any moment and he felt obliged to catch it before it hit the floor. The door opened and a push cart with two silver domes, and fresh brewed coffee. The white sheet flared into the air literally pushing him backwards. His eyes couldn't believe what he was seeing or experiencing. This all felt like a bad dream. He pinched himself on the leg hard enough to imprint fingernail marks. He sighed.

The General sat down man to man with him. He rested his elbows on the neatly white sheet that covered the once beat up, disgusting table that had old brown blood stains that was engraved by the markings of tortured inmate's teeth and nails. He was forced to ask himself, did he know he had come to assassinate him?

The domes were removed. The steam floated towards the ceiling. The beautiful imported silverware was placed next to them both.

"Kalargo, we will eat and discuss business..." before he could finish, the plates were placed in front of them, and breakfast was served. "...how do you like your coffee?" the General poured his coffee first, and then his own.

He grew some balls and raised his hands and pushed his seat back from the table. Before he could get a word out of his mouth, the guards became attentive, and ready to protect the General.

"Listen son, Relax I don't do this for many people..." he looked around to prove it. The guards agreed with a head nod. Two of the guards slowly pushed his chair towards the table.

He looked at the food and licked his lips. "So what's with the special treatment? What have I done to deserve this?" he slowly picked up his knife. One of the guards pushed his cup of coffee closer to him.

"Well, for starters..." the General stopped, "...how do you like your eggs cooked?" he searched his soul with his eyes above his shades. He slowly removed them to eradicate his untrustworthy appearance that he somehow thought he could simply erase as if it was chalk on a blackboard.

"Scrambled eggs..." the chef began to cook his breakfast on a portable cooking device. He reached for the sugar, cream, and prepared his coffee. He stirred it with his knife.

"Toasted bread?" the cook asked.

"Yes." He relaxed and thought. 'If he wanted me dead, I wouldn't be in this room having breakfast, now would I?' he thought that made since.

"So, my first question is…" he cut half of his steak and stabbed his fork into it and placed the other half onto Kalargo's plate.

"Where did you learn to fight like that?" the General had a smirk on his lips, spooky but interesting.

"I saw how you…" He moved his knife and fork through the air over his food like he was mimicking his martial arts moves. His smirk developed into a huge smile. His excitement grew with his loud voice in tow. Then he toned it down to a whisper. He cut a small bite size of medium rare steak, and pointed at him. "…where did you learn to do that Bruce Lee stuff?"

The cooked slowly pushed off his scrambled eggs onto his plate. He quickly thought and chose his words carefully. He knew most likely have to explain in greater detail if he told an unbelievable story. So he kept it simple.

"I am a huge fan of Bruce Lee. I have every movie he has ever made. Every since I was a little kid I wanted to be just like him." He sighed softly and quickly reached for his coffee. The room went silent for minutes so it seemed. The guards looked at him as if the General was going to kill him thinking he was stupid enough to believe that crap. He was the only one to appear to be moving. Even the General looked frozen, he felt like this was the perfect time to escape.

The General burst out with laughter. His hands slammed the table. He couldn't hold it no longer, threw his head back and let it out.

"You son of a bitch…" He pointed that damn knife at him again, "…you almost had me fooled!" his laugh became an irritable ear rash. He promised to never tell him anything funny ever again.

He held his potbelly. "You are also funny."

He quickly denied that just to keep him from doing that silly laugh. The General looked at him with a serious eye from his good-looking side, like he really had one. He shook his head and not believing the crap that was coming out his mouth. He sighed and ordered the chef to cook two pancakes. "You care for some?"

Kalargo looked at the General, looked at the chef, "Why not? So…" he rubbed his face with both palms of his hands to clear his eyes of happy tears, and reminded him that he had his teeth kicked out by slowly running his dark crusty white tongue across his front edges.

The General pulled a used toothpick from his top pocket and drove the tip of it between his teeth. He examined the left over steak on the tip of the toothpick and licked it off. He offered Kalargo his toothpick to use. He rolled his eyes like a bitch and refused.

"I am here to proposition you." The General put his toothpick back into his front pocket.

Kalargo's eyes followed his hand and asked himself, 'When will he finally throw that toothpick away?'

"I would like for you to work for me." The General let it all out with a cunning smile as if it was a small and simple gesture.

He really could not believe what he was hearing. He sighed deeply, and felt like he was going to be enslaved. He rubbed his forehead, and swallowed rooster size egg of phlegm. He really didn't understand.

The General held up his hands to prevent him from speaking. "Before you speak, just hear me out. Your skills are definitely genuine. The way I see it…" he sort of led to an ultimatum, "…you can choose to do your six months in this…" he looked around the obviously disgusting room. "…or." He paused as he drew small circles with his right index finger on the tablecloth, "Or you can choose to train my elite group of soldiers, not more than three hundred men. Wait, before you respond, they are well trained, disciplined, and whatever they learn from you. They will teach the rest of my army these fighting skills."

Kalargo eyes were frozen in time, but quickly melted with joy. This will give him plenty of opportunity to assassinate him. He placed his right hand across his heart. "General… it would be an honor to work for you." He put his hands together in front of him and bowed his head. They stood up from the table.

"At all times you will have four armed soldiers that will shoot to kill. They won't need my permission to kill you if you try to escape."

They walked out of the room. Kalargo's left hand was placed behind his back to secure them with handcuffs.

The General look at the soldier and waved his finger. "There is no need for that. You have permission to kill him if he tries to escape."

Kalargo smiled at the soldier, and he realized that he was one of the soldiers that he gave a good kick to the nose. He sighed and walked behind the General in his trail of cigar smoke.

Chapter 19

Seoul, South Korea

The phone rang four times before Mugumbi said. "Hello."

Na Min held the receiver with his right shoulder, "Yes Mugumbi, I hope I didn't awake you."

Mugumbi cleared his throat, "No, not at all, have you heard anything from Kalargo?"

He paused, "Yes…" He inhaled profoundly, "…he was in the hospital…" he was interrupted.

"Hospital, what happened?" Mugumbi asked with concerned.

"Well according to my sources, he was beaten pretty badly for fighting with some soldiers. But over all, he will be ok."

Mugumbi sighed, "Yes, that's my boy."

The tone mellowed downward and he broke the news. "But I do have an executive party for you to attend in Miami. Go ahead and arrange for your flight two weeks from today. I will have your party profile ready."

"Not a problem Na Min." His voice sounded like he had a smile and relieved to know his nephew was alive.

He let out a burst of morning breath before he stood up to stretch. He looked over at his wife and covered her half naked body. She moaned and pulled it further to cover her almond eyes. He reminisced the first time they met ten years ago, and smiled. He kissed her on the forehead. It felt good to be still in love. He searched the floor for his gym shoes and prepared for his morning exercise.

*   *   *

Miami, Florida
Two weeks later

Flight 2047 landed at Miami international airport, Mugumbi raised his hand for a taxi, "Taxi!"

The yellow cab with the numbers 305444444 painted across the door. "No luggage Sir."

"No, just my carry on, I'm headed to the Marriott on Biscayne blvd."

The driver quickly slipped the gear into drive. "Yes I know exactly where that is." The driver listened to Creole music.

"Are you available in the day time?" Mugumbi asked.

The volume lowered as he made eye contact through the rearview mirror. "Not usually, I have a second job from four thirty in the morning to three thirty in the afternoon. But I'll give you my cell phone number just in case. Are you here on vacation or business?"

Mugumbi's eyes searched the city's skyline as the taxi pushed through traffic on the Dolphin expressway. He returned his attention to the rearview mirror.
"Hmmm, I guess you can call it that. Hey I may need a good tour guide. It's my first time in Miami."

"Oh, ok…" the strong educated Creole accent rolled off his lips.

"Where are you from?" Mugumbi asked him.

"I am from Haiti, and you?" he thought about how good he spoke English, but didn't mention it. "Well, Africa via South Korea."

The taxi driver was surprised. "Wow, how you like South Korea?"

He rested his head back on the seat. "I love it. I've lived there for fifteen years."

The driver was very surprised, "What, How?"

"Do you speak Korean? I imagine that you have to if you have lived there for that many years."

"Yep, I speak it pretty good." He closed his eyes and jetlag rode his body to sleep like a dose of medicine. His response was evident that sleep was needed as he mumbled out loud. "Yeah, I love South Korea." He was out for the rest of the ride.

*   *   *

The next morning he woke up to a dark room only to realize his face was buried into his pillow. He moaned, lifted his head and turned it toward his left shoulder. He sat up slowly and massaged the back of his neck with his right hand. He twisted his neck until it popped like knuckles. He noticed himself in the mirror.

The wrinkles beneath his eyes and neck are more noticeable. "Damn, I'm getting old."

He stood up and stretched. He walked to the bathroom, sat on the toilet and relieved himself. He reached between his legs, plucked out the floating balloons of heroin, and tossed them into the sink. He sighed and jumped into the shower. As he walked out of the bathroom, he noticed a vanilla envelope that had been pushed beneath the door. He paused and let out his breath as he tossed the hotel robe on. He approached the door to look through the peephole. There was no one. He picked up the envelope and tossed it on the bed. He reached for the hotel phone and pushed zero.

"Yes hello, I would like to order breakfast." He stood and rubbed the towel to dry his hair. The front desk transferred his call to the restaurant.

"Yes, how can I help you?" the voice asked.

"I would like to have three scrambled eggs, two sausages, orange juice, milk, and a bowl of honey nut cheerios." His said.

"Will that complete your order?"

"That's it. How long will that be?"

"No longer than twenty minutes." The voice on the phone said.

"Thank you." He put the receiver down; he rubbed his aging face with both hands. His five o'clock shadow and mustache was sprinkled with gray hairs. Suddenly, he sighed deeply and looked at the envelope.

"Well. Well, let's see what we have here." He opened the envelope and looked at the picture. It surprised him that the target was black, but thought nothing else of it. He mapped out the address and found it to be on an island. He held a key to a storage that contained a variety of things he would need.

He paused for a moment, and felt that creepy feeling that addicts feel. It was like an alarm clock that told him it was time to get high. He crossed his legs and used his left thumb and index fingers to massage the bridge of his nose. He rubbed his shoulder and realized that he could no longer prolong the anticipation. Once before, his mind had fought a warrior's battle to be drug free, but his body submitted like a wet paper bag.

The balloons of heroin were speaking to his mind like unwanted voices. But they were only horror voices when he tried to fight that edgy feeling off. When he gave in, it was like a charming seductive concubine whispering in his ears.

"Touch me, I love you, no one touches you like I do. You can hug me." It was a creepy love hate relationship between them two. The embrace of this chemical love was an ultimate high.

The bathroom appeared to glow with a different light. He stood and walked like an abused dog with his tail between his legs, a weak man in love, walking with center blocks on his feet. Only when he is alone he felt like he was getting married, his sweat felt different. He sighed and knew that he was small compared to those purple balloons that lay in the sink.

He looked at himself as he washed the balloons. He sighed and reached for his get high kit. He shook his head and knew what he was about to do would really be stupid, but he did it anyway.

"I can't stand this bullshit. I quit."

"I... quit." He leaned over the sink and closed his eyes. His fear of sickness punched him in the stomach. He grabbed some tissue to wipe his eyes and blew his nose. The symptoms had begun already. He flushed the balloons down the toilet.

"I have to fight this. I can do it." He walked out of the bathroom to go over the profile of his target. He was confident, but scared.

*   *   *

The small tourist boat cruised slowly away from the Bayside Mall as it made its way towards Star Island. He sat in the back with his camera around his neck. He took pictures for notes to go over later.

"Is it always this hot?" he fanned himself and wiped his face with a hotel face towel. Everyone looked comfortable besides him. He sighed. The back of his shirt, armpits were wet.

The Biscayne Bay was beautiful, the cruise ships were larger up close and the downtown skyline was picture perfect. Two dolphins followed the boat as it passed under the Macarthur causeway bridge. His camera clicked away. As the boat circled the bay of Islands he noticed that Miami Beach was closer to Star Island than Miami. He zoomed in through his camera lens at the docked area of yachts, jet skis, and sailboats. He eye balled the distance and calculated how long it would take to cross the bay from Miami Beach under darkness. The island was secured by rent a cops that guarded the only two-lane bridge, so driving across was out of the question.

The tour guide's voice over the speaker directed the crowd's attention to several multimillion dollar celebrity homes in particular. The sound of shutters of cameras clicked wildly.

He pulled out a small roll of tissue, wiped his eyes, and blew his nose. These were the beginning symptoms of withdrawal. He felt horrible and couldn't wait to get back to shore. He thought about the good dope that he had flushed down the toilet, just stupid. He sighed and thought of going to rehab.

Later that night he tossed and turned as he dreamed of being in a circle with super heroes at the Narcotic Anonymous.

Spiderman stood and said, "Hi, my name is Spiderman." the crowd at the meeting responded in sync, "Hello Spiderman."

He looked sad and dirty. "Well I have been clean for six hours." The group applauded. He held his head up, "I was hooked on pills. I know it won't be easy, but I'll keep coming back."

The NA group responded, "Keep coming back."

Out of nowhere, Superman stood, "Hello, I am Superman." He spoke with a struggle in his voice. His costume was filthy. His face was sunken in from massive weight loss. His five o'clock shadow and arid lips showed that he was in bad shape. His tights sagged off his ass. His muscles had been deflated.

"Today I am clean. Yesterday I was a crack head that tried to take over the world." He paused and sighed, "I have been smoking crack for twenty five years, but yesterday I…" he started to cry, someone in the group said, " Take your time Superman."

Then wonder women gave him a napkin, "It's going to be okay, we all have problems."

Superman opened his eyes and looked at his peer group, even his archenemy was in the circle, Lex Luther. He continued.

"I didn't notice..." He paused and formed his left hand into a weak fist. His bones protruded his skin. He held it tightly, "God damn it. I am Superman!"

The voice of Batman encouraged him to continue, "Keep talking my brother. We understand."

He pounded his chest and looked at Batman and thanked him with a wink from his black eye.

"I knew my habit was bad when a little kid asked me, where was my cape?" he wiped his eyes of tears, "I was so high. I told the kid to buzz off." He sobbed.

"What you think I need my cape to fight crime and fly mother fucker. I am Superman. You snotty nose bastard!" his heart was obviously torn apart. The crowd moaned in disbelief. He let out a sigh and raised his chin from his chest, "I know, I know, for the first time in ten years I have not flown, saved lives or made a citizen arrest." He blew his nose on his dingy "S", "I found a pawn receipt that dated five years ago. Can you believe I pawned my cape? So, today without taking too much of your time, I just wanted to say that it was time for a change. I put my crack pipe down; with your help and support. I hope to be back flying the skies and saving lives, with that I will keep coming back."

Mugumbi sighed and laughed at his crazy dream. He looked at the clock and stood from the couch. He opened the sliding glass to the balcony. The city came alive, and smell of salt water rushed him. He leaned on the rail.

"Tomorrow night would be a perfect time to have this party." He spoke out loud and thought of those purple balloons.

Hours had passed when he returned from the storage. He placed a black tote bag that contained his hit man gear on to the bed. He flipped it over to dump everything on the bed. Two guns with silencers, bullet proof vest, brand new pair of eleven size casual shoes; that was one size bigger. He ran his hand through the tight curly wig and put it next to his black mask. His black gloves were pre printed with fingerprints of a foreigner that can't be traced. He collected fresh cigarette butts from a bar on the way back to the hotel. He looked at his black top and bottom long johns and thought of a plan to how they will be best used. He unfolded a huge zip lock plastic bag and stuffed it with his shoes, a pair of jeans, pullover shirt, and a Miami heat ball cap. In a smaller bag, he stuffed his identification, cell phone, a small container of igniter fluid, and a lighter. He neatly placed everything in the tote bag and zipped it. The sigh of frustration vibrated his lips. He rubbed his face and wiped his runny eyes and nose on his sleeve of his shirt. His symptoms of withdrawal were getting worse.

Just before the sun was swallowed by the horizon, the streetlights slowly flickered on and the night sky creped from the east. He put his long johns on first, and then donned his outer layer to wear to his destination. He placed his knees on the floor, closed his eyes and said a prayer. He slowly placed the palms of his hands on his forehead, slowly pulled down his mental transformational mask, and he was ready. "I can do this."

The taxi made a right turn on Alton rd. and fifth St. on Miami Beach. He gave the driver a twenty and told the driver to keep the change. He walked into the seven eleven store, purchased a drink, and a Bahama Mama hot dog. He headed towards the boating dock behind the condominiums on west Ave. He took a seat on the edge of the dock and observed, waited for an opportunity, and it came. A fisherman cleaning his small motorboat removed his fishing poles, and tackle box.

He looked around for surveillance cameras. He made his way to the parking garage. He tossed the last bite of his hotdog in his mouth. In the shadow of darkness, he slipped his gloves on and twisted the silencer on his pistol. He sighed and double-checked for possible witnesses. He crept up with his pistol tucked in his armpit. He walked past the boat and pretended to be lost.

"Excuse me, are you giving rides on the Biscayne Bay?" he looked around and a quick glance of the balconies. They were empty.

The fisherman smiled and looked him in the eyes. It all happened so fast, it sounded like a thump. The fisherman's body fell forward of the boat. He jumped in and started the boat and quickly left the dock before anyone noticed.

In the middle of the bay, he shut the motor off. It was darker than expected, and the silence was peaceful. He took off the outer layer of clothes, put on his wig, and black stocking mask. He donned the bulletproof vest, and stuffed the two pistols into the pockets on his vest. He pulls the gps to navigate the address.

"One, two, three, four, and five..."He pierced his eyes through the mini size binoculars. "That's it." He mumbled his words. He started the motor and went full speed ahead until he felt the need to be quiet. The wind blew across his face as the front of the boat lifted upward. When he got to fifty miles per hour, he shut the motor off, and glided half way. He looked around through his binoculars, and saw no one. He paddled the last two hundred meters. He was exhausted from paddling.

He reached the boardwalk behind the eight bedrooms, four baths, and four-car garage home. He climbed out of the boat and tied it to the dock. He quickly hid behind the bushes that lined the wall of the house.

He tried to control the rise and fall of his breathing. He counted to sixty slowly. He got on his knees and crawled towards the patio. He looked up and noticed the television upstairs in the master bedroom. He started to get nervous as the butterflies began to float throughout his stomach.

He sighed and realized it's now or never. He tightens his gloves and pulled his pistol. The French doors to the kitchen were open. He looked at his hands. They shook like leaves on a windy afternoon and his paranoia started to play with his mind. He thought about how stupid it was to flush his dope.

He stepped in and looked for a place to hide. He peeked around a wall that led to the living room. The smell of stew boiled on the stove, uncut Cuban bread, and a half peeled banana on the granite counter. He let out a huge sigh; someone was going to return to check on it.

Beneath his breath he sang a song from back home, it kept him calm. A voice grabbed his attention to the upstairs. He quickly tiptoed and stopped at the top. He let out a huge puff of breath as his melodic tune repeated. He found a dark corner and stuffed himself into it to be invisible. The hallway was lined with life like statues of various warriors of history. The ivory marble tiled floors were throughout the second floor. He kept the tune flowing. The television blared, as he got closer. He softly pushed open the first bedroom door enough to see a child on her bed watching TV. The third bedroom was unoccupied. He stepped in, shut off the light, cracked the door just enough to keep an eye on the hallway. He bounced his head to the beat, tapped his pistol on his thigh, and waited.

Suddenly, he saw the kid walking towards him and reached for the door. He stepped back as far as the wall would allow, in shock he stood there behind the door. The kid grabbed a doll off the bed, and left the room. He sighed and slowly closed the door enough to see the hallway. He swallowed a huge ball of luck; his heart pounded his chest hard. He raised his mask to wipe his sweat, and gather his thoughts. From the door he could see the shadow of someone walking around the master bedroom. He got his rhythm going in his head, and counted to five. His sigh was long and hard, but confident. He opened the door and the curious kid stood there looking at him.

Without hesitation, he simultaneously put his left index finger to his lips, and the tip of the pistol nudged into her right eye, "Shhhhhh!"

He quickly grabbed her with his left hand covering her mouth. "Don't say a word!" he whispered. She wet herself and it flowed on to the floor. She began to cry. He pushed her into the bedroom.

"Who is in the other bedroom?" he demanded.

"My father." Her tears pooled her eyes, as her lower lip quivered.

"Is there anyone else in the house?" he peeked through the crack of the door. He knew time was not in his favor. She shook her head left to right. He quickly grabbed a shirt from the closet to use to tie her hands, feet, and to gag her mouth.

He walked towards the master bedroom. The door was closed, the music blared. He opened the door and aimed his pistol. There was no one. He looked around the room as he headed to the bathroom. With his left foot he pushed the door open.

"Don't move!" he told him. He stood there in all black long johns. His target damn near fell off the toilet, dropped his magazine and held his hands up to plea for his life. He was every bit of four hundred pounds.

"I don't want to die like this! Please!" His hairy legs shook from fear, his voice sounded dry and he knew death was eminent.

"Can I please put some clothes on?" his tears fell like his little girl's did. Mugumbi kicked his boxers toward his feet.

"Put those on!" he waved his pistol nervously.

The target slowly reached for the roll of toilet paper. He sobbed.

"Hey motherfucker! You won't need that, put the boxers on!" Mugumbi demanded.

The target heard that he had an African accent. "Where are you from my brother?"

Mugumbi tapped his left foot up and down. He felt sympathy for him.

"I can hear it when you speak. Why are doing this to another African bother?"

Mugumbi hesitated; his index finger rubbed the trigger ever so softly. He took a deep sigh and aimed.

"Wait! Please wait! Can you at least tell me why this is happening?" He slowly tried to stand, before he got a response. But his legs were too weak. His body felt heavier. He pleaded as he used the sink for leverage to help him stand like a man. His body shook like cow tits on the run from a horny Bull.

"Ok, ok." His breathing was hard and sporadic. He tried to catch his breath. He wiped his tears with his forearm.

"What have I done to deserve this?" his voice cracked. His heart pounded his temple. "Please, I'll give…give you anything." He stuttered, lips moved faster than his words could fall from his mouth.

"I don't want to die, God, please." He begged like a whimpering innocent big-eyed defenseless puppy.

"Can I see my daughter? I just… want to kiss her good bye." He softly spoke. "Where is she?" he slowly walked towards the door. He wanted to let him know that he had not harmed her.

"She is ok." Mugumbi told him.

"Please, can I see her? I just want to let her know that I will always love her."

Mugumbi backed away not understanding why he felt so compassionate and obliged to respect his wishes.

"Follow me." He pulled out his second pistol and guided him like a Boeing 747.

The life size chief Indian stared him straight in his face. He stepped over the puddle of piss. The room was lit with the hallway light. The nine year old was hogged tied, blind folded, and gagged with a dirty sock in her mouth. She was wedged between the bed and the far wall.

"No!" he made his way towards her. He moved the bed like it was a cot. He took the sock out of her mouth and lifted her as he sobbed. He removed the cloth from her eyes and bear hugged her.

"I love you so much. I am so sorry…" his sobs continued. His kisses were out of love.

"Hey, hey that's enough!" He prevented him from removing her restraints. He sat on the floor and held her close. Tears fell with a horrifying look in her eyes. She began to scream. He hugged her tighter. She saw her favorite Barbie on the floor. She wanted to pick it up.

"Daddy, help me." She whispered in his ear.

Suddenly, there was the sound of footsteps coming up the stairs. The shadow stopped at the door. "No!" She ran in to rescue her daughter. She was outraged, too scared to fear death. She charged Mugumbi and scratched his chest and neck.

He shot her two times in the chest. He stepped out of the corner of darkness, nervously shaken. His breathing was heavy. The room was loud with screams. The target launched at him like an angry elephant, but to no avail, he was shot four times. The weight of his body weighed him to the floor. His blood soaked his clothing. He dragged himself from beneath the target. He sighed deeply and counted backwards from twenty to zero. He closed his eyes and sat on the bed. He rested his left foot on the target's leg.

"Fourteen, thirteen, twelve, eleven, and ten…" he can hear the little girl sobbing from the floor, "…three, two, and one." He pushed the silencer across his temple. He thought about his dope.

He stood up, stepped over the two bodies to get to the little girl. He had this sick feeling at the bottom of his stomach and pulled the trigger two times.

"Damn it…" he looked at himself in the mirror. He sighed. "Stupid bitch!" He ran down the stairs to the kitchen in search of some sort of knife. He returned with an electric knife and cut off both of her hands from the wrist to keep his DNA from being found beneath her fingernails. Then he fled the scene.

The boat was going as fast as it could. The throttle was all the way forward. The wind pressed his face until the motor began to sputter. He came to a sudden glide across the Biscayne Bay. He had run out of gas.

"What the fuck!" He yelled and grunted. He tried to crank it several times; it only pissed him off more. He sighed; it was dark, quiet, and scary.

"Damn… someone is coming!" he quickly laid himself down in the boat. The sound of the boat passed him, but slowed to return.

"Please keep going. Please don't turn around." The motor gradually came to a purr as it pulls along side of it.

"Is any one there?" the fisherman asked without a flashlight.

Mugumbi raised his right hand and pulled the trigger. The fisherman fell on to his back. Before the captain of the boat could aid his friend, he fell with a wound to his chest.

Mugumbi threw his belongings aboard and headed to the Venetian causeway bridge, dumped the boat, carefully removed the finger tips from the hands, tossed them into the Bay, and later flushed them down the toilet of a restaurant and escaped capture.

Chapter 20

Honolulu, Hawaii

Six months later

Jamie sat in the martial arts office chair at the computer, ignoring her vibrating cell phone. She thumbed through membership applications and entered their information into the database. She sipped her orange juice and sighed at an unfamiliar number that had called three times already.

"Hello." She sounded like she didn't want to answer the call. The voice excited her with a loud scream.

"Girl! Where have you been?!" I was wondering what happened to you." She leaned back into the chair. Stacy's voice was good to hear.

"Well, I took your advice." She sounded happy.

"Girl, you didn't call. You changed your number…" Jamie was happy to talk to her.

"Why you didn't answer your phone?" Stacy asked.

"Girl, I didn't recognize your number, and I was on the computer trying to concentrate." She took in a deep breath, "…and you already know how I am with computers. So…" She kicked off her shoes, and turned the chair around in a slow full circle.

"I have so many things to tell you." She interrupted Jamie.

"Well, let me just clean the wax out of my ears." They both laughed.

"Well first and foremost, I went into therapy. And…" she was interrupted.

"So how did that go?"

"Well… it was very helpful. It helped me deal with a lot of issues, and it allowed me to meet others that are like me." Stacy explained.

"I am so glad to hear that." Jamie crossed her left leg over her right. "Stacy, I was so worried about you. I was really hoping that you had not done anything stupid." She paused. "Like parachuting and not pulling the string." They both burst into laughter.

"OMG let me tell you about my new boyfriend!" she burst it out like she could no longer hold it in. "Girl, he is so all that with a honey chocolate flavored banana with caramel running down the side..." she screamed, "...on my mother fucking hand, bitch!" She paused to take a deep breath. "He is from St. Croix. His accent is so romantic."

"Where did you meet him?" Jamie asked.

Before Stacy could answer, "Girl I hope you told him."

Stacy laughed. "Jamie, you will not believe it." She took a drag from her cigarette.

"When I told him..." she let out a stream of smoke, "...about me."

"What did he say? I want to know." Jamie couldn't wait.

"Just calm down and let me tell you." She held on to the anticipation for as long as she can.

The office phone rang. She picked up the receiver "Please hold."

Jamie was more curious and anxious. Stacy giggled.

"So you told him about your thing?" Jamie asked.

"Yes of course, and it was the best thing I ever done." Stacy was over the top happy.

Jamie's ear was sucking the earpiece like she was thirsty for more details.

"Now listen, at first I did not tell him, you know, but he wanted to kiss me. I told him that I have something to tell him." She took a long drag from her cigarette, "I really have to share this part of my life with you before we take this to the next level. The last thing I want to do is to lead you on or play games with you. I have no idea how you will take this, but we need to talk about it." Stacy paused.

"So, what happened?" Jamie stopped rotating in the chair and braced for her response.

"Well I asked him had he ever seen a large, long clitoris before. He said yes. I came straight forward with it..." They were like teenagers, excited and on the edge of suspense.

"And..." Jamie broke the silence.

"Girl..." she wedged her face into the pit of her elbow with fear of what would be said next.

"Did he ask how big?" by now her finger nails were at the edges of her teeth.

"Girl let me finish…" she smashed the butt out into the ash tray, "I told him that I was all female, but my clit is a little abnormal." They burst into laughter. "Now, keep in mind, all this was in the parking lot of the mall." They laughed like cute hyenas. Jamie almost fell out of her chair. Stacy choked on her smoke.

Stacy sighed heavily. "He wanted to see it, girl! I was so embarrassed, but I felt so comfortable with him. I … I let him see it." She could barely contain herself.

Jamie was damn near on the floor, holding her stomach from the cramps of laughter, "What! You got to be joking?"

"He was just a freak. He asked could he touch it, and when he did. It got bigger and his eyes grew wider, like what the hell. He positioned my right leg, pulled my ass closer and begged, 'please let me lick that beautiful motherfucka' I was so wet, my mouth was wide open, lost for words. I didn't say go ahead, or refused. My body went limp, my head went back, and he took control like a beast." She pulled a cigarette out of the pack with the tip of her fingers, lit it and sucked on it hard. "Bitch, I thought the damn car was floating." she was interrupted with a huge gasp of surprise.

"No way! What did you say?" Jamie held on to the edge of the desk for dear life.

"What! For thirty minutes, nothing was said. I felt like I was on a pedestal. Girl, right there in the parking lot of the mall. He got down. I mean, it was unbelievable. He had me at hello, bitch!" she screamed. "Aaaaah!"

Jamie was so surprised. "But wait, wait a minute, and how long did you know him?" the phone was silent, but not for long.

"Not long enough!" she said it with confidence.

"I am hooked, bitch!" she calm herself down, took a deep breath and fanned her face.

"So it sound like you two are pretty serious?" she sat back into the chair.

Stacy looked at the phone as if Jamie could see her face.

"Jamie, girl if I find out… Now listen to me carefully. If I find out that there is another big clit bitch within a five hundred, no a thousand miles, bitch I just may have to go kill that hoe." They laughed so hard, she was finally happy, and nothing can take that away from her.

"Jamie, I am so happy."

"Damn I wish I can say the same." The subject had changed.

"Where is Kalargo?"

"He has been in Africa for five months. I have not spoken to him. It's almost like he doesn't exist. Girl I have lost weight. I look a hot mess." Stacy can hear the stress in her voice.

"Did he say why he was going to Africa?" Stacy asked.

Jamie rubbed the back of her neck. "Some type of research, yeah research my ass."

"No letters, phone calls?" Stacy asked.

Jamie placed her elbows on the desk. "He did say he would be able to retire when he return."

"What kind of work his father does?"

"He is the CEO of Net Rem Grat logistic in South Korea."

"Girl he might have a wife in Africa that he has not told you about."

Jamie quickly disagreed. "He has no other family besides his uncle. His family was killed in genocide."

"Well..." Jamie sighed. "At least you are happy. Now that, is some good news."

"So when are you able to come to San Diego?"

Jamie looked around the office and knew it was impossible, just too busy. "Not sure, I am running the fitness center." She said with a skeptical facial expression.

"You got to introduce me to your boyfriend, when are you coming back home?"

"Well I have two more months of therapy. Anytime after that, I will keep in touch." They both said their good bye.

* * *

Jamie sat at the computer dazed, and knew that there was nothing she could do but wait. She had not heard from Na Min in two months. She looked at the clock, it was 3pm. She quickly grabbed the receiver and dialed his cell phone. She hesitated on the last number. She pushed her right index finger across the number. Finally, she pushed it and the ring tone seemed louder than usual. She sighed heavily. She leaned back into the chair and held on to what felt like her last breath of hope, before putting the receiver down, she paused. Her feelings were shattered into a million pieces. She slammed the receiver down and pushed away from the desk. She covered her misty eyes with the palms of her hands and pushed her tears towards her ears. She smeared her mascara and masked her face like a raccoon. Her runny nose convinced her to go to the bathroom.

Over the sink she stood in front of the mirror and tried to damp dry her ridiculous look. She shook her head, and sighed. She reached for the facet with her left hand to run the water, and checked the temperature with her right. She splashed her face several times. As she reached for the towel, the phone rang. She snatched the towel and ran to the phone.

"Honolulu fitness center, how can I help you?" she swallowed a gulp of hope.

"Yes, Jamie." the voice was Na Min's.

She thanked God it was him, "Na Min... yes I hope I did not interrupt you." she said with the up most respect.

"Of course not, is everything ok?" he asked and multitask a meeting in D.C. The voices in the background were more important than hers.

She hesitated, and was interrupted.

"Jamie..." as he spoke to a colleague and returned to her, "I have not heard anything, but you will be the first to know. I do apologize. I am sure he appreciates everything you are doing." He stressed to her. He quickly cut her short.

"Listen, I have to call you back." he said as he and his colleagues approached the entrance to the Pentagon.

After a long forty five minute walked, he arrived to the area of the Pentagon where their meeting will take place. The office had an oval smoked glass table with black office chairs that surrounded it. The four plasma screen monitors hung close together on the wall. Each position had a small laptop for access to information on the oval table.

He shook hands with several people whom he had not seen in years.

"Na Min." firm handshakes. "Wow, it's been, what, five years?"

He smiled, "Just about. I see you taking care of yourself." he said to a friend from the farm, which stood for Central Intelligence Agency training in Virginia.

As others mingled in their groups, they slowly assumed their locations according to where their names were on the table. The members of this Top Secret meeting consist of

N.F.I.B. National Foreign Intelligence Board
I.N.R. Bureau of Intelligence and Research
D.I.A. Defense Intelligence Agency
M.I. Military Intelligence
R.I.O. Regional intelligence of the Orient

Finally, they sat down and whispered among themselves. Suddenly the room fell to silence when the door opened and the President of the United States entered.

They all stood, "Have a seat gentleman." The President slowly sat down and pulled himself towards the glass desk.

"Ok guys, what do we have on Kim Jong Il?" he sighed and opened the folder in front of him.

"Well Mr. President..." Mike Tonki from the Defense of Intelligence Agency. "We have evidence that in Dec. of 2002 following revelations that the (DPRK) was pursuing a nuclear weapons program based on enriched uranium in violation of the 1994 agreement with us to freeze and ultimately dismantle its existing plutonium- based program, North Korea expelled monitors from the international non-proliferation treaty. In mid 2003, Pyongyang announced it had completed the reprocessing of spent nuclear fuel rods to extract weapons grade plutonium and was developing a nuclear deterrent." he flipped over a sheet of paper.

"Since august 2003, North Korea has participated in the six party talks with China, Japan, Russia, and U.S. to try to resolve this stalemate over its nuclear program." he stood up passed folders to everyone.

Before Mike sat down, "The fourth round of six party talks was held in Beijing during July and Sept 2005. All parties agreed to a joint statement of principles in which, among other things, the six parties unanimously reaffirmed the goal of verifiable denuclearizing of the Korean peninsula in a peaceful manner in the joint statement, as he sat down and looked at the President.

"The DPRK committed to abandoning all nuclear weapons and to IAEA safeguards." he said.

Na Min sat quietly, and listened well with his undetectable bug that the North Koreans gave him. He was the ultimate mold. The highest ranking mold you can plant among double agents.

Mike continued his analysis, "Joint statement also commits the U.S. And other parties to certain actions as the DPRK denuclearize. We offered a security assurance, specifying that it had no nuclear weapons on ROK territory and no

DPRK will take steps to normalize relations, subject to the North Koreans implementing its pledge denuclearize and resolve other longstanding concerns. While the joint statement provides a vision of the end-point of the six party processes, much work lies ahead to implement the elements of the agreement."

The President looked around the room. "So can anyone tell me what Kim Jong Il is up to? Na Min do you have any other evidence of nuclear proliferation?"

He took in a deep sigh. "Mr. President, Kim Jong Il is definitely up to something. There is movement of an approximately fifteen thousand troops along the west Kaesong border and from the satellite images of missile launchers have been repositioned. We know for a fact that North Korea is selling missiles to various unstable countries in the Middle East. Due to their desperate economic conditions, the industrial capital stock is nearly beyond repair as a result of years of under investment and shortages of spare parts. Industrial and power output has declined in parallel. Despite an increase harvest in 2005..." He flipped a page and continued.

"Now because of assistance from South Korea and an extraordinary mobilization of the population to help with agricultural production, the nation has suffered its eleventh year of food shortages because of ongoing systemic problems, including a lack of arable land, collective farming practices, and chronic shortages of tractors and fuel." He flipped the third page.

He looked around the room above the rim of his glasses. He returned his focus on to his pages that he read from. "Massive international food aid deliveries have allowed the people of North Korea to escape mass starvation since famine threatened in 1995, but the population continues to suffer from prolonged malnutrition and poor living conditions. Large scale military spending eats up resources needed for investment and civilian consumption. In 2004, the regime formalized an arrangement whereby private farmer markets were allowed to sell a wider range of goods." He took off his glasses and squeezed the bridge of his nose.

"Gentlemen, I say all of this... the dictator of North Korea is desperate, and..." he paused. "And willing to try anything to pull his country out of this hell they are in." He looked at the President of the United States.

"I truly believe the proliferation of his nuclear programs continue to grow. He has tested medium range missiles in the peninsula. Now there is evidence of them building long range missiles that would be capable of reaching the west coast in less than seven years..." he was interrupted. He held his pen up to his lips and shook his head in disappointment.

"And once they find this plutonium, they will be well on their way?" the President asked.

"Sir, they will have a minimum of five nuclear warheads capable of reaching the American soil." he said.

Air Force General, Paul Bugat of military intelligence "Mr. President, North Korea has been a main supplier to countries in civil war for the past twenty five years. It would be the perfect timing for any one of the terrorist groups to obtain a nuclear device. It's not like they don't have the money. They just have not had anyone to sale them a nuclear warhead, and once the North Koreans test the nuclear warhead for the world to see. The auctions for nuclear warheads will be up for sale to whoever has the money."

The room fell silent. The president leaned forward and placed his face into his palms of his hands. "How close are we monitoring them?

"Very closely." said Na Min.

"Can we just take out the nuclear plant?"

A voice from the opposite of the table spoke, "Yes, but if we do, that would be more than enough reason for them to attack South Korea, and Japan. Even if we made it look like an accident. It would raise questions. We have to use the six party talks to come up with a diplomatic resolution." said the defense intelligence.

"Well, I guess we have to wait, but keep me informed. I..." The president paused and looked at his watch. "...I have a meeting at 2pm." he stood up and grabbed his folders. Everyone stood at attention as he exited the room.

*   *   *

Na Min stood outside the Pentagon. He looked up at the partly cloudy sky. He felt a ten mph breeze from the west. He slowly looked over the parking lot for his rental car.

"Oh there it is." he walked past several cars, and suddenly thirty feet from his car. His cell phone rang. He stood facing hwy 395, he smiled.

"Hello honey." he preceded towards his car.

"I just called to say hello..." before he could say another word, a breeze lifted his collar. "Baby I just wanted to hear your voice."

His memory re-winded like a 1970 cassette tape back to when they first met. Her Latin accent filtered the ear piece and warmed his soul. He reached into his left front pocket of his navy blue slacks that matched his jacket. He rubbed his finger across the rental car remote, as he engaged in a loving conversation with his wife, just before he pressed the button with his thumb, he paused. He swallowed, he laughed after she told him a short joke. He proceeded towards his rental.

"Na Min." a voice from behind him interrupted his phone call. He turned around. This person took his smile and crumbled it to an unexpected frown.

He quickly put his index finger up towards Agent Craig. "One moment." he gestured. After he said good bye to his wife, he slowly put his cellular in his front left pocket.

"Hey I hope I was not interrupting you." Agent Craig said.

He smiled candidly. "Are you up for a drink? Maybe we can catch up on old times?" he said as he scratched his upper left chest, and combed his fingers through his hair. Craig's dark gray conservative neatly pressed suite and perhaps straight off of a J C Penny's rack fitted him well.

His weight gain showed his lack of enthusiasm for physical fitness. He was always a heavy sweater with sweat on the tip of his nose, and between his double chin that left a ring around his collar, he work for National Foreign Intelligence Board, a body of the government formed to provide the director of Central Intelligence with advice concerning production, review, and coordination of national foreign intelligence; the national foreign intelligence program budget; inter agency exchange of foreign intelligence information; arrangements with foreign governments on intelligence matters; the protection of intelligence sources or methods; activities of common concern; and such other matters as are referred to it by the D.C.I.

"Sure, why not." Na Min looked down at his watch.

"Are you at the Marriott across the street, Army Navy street, right?" he asked Craig.

"Yes, room 814, it's a bar in the lobby." he nodded his head, rubbed his nose. The sound of his car door unlocked.

"Sure why not, I will call you about 7pm." they both agreed and jumped into their cars. As he drove through security, he mumbled. "I just don't trust him. I swear I don't like his vibe."

He looked in his rearview mirror. "Yeah, he's apart of N.F.I.B., that's another reason I don't need him snooping around." he spoke to himself.

Na Min had been a double agent for more than twenty years and trusted no one. He felt like Craig was being forward about having a drink. The last time they saw each other was in Central America. He had witness him pull the eyes out of an El Salvadorian rebel.

"Thank God that was after he tried to kill me. Now that was a miracle..." Shook his head and gestured, "Bad luck for him. He ran out of bullets." he thought and spoke out loud.

He sat in his car going over one of many of his experiences. This rebel was pissed and determined. He fired one round into the air, and yelled for me to stop, but Na Min kept moving. The next two rounds zipped by his head. He was so scared. He forgot to breath.

Na Min gripped the steering wheel and gritted his teeth as his mind raced with anger. The rebel pulled the trigger and the clacking sound of the AK-47 made them both sigh. They charged right at each other. He swung the butt end of the rifle at his head. He round house kicked the AK-47 to his left and came quick with a right foot as hard as he could to his ribs. He fell, before he could recover, he kicked him in the throat. By then his adrenaline was high as a kite.

He looked crazy talking to himself the entire drive to his hotel. "I jumped on top of him with my knees on his shoulders, jabbed his throat again. I jammed my thumbs into his eyes until my knuckles were covered with blood. The sound of screams was undesirable. His body tossed me off of him. I fell to my right side, it was a mess. I looked over my shoulder and there he was, Agent Craig. I don't know what all he saw, but he never spoke a word of it."

He came to and realized that he arrived to the hotel parking lot. He had no idea how long he had been sitting there. He looked around the lot and thanked God he was alive.

"If I wake up early, I can stop by and place flowers on my kid's grave." he walked away from the car.

* * *

Gambia, Africa

Kalargo awaken by the sound of banging at his door. His studio apartment was his holding cell until he finishes training the three hundred troops. Four months had past and he was pissed.

He opened his eyes and seen a note that had been slipped under the door. He looked at his clock and covered his face. "Damn." he looked down at his left elbow and rubbed his bruise. He sighed. He walked over and picked up the note and read it. He smiled.

"Now this will be interesting." he sat on the bed and once again plotted how he would kill the General.

The clock displayed four am; he unfolded the note and reread it. He could not believe the General wanted to have an expedition to show the progress of the training of the troops. The whole town will be there. What a great opportunity this will be. He tossed the note in the trash.

He had to prepare the troops for a once in a life time event, and knew it would be big. For the first time he was happy to have the chance. The banging at the door did not bother him. He was dressed and ready. The sound of the keys unlocked the chain that secured the door.

"Kalargo is there anything you need for today's preparation?" the soldier asked.

"Yes, gather the men, all three hundred of them, have them meet me in the gym." he sat down to eat his breakfast.

"Coffee?" the soldier asked.

"Yes, and cream." he put his grape jelly on his toast.

In the gym he stood in front of the troops, "In two weeks we will have an expedition. This means the best out of three hundred will be allowed to show off their self defense skills to the General and the King of The Gambia." the sigh of three hundred troops said they were excited.

"I am looking for the top fifty. Raise your hand if you want to participate?" almost all of them raised their hands with excitement. He quickly picked two men and told them to come forward. He motioned his hands to form a circle. He stood between them and explained.

"What is the number one rule in self defense? Anyone?" he turned to the crowd.

Everyone yelled, "Protect yourself!"

"You, in three seconds I will attack you." he turned his back to the soldier and spoke to the crowd.

"At no time should your guard be down." he turned around and punched the soldier in the stomach, chopped him across his throat and broke his nose. He fell to the ground. The gasp in the air was breath taking. Now they knew he meant business. The second soldier stood in the ready position.

After four hours, he finally had his fifty soldiers that will participate. They all were hurt, bleeding, and suffering from some form of pain. None of them knew how to fight, but he had fun just kicking their ass around like rag dolls. He made a very good example of the soldiers that beat him in the back of that truck. They were taken to the hospital.

Out of nowhere the gym was silent, "Attention!" all the troops stood still as the General walked through the crowd. His guards made the way. Kalargo walked up to him and shook his hand with a smile.

"I see you are doing a fine job. One day I will have finest fighting troops in Africa. "I come to see a small demonstration from my fighters to be." he let out a puff of smoke.

He knew these sorry troops were not worth watching, so he explained to him that the best fifty that will perform in the expedition are now exhausted. However, he will not be let down.

"Fight, fight, fight! I came to see a fight." he picked two men from the crowd. "You and you, up here" they both ran to the front of the crowd.

"Yes sir!" they stood ready.

"He is the enemy. I want you to kill him. He is trying to kill me. If you lose, your family is dead." he looked at the other soldier. "Today, you will die."

Kalargo was disgusted, just could not believe what he was hearing. He knew he had to get rid of this guy.

Chapter 21

Expedition day

Kalargo gathered his handpicked fighters to talk about what looks good for entertainment. "Now guys, we have to make this look good, look real, and most or all, entertaining."

He pounded his fist in his right hand. He meant business. He went over all the moves in slow motion, on how to entertain the crowd. He looked at his watch and sighed.

"Well, I will see you guys in four hours, do your best, and make the King proud."

He had to prepare for his escape. This night would be his only chance. For the last three nights, the General had invited him for drinks. He knew after the expedition with the large crowd it would take the focus off of him, making it easier to assassinate him.

He arrived at his studio apartment, two soldiers stood outside and one at the rear. He wiped sweat from his forehead and took off his shirt. He looked in the mirror and shook his head. The butterflies in his stomach began the feel like the tail of a rattle snake. He had already made up his mind how he would kill the General.

The soldiers stopped frisking him three months ago. He had been grinding a butter knife to a point like a shank, adding a hard dried toilet paper for a handle. He pushed his hand between his mattresses, where he cut a hole to hide it. The grip was a perfect fit to his hand. He let out a deep sigh, and cleared his throat. He imagined how he was going to kill the General. The timing has to be right. He knew that he may not have much time to escape. He sighed and walked over to the window and rested his head on the glass. His hands shook. He could not believe the situation that he got himself into.

He looked at the clock, three more hours. He decided to meditate. He crawled to the floor to try to gain some type of control of his emotions. He felt out of whack. He closed his eyes, tuned out the voices outside his door, the air compressor outside his window. He sat in the same position without moving. His breathing slowed down, and one by one the butterflies flew away.

The deep sound of banging on his door opened his eyes, "Twenty minutes, be ready." the voice of a soldier said.

He had fallen asleep sitting in the Indian position for two hours. Finally, he was mentally ready for what he had to do. He stood up and stretched, cracked his bones in his neck, arms, back, and ankles. He snatched his shirt from the chair, and tucked the shank in his third pair of underwear. He paused just before knocking on the door to let them know that he was ready. He took a deep breath and knocked.

He spoke to the soldiers like he had known them for years, told his last joke, sipped from their liquor bottle. He knew if it came down to it. He may have to kill one of them to escape.

"So, this is going to be a good fight?" the driver asked.

Kalargo took a long drink from the bottle, and sighed. "You will see very good fighting. They have been training well." he gave a thumb up.

They arrived to the gym to a crowd of people; lines were wrapped around the corner. The red carpet was laid for the King, and soldiers were everywhere. He looked around and doubted himself of the easy escape.

The crowd cheered his name like he was a celebrity. He quickly came up with a plan. He called over a soldier.

"Hey I need you to stand by me, no matter what, don't leave my side."

"Is the crowd to much to handle?" the soldier asked.

"I don't handle crowds to well; I get sick to my stomach." Kalargo said.

The soldier was delighted to stand by him to keep him safe from the crowd.

The stands were filled with people, chanting. The General entourage arrived, the crowd went crazy. The support and love they gave the General was huge. He could not understand what they chanted.

The General shook hands with him, waved to the crowd went up on the stage and grabbed the microphone.

He calmed the crowd down and introduced the King of the Gambia. The curtain slid apart and there he was. He was old, very dark skin, and covered in metal that wrapped his arms from his hands to his elbow. He nodded his head and waved to the crowd. His security was around him, well armed. The General waved for Kalargo to come to the stage. The King had heard so much about him. He wanted to meet him in person.

His butterflies came back like angry bees. The King raises his right hand that held a royal pinky ring. Kalargo slowly kneeled to one knee and kissed the ring. The King then held his hand out to shake his hand. When they shook the crowd went wild, chanting the tribal slogan. The King held his hand; looked at him and said something in his native tongue, Jola.

He did not know what to do. The King looked him up and down, searching for tribal markings. The King appeared suspicious of him, he started to sweat. He pulled him closer, smelt his body odor, rubbed his old wrinkle hand across his jawbone, and looked behind his ear. He smiled and let his hand go. His teeth were not royal like. He appeared ill and smelt horrible. He noticed the metal that wrapped his arms were pure gold.

The General walked over, "Kalargo!" the crowd cheered, and stomped their feet on the bleachers.

After two hours of fighting. The King called over a servant and whispered in his ear.

The servant grabbed the microphone and told the crowd that Kalargo would be fighting three people. The crowd went wild.

He was shocked by this and was not prepared. The King chose three people and raised his hand. As he moved around the mat, the shank rubbed his thigh. He knew if it fell from his pants, the whole plan would be spoiled.

The first kick attacked his right leg, the shank cut his thigh. He blocked it and hit the guy in the throat. From behind, his left foot was kicked from beneath him. He fell and recovered quickly. He used his left hand to block a punch to his nose, and threw a hard punch to the ribs, kicked him off his feet, and pounded his elbow down to his chest. The soldier curled with pain. A strong left foot caught Kalargo across the face, busted his lip. But he held the shank in place.

"Three more people, he is good. I like him." The King said.

Kalargo was on his knees, exhausted; all three men were down and moaning. From behind he was kicked on the left side of his face. He rolled over on the mat. His eye had swollen shut. From one eye, he looked up as one of the soldiers grabbed his collar and went for his throat.

Kalargo quickly blocked his throat in time, grabbed his groan and twisted hard. He screamed and fell hard to the floor.

He was pissed, hurt, and bleeding. The shank was still in place. Suddenly, a soldier jumped him from behind; he quickly tossed him off and pounded him in the chest. He blocked a kicked from the last soldier and round house kicked him to the face. He flipped around and fell to the floor, out cold.

He was breathing hard, tired, and angry as hell. The crowd was cheering, stomping their feet on the bleachers. The General and the King applauded. Six soldiers on the floor, and he slowly stood to his feet.

He raised his hands and bowed to the crowd. He turned around and bowed to the King.

The General walked on to the mat and shook his hand."You were great, and taught my men well; go ahead, get cleaned up and meet us for dinner."

He was escorted out of the gym. Blood from his thigh soaked his pants as he waved to the crowd; he was a hero in their eyes.

*   *   *

Kalargo was a free man as he walked unescorted into the General's house. He looked around in search of escape routes, and closets. He smiled as he was greeted by soldiers that once guarded him. They shook hands and patted him on the back; native music by the live band, the smell of food was throughout the house.

The dinner table of twelve stood and applauded him as he entered the room. The General walked over and pulled his chair out for him.

"Kalargo, you are more than welcome in my house." he pulled his cigar from his lips.

The silver domes of food were uncovered, as plenty of wine was poured. It all reminded him of his younger days. He had not had these flavors in his mouth since.

He took a deep breath, "I would like to say that you guys have treated me well, but I will not miss you guys." with a smile. The room burst into laughter.

"Well, anytime you want to come back after this war. You are more than welcome." The General said.

They ate and enjoyed the entertainment.

Later that evening, everyone said their goodbyes; He asked one of the guards to give him a ride back to his quarters. He carried his bottle of wine in his hand. He staggered into the truck.

"Hey, I want to thank you for the ride." shortly after they pulled out of the gates of the General's compound.

"Holly molly." he squirmed in his seat. "I got to use the bathroom, it won't take long. Just pull over here. This is perfect." he barely was able to hold himself up as he slid out of the truck.

"Damn, I did not know that I was this wasted." he fell to the ground. The soldier ran over to help him.

He looked at him and apologized. From the right side he slammed the bottle of wine across his head. The soldier was knocked out cold, quickly removed his clothes and put on the uniform. He pushed him down the hill, and headed back to the General's compound.

He parked the truck a couple of blocks away, jumped a wall, and climbed a tree to gain access to an upstairs bathroom window.

He sighed and slowly walked toward the door. He could hear voices and realized he had nowhere to hide. His hands began to shake from fear. He felt almost sick to his stomach.

His mouth was dry; it felt like he tried to swallow his tongue. The voices had traveled further away.

It felt like minutes had gone by. He stood behind the door with his eyes closed. He came to and realized he dosed off to sleep. He listened with his ear to the door. The bedroom light came on from beneath the door. He started to breath abnormal. The sound of a person walking around can be heard.

He cracked the door to see what the General was doing. He slowly and quietly walked over to the bed and stood over him. He was so drunk. He had no idea that Kalargo was standing over him for three minutes.

With tears in his eyes, he slammed the shank into his chest five times. The sixth time he held it down with the weight of his body until he took his last breath.

He quickly escaped through the bathroom window, leaped across the cement wall and drove away. He came upon the soldier that he had left on the side of the road. The head lights blinded him as the truck approached him. The soldier waved him over.

"Help me, help me!" he held his hand up above his eyes to dim the bright head lights. He pretended to help him until his right fist clobbered him across his temple. The soldier fell to the ground. He dragged him to the side of the road, took his clothes back and dressed him in the bloody fatigues. He moaned.

"What happened?" he raised his head. He clobbered him once more to the chin.

He dumped the truck and continued on foot to his stash location. He sighed when he found it untouched. He dragged it further away from the road to be undetected. His hands were shaken. He just did not feel well. He swallowed his dry. He had taken several deep breaths to no avail. He tried to hold it, but couldn't. He rolled over to his left and vomited. He used his sleeve to wipe his mouth, but more came out. He was pissed, and disappointed with himself. He just couldn't understand that his worries are over, but far from freedom.

He quickly opened the container and pulled out the satellite phone. He hit the redial button, and nervously waited.

*   *   *

Honolulu, Hi

Jamie stood in front of the mirror applying her makeup. She heard her cell phone vibrate on the counter.

"Hello..." with one hand she smeared her lip gloss across her lips.

"What time will you be here?" Stacy asked.

"It shouldn't take that long... Are you dressed already?" Jamie slipped on her sling shot thongs.

"Yeah, I am putting my hair in a bun, but I still have to decide what skirt I'll wear." Stacy said.

"Girl, I thought you were ready. You know it take you awhile... hey hold on I have a call coming through." Jamie sighed and quickly decided to change her clothes.

"Hello..." She unbuttoned her dress with her right hand and held the cell phone in the other. The pause on the phone frustrated her. "I said hello, is anyone there?" just before she hung up, there was a voice that pushed her backwards. Her heart dropped like crystal glass. She looked at the caller id, it had all zeros.

Her eyes grew big, "Hello..." she said softly.

"I love you Jamie. I love you so so much." his voice sucked the breath from her lungs like a burning room filled with smoke. She grabbed her chest and melted to the floor. Her eyes pooled of tears.

"Can you hear me? I am so sorry..." Kalargo's voice sounded weaker than before. The satellite phone had a periodic sound of static.

She tried to reply, but could not pull herself together. She was only able to burst out a horrible scream. She cried in disbelief, hyperventilated and tried to say I love you, but it came out loud and horror like.

She cleared her throat, "I thought you were dead! Oh my god, baby, are you coming home?!"

"Yes, yes, I am coming home." he sighed with relief. Neither of them could believe they were speaking to each other.

"It's been six months, I have been waiting for your call!" she could not hold back her tears. She lay across the floor. "I love you, I love you, I love you so much, please come home!" she screamed at him. The static had gotten worse, so he decided to save the battery time for later.

"Hey listen, I have to call my dad."

"No, don't hang up, I want to talk you."

"I know but I have to call him so he can prepare for my departure out of Africa." he stressed to her how important it was.

She pouted her lips and licked her tears from her upper lip.

"You promise to call me back?"

"Yes, not only that, I promise to see you soon." the line ended.

He gripped the phone with anger and closed his eyes. He exhaled deeply and dialed Na Min's number.

After no answer he tried again, and again. He looked up at the early morning sky. His watch displayed two o'clock. He calculated the hours and figured that he had to be sleeping. He gathered some items and tossed them in his back pack, tucked his pistol in his waist. He used the northern star as his guide and headed west.

After three hours on a dirt road he ducked off to the side to try to call him. On the first ring he was relieved to hear his voice.

"Thank God you answered the phone. Hey listen, the land is clear and ready for the caterpillar." He used the code to notify that the General is confirmed dead and he was ready for extraction. He was excited and he sat in a small creek along the road. He listened very carefully for his next instructions. He had a smile.

"Yes I can hear you." Kalargo glued his ear to the phone. "No! No!" he said with an unexpected tone that he could not hide.

"Kalargo, don't tell me you left without the gps beacon?" he did not wait for his respond. His voice told him he had left the gps beacon with his belongings hours away.

"Do I need it?"

"You bet your ass you need it, how will you be found! Go back and get the beacon! Time is limited. Your scheduled pick up is eight hours from now. It should take you... Just about that..." Na Min paused, counted his fingers.

"Kalargo..." he had some bad news and did not want to tell him. The silence on the phone was as scary as it could get. "I don't think you will be able to make the window for extraction." before he could finish his words.

He quickly headed back for the gps beacon. He was running and explaining how he could make it."No, I am coming home! I am ready; just tell them that I will be there!"

*   *   *

Seoul, South Korea

Mugumbi was exhausted when he arrived from Miami, besides fighting the demons of getting high; he was desperate to find out the news on Kalargo. He turned the key to his home and slowly walked in to the kitchen and surprised his wife.

"Hello you sexy Almond of joy." she quickly ran to him and bare hugged him of his last breath.

"I thought you were going to call me?" she lifted her body on to his. He dropped his bags and carried her in to the bed room.

"Well, I changed my mind and decided to treat you with the unknown." they fell on to the bed and kissed.

She pushed his shirt upward from his belt to his chest; he French kissed her like he was in need of oxygen. She pushed away for air. She licked his salty abdominal. He reached for the lamp and switched the light off as the moans deepen and love escalated.

The room was hot; their bodies were sweaty as they both reached their climax. They spooned their bodies next to one another as they gasped for air. The phone had rung several times, but ignored it.

"Is the air condition on?" He asked.

She smiled."Of course..." they both laughed and slid their naked bodies off the bed. So exhausted, they didn't moved from the floor.

"I love you." he said.

She looked him in his eyes. "I know you do..." she was interrupted by the phone. But she said it anyway. "I will never stop loving you."

She slowly, but forcefully pushed her naked body from the floor and pranced across the room to lower the temperature on the air condition.

The phone rang and he reached from the floor and dragged the receiver from the night stand.

"Hello." he let out a huge sigh of exhaustion.

"Well, well, you won't believe who I spoke to earlier." Na Min had a more cheerful voice than before.

Mugumbi was excited to hear from him. "About time, now if I had went. It would have taken me less than a week." he smiled and said as a joke. "So, when will he be back in Hawaii?"

Na Min laughed," Well, that's if he can make it to his extraction on time. He is late by ten minutes. He will have to wait another two weeks."

"Wow, what make you think he won't be there?"

Yuki sat on top of him and rubbed his chest and grinded her groan against his, pinched his sensitive nipples really hard. He swatted her fingers away.

"Well, he left without the gps beacon, and he is already eight hours from extraction. He just may not make it." he went on about how he will be extracted.

She reached over to the night stand and pulled out her kit and needle. He was immediately distracted and already weak to his jitters. He waggled his left foot and barely held the receiver to his ear, but responded accordingly, "Sound like he is not out of the woods yet."

She prepared the heroin and lit the spoon with the flame. It sizzled and bubbled a dirty brownish color. His eyes opened wide. He could not fight if he had tried. She wrapped his arm tight; veins ballooned upwards like roots of a tree.

"What's my daughter doing?" Na Min asked.

He was lost for words; the needle was in his vein. "She... Well..." he took a swallow of guilt and disappointment. He wiped his left eye of a long tear. He didn't know if it was from the heroin or the fight to stay clean. He asked himself why? He looked at her and whispered in her ear, "I love you."

"She is preparing some food?" He felt like a weak junkie and dog food was his fix; heroin.

"Well, I am pretty sure you are tired from all the travel. Tell her to call me when she gets a chance." Na Min said.

"I will have her call you." they ended the line. She took the receiver from his hand and hung the phone up. She had the rubber strap tied and wrapped around her arm with the end tightly held between her teeth. She took no time before she had the needle in one of her small worm like veins.

She inhaled deeply and took her time as the heroin polluted her body like a living fungus of maggots that slowly ate away at her soul. She enjoyed that feeling, just short of loving him. They both relaxed in the nude until the substance of time was forgotten.

*   *   *

Na Min sat on the edge of his bed with a lot on his mind. His wife walked in the room, with his Ginifer and orange juice. "What are you thinking about?" she grabbed the television remote and searched for her shows.

"Not much." He sipped his drink and wiped his left hand across his mouth. He tried to relax but couldn't. He was stressed about the blood he had just seen in his urine. The pain and unusual amounts of trips to the restroom, but could not find the balls to let her know that he had not been feeling well recently. He looked at her and took a deep breath. His head dropped as he felt compelled to let her know, but not after he swallowed a good amount of his drink.

He stood up and looked at her, "I ..." he tried to shake the nerves of bad news off of his back. It felt like a heavy load of unwanted cargo about to derail.

"There is something..." the phone interrupted him. He pulled it from his pocket and held his index finger up to signal for her to wait a moment.

"Thank God you called!" Na Min said.

"Where are you Kalargo?" he sighed and smiled that he had not revealed his illness.

Kalargo was out of breath, running through a short cut across a wet terrain. "I am trying to make up time!" before he could respond.

"I am running across some farm land. I think it some rice patties, but I am four hours away from the extraction." he jogged and jumped over several fences, creeks, before falling to the ground. He was muddy up to his chest.

"Sound like you're making good time." Na Min walked out of the room.

"Hey listen, you need to get on one of the roads. It would be a lot quicker for you to catch a ride, just make sure you not going in the opposite direction."

Kalargo fell down to his stomach, exhausted. He tossed the back pack and rolled over to take a break. The sound of cow bells can be heard in between his breathing. He crawled a little further. "Another farm." he wiped his sweat with his forearm. He dragged himself up from the tree line. "I will call you back!"

The small village welcomed him with open arms and waved good bye as he rode away with a bicycle.

Chapter 22

Kalargo looked at his watch and sighed. It was three in the morning and he needed to rest, but could not take the chance of missing the time line. He stopped to take a piss. He noticed that it rolled down hill. He had just realized that the inclined was making him extremely tired. He sat down and laid on the back pack with his arms spread out like a cross. His heavy breathing sounded like a hurt elephant in need of water. He was drenched with sweat. He slowly pulled the map from his back pocket, placed a mini flash light between his lips. The pain of his jagged teeth reminded him of the need of a dentist. He totally had forgotten how his mouth looked. He focused on the map. He just wanted to go home.

"Damn..." he pulled himself up off the ground and shook his head, "...I can't believe that I am still two hours behind!" he folded the map and stuffed it in his back pocket. "Come on, no time to rest." he snatched the bike up off the ground and jumped on it like fire was on his ass.

The dirt road of rocks and pot holes was taking a toll on the bike and him. He struggled to push forward. But he knew that he was close to the hill top. He could see it. The full moon made it easier to travel but nothing more. "Come on!" he peddled harder; three to four peddles at a time. His palms were sliding off of the handle bars. His body was trembling, and shaking like he no longer had control.

Suddenly, he heard a noise. He stopped. He put his left foot on the ground. He licked his lips of sweat, and wiped his forehead. He shoved his right index finger in his ear to clear it of dirt and ear wax. He placed his hands behind his ears to improve his hearing. He thought he had heard a helicopter. He sighed and grabbed his chest. He looked at his watch and swallowed the fear of being left behind.

He continued to climb the hill with every grunt, with twenty five more minutes to go. The more he climbed, the narrower the trail became. The edge of the hill had gotten more dangerous. He stopped and looked up, again he thought he had heard something. It came from his back pack. He took it off and went through it. The gps beacon had automatically activated. His eyes became big. He knew he needed to hurry up and climb the hillside. He tossed the bike over the edge. Out of nowhere, a huge helicopter passes over him. He screamed and waved his hands.

"Hey! I'm right here!" he climbed the hill with all his strength. His fingers were used like mountain lion claws. He used tree limbs to brace his weight. His finger nails were black from the soil.

"Please, I'm right here!" he jumped as high as he could.

The helicopter drifted away slowly from the hillside. The back of the helicopter hovered toward him. By the time he arrived, the helicopter had drifted to far away looking for him. His voice was never heard.

He threw the back pack down and dumped everything on to the ground. He grabbed a flare gun and fired it. The night sky was like five full moons. He fell to his knees and leaned backwards. He knew that this was the last thing that he could do to be rescued.

His eyes filled with tears as the helicopter disappeared behind the mountain side. He gritted his teeth with anger, and fear of being left. He screamed to the top of his lungs.

The sound of the chopper faded in the distance. He reached for the satellite phone, but he paused. In the far distance just over the hillside, he could see a tiny figure in the sky. The flare was still bright. It was the helicopter slowly returning. He lost his breath with every scream. There were no flight lights flashing to keep it from being seen.

He quickly grabbed his harness from the backpack and tossed it on. He could see the huge basket being pushed out and dangle in the wind of the rotating blades. Two hundred feet above him, he took a deep breath.

"Come baby! Don't spin!" he grabbed it and places it on the ground, falling in with the back pack, tired and out of breath. The rise of the helicopter smoothly took him off into the sky. The glide across the early morning sky was very peaceful. He said a prayer as it climbed higher than two thousand feet. Finally, a hand pulled him into the cabin of the helicopter.

"Did you need a ride?"

He rolled out of the basket and wanted to hug the plane captain. So he did and shook his hand.

"You guys are life savers..." before he could say another word, he was tossed a brown paper bag, with an apple, ham sandwich, and orange juice.

He rubbed his tongue across his lips, and placed his face in the palms of his hands and cried. He could not believe that he had made it. His tears of joy and knowing he was getting the hell out of there was too much, just wanted to curl up, close his eyes, wake up in his bed.

He was handed a set of head phones with a mic to communicate with the plane captain.

"We have a long ride, four and a half hours. If you want, you can get some sleep. Let us do the rest. You look like you had been through enough."

He nodded his head, closed his eyes, bit into his apple, cried and wished he had teeth.

*　　　　　*　　　　　*

The King screamed and slammed his fist down on the table, "Can't be true! Find Kalargo! I want him in front of me."

He sent a team of armed men to his sleeping quarters. He blocked all roads in and out of the city.

"It has to be him, I knew it was too good to be true." he wiped his eyes. He just could not believe his only brother is now dead. "When you get there, collect DNA! I want to know who he is and where to find him!"

The King walked into the kitchen. Pissed as hell, he barely stood strong, but manages to wipe the table with his arm of all the food to the floor. The loud commotion had people running to his aid. They thought he had fallen. "Paul!" he yelled.

Paul came from behind just before he collapse to the floor. He held the King up and carried him to his bedroom.

"I swear! He can't hide. I will find him and I will skin him alive." he grabbed Paul's shirt tightly.

Paul spoke softly, "We will find him. No matter where he goes. We will get him."

The King became speechless, shook his head as he was lowered into the bed. He gritted his gums. He pulled Paul by the shirt until their lips were inches away.

"Paul, promise me you will find him. I want you and Wataami to look for him like he is an underground ant. Bring him to me, if it's the last thing you do." Right then and there, Paul had a new mission in life, to bring Kalargo to the King.

Paul arrived to the efficiency where Kalargo slept minutes after the team of men. He immediately told everyone, "Don't touch anything!"

He carefully sifted through everything that was left behind for his DNA. He bagged the bloody bandages, hairs from the comb, drinking glasses for finger prints. He looked for any written clues that may give an idea to where he may be going.

He walked over to a small pile of dirty clothes. He pulled his ink pen from his left pocket and lifted a pair of underwear. He held them to his nose and inhaled. He knew right away that his DNA was left behind. He tossed them in the bag.

"Ok, we have what we need. Now let's hope that we can find him." he grabbed the bags and told everyone to wrap it up.

Paul walked out of the efficiency and looked into the night sky, "I will find you. You can't hide now."

Paul stood 5'11, 235 lbs, just had his fiftieth birthday two weeks ago. His rounded face and chubby gut, was balanced out by his broad shoulders. He shaved his head and dyed his facial hair to appear younger. His dark walnut skin complexion and blood shot eyes made him appear high or drunk. His father was a good friend to the King and after his death, he looked up to the King as a father figure. To make it worst, the General was a childhood friend.

He rubbed his right hand on his five o'clock shadow and stood in front of the pickup truck. He lit his cigarette. "Wataami." he scratched his head. The sound of the driver door opened. "What are you thinking?" he sat in the driver seat.

"You think he did it?" he looked at Paul.

"Of course, and we are going to kill him." he tossed the bags on the seat and slowly slid in.

"Well, hey I'm ready for whatever." he cranked the truck and drove off.

Paul's cell phone rang. "Hello."

"Hey Paul, we have your cousin here in bad shape he claim he was attacked. But his memory is a little fuzzy."

"Ask him if Kalargo was around?" he leaned forward in hopes that Kalargo's name would come up. He slammed his palm on the dash board.

"At the moment, he is going in and out of conscious. He was hit pretty hard. He got a huge bloody hole across his head. If you want, you can meet us at the hospital." the voice said.

"I'm on the way." he waved for Wataami to head to the hospital.

He ran through the hospital doors in search for his cousin. "Where is he?"

The nurse held him back, "Sir!"

Paul passed her desk looking for him.

"Who are you looking for?" she asked.

"Gene!" he yelled his name. He slammed his fist against the glass. "Gene!" his eyes watered. He grabbed his shirt. Gene's body was covered underneath a white sheet with stains of blood."Noooo!" he screamed out loud.

The doctor came out, "Paul, I'm so sorry. We tried everything to save him."

Paul wiped his face with his palms in disbelief. "Can I see him?" he clinched his arms around his chest. His tears fell as he balled his fist in anger.

The doctor slowly removed the sheet.

Paul fell apart. "No, no! Gene, oh my God!" He walked out of the room and leaned on the wall with his head in his hands.

Wataami hugged him, "I swear we are going to get to the bottom of this. I promise. Someone knows something." they walked him out of the hospital.

"He was such a good kid. He bothered no one. He did not deserve this. Especially like this." Paul's breathing was heavy. He swallowed the pain that held his throat together. He sat in the truck and just leaned his head on the head rest. His eyes closed as the truck sped off in to the early morning sun. The moist breeze across his face calmed him. He was quiet.

"That motherfucka! When I get my hands on him!" Paul rested his head and closed his eyes with anger.

*   *   *

Indian Ocean
U.S.S. Carl Vinson
Two weeks later

The aircraft carrier was loud and very much alive at three o'clock in the morning. Kalargo rested in his rack below deck. He was so amazed to how this huge ship of five thousand sailors operates at sea. The coffin like racks were small, but he had his privacy. He was restricted to the sleeping quarters and the chow hall. He had seen the dentist and had his chipped jagged teeth removed. The food was awesome and every once in awhile airman Crockett would give him a tour of the ship, go to the gym, and hang out aft of the ship to watch the airplanes land.

"Knock knock, it's your tour guide." Airman Crockett said.

Kalargo pull his curtain back just enough to talk to the airman. They both laughed.

"Hey, I'm going to breakfast in a couple of minutes, you going?" Airman Crockett said.

He pulled the curtain back further and smiled.

"Damn, I can't help but to ask what the hell happened to you?" Airman Crockett held his hands up like he had given up on guessing.

Kalargo crawled out of his rack and sighed. He stretched his body using the adjacent racks in front of him, kept his voice down. He did not want to wake the other sailors. He looked at the airman and just shook his head. "Let's just say that sometimes there are things you can't talk about." his accent with missing teeth was like a drunken daffy duck. He slid his pants on and pulled a fresh t shirt from beneath his pillow. "What they got for breakfast?" he grabbed his tooth brush.

"Well, there are certain foods that I just can't talk about?" they both burst out grinning.

The chow line was short and the food was fresh. They sat down across from each other. "You ever get tired of being at sea?"

"Hmmm, Well once you get used to it, it doesn't bother you too much. Besides, I'm never really at sea for long any way. I'm usually on land. This is temporary for me. Now these guys, Yes, I do feel for them. They are actually stationed on the ship for two or more years." he slid a fork of eggs in his mouth. He shook his head. "Now that would take some getting used to."He pointed the fork at him. "By the way, you should be going home in a day or two." he took a drink of his orange juice.

Kalargo eyes got big. "Wow."

"That's what I said. Your first catapult from an aircraft carrier, not many people in the world get to experience that." he looked at him. "You are talking about a roller coaster ride."

He looked at the airman in the middle of his bite of his pancakes. "What is that like?"

The airman slowly took a bite of his pancake. "Some things a man just can't talk about." they both started laughing.

"Well at the moment we are in the Indian ocean. When you take off from here you go to an island call Diego Garcia. From there you will fly to the Philippines. From what I understand, this seems to be some kind of a special trip." he sat his drink down and cripples his lips. "Man, who are you? I've seen some weird shit come on this ship, but you got to be the most interesting. You was not pick up from an airport and you not going through customs to get in to the Philippines." before he could continue his theory. He stopped him.

"Listen, you seem like a cool dude. Keep in touch, when you get out of the military, I should be able to tell you a great story, but for right now, for my safety and yours. I rather not talk about it." he held out his hand to shake on it.

The airman sighed and looked him in his eyes. He shook his hand. "You know what. I normally stick to my business. But..." he was stuck for words. "...I have never seen a brother not in uniform who was giving the level of respect like you have gotten from the officers on board this ship. I hope you can understand how intriguing this is." he stood from the table. "And you look like hell."

"Yes, now that I can understand. And believe me, the day I tell you my story, it will blow your mind." Kalargo said.

The next morning on the flight deck just before the sun could light the sky. Kalargo was breathing heavy. He had every right to be nervous about taking off of a flight deck that was only three hundred yards long. In a plane that looks too slow to take off. He walked over to the island of the flight deck with the airman. "So this is what you do?"

"Yep... I make sure there are no obvious problems by doing an inspection, no leaks, and etc." they casually walked around the C-2 turbo prop cargo plane. He pulled and tugged on various parts; check the lights on the wings.

A group of other passengers arrived. The load master started to load the plane with cargo and people. He called Kalargo over to him. The sounds of jet engines were getting louder as they prepared for their first flight of the day. It felt like a real airport. Everyone had a job to do. The aircrafts were tied down with big chain to keep them from rolling when the ship rolls. He saw mechanics standing on top of park aircraft.

He walked over to the tail gate of the C-2. He noticed that all the seats were facing aft of the plane. He thought it was odd. He was giving a pair of cranial with ear muffs to protect his hearing.

"You can sit wherever you like. He slowly walked over to a window seat. The airman boarded the plane.

"It was a pleasure to see you again." they shook hands.

"Be safe, I'll call when I'm back in the Philippines." the thunderous sound of the first jet had catapulted off the deck. The auxiliary unit was ignited and the interior lights come on. The airman walked off the ramp to proceed with his duties.

The load master gave instructions on the procedure for takeoff. The C-2 taxied slowly into position. It was two aircrafts from takeoff. After four minutes, he can see the men standing around the flight deck. He noticed how the men in yellow jerseys had control of the take off.

Suddenly, the power of the turbo props were in full throttle, the loadmaster held his hand up, and when it dropped everyone leaned forward as far as they could. The force from takeoff pulled him so hard. It felt like his eyes were being pulled through his flight deck goggles. In a matter of seconds, it was over. The C-2 was slung off the aircraft carrier as if it was in a sling shot. It felt like a violent rollercoaster ride. He felt the plane dip towards the ocean once it left the deck. But it slowly climbed, as he gained confidence that he was going to be ok.

He looked out of his window as the plane banked a left and climbed several thousand feet. He could not believe that he was just on that tiny aircraft carrier.

Chapter 23

The long flight to the Philippines had achieved body aches from sitting on the uncomfortable ride. They landed once in Diego Garcia to fuel, two hour delay, and back over the Indian Ocean. He leaned forward and rubbed his neck, and stretched. Earlier the loadmaster handed out brown lunch bags filled with a fruit, cold cut sandwich, and drink. He sighed as he opened his cold cut. The loadmaster master walked through to inspect.

"Hey, how much longer?" he chewed a big bite of his sandwich.

"Six more hours before we arrive, you can stand up and stretch your legs." it was like he was giving permission to run free.

The sun slowly dipped below the clouds, and drifted below the horizon. He could see lights on the islands below. He knew they were getting close.

He had dosed off for several hours and was awaken by the wheels touching the run way of Cubi Point Naval base.

The aircraft taxied toward VRC-50's hanger bay. He unbuckled his harness when it came to a complete stop.

"Welcome to Cubi Point boys and girls." the loadmaster said as the ramp lowered to the ground.

He grabbed his back pack and stepped off the ramp. The night sky was clear of clouds and warm. He inhaled deeply, smiled, and gave a sigh of relief.

"Never been so happy to be back in the Philippines." he pulled his satellite phone to call Jamie.

"Kalargo! Kalargo! Over here!" he heard his name being called. He really felt like he was hearing things. So he dialed the area code 808.

"Kalargo!" he looked beyond the flight line towards the parking lot.

"Holy shit." he could not believe who was waiting for him. "What the hell you doing here?" he walked through the gate. He hugged Jenko and patted him on the back.

"Long time no see. As soon as Na Min told me you were flying in. I rushed over to pick you up. How was your flight?" Jenko said.

"Damn I can't believe this." Jenko stopped him before he tossed his back pack on the back. He looked at him."What the hell happened to you." he noticed he spoke funny. "Damn! What the hell happened to your mouth?"

Kalargo tossed his belongings on the back seat, rubbed his left index across his eyebrow. "It's a long story, just thank God I'm here to see you." he sighed.

Jenko seen in his facial expression that he had been through a lot and probably did not want to talk about it. "Well Maria has cooked dinner for us. I know you must be starving." he drove off.

"Maria?"

"Oh, I never told you. It's hard to believe, but I'm a married man now. And she is pregnant, with a boy." he sounded so excited.

"Wow, so you found the right one?" That's incredible." He thought about Jamie. "Nothing wrong with that..." He smiled. "...I got plans to marry Jamie. She does not know it yet. I think I'm going to pop the question when I get back." he looked out of the window.

Jenko looked ever so happy.

They arrived to Jenko's house on a small farm. The smell of pork adobo lingered the air.

"Smells good." Kalargo said.

As they approached the door it swung open. "Daddy!" Two kids ran out to grab his pants leg. They both rode his leg as he walked in the house.

"And these are my kids from... you remember Heather?"

"Oh, yes I do. Whatever happened to her?

"She passed away from a car accident."

"So sorry to hear that, I never knew." they walked in as he dragged his way in.

"Ok that's enough of that. I told you about doing that." his wife walked in from the kitchen with a kitchen towel across her shoulder.

"And this is my lovely wife, Maria." she looked hot as hell, just beautiful with almond eyes, dark complexion. They shook hands.

"Dinner will be served shortly." Maria said.

"I have to wash my hands." they both pointed in the same direction to the bathroom.

After dinner they sat out on the back porch and caught up on things, and tossed back a couple of beers.

"Kalargo." Maria interrupted their conversation, "I put a blanket, towels and a new toothbrush in the third room on the left. Feel at home." she stepped out from the sliding glass and gave Jenko a hug and a kiss.

"Me and the kids are going to bed now. I'll cook breakfast in the morning. What time is your flight?" She asked.

"Eleven." Kalargo looked over his shoulder.

She entered the house, "You like your eggs any certain way?"

"Scrambled."

*   *   *

Honolulu, Hawaii
Honolulu International airport

Jamie ran towards Kalargo with open arms, huge grin, with tears in her eyes. They hugged like there was no end. She removed her shades and grabbed his face and pulled him as close as she could. Their lips were like one. Her makeup smeared from her crying.

"I'm so happy you are back! I love you so much." she was so happy just to be able hold him tight again, to rub her hands across his body. But she took a step back and got a closer look at his face. She burst into tears. The scars on his face were horrible sign of the adversity he had been through. With her thumbs she pushed his upper lip up and his front teeth was gone. She was devastated.

"What happened to you?"

He grabbed her face with his hands, wiped her tears and pushed them from her face. It was obvious that she was hurt that he had been through a lot.

"Baby, I thought you were not coming back. I thought you had died over there." Her face frowned with horror, sadness and empathy.

He picked her up in to the air and sucked on her navel and hugged her tighter. "I would have let nothing stop me from coming back." he spun her around in a circle. "I love you more than anything." In the middle of the airport, he got down on one knee.

"Will you marry me?" there was a pause.

She almost lost her mind. She was scared to say yes. But knew the word no was not an option. She jumped up and down.

"Yes, yes of course I will!" the crowd in the airport exploded with joy and applause.

They went home to celebrate.

*   *   *

One month later

Kalargo stood in front of the bathroom mirror admiring his new set of teeth. He sighed. It was amazing how they replaced his teeth and they look better than his originals. His favorite song came on the radio. He closed his eyes and repeated the lyrics. He snapped his fingers and danced his way out of the bathroom.

"This is my song." he thought about how happy Jamie is to be engaged. They would grow old and live happy. He grabbed his backpack and dumped everything on the bed. He decided to give her the engagement ring. He noticed the ten page letter that he had not read yet. It brought back bad memories. He sighed and held the ring in one hand and the letter in the other. He felt like he had an obligation to take care of, just the mere fact that he made it back. It could have easily been him to die over there.

"And he was married." so he knew that his wife was waiting for that one day when her husband would walk through those doors and say. "Honey, I'm home."

"Wow..." he looked at the clock. He had time to book a flight to Chicago and later meet with Jamie. So he did.

Chicago, Ill.
Two days later

He landed at the O'Hare International airport. It was 23 degrees with snow flurries falling like feathers. It was five days before Christmas and his round trip ticket leaves tomorrow morning.

"Taxi!" he climbed in the back seat and gave the address to the driver. "Is it far from here?" he closed the door.

"About forty five minutes." he drove off.

He had no idea what to think, to do or how she would react. He got nervous. He sighed and rested his head on the seat. He pulled the letter out of his back pocket and unfolded it. He felt wrong for wanted to read it. But his curiosity asked him, 'who is this fellow?'

He was interrupted, "First time in Chicago?"

Kalargo was sad the first five lines had his eyes wet."Yes, it's my first time to Chicago."

"Must be a very short visit to travel without luggage." he pushed through traffic and jumped on the expressway.

This letter was so hard to read because this could have been him. It was him, but, he felt lucky that the General saw something in him to save his life. He scratched his forehead. The bond he had with his wife was an admirable relationship. He thought of Jamie. Just to know that you have someone waiting for you under these circumstances.

He started to sweat. He let the window down for fresh air. He folded the letter, closed his eyes and shoved it into his inner coat pocket. It was too emotional. It brought back unwanted memories. He felt the pain through his words. He had no idea how to explain any of this.

The taxi exited off the expressway and maneuvered its way into a nice middle class neighborhood. He wanted to put the letter in the mail box and ride off. He sighed and couldn't do that. He promised if he made it home he would bear the bad news.

He sat in the car as he looked the house over. Snow covered the lawn and roof; he could see the lights on the Christmas tree in the window.

"Well this is the address, right?" the driver turns around to
verify with him. "That will be sixty dollars, cash or credit?"

He gave him a hundred dollar bill. "Keep the change." sitting there in awe... He tried to open the door, but it felt stuck. He cleared his throat and pushed the door of the taxi open. He slowly walked up the walk way. He heard the taxi drive off and he felt alone and cold. He slowly and softly pushed the door bell. But to no avail, it was the loudest door bell he had ever heard. He could hear the footsteps walking towards the door. She was talking to someone.

"Can I help you?" she held the cordless phone to her ear.

He wanted to run. "Hi." he thought about how to start this conversation. "Are you..." He cleared his throat, "Margret?"

She told the person on the phone to hold on and put the phone behind her back.

"Tim sent me." before he could say another word.

"Hey, I'll call you right back." she looked him in his eyes and tilted her head. "How do you know him?" she became defensive at the door.

"Well I met him in Africa and..." he didn't want to just give her the letter and walk away. She deserved more than that. He was getting cold as he stood outside. He clutched his hands together.

"He wanted me to give you something." he blew on his hands to warm them.

She looked around for his car. "Where is your car?" she looked down the street.

"Do you mind if I come in for hot tea?" he said.

"Yeah, come on in." she stepped aside as he passed her and waited for her to offer him a seat.

Moments later she returned with two cups of tea and sugar. "Have a seat, your name?" she sat across from him.

"My name is Kalargo." he looked around the room at the pictures of her and Tim.

"Well..." he reached in his coat pocket and pulled out the letter. "He told me to deliver this letter to you." he sipped on his tea.

She knew that this could not be good news. Her eyes pooled of tears as she reached for the letter. She started to breath heavy. She cried, but held it together. She slowly unfolded the letter. The first stream of tears rolled down her face like acid. She stood up and walked towards the bay window.

Kalargo grabbed a Kleenex tissue and gave it to her.

She dropped the first page to the floor. She held her mid-section as the third page fell to the floor. The loud moan of a broken heart can be felt in the living room. Her heavy breathing became intense. She grabbed her chest as the sixth page floated towards the floor. She fell to her knees before it landed with an outburst of anger. The last page was crimpled up in the palm of her fist.

"Nooooo!" she begged with her head down. "Nooooo! I can't believe this." she looked up at the ceiling.

Kalargo walked over to her and picked her up from the floor, not knowing what to do.

"Oh my God! What Am I going to do? He was my everything." he put her on the coach and gave her more tissue. She cried hard and long. Two hours had passed and he felt like he should leave.

"I am so sorry for your lose." he stood up. "Is there anything I can do for you before I leave?" he headed towards the door.

"On the shelf, there is a book..." she pointed. "These will be the longest days." Her moans were just as painful to hear as to watch her endure his death. "Can you help me find it?" she walked into the bathroom and slammed the door. Her cries crew louder.

He held his hands up in a desperate attempt to quickly find this book. He found it and pulled it down from the fourth shelf from the top. It was very dusty and something was wedged between the pages. He opened it, as the pages cracked apart from years of being unused.

The book contained several letters and a key. Just before he was going to tell her that he had found it. He noticed the names on the letters. He thought it was strange.

"Bradley Son Chi." he looked at the address. "From South Korea?" he recognized the name, but could not put it together. He heard the bathroom door open. He quickly tucked the envelopes in his coat pocket. His mind was racing. His hands shuck of fear. Just in time, he turned around.

"Here it is, I found It." he cleared his throat and sighed. He was really ready to leave.

She grabbed the book and took the key down to the basement. The key was to a safe hidden behind a metal locker.

He called for a taxi and stood in the bay window.

"Kalargo!" she screamed for him. He ran down the stairs. "Yeah, you called."

There she was trying to move the metal cabinets that blocked the safe. "Can you help me move this?"

"Of course." With a little extra man power, the safe was cleared.

She slid the key in, turned it, not knowing what to expect, she slowly opened it. Papers, bank accounts, she stood up and walked towards the light.

She dropped the first paper to the floor. She quickly pulled another. She could not believe her eyes, four bank accounts in Europe and one in the Cayman Islands with a total of three million dollars. She cried. Beneath the papers were three bundles of cash. She looked up at him.

"This is for you."

He stood back and refused. "No, that's all yours." he heard the taxi blow the horn. The bundle of cash was ten thousand. He did not feel right accepting her money. She thanked him for doing what he did. He hugged her and said good bye.

*   *   *

Honolulu, Hi

One year later

The organ played, "Here comes the bride." The beautiful fall weather was perfect, partly cloudy with a breeze from the west. The open windows of the church gave an outdoor feel. Their friends flew in from around the world. Her mom and dad were very proud of them both.

She stood at the altar in a stunning white gown with crystal studs that lined her mid-section. Her veil sheered her face as she looked down and rubbed her stomach. Her amorous glow was like a rainbow.

Kalargo stepped up to the altar to Jenko and shook his hand and congratulated him, and stepped aside.

Behind them in the first three rows sat his father, he was so proud, his only son. His memories of how he raised him from a kid to a man frequently came to mind. The years went by so fast. The sound of the organ stop playing, the four ceiling fans turned in sync. Kalargo sighed and grabbed her hand. She looked over her shoulder.

The priest began his sermon and moments had passed before he knew it, he was reaching into his chest pocket for his vows. He cleared his throat and read from the index card.

"Jamie... I stand here today in front of our world of peers and love ones. Today is that day that we have dreamed about." he sighed and held back his tears. "Today, we love each other like we did four years ago. I gave you my heart, honesty, loyalty, and most of all my love. I've made it my duty to cherish you and never let you down. No matter what our differences are. Nothing comes before our love."

Her tears fell steady. She knew he would make a great husband.

He put the card in his pocket. "Jamie, I can't live without you. You are the piece of my puzzle that completes my life."

The priest was crying when he asked for the ring, and Jenko gave it to Kalargo. The five carat ring was attached to the three carat engagement ring. The I do's was said and simple French kiss followed.

Hours later

The wedding reception was held at their new Tuscany designed, five bedroom home, the four bathrooms were designed from a magazine, and the three car garage could fit a trailer. The fitness room was the size of the average living room, and the infinity pool that was shared with tropical fish that over looked the Pacific Ocean would give a person with Down syndrome a seizure. It was furnished with foreign interior decor; with French doors, as well as granite and moldings were throughout the mansion.

Their friends and family enjoyed the catered food, fine wine from France and the smell of scented candles.

"Toast! Toast!" They chanted.

He stood up holding his glass in the air."Well, he looked around the spacious living room. The waiters were bringing food from the kitchen."Where is my wife?" the crowd laughed.

"Jamie my dear, there she is..." she walked over to him and put her arms around his waist. She smiled from ear to ear. "I want to give thanks to the one guy that made all of this possible." he pointed to Na Min and his wife that sat next to him on the German chocolate love seat. His receding grey hair line gave his age away. He held a dinner plate in his left hand and a fork in the other. He chewed like a bull. He stuck his fork straight up and down in his potato salad and grabbed his glass of Genifer and orange juice to raise it up in the air.

"I stand here today and I can honestly say... You." he pointed. "I give you my heart and respect, blood, and tears, without you... Who knows where me and my uncle." he pointed to Mugumbi and Yuki."Oh... by the way, I include Yuki in this toast. She introduced us to her father when we were in desperate need of help in a foreign country that treated us like aliens." He laughed and the crowd followed. He sighed. His eyes became red as his tears of joy streamed his face.

"I just want to say thanks and..." he wiped his face with the pit of his elbow. "I'll never forget. My door is always open to you guys."

Later that afternoon the crowd slowly departed, most of the remaining watched movies, or sports in separate rooms.

"Oh my God, I have to put this in my photo album." Jamie said.

Yuki sipped on her vodka and cranberry, tipsy as she could be."What happened to last year's photos? I did not get a chance to see them. You guys went to Costa Rica, Panama and Peru, right?"

Jamie quickly directed her to the lower drawer of the entertainment center.

"Here?" Yuki asked. She searched and found more than she had asked for, lifting the green sparrow albums that contain the three letters from her father Bradley Son Chi.

She paused and wondered why her father's name would appear on these envelopes. She looked at the date. It was over thirty years ago. She rubbed her hands across them, and grabbed her chest. She looked over her shoulder and noticed that everyone was deep into laughter. She quickly tucked them. "Yes, I found them." she walked back to her seat with the photo album close to her chest. Her heart was pounding, but her body language was undetected. She sat next to her husband who was laughing. She smiled and rejoined the conversation.

Yuki's pink blouse and loose white pants matched her three inch white bamboo open toe shoes. She sighed as she opened the album. She looked at Kalargo and Jamie, and asked herself, 'What the hell is going on?'

The letters bulged her pants and blouse enough to occupy her mind. She tapped her left foot nonstop and sighed again. No longer interested in the album, but pretended very well... "This is...a nice picture. What kind of camera you took this with?"

"Look." she showed Mugumbi.

A whisper in a back room didn't go unnoticed. "Congratulations girl..." she gave Jamie a hug. "I am so, so proud of you, look at this house." Stacy looked up at the vaulted ceilings and over her shoulder. "I am so jealous." she said sarcastically. They both peeked around the corner into the living room like they were up to no good.

"Oh my God, he wants to marry me girl." Stacy danced frantically with joy.

"Do it Stacy..." she urged her. They held hands to her chest, and leaned against the wall for hope, and a prayer that everything goes through. Her eyes became tearful. "Don't cry, I know he will, listen. You were the one that said you both are a perfect match. Also, no one else can understand you like he does." they both sighed at the same time and rejoined the reception.

Jenko stepped to Kalargo the sound of their glasses chattered as they touched.

"I got to tell you... I thought you would never tie the knot." they both stood overlooking the living room from the stairs. "You have really come a long way. I am..." he swallowed his pride and true jealousy, "…very proud of you."

"Thanks, you have always been a friend since we were kids in South Korea." he gave him a hug, and patted him on the back.

Jenko looked at his watch. "Well, it's also about that time."

"So soon..." Kalargo sighed and wished he had more time.

Finally they said their goodbyes.

Chapter 24

Three weeks later

The first class flight back to South Korea was smooth. While Mugumbi slept the entire way, Yuki did not get a wink. Her burning desires to read her father's letters were like fire ants in her pants. She sighed and let the air vibrate her lips. She looked below out the passenger window at Seoul. She put the airline magazine in the slot behind the seat in front of her, and waited for their landing.

She had not opened the letters, but every moment of every day she looked at them, held them in her hand, and at times carried them in her purse as a sentimental object. Another week had passed when Mugumbi returned from a trip exhausted. He kicked off his shoes at the door.

"Hey..." he planted a big kiss on her forehead and then her lips.

"Wow." he looked down at his watch. "Mail came already?" he put his carryon bag on the kitchen table.

She smiled like a grown up would with child like proclivities. "No actually..." she paused and thought about how she acquired them. She sighed and pushed her right index finger across the white table cloth, and proceeded to tiptoe her fingers to her tea cup. She carefully sipped a little. She thought she could think of a quick lie, but to no avail. Her mouth open and nothing came out.

He flipped over the letters and read the names and addresses. "Wrong address?" he frowned with a surprise look on his face. He lifted one of them to verify what he thought he had read. "Chicago?" he looked at her.

She slowly looked up at him. "Look at the date." she insisted.

"Where did you get these?" he placed them down on the table.

She took a big gulp of her tea and held her blow fish like cheeks until she swallowed. "What else do you see? Anything that would ..." she twisted her neck a little to the left and then to the right, before she got on his nerves, he interrupted her.

"Ok it was sent to Chicago from South Korea. It's over twenty years old and it's not yours. So what are you doing with it?" he walked away to fix a sandwich.

"You see the sender's name?"

He spoke over his shoulder from the kitchen. "What about it?"

She sighed heavily. "These were sent by my father."

He stood with the refrigerator door open. "What! Your father is Na Min. What are you talking about?" he pulled out a loaf of wheat bread, cold cuts and condiments.

"Listen I told you he adopted me, my father was his partner, and he died in a shootout." She frowned and squinting her eyes. "You know a fallen hero." She leaned back into the chair, proud.

He leaned on the door entrance to the kitchen and took a huge bite into his honey mustard, turkey cold cut. "This is good." he mumbled. "So how long have you had these letters? You seem like it's all new to you." he looked down at the dark wooden floor. A couple of drops of honey mustard fell between his dusty brown leather sandals. "Damn..." he noticed he didn't miss his white shirt. He sighed.

"You think I should open them?"

He tossed the last of the sandwich in his mouth and shrugged his shoulders upward. "It's not like you would get in any trouble."

She sighed with excitement, but thought about it, just before she slid her index finger to open it.

"So where did you get them?"

She stopped. "If I tell you, I would have to kill you."

He sarcastically threw up his hands. "Ok, Ok I understand. I don't want to know. I love you. It's no need to kill me." he laughed and walked out of the kitchen.

Days had passed before she opened the letters. She carefully pulled the pages from the envelope. She stopped and quickly wanted to make sure that she had them in order by date. "Damn!" she put them in order and opened the first one by its date.

"Well daddy, these are your last words. So what do you have to say?" When her eyes begin to read, her lips spoke silently. "Wow..." she continued to read.

She stopped after the first page, front and back. She rested her soft fist on her forehead. She paused, and looked at the date on the envelope, then sipped on her cold tea, her mouth crimpled in disgust for a fresh pot, but the words on paper paralyzed her. She sighed and struggled to put the first page down. She quickly flipped the third page over and read it like a romance novel. She stood up and walked over to the bay window with her hand over her lips. She sat on the ledge with her legs into her chest. She pulled her long sky blue dress between her legs to get comfortable. So far, her mother had died in a car accident and he blamed himself. He had tried to explain to her that he no longer had anything to do with his previous wife and son. But when she had come looking for him she thought he invited her. And when she found out that he had previously married an African woman, her true racist tongue lashed out at him in disgust. She thought he was in a hotel with her. No matter what he said, she insisted on meeting him. The more he told her it was a bad idea. The more she felt like she was with him. Convinced that he was cheating on her, she drove the lonely dark road across the Sierra Mountains from Sacramento to Lake Tahoe on highway 50.

Yes it was true that his ex-wife had come to Nevada from Africa. She was dying of cancer and begged him to take their son while she continued with chemo therapy. He took out a second mortgage on his home of eighty thousand dollars and told them he never wanted to see them again. They were embarrassing him.

She had beaten the cancer and met a wealthy Caucasian businessman and moved to Asia and never heard from her again. He regretted his actions, losing his wife and a son; all in one month bothered him. Several years later, the cancer had come back stronger. She died asking for him.

"Wow, I have a brother." she looked at the date again and counted her fingers. "I was three years old." The fourth page floated to the bottom of the floor board. Her eyes burned of tears, and pages lay scattered on the floor beneath her feet. She used her dress to wipe her eyes and nose. It was too much for her, she had to take a break.

But the seventh page had her wanting to know more. She walked over to the kitchen, poured a cup of tea with a page in one hand and pot in the other. He searched for his son to unite them, but the damage had been done.

The last page fell to the floor. She was hurt with anger that boiled in her mid section. She just could not believe that she had a brother. "Damn!"

Mugumbi came into the living room. "What's wrong?"

He saw that she was upset and gave her a hug. She burst out into tears like a broken dam. She looked at him with her lips on his cheek and could not tell him, not yet. She hugged him tighter. He rubbed her back and comforted her.

She desperately wanted to know more about her brother and father. She knew how difficult Koreans are and can relate to how her father's wife would not have taken this lightly. Most Koreans are never exposed to any black people. They look down on their own kind for having too much dark skin. Considered dirty, untrustworthy peasants, to this day some still believe that blacks have tails like animals, of course something that was put into their heads by others. The derogatory comments from her friends and strangers when she first met Mugumbi were none stop. People whispered when they were in public. They feared walking close to him thinking his dark skin would dirty them. It was fortunate that she had traveled and lived in Africa. No matter how upsetting it was, she shut them out, but to turn your back on your own son had to be painful for her father. She asked herself, how he could have done such a thing.

She looked at the remaining envelopes on the table with fear, and turned her head away, scared of what was to come. She never thought of the consequences of reading these letters or the emotional part of snooping through someone else's mail. But this is history, her history. The missing chapters of her life are in these letters. She had had enough for now. She slowly walked into the bedroom and crawled under the blankets and closed her eyes and forced herself to sleep.

*   *   *

Honolulu, Hawaii

Two months since their marriage Kalargo's double vision came and went. But the pain behind and above his eyes was almost unbearable. The pressure of the headaches felt like his eyes were pulsating. Lately he wore dark shades to reduce the sensitivity. He stood in front of his car with hands on the hood for support.

"Jamie!" he quickly tried to return into the house.

She found him passed out in his rose garden. "Kalargo!" she ran over and lifted his head. "Kalargo!" she dialed 911 from her cell phone. His eyes had rolled to the back of his head. She tried to lift his head to comfort him.

Later that afternoon Dr. Conway came out to the visiting room. "We are doing everything we can. Your husband suffered from an aneurysm. Now there is a new treatment called coil remobilization or what we call endovascular coiling. It sounds difficult but it's an easy procedure. He'll be up and running in no time." he raised his eyebrows with concern. "However, we are also doing more test to find out what caused the aneurysm."

She slowly wiped her tears. She was alone and scared. She spoke with her hands over her mouth. "Is he going to be ok?" she sighed nervously and wiped her face.

Dr. Conway looked at his watch. "Listen... relax, I'm going to prepare for surgery and ..." he comforted her that everything will be fine. "It should not take... give or take six hours. I'll have a nurse give you food, pillow and a blanket." they gave a grim smile and prepared themselves for surgery.

Jamie woke up nervously and concerned. Her watch had to be wrong or she over slept, eight hours had passed and no one was there to explain how successful the surgery went. She stood and tossed the charcoal grey wool blanket on the pillow. "Excuse me!"

The nurse placed the earpiece of her phone on her left shoulder.

"Is Mr Choi out of surgery?"

The nurse gave her the index finger in a polite way, a gesture to quietly say hold on. "I'm pretty sure... let me page Dr. Conway."

She sighed and tapped her watch and compared it to the clock on the wall. "Hmmm... same time." she walked over to the water fountain.

"Mrs. Choi..."

She quickly turned around with dripping water from her bottom lip. She used her forearm to dry her mouth.

"Did I say it correctly?"

"Yes" she nodded her head anxiously.

The doctor approached her with his mask ruffled at the bottom of his neck. "You can see your husband now."

"Thank you Lord." she wobbled her way toward his room. Her stomach protruded her maternity dress, adding a bad night of sleep, she felt awful. The nurse pulled the curtain and there he lay. His head was wrapped with a bandage. She wanted to cry. "Kalargo..." she cautiously approached him. "Can he hear me?"

"Yes, he might be a little out of it, but he'll come to soon." The nurse placed his medical chart at the end of the bed.

"Baby, I'm right here." She held his hand. He responded by squeezing her hand and smiled. "How are you feeling?"

He moaned, "A huge headache."

"You'll be out of here in a couple of days." She assured him. They both smiled and couldn't wait.

Two weeks later

The phone rang and she answered, "Hello."

Dr. Conway greeted her. "Mrs. Choi, how are you doing?"

She responded with a pregnant pain and awe, "Could be better, one moment." She took the cordless phone to him and left the room. She returned with hot tea for the both of them.

"Well I have an appointment for tomorrow at 3pm." Kalargo carefully grabbed his tea cup.

"Follow up?"

"He just wanted me to come for blood work. He asked if you could drive me. I guess I should not be driving yet," he sipped his tea like a kitten laps hot water, "Hot."

She agreed, "Well you are still on medication." They both sipped their tea.

Inside the Dr.'s office was cold and uninviting, white painted walls with large photos of anatomy parts of the human body. The medical table he sat on had a white wax sheet of paper that rolled out and thrown away after each use. Jamie sat next to him in a small spin around chair that glides across the floor. After looking at the posters their eyes connected, they both sighed just before the doctor opened the door.

"Hello hello," he carried his medical chart that rested on top of his belt buckle, "how do you feel?"

"Well a little under the weather, but ok."

He removed the bandage from his head, "Not bad, not bad at all," he tossed it in the red hazardous container, "its healing quit well, don't need that anymore."

He pulled out his mini flash light and raised his left eye lid, and then the right eye lid. "Open your mouth."

He thought about the doctors in Africa that grossed him out.

"Lift your tongue, say ahhh." He pulled out another instrument to examined his ears. "Do you feel anything here," he rubbed behind his neck, "what about here?" he closely examined the staples from his surgery."

He sighed and leaned on the medical counter, "Well, your blood work has come back," he looked them both in the eyes, "I have some good news and bad news."

"Well, I just had an aneurysm, so it can't be any worse than that," he looked at Jamie as she grasp his hand, "so give me the bad news first."

He paused, "Well Mr. Choi, you are HIV positive."

His eyebrows dropped like a bridge as his eyes fought to hold them open. "The good news, with the new technology and treatment that we have today, you will be able to survive and live a long life."

She grabbed her belly and fell on to him. She had a one night stand and must have given it to him. But she had no way of telling him, at least for now. She held this secret until she could reveal it to him.

"Mrs. Choi, you would have to undergo test. It would be for your protection, if you are negative you can start protecting yourself and the baby." He pulled out the needle and the tube to take her blood. She cried. She felt like she had let him down. The room seems to get smaller. The nurse came in to draw her blood.

His tears fell as he rubbed her belly. He put his arms around her and hoped that he did not destroy his family. He tried to think how this could have happened to him. She was the only person he had sex with. He just could not understand. He felt betrayed as his blood boiled.

The doctor handed them both a napkin. After her blood was drawn, they were in the room until they were able to drive home.

Later that night, they lay on the kitchen floor in front of the refrigerator as they cried and held each other. Their bodies were too weak to walk, so they rested. The outburst of frustration and anger from them both, "Why us?!" she pounded the floor and his chest. "Why, why!"

"I know sweetheart." He grabbed her by her head and brought her closer. He rubbed her belly and his tears flowed after he thought of his son.

She grabbed his face, "I love you Kalargo." she wanted to tell him about the affair. "I love you so much." But she could not do it. It was too painful. They felt like broken pieces of a puzzle, shattered glass as the travertine tile welcomed their sorrow. "I am going to die!" she screamed. I can't take pills!" she pounded his chest.

"Don't say that, don't say that!" he looked her in her eyes, "it's not over, you understand me? It has to be another way to take this medicine." She cried uncontrollably. "You may not have been infected." he embraced her, "don't give up on me baby. I can't lose you. I can't."

She lifted her heavy head from his chest, "We've been together more than two years." she just could not tell him about the affair. They cried themselves to sleep.

Hours later, the sound of a loud noise woke Kalargo from his sleep. "What the hell was that?" he stood from the floor. "Jamie!"

He searched the house, "Thank God." he walked into his office. "No!" he yelled. She lay across the floor, blood splatter on the wall. She used his .45 caliber to shoot herself in the mouth.

"My God! Why did you do this," he lifted her head, "Jamie! You did not have to, " he held her in his arms. He shook her hard, "Stupid, stupid thing. You didn't have do this." he reached for the phone that was off the hook on the floor. He punched 911, but he didn't want to live without her. He cried out an uncontrollable burst of anger begging her to come back. He shook her none responsive body.

"Jamie, please!" her blood was all over him. He started CPR and tried to resuscitate her. "No! You are not dead! Now Jamie, you listen to me," he spoke as he pumped down on her chest. "One, two, three, four and blew in to her mouth. After fifteen minutes, he collapsed on top of her.

"Jamie, do not leave me!" he yelled out to her. He lifted his head off of her chest. The sound of the ambulance sirens were getting closer. He thought of the police. He quickly picked up the Chinese mouser Shanei .45 caliber and read it the stencil. "Life or Death...you choose. " His eyes showed fear as he placed the barrel of the gun in his mouth. His hands trembled as he let out a deep sigh. He looked at Jamie.

He squeezed the trigger, 'click, click, click' the gun was empty; she took out the bullets and hid them. Na Min burst into the office as he pulled the trigger continuously.

"What the hell are you doing!" he spoke in Korean. He slapped the gun from his hand and grabbed him tightly.

"She is dead daddy!" he fell over onto her body. "She's gone!" her blue eyes made contact with him for the last time.

"Come on son." he picked him up from behind and walked him in to the living room as the paramedics worked on her and to try to save the baby. They got her to the hospital in time to save the him; she lived on life support for two weeks before she died.

He found out later that she was HIV negative.

Chapter 25

Gambia, Africa

"Your majesty," the servant walked over to the King of Gambia. He lay in bed with two fluffy pillows behind his neck. His body was weak due to an illness. The oxygen mask frequently placed over his nose and mouth to assist his lungs.

"Your breakfast is ready." Paul stood beside his bed with a shiny silver tray and dome. His servant wore all white cotton gloves. He was twenty years younger than the King, but strong and alert.

"Paul." the King called his name and held the oxygen mask in his right hand. The white sheets and pillow cases were neat with minimum disturbance. The King size bed can hold up to four adults, but he was alone. His six wives, thirty two grand-children were murdered over the last fifteen years. General Kakambo-his last brother killed- was his last relative up for the throne. He was unable to have kids.

"Paul, I want you to sit at the table." he gathered enough strength to bring himself to the edge of the bed. Paul quickly sat the tray on the night stand. He lifted him by placing his hands underneath his armpits and raised him slowly. The oxygen tank trailed them as they carefully made their way to the dinner table. His weak bladder soiled his pajamas in the night. He slowly sat down as if he was on a porcupine and sighed like he had finished a marathon. He desperately placed the mask over his nose and mouth.

"Are you having orange juice and fruit punch, your majesty?"

He nodded as the mask fogged. In his left front pocket he pulled out an envelope and tossed it near his silverware. He stared at it. He placed the mask down on the right of his steamy plate of soft scramble eggs, turkey bacon, grits, and wheat toast.

Paul stood near in case he needed to feed him, but not today. He had more energy than usual. He stuffed his food and used both of his hands to bring the glass to his lips. He starred at the envelope and took another sip. He put his palm on the envelope, then sighed, and placed his hand back on the trembling glass. His grey hair was dotted with black strings of hair. His small frame body allowed his veins to show on his hands like roots that crawled from a tree. His throne was in jeopardy. "Where is Akette?"

"Your majesty, he's on his way?" he assured him. "Is there anything I can do for you?"

"Can you bring him home?" Every once in a while, the King asked for someone to bring home a son, but they knew he was the only living relative. He out lived everyone.

"I'm hot." minutes later he was being fanned with huge hand held fans. "Paul," he leaned over. "Can I trust you?" he stopped chewing his food.

Paul looked into the King's eyes and wondered why he would ask such a question.

"They don't want me in power. They have killed every one of them. Do you have any idea whom I'm talking of?" the King ask?

He stood tall and relaxed his posture. The King's left hand pulled his coat and directed him to sit. He refused and looked around the room at the others. No servant sat with the King, never. He's been there more than twenty years as a friend to his deceased father and has never sat with him.

"Sit!" he said with a bent out of shape upper lip.

"Your majesty, I am Paul, your servant," he thought perhaps he was slowly losing his mind. He went down on one knee.

"Can I trust you?" the room was silent. "Has Akette arrived yet? I am waiting on Akette."

Paul took the glass from his hands, "Are you ok your majesty? You can always trust me."

"With my life, I can trust you?" he held Paul hand in his. On behalf of your father I have protected you all of your life. I have kept you from harm's way," he coughed as he reached for his mask and inhaled. "I have never asked of you for anything, however," he had begun to sweat as he inhaled once again. "I know that I can trust you with my life," he grabbed Paul's chin and raised it. "What I want you to do may get you killed."

"Anything your majesty, no matter what it is, I will give my life if that's what it take." Paul said.

He touched his chest and rubbed his left index finger across his tribal marks. His chest rose when he was short of breath. He reached for his mask like he was drowning. "How far away is Akette?"

Paul quickly snapped his fingers at the other servants. "Find him now!"

"Take it easy your majesty, you must not excite yourself."

He found the strength to bring his left hand across the table and violently dragged and threw everything off the table. The loud high pitch sound of silverware and glass scattered the old wooden polished floor. "Bring him home! Akette!" he spoke with the mask just far enough from his mouth to be heard throughout the Palace. He slammed his left fist down, he anguished through his crooked lips and squinted eyes that meant business.

"Please, calm down, this is not good for you to be excited. The doctor said," he was interrupted.

The King raised his index finger, and pointed it at him. "You find him, you find him," his bottom lip trembled. His finger touched his emotional side of him. ''You owe me that much."

Paul wanted to cry as his eyes became wet. He just didn't know what to do. He felt sorry for him.

A loud commotion came from down stairs. The sound of many wild mustangs pounded the wooden stairs. Suddenly, eight men burst into the dinner room. They all pushed and trampled over each other. Their heart beats race all at once. One person spoke for them all. "Your majesty, we have found him."

Akette walked in and noticed the mess on the floor; he tiptoed through and picked up the envelope from the floor. Everyone stood back and gave them privacy. He pulls another folder from his pants. He whispered in his ear and brought a smile to his crooked lips that had been warped like wet mildewed wood. Finally, he gave him the folder. The sound of it being opened echoed the room.

The King read and nodded his head. He closed his eyes and held it close to his face. He reached for his mask and looked up at Akette. Then he read more, and starred
down the long dinner table. He sat the letter on the table faced down. He pulled Akette close and whispered in his ear for nearly fifteen minutes. The room was so quiet, the mice were listening. Akette's eyes opened wide as he looked at Paul. He grabbed his chin and pointed his finger at him. "Paul," he also pulled him close and whispered in his ear. After ten minutes Paul's eyes opened wider than Akette's did.

He pointed his finger at him and reached for the envelope. Akette passed a lit candle to Paul. He held it for the King to burn the letter. The ashes floated to the floor. They lifted him and slowly walked him to his bed with his oxygen tank in tow.

"Don't forget." he said. He crawled beneath the sheets and they tucked him in.

Their last words, "We will never forget your majesty."

He reached beneath his pillow and pulled out an eight by ten manila folder.

"This contains everything you will need, good luck." they both walked out of the room on a mission for the King.

*   *   *

Honolulu, Hi

Kalargo lay in his bed in a dark room for days now, and thought how this could have happened to him. Underneath his blankets, he sighed and moaned. He felt alienated, very different from how he had felt before. He thinks of the millions of people that have died before him. He had not eaten, or shaved in awhile. He felt healthy and normal, but mentally, he felt everyone looked at him differently. He hid in his home, to avoid the mental pain that accompanied the disease.

His wolf man jack beard and hiding in his house would give that illusion of out of sight, out of mind mentality. But, he also knew he had to fight, for his son and his life, it's not the end of the world, and allowing himself to be depressed will kill him before the disease would. All of his phone lines were disconnected; his father came to check on him. He spoke through the door and told him he did not want to be bothered. He wanted to be alone. Him and his new born son, for the sake of his baby boy, he had to snap out of this depression.

He tossed the blanket off of him and opened his eyes. Shadows of the sun danced across his feet as it tried to give light to the room. He sighed as he looked at his parade of prescription bottles that reminded him that he had to daily consume. He shook his head with sadness. His throat was dry, teeth coated with bacteria film from lack of brushing. He crawled out of bed to the floor in a meditation position, afterwards, some martial arts movements to stretch his muscles, and loosen him up. It was good for him; it took the disease off of his mind, so he continued. He sliced the air with hands and kicked vigorously above his head. His muscles began to glaze as he shadow kicked and punched.

He dropped to the floor with his chest inches from touching the carpet and counted his pushups out loud. He rolled over on his back and followed with sit ups. It was then he had realized that he was being too hard on his self, feeling healthy and strong, flexed his muscles as sweat dripped from his nose, chin, eyebrows, and looked at the bottles. He decided that he could live and love his life. "No shame, no surrender," he grabbed his bottle and popped the cap off and tossed his first pill. He snatched his Luke warm bottle of water and chased it with a swallow as he held his head back. He took all of them the same way.

He walked over to the mirror and touched his face. This day will be the beginning. He inhaled deeply and released it slowly. "I can do it."

He rubbed his wolf man jack and picked up his toothbrush. He knew this day will be the first day of his new life.

His son started to cry. He lifted him up and smelt him, "Well, I can always tell when you have made a mess." He smiled and held him inches from his face, with baby talk as he flew him through the air like a plane.

"Yes, I love you. Yes I do." He looked him in his eyes, "I'll never give up on you."

Kalargo jr. smiled, and started to cry again. "Ok, ok, I'll change your diaper; stop being such a cry baby."

*   *   *

Seoul, South Korea

Yuki was finishing the second envelope as she turned the last page over, "Wow, this is interesting." she shook her head and quickly ran into the kitchen and snatched another envelope from the table like it had no right to be there. The table cloth lifted followed by the breeze she created. She put her finger on the date," Yes," and counted the days between the two. She used her fingers to be precise, "exactly forty five days." she cleared her throat and twisted her neck.

"Ok," she opened it and pulled the pages out. The first sentence opened her eyes wide when it said, 'I am going to die over here! I need immediate extraction!'

She carefully read and walked slowly throughout the living room and found herself sitting in front of her tub that she had prepared earlier. The bubbles were fresh and the bath water was just hot enough. She slowly read and removed her clothes. She ran her hand deep in to the water and followed with her feet. She tossed a page to the floor as she dipped her body into the bubbles that came up to her chest. It was almost as if he was whispering in her ear. She felt helpless, that he needed help, "What is going on?"

She folded the pages, placed them aside, overwhelmed and unable to read more. But so far, these letters does not match her adopted father's story of him dying as a hero.

"A great hero," She could not bring herself to finish reading the rest. She slowly drowned her tears away as her head went beneath the water. She came up to breath a couple of times as time slowly passed. She sadly lay in the tub of vanishing bubbles, eyes closed, with her left leg hanging outside the tub, her right knee was just above the water and her chin lined the water line. She had took a hit of heroin, with the elastic still wrapped around her left arm and the needle on the floor on top of the folded pages. She was angry and disappointed that no one seems to listen to him or come to his aid. She could hear the rain drops tap on the window, making it more depressing. She now knew she has a brother somewhere out there.

She slowly went over the story that she had been told. It did not make sense after comparing them to what she had read. "That lying bastard." she nodded off into her high. She wanted answers and deserved to know why. She raised her right arm as the water raced back into the tub. She rubbed her face, but nodded again, leaving her hand resting on her face.

"I should kill that old..." she slurs her words, " ...revenge, and an eye for an eye." she had been told these lies all these years. She took a deep breath and submerged her head below the water line and allowed her bubbles to float to the top.

Mugumbi walked in, "Do you mind if I join you?" with a glass of wine in each hand.

She raised herself up and wiped the water and bubbles from her face. "Of course." it was just in time to hide her tears.

Later that night, she sat at the dinner table holding the cordless phone in her hands. She dialed Na Min's number but ended the call. "What would I say?"

She put the metal extractable antenna between her front teeth. Finally, she built enough courage to actually speak to him. She sighed heavily, ended the call, and threw the phone across the living room, didn't bother to watch it dance across the wooden floor. She folded her arms and buried her face into the pit of her elbow. She felt empty and deceived, but more so, betrayed.

She wanted to know why he would keep her away from her family. "I can't believe that I lived with my father's murderer." she sobbed, and mumbled beneath her breath to promise to confront him with the letters. She used the palms of her hands to push the tears towards her ears. She touched a wallet size photo of her dad and shoved it in her back pocket.

"Honey, are you hungry?" she said loud enough to be heard throughout the house.

*   *   *

Na Min was down on one knee behind his office desk with his left arm half way in the ventilation duck. He pulled out a retractable cable. From his desk he grabbed a brown pouch and took out his snug nose .38 caliber, made sure it was loaded, attached it to the cable and check to see how well it worked.

"Not bad," he pulled it out once again. He tinkered with the door because it didn't close after the cable retracted. He wanted it to close and appear unbothered with. He sighed and decided that he would figure it out later. "Hmmm, how can I make this close and spring back into the wall and look natural?"

He stood up as he held on to the desk for balance, 'I am getting old.' even though he was in great shape. His joints were a little different as the years had passed. He flopped into his chair and looked at the hole in the wall, threw his hands up as in to surrender for now. But that hole in the wall brought back memories of the tunnels that the North Korean agents had built to smuggle, and secretly cross in to South Korea.

These tunnels were well built with sophistication. They were dark, clammy, with dripping water that fell through the cracks, built in the early sixties to infiltrate South Korea. The North Koreans claimed they were for coal mining, however no coal had been found in the tunnels that were dug through granite and painted black to give the appearance of anthracite.

Originally they were built for a military invasion route by North Korea. Each shaft is large enough for an entire infantry division to pass through in one hour, not big enough for tanks or vehicles, but reinforced with concrete, electrical power, and lighting. Weapons storage locations, sleeping quarters, a narrow gauge railway with carts had been installed. He thought about how he had crossed over in tunnels that had not been found.

He looked back at the ventilation duck and something came to his mind, "Hmmm, I think I know how to make this work." He decided to replace it with a modified door that look like a ventilation door. He snapped his finger with a better idea.

His wife knocked on the door before she entered, "Are you busy?"

He quickly moved his chair in front of the hole in the wall.
"Hey honey, how you feeling this morning?"

She sighed as she walked over to his desk, "Have you spoken to Yuki? I think she tried to call, but when I answered, the line was dead." she rubbed her left earlobe to adjust her four carat earring.

"Hey, I have an idea," he stood up, "you still want to go to that coffee shop, you know the one with those bagels that you like?" he kissed her on her lips and rubbed her back as he guided her out of the office.

"Oh wow, it's been awhile since we've been there. What made you think of that place?" she embraced him and rubbed his chest.

"Well, the weather is stunning, and I thought it would be a great time to take advantage of it, you know…" he put his mouth on her earlobe and blew in her ear. She cringed and became so sensitive, "…grab a seat outside and enjoy the view."

"That sounds good, let me get my purse and put a little make up on." she happily dashed into the bedroom.

He quickly returned to his office and replaced the ventilation cover.

"I'm ready." Moments later, she came into his office, "There you are," she paused, he was on the phone.

"Yuki, I was trying to return your call..." he looked up at his wife and frowned, "well, I'll be stepping out for a while, you can call my cell if you need me." he placed the receiver down, grabbed his keys and held them up, "Can't leave without these." as he headed towards the door.

*   *   *

Honolulu, Hi

Paul and Akette sat in an American restaurant for their first time, "So, this is America," Paul held his glass of dry white wine over his lunch.

Akette smiled, "Who would have ever thought." Their table over looked the sand that led to the smashing waves. They sipped and ate until they were content.

"Let me see the manila envelope." Akette requested.

Paul pulled it from a black leather brief. He pulled out pictures of Mr. Choi. "Do you remember what he look like?"

"I'll keep this one." he looked at it for a moment. Akette pushed his plate to one side of the table and replaced it with a wireless laptop. "Well, let's see how we can locate him."

"First, we will check county records, marriage license, property records, business license, one of them have to pan out." they both crossed their fingers, "It'll be like a needle in a hay stack."

Five days later, the Queen Liliuokalani Freeway was heavy from the rush hour traffic leaving downtown Honolulu. Kalargo drove his three week old Carrera Porsche towards downtown. He zoomed past cars like a professional driver. He smiled and tuned the world out to Jazz. He felt good, no wonderful. He had just received good news from his doctor and better news that Germany has a medication not yet approved by the Federal Drug Administration. It proclaimed to cure him of H.I.V. for life. But it was in its pretrial stage. It had only been tested on rats. In four months they will be testing monkeys.

"Get out of my way!" he smashed down on his horn, and smashed the pedal to the floor, seventy mph to one hundred twenty mph.

"Now that's what I'm talking about..." he looked over his shoulder, "...fall back from the chuck hole, idiot!" he felt untouchable. He wished the drive from the fitness gym had more distance in between them; a twenty minute ride was only three hundred seconds to the exit. He exited the highway and pulled into a gas station.

Moments before he opened the door he noticed a blue impala that he had seen earlier leaving his house. He laughed, "Can't keep up with a Porsche, are they crazy?" he spoke to himself and shook his head.

"Kalargo, how's your day?" the cashier asked.

He smiled, "You see my new ride?"

The cashier eyes opened wide, "Wow, that's yours?"

"Come check it out." he insisted.

The cashier called for his assistant to take over the register. "Incredible, is it fast?"

Kalargo chuckled, "Ask those detectives. They have been tailing me since I left the house,'" they both chuckled, "look at them, they riding in a car and they still look like tired greyhounds chasing a rabbit." he jumped into the driver seat. The trail of burning rubber was enough to hide the Porsche. He was expecting them to pull him over sooner or later for reckless driving, but good news like he had received was worth a ticket. But he started thinking, if they were the police, they would have stopped me by now. His defenses began to raise flags. He quickly dialed Bennett's number on his cell.

"Hey, Bennett, you busy?" he told him where to meet him and the circumstances. He slowly drove towards Chinatown.

Akette and Paul patiently followed Kalargo until the right moment to approach him.

Bennett was in the position and finally made his way to Date St.

They followed him patiently, a left on Palani ave.

In his rearview mirror Kalargo saw the impala kept straight. "Damn it," he punched the steering wheel with his fist. After he made a left on Winam ave., Bennett pulled up alongside of him with four Polynesians.

"Howzit, " Bennett jumped out of his car and looked around, "Where are they? You lost them?" he chuckled, "you need to slow down in this thing." he looked inside, "you headed to the gym?" before he could speak," I'll ride with you." he told Daren to take the wheel.

Kalargo headed towards Mamala Bay, "So this is what Porches feels like," he rubbed the seats like they were the skin of sexy woman that moaned to his touch, reclined himself, "I like this." he wiggled his butt in to the seat.

"How long have we known each other?" Bennett cracked open his left eye, "Got to be over ten years, at least."

He made a right on Kuhio ave, before he could say another word; he saw the blue impala, "There, that's them."

"Who," he raised his seat.

"There they are, the people that were following me." Kalargo said.

"Pull over there, next to them." he pointed his hand towards the impala and the Polynesians hopped out of their van.

Paul and Akette walked out of the ABC store, they were surrounded by four big Polynesian with pistols in their rib cages. They reached for the sky and dropped their drinks, chips, and cigarettes.

"Put your hands down!" they were forced in to the van, "What the hell you want?"

Paul tried to point to their car. Daren hit him on the back of his head with his pistol, "Speak up killer!"

"Damn, not right here," put them in the van. Paul's English came out with a heavy broken accent.

"Where the hell are you from?"

Akette's English was better, so he spoke up, "Gambia."

Daren slammed the van door. "Drive around the block a couple of times," he called Kalargo, "What you want me to do, kill them?"

He followed the van, "I want to know why they were following me. Torture them until they talk. Do they speak with an accent?"

"Hell yeah, they said Gambia," he gave the signal to torture them. They were willing to talk, but didn't have a chance to explain anything. They were stomped and pistol whipped. Kalargo can hear them screaming through the phone.

"Hell yeah, they came all the way here to kill me; this will teach them a lesson. Tie them up real good."

"Where is," before he ask for Mr. Choi?" Daren popped him in the mouth. "Shut up and put your hands behind your backs.

"Wait, we must speak to Mr. Choi, it's urgent..." Akette spoke quickly, "...it's important!"

Bennett smacked him on the side of the head.

"Shut up, you stank," he gasp for fresh air out of the little side window that didn't really work. "You people don't use deodorant?"

Kalargo was sure they were there to revenge the General's death. "Damn, take them to exit 19, Hwy 3. I got something for them."

Thirty minutes later the van pulled off on a dirt road in the middle of nowhere. The van door opened up, they were blind folded, gagged, and tightly tied up, "So these are the assassins?"

"Get their ass out of the van," they were pushed out by foot as they fell on to the ground, bleeding, and swollen faces.

"Go ahead and put a bullet in their heads." Kalargo stood back to avoid blood splatter. Daren's pistol jammed.

"Damn, what kind of gun you got?" Bennett pulled his pistol out and aimed at Paul's head.

"Hold on, I want to know how they found me?" he walked over and pulled the gag out of Akette's mouth.

He immediately begged for their lives, "Please, just listen to us, we can explain. We are not here to kill you. It's our honor to deliver this message to you."

He laughed, "Message my ass. Where is the message, on the right or the left side of the bullet?" they all laughed as they squirmed and pleaded.

"You think we are stupid." he kicked him in the ribs. Akette curled up in pain.

"Just listen to us," he took a breather, a quick one, after he swallowed some of his own blood He was sweating like he was in a sauna. "Where are the weapons? We came here to kill you, right? Where are our weapons?" he pleaded.

Daren finally got a shot off into the ground next to Paul. "I got it to work. Put one in his head?" he scared everyone. He put the muzzle to Paul's temple. "Just say the word." he gritted his teeth and wanted to prove his loyalty. He pulled his bottom lip with his upper teeth.

"Hey, fall back before you kill someone." Kalargo said.

"Who sent you?!" Kalargo walked around them both, "I said who sent you?"

Daren danced around them as he pulled and tugged his groin area, "Aah, just let me squeeze one in his head! I bet one of them talk!" it was obvious he had never killed anyone before.

"Your own father."

Kalargo eyebrows fell down to his eyelids. "Stop it! I'll put a bullet in you right now!"

Akette spoke quickly, "Listen, " he spoke in his native tribal tongue, Jola.

"Na Min would not do this to me," he smacked Akette across the jaw and gagged him.

He pulled the cloth from Paul's mouth and removed his blind fold, "Speak and speak quickly, now who sent you?"

Paul looked up at him, "Your father."

"Damn, Kalargo, your own father wants you dead." Bennett said with disappointment.

Paul shook his head, "No not dead, he wants you to come home."

Everyone stepped back as they tried to process this crap, "What the hell are you talking about?" You need to make sense," he rubbed the muzzle of his gun across his forehead in frustration.

"Listen, reach into my back pocket. I have a picture of you. In the car I have all the documents to explain."

Kalargo reached and pulled the picture from his back pocket. "Any killer would have a picture." he threw the picture into his face."

"Your father is very ill. He needs you. We need you." Paul said.

He stopped him from talking and sighed. "What do you mean?"

Paul looked at Akette for the ok to tell him. "You are the son of King Bawee Shabonee. He requested that you return home. It's urgent. He's very ill."

"Kalargo, do not tell me you are going to fall for this bullshit. These guys were going to kill you as soon as they had a chance. I'm telling you. We need to kill these bastards before it come back to haunt you." Bennett said with a convincing voice.

Kalargo put his index finger to his lips to hush him, "Shhh!" He tried to speak his native tongue. He was horrible but he knew that only a hand full of people spoke it. But he could not understand his born language, he spoke four languages, and not his own. He was frustrated. "Damn!"

"My parents died when I was, what seven years old," he threw up his hands, "what, how can I believe you are not here to kill me? So far, this is not looking good."

He took the gag out of Akette's mouth. "Everything you need is in the car in an unopened envelope in the trunk."

Daren kicked him in the chest. "Where are the keys?"

"Are you crazy?!" Bennett tried to warn him.

"Daren, you are going in the trunk. Let's go."

"Damn!" he lowered the gun and tucked it in his belt, took the keys from Paul's left front pocket. He told everyone to sit tight and don't let them take a piss if they have to.

Kalargo and Daren drove back to Waikiki. He pushed the Porsche to its limit. The blue impala was parked behind the corner store.

Daren hit the button to open the drunk. He looked at Kalargo, "No boom yet."

They both walked over and looked. There it was on the floor of the trunk beneath the spare tire. He sighed and slowly reached in nervously. The closer his hand got, the harder his chest pounded, just before he grabbed it, his phone rang. He was startled. "Damn it."

"Yeah Bennett…"

"Is everything ok?"

"I'll call you back."

He quickly called Mugumbi, but no answer, "Damn. Come on, answer the damn phone." he begged to hear his voice, "Nothing."

He finally grabbed the envelope. They both rushed back to the Porsche.

Five minutes later

"Wow." he picked up the phone and called Bennett. "Hey, let them go."

"What!"

"You heard me! Let them go! Bring them back here. I need to talk to them." he ended the call. He shoved the papers in the envelope and tossed them on the dash board.

"What's wrong? You ok?" Daren was concern, but not to nosey.

He reached in his pocket and sighed. "Daren, here take a taxi home." he gave him a hundred dollar bill.

"But," he was interrupted.

He gave the money back, "No, I'll wait until Bennett get here!"

"If you choose, but you can keep the money."

He got out of the car with a million things on his mind. But he could not figure out why Mugumbi was not answering his phone. He hesitated about calling Na Min. It would shake him lose to know the breaking news or even if it's true. He looked into the sky, "God, give me a sign. Tell me something."

The van pulled into the parking lot next to his Porsche. He stood on the steps of the restaurant. He waved his hand to Daren to bring the envelope and for Paul and Akette to come over.

"Hey, Daren is he ok?" Bennett asked.

He raised his eyebrows and shrugged his shoulders, "He read something in the envelope and gave me a hundred dollars to take a taxi home. But I refused."

"Did he appear upset?" Bennett asked.

"No, not at all, more like shocked."

"You want us to wait out here just in case?"

"No, you guys go ahead. I'll hang around. If we need you, you'll get a call." Bennett waved them on.

They drove off and he lit a cigarette and waited.

Four hours later, Bennett was surrounded by butts that he tossed down. He grew impatient and dialed Kalargo's cell, no answer. He looked into the restaurant. He sat with Paul and Akette like he was in a profound conversation. He held documents and photos in his hand that obviously really meant something.

He didn't want to be rude by barging in, so he waited. He seated himself on the other side of the restaurant and ordered food.

Two hours before closing, very few customers, from the distance, he heard Kalargo give his cell number to them. "In the morning I'll pick you guys up."

Kalargo reached out to shake their hands. But they both had the same reaction. They bowed and kissed his hand.

Kalargo walked over to Bennett, "Now what the hell that was all about? You look like you saw a ghost." He asked as they crossed the street.

Kalargo put the envelope under his armpit and reached for his keys. "This is crazy. I'll get down to the bottom of this." he pulled out his cell phone. "Hey..." he looked at him just before opening the car door, "I just got some incredible news, that my biological father is alive, but very ill."

He looked at him, "I thought Na Min was your dad all this time." they both laughed.

"Now that's some damn news." they both closed their door.

"I mean, that would mean good news right?" he expressed excitement.

"But that's not the good news." he put the envelope beneath his seat and put the key in the ignition.

"So what's next?" Bennett rubbed on an annoying pimple in the vanity mirror.

Kalargo looked at him and just shook his head and sighed.

*　　　　*　　　　*

Seoul, South Korea

Na Min sat in a coffee shop, nervous and impatient. He looked over his shoulder, "Can I have more sugar?"

He waited for a drop from Zang, late but not unusual. He looked at his watch, five more minutes."

The waiter returned with sugar and a small note. He added more coffee and sugar, then read the note, 'Two blocks east make a right, four blocks south, make a left, red sonata, drive two blocks south make a right, park under the parking garage. Leave package under the seat. Call me later.'

He folded the note and held it in his palm. He slowly looked around the coffee shop to see if anyone watched him; just college students at their wireless laptops with their brewing cups of coffee. He stood up and sipped his coffee as he headed towards the door.

It took him no time to arrive in sight of the red sonata. He stood at the corner and sipped his coffee while he observed the area around the car. Across the street a man sat in his car, beneath his door were several cigarette butts, and another hanging from his lips.

He crossed the street away from the car pretending to look for an address. Out of nowhere some kids burst from the door of a bakery shop nearly bumping into him. He quickly entered the bakery shop and sighed.

"Yes, two donuts with the cream fillings please." he looked out the bay window.

"'Will that be all?"

"Yes, can I get a fresh cup of coffee?" he gave him his cup for a refill. "How much will that be?" Just before he paid, he heard a car horn; a young fellow came out the building across the street and got into the car with the waiting man with the cigarette hanging from his lip. He quickly yanked the gear into drive and pulled out into the street without looking.

Na Min stood at the window of the bakery with his half of donut and coffee in the other. He exited the bakery, double looked down the street, second floor windows for suspicious activity. He quickly gobbled his second donut and licked his fingers of glaze cream as he walked over to the red sonata, opened the driver door, reached under the mat for the key and started the car. He positioned the seat and mirrors with his left hand. He sipped his coffee, put the car in drive and drove off.

He pulled into the parking garage and circled his way to the third deck. The half empty deck spooked him when he saw four guys talking outside their vehicles.

He sighed and glanced away. He found an empty parking space two spaces away from the elevators and stairway. He shut the engine off, and looked around before pulling out a Manila envelope. He slid it beneath his seat and tucked the keys under the mat. He reached down and pulled the level for the trunk as he watched it open from the rearview mirror. He drank the last of his coffee, folded the cup to place it in his pocket and wiped his finger prints from the car.

He went to the trunk and pulled out a briefcase. He weighed it manually, "It feels about right." he quickly closed the trunk and took the stairs. "Taxi!" he jumped in the taxi, "downtown." he sat behind the driver with the briefcase on his lap. The latches popped open as he slowly opened it. He was looking at two hundred thousand dollars of counterfeit money. In a small valve he pulled out contained four uncut rough diamonds the size of marble stones. "Wow..." he whispered. He smiled and relaxed as he closed the briefcase.

Chapter 26

"Na Min, can you talk?" Mugumbi's concerned voice came across as troubling.

"Well, I'm boarding a flight to Japan," he paused a moment to give his boarding pass to the flight attendant.

"First class." she said and directed him to the huge comfortable seat.

"Yes," he returned his focus to his phone call. He reached and tossed his carry on above his head. "What's the concerned voice for?"

Mugumbi had to take a deep breath, but he spoke. "It's Kalargo, he left some message on my phone." he paused. "Somehow two men from Gambia are in Hawaii." They both paused.

He slowly sat down and wondered as a sigh exuded as he thought about what he would say next. The passengers slowly found their seats, as he felt like his world was slowly changing.

"Listen," he looked out the window and saw the ground crew preparing the aircraft for launch. His voice was lowered as he spoke. "You have to get to Hawaii and take care of these idiots before they kill him." he held his face in his hand.

"Now that's what I had in mind, but I wanted to run it by you first." Mugumbi confirmed his intuition.

"When you locate them, get rid of them." he waited for a response.

"Not a problem."

"Do you remember the address to the house, you can take them there, you know what to do from there, and whatever happens, insurance will take care of the bill. You understand what I mean by that?" the plane had taxied on to the tarmac, "Call me when it's done." he was politely asked to end his call by the flight attendant.

"I'll call you when I arrive." Mugumbi said.

They ended their call.

*　　　　*　　　　*

Honolulu, Hi

Kalargo sat quietly in his office with Paul and Akette in front of him waiting for him to decide to take the DNA test. He broke the silence with an exhausted sigh.

Paul scratched his chin with his left index finger, "Hey, what could it hurt? If you are not related, we leave Hawaii. But you are..." they both looked at each other.

"Your Majesty..."

He interrupted them. "Hey, cut that out."

"Sir Kalargo, you were in Gambia. You left your blood stained tissue in the bathroom." Paul sighed.

Akette leaned forward, "Sir, take the test and you'll see for yourself."

Kalargo held his hands up and silenced them both. "Ok, ok I'll take the test."

"Yes!" they both were excited. "You will not regret your decision." Paul stood and bowed.

"We will see you when the results return." he gave him the kit to take a swab test and to mail it himself.

"You will need this to match your DNA," he also gave them their hotel room number, "call me at the hotel."

"You guys are going to be here until the results are in?" Kalargo asked.

"Whatever it takes." they exited the office.

As they walked out he buried his face in his palms and sighed. "This is too stressful." Kalargo said. Before the door closed completely, there was a knock; he shoved the folder in the center desk drawer. "Yes, come in."

Bennett entered with his head first, "You ok?"

"Oh, yeah, come on in, have a seat."

He walked in with his left hand rubbing his earlobe. His white sleeve button down shirt went well with his long jean shorts. He flopped into the warm leather chair that Paul had sat in. Before Bennett could speak...

Kalargo leaned back into his office chair."I am starting to believe that my father is alive." They looked at each other. "But I will know for sure after I take the DNA test," he stood up, "I need you to take over until I come back. Hopefully, I'll be back before the four o'clock training class." They stood up and walked out to the car, "Can you imagine me, a King?"

"Well, I am trying to visualize that. I can't see it." Bennett lit a cigarette as he drove away.

*   *   *

A cpuple of weeks had passed and Kalargo was expecting his results any day now. He paced the floor enough to leave his shoe prints. He tried to get a hold of Na Min or Mugumbi. "Damn, someone needs to explain what the hell is going on." he threw his hands in the air in frustration. There was a knock at the door. The door was snatched open.

"Damn," he sighed. He thought it was the mailman.

"Well damn to you." Bennett said.

"I thought you were the mailman." He let him in like he was tweaking on drugs, he paced the floor with hands on his hips, "You know all day I've been trying to remember my childhood," he paused and half way sat on the corner of the desk, "Nothing comes to mind, you would think if my father was the King. I would know this, right?"

"Maybe, you have to jog your memory, how old were you when you left?" Bennett stood up to prepare a stiff drink, "You care for one?" The ice dangled into the glass.

"You see that's why I need to talk to Mugumbi. I can't remember anything before that shack we lived in," he nodded his head trying to reassure himself.

"So Mugumbi is the missing link," he sipped slowly, "and he never said anything, because if he's your uncle, that would make his brother your father."

They both looked at each other as if a light bulb came on, a bright light bulb. The moment of silence made the office much smaller.

"Well..." before he could say another word, "that's the mailman!" They both rushed out the office, breathing heavy; Kalargo's hands trembled as he ripped open the letter. They both entered the office; Bennett looked over his shoulder, but to no avail.

He turned his back, totally forgetting about him. The sound of the letter in his hands rattled the office. He sighed and took a seat, slowly raised his head. The eye contact that he made with him was not good.

Bennett quickly downed his drink, frowned as his throat, and chest burned. He shook his head."Well," he sighed. "What does it say?" he asked.

Kalargo held his hand up to silence him.

"What if Mugumbi is not your uncle?" There was a knock at the door.

"Damn! He is my father." Kalargo said.

"So who is Mugumbi?" Bennett stood up to answer the door; it was Mugumbi's face that froze his emotions in place.

"Well, are you going to let me in?" he reached out and hugged him, "long time no see." Bennett's smile was not genuine, as his heart skipped a beat.

"Of course, come on in my brother." he sighed and thought if he is not his uncle, then who is he?

Kalargo had stuffed the papers in his desk drawer, scared now to face him, not knowing who he really is and afraid to ask. But he must know something. He felt betrayed, hurt, as he sat down. He wanted to know who is Mugumbi. But he could not gasp the breath to ask him. He wanted more information before he can point his fingers at anyone.

He sighed, "So, I am surprised to see you. What brings you to Hawaii?" they hugged.

"Well I had some business to take care of, and decided to stop by. I got your message." He sat down where Bennett had sat; the seat was warm and comfortable.

Bennett stood behind him, gestured not to say anything about the DNA.

Mugumbi felt something was going on and turned to him.

"You want a stiff one," Bennett almost pissed on himself, "got vodka, beer?" he cracked the ice tray.

"Yeah, give me an orange juice and vodka, hold the ice."

Bennett hands shook like a leaf on a cold Chicago day. He dropped an ice cube and sighed to relax himself.

"Here you go." it was filled to the rim as he tried not to spill it.

Kalargo looked at the clock and tried to hold a conversation. "How is Yuki?" His mind was racing as he desperately wanted to call Paul and Akette.

"She is doing fine..." he sipped his drink and frowned, "damn this is stiff," he coughed as his throat burned," what happened to the juice?" They laughed.

Kalargo could see Bennett's lips moving. "He is not your uncle." and crossed his throat like he had a knife.

Mugumbi was rambling on about the new car he had just purchased.

He was so uncomfortable talking to him, now he knew there was a chance of him not being his uncle. Any moment now the phone should ring, Paul and Akette would knock on the door. He twisted his neck and back. He burst out with laughter as the joke vibrated the office. Bennett didn't find it funny, but he laughed hard with him. Kalargo wanted to jump over his desk and choke the truth out of him.

Suddenly, Kalargo received a text, maybe it was Paul? He looked down at his phone and almost read the text out loud.

Bennett choked off his drink as it comes out of his mouth.

He slowly put the phone back into his pocket and took a deep breath. He shook his head and smiled. Mugumbi laughed as he finished his story.

Bennett sent him a text that told him to get his DNA, and test it to see if he is even related at all.

What a brilliant idea Kalargo thought as he stood up, "Hold that thought, I got to use the bathroom."

He sighed as he closed the office door. He gave a fist pump to the idea of getting his DNA. He walked around, outside, inside the facility and then he came up with an idea. He swallowed a lump of marbles because this was brave, but also easier than expected.

He had realized that Mugumbi had a runny nose. He would keep the tissue and use it for the DNA comparison. Just before he returned to the office, he texted Bennett the plan. He walked in.

"I just don't understand why it's so hard for them to keep that back room clean." he expressed his anger and flopped into his chair.

Mugumbi rubbed his nose; they both looked at each other. He pulled out a box of tissue.

"Here you go," He pushed the trash basket closer to him with his feet.

Mugumbi reached in his right pocket and pulled out a handkerchief and sneezed into it. Once again, they looked at each other disappointedly. They both sighed. He shook his head and thought that this is going to be harder than he thought. Bennett quickly thought of something, he texted him as he entered the bathroom.

He sighed and looked at Mugumbi, "You know this idiot have been taking money from me. But I can't prove it."

Mugumbi was shocked, "What! No way, for how long?"

"Not too sure, but I can't prove it. It's either him or somebody else." Mugumbi saw how upset he was about the situation.

"Hey you want me to deal with him?" his eyes looked evil and glossy. "I never liked him anyway."

"No, let me deal with him, he is my friend." He slid down in his chair.

"That's the problem, you can't properly handle this. Listen, I will make this hamster talk. I got this torture technique I am dying to use." he looked excited.

"Calm down, relax. I am not sure if he is the one we are looking for." he tried to calm him.

"Well…" he took a sip of his drink, "…just let me know when, it's whatever. I got your back."

Just before another word was spoken, the door opened as Bennett walked in. "You are right about them not keeping up the bathroom. I had to freshen up the bathroom, pick up the dirty towels."

The room was quiet. Mugumbi sat there waiting for Kalargo to say something about the missing money. He rubbed his hands together; sucked air between his teeth, his left foot constantly tapped the floor.

"Hey, you guys want another stiff one?" Bennett asked.

Mugumbi could not contain his anger, "Yeah, while you at it, give this man his money you took from him." the office was silent.

"What did you say?"

"You heard me, the damn money that's missing."

"You accusing me, you don't know what you are talking about!"

Just as he stood up, Bennett swung on him, and they began to fight, Kalargo wedged himself between them before it got to serious. They knew in order for this to work, he had one chance to draw blood and hoped he can be convinced that it was all a misunderstanding.

Mugumbi had him in the head lock; somehow he was flipped over and threw more punches. He saw blood on the floor, but didn't know whose blood it was. Kalargo quickly jumped in, Mugumbi nose was bleeding, it was time to stop it. They looked like they had won a prize at the carnival.

"Enough, enough," Kalargo held them apart.

"You got some explaining to do!" Mugumbi said.

"Hey! I told you that I will handle this!" Kalargo said.

Bennett fell to the floor; he pretended to be hurt so Mugumbi will feel that he got the best of him. "I think you broke my ribs," he inhaled with difficulty. He held his ribs.

"Good, I got more for you!" Mugumbi said and held his head back.

"Here, take this." Kalargo gave him a towel. Mission accomplished.

*　　　　*　　　　*

Paul woke up from an induced drug that knocked him out, eyes blind folded, feet and hands tied up, mouth taped, he noticed that he was on a mattress. He yanked his hands, but they were somehow tied to a pole above him. He used his shoulder to slide his blind fold just enough to see out of one eye. The room was blurry from his eyes being covered, but slowly adjusted. He was scared and tried to snatch his way loose. He looked around the room, it appeared to be a vacant house, the smell of fresh pineapple was strong, and he figured that he had to be far from the city. He looked down at his pants and noticed that he had soiled himself; the smell of urine had already adjusted his senses.

The windows was boarded, the table lamp was on. He tried again to wiggle his way free, but only exhausted himself. The only thing he could think of was dying there in the middle of nowhere. He wiped his sweat with his shoulder. He noticed how old the pipe was near the floor. It gave him hope, but did he have enough time.

He was drenched in sweat, the pole loosening; the rust was giving way to his strength. If he could just get free, his hands could easily be untied. The pipe was a lot more durable than he had expected. But he knew that help was not on the way.

Mugumbi sat in the Burger King lobby eating his meal. He looked in the window reflection at his bandage that covered his nose. He shook his head, "That mother..." there was kids sitting behind him, so he decided to respect them by keeping his vulgar to himself. He stood up and walked over the counter to order another meal to go. When he returned one of the kids was eating his fries. He paused and shook his head. His mother apologized, but he just cracked a smile, "That's ok, he can have them."

The little boy smiled but hesitated. "What did I tell you about that?" his mother grabbed him by his arm.

"No that's ok, he can take them." he noticed that they were just sitting there with no food and had not ordered since he had first arrived. He reached in his pocket and slid her a hundred dollar bill.

"I can't take that," she pushed it away, "I just can't."

Mugumbi came up with a bold face lie, "Where I am from, if someone give you something and you touch it, it's ten years of bad luck if you give it back..." he looked at her with a serious look, "and that's bad luck for the both of us."

She sighed, "Well I guess that's why the last ten years have been bad luck for Me." she hugged her son, folded the money and shoved it down her bra.

"God work in mysterious ways." he grabbed his bag of food and walked out to his car. She promised to never turn another blessing away.

He drove for almost an hour when he decided to stop at the roadside vendor for fresh fruit. He picked a package basket and tossed the vendor a twenty.

The vendor looked at him, his nose in particular, "Are you ok?" He handed him a couple of extra napkins. "You have blood coming from your bandage.

He grabbed the napkins and held his head back to stop it from ruining his shirt, but it was too late. "Damn it!" he sighed with anger and snatched his basket and change. He was so pissed about his shirt that his wife had gotten him. He sped off into traffic with no regard for others; dust overwhelmed the vendor as he gave him the middle finger.

As he slowly drove the dirt road, he looked in the mirror to check to see if the bleeding stopped. He was thankful. He was minutes from the house. He slowed down to see if anything had been moved from the porch. He had arranged some bottles of water and a vase that would fall over if disturbed.

He stopped in front of the house and paused. Birds flew the partly cloudy sky. The breeze reduced the ninety degrees to a comfortable eighty six degrees. His nose was itching, but no way to scratch it.

He pushed the trunk button and opened the car door. He placed the basket of fruit on the porch. As he returned to the car, he touched his nose to make sure he was not bleeding through his bandage again. He reached in the trunk and pulled out his bag of torture tools that he had purchased from a thrift store.

He opened the door to the house, tossed his tool bag on the floor and returned for the food. He tossed his keys on the end table. He walked over to a closet and pulled out an old car battery charger, placed it next to a metal chair. He placed his bag of tools on top of the dinner table to examine each one, meat cleaver, hammer, saw, barb wire, cordless sander, kitchen knives, ice pick, bottle of alcohol and fresh lemons.

He grabbed the bag of food, keys, and walked over to the room. He opened the door and his heart fell to his stomach. Paul was gone.

The bag of food fell to the floor, his heart pounded through his chest. He immediately pulls his gun from his belt line and returned to the living room. That was the last thing he remembered.

Paul knocked him out with a small pipe that he had freed himself with. But he quickly recovered as Paul tried to tie him up. He grabbed Paul by the shirt collar and punched him in the throat. They violently wrestled on the floor. He punched Paul in his mid-section. He grabbed his rib cage and fell to the floor.

Mugumbi kicked him, but he held on to his foot and swept his remaining foot from the floor. His ankle twisted in his hands. Mugumbi screamed in agony, before he knew he was kicked on the nose.

"God, my nose!" he screamed, and grabbed his bloody nose that soaked his hands.

Paul quickly jumped on top of him and weld on his face. His final blow knocked him out again. He took no chances, quickly tied his hands and feet.

"So you want to torture someone!" he yelled out in anger. He was pissed. His cut on his ear dripped, the scratches on his face stung. He licked his swollen lip; he grabbed a knife and began to torture Mugumbi. "I am going to kill you slowly! You bastard!" without hesitation, he sliced his left side of his face. "Who the hell are you?"

Mugumbi slowly came to; his eyes opened to a blurry room. Paul tossed a pot of hot water on him from the micro wave. He screamed and fell to the floor, realizing that his hands were tied behind his back. He tried hard to break free from the rope. He mumbles some words and thought that the situation was not looking good. The pain his body was in was unexplainable. His blood clogged his breathing through his broken nose.

"You heard me, who the hell are you?" he sliced his rib cage to get his attention. He tossed and turned on the floor as he tried to get away from him.
"Stop, please stop!" he begged.

Paul heard his accent and wondered where he was from. He violently grabbed him by the throat, cutting off his air supply. He held him with two hands.

"What the hell were you thinking?" he whispered in his ear, the veins in

Mugumbi's neck were under severe pressure. He can feel his wind pipe began to collapse. He looked in Paul's eye for the last time, as tears came from his eyes, but he was not going to let him die so easy. Not without knowing who he was and why he wanted to kill him. He let go of him and fell beside him.

"You think…" they both were breathing hard, "…I was going to let you die this easy." He looked him in his eyes, "Oh, you got a lot of explaining to do!" he gritted his teeth with anger.

Mugumbi moaned in pain and gasped for air, his life had passed in front of him. He tried to talk, but his wind pipe was slightly damaged.

Paul pushed himself up and off of him and walked over to the table of tools. He picked up a saw, "Not yet." He picked up a twelve inch metal wasp with deep grooves that put a smile on his face. He slowly rubbed his thumb across the razor sharp grooves, he sighed with a grin. Something grabbed his attention from the corner of his eye, "So you actually came with food." he grinned.

"What kind of human are you?" he walked over to the bag, snatched it from the floor, open it. "You no good bastard," he took a bite of the burger through the paper that wrapped it. He held his head back, not realizing how hungry he was. He held the burger in one hand, and the wasp in the other. He moaned as the flavors burst in his mouth. He walked over to Mugumbi and slapped him across the face with the grooves of the metal wasp.

Paul looked at the scar the grooves had left on his left side of his face. "I told you…" he took another bite of the burger with mayonnaise in his mustache, "…you will talk." He hit him again across his left ear, almost taking it off. Mugumbi moved in time, but gauged the back of his head.

The cry for help went unheard from this house. Mugumbi kicked as hard as he could, but unable to break free; his ankles were chained to the legs of the chair.

"What is your name?" Paulsaid with a whispered voice.

Mugumbi's throat was in so much pain, "Mugumbi.", he murmured under his breath.

"Why did you kidnap me?" Paul frantically searched the house, from the bathroom to the kitchen, "I can't hear you!"

He grabbed a bottle of green rubbing alcohol, slowly walked over to him. "Why?" he unscrewed the cap and sniffed the bottle, threw a little on his face.

Mugumbi bucked and jumped around wildly.

Paul mounted him like a pissed off bull, with his knees on his shoulders to pin him down. He grabbed each eye lid and poured alcohol in them. The yelp of

Mugumbi described the unbearable pain.

Paul grabbed him tightly and opened each eye lid, inhaled deeply and gathered as much saliva from the back of his throat, hocked the best of it and oozed it slowly into his eyes to soothe the pain, lubricating his eyes.

The high pitch scream vibrated the windows as he tossed and turned to be let go. Paul kicked him in the ribs and poured more alcohol on him.

"Why did you kidnap me?" he grabbed him by the throat. He could see that he wanted to talk. Paul stood over him with his left hand behind his neck and pretended to pour the alcohol in his eyes for a second time. Mugumbi violently struggled between Paul's legs. "Why! Stop trying to be a tough guy!"

His lips began to move, as he swallowed, "You came to kill Kalargo!"

"You dumb fuck! Why no one believes me!" he grabbed him by the nose, twisted it, and snatched his fingers away. "I am the servant to the King of the Gambia. I was sent here to bring his only surviving son home. The King is his father. He is not in good health..." he put his foot on his throat, "...now tell me the truth." he allowed him to breath.

"Why would someone want to kill the new King of the Gambia?"

The pain diluted the words from Mugumbi's lips. He took a small swallow of blood. He could not tell him the truth, but he had to tell him something

Paul grabbed him by the throat, "What's your name?!"

"Mugumbi." he barely said.

"What part of Africa are you from?!" he walked over to the table of tools, picking them up one by one.

"The Gambia." the blood covered his face and clothing. The humidity set in as their sweat wet their clothes like hard working men.

"The Gambia?" Paul put the ice pick in his left pocket. "Do you know Kalargo?" He walked over to him and waited for a response. He wiped his face with the shoulder of his shirt.

"Yes." Mugumbi coughed up some blood as he tried to breathe through his mouth.

Paul pulled out the ice pick, "Now, I told you I would get the truth out of you." He looked at him with the ice pick and savagely stabbed him in the right thigh. "You little piss ant, tell me the truth or I will end your life right now!" he pulled it out and threaten to stab him again.

"Please!"Mugumbi begged him. "I..." his tears fell as he cried and begged for mercy. "I swear to you. I am also the servant of the King of the Gambia." he took a deep breath and cleared his throat. "It was I who sneak him from Africa. It was my duty to look after him, protect him from harm. I heard you were here to kill him! I kidnapped you to find out why you were looking for him."

Paul looked at him like a curious dog, "So you are not mentioned in none of my papers from the King himself?"

"You got to think my brother. All this happened more than thirty years ago!" Mugumbi tried to sit up and crawl towards the wall. He spat on the floor, as he frowned from the cracked ribs cage.

Paul looked at his bloody hands and dropped the ice pick to the floor. He paced the floor with the back of his left hand against his forehead in disbelief.

"So you are trying to tell me, that you are the one who took him out the country?" he leaned against the wall and slammed his fist. He felt bad and did not know how to apologize to him. He quickly picked him up from the floor and untied him.

"I have to apologize. I know you would have done the same thing if you had the chance to escape." he untied him and tossed the rope to the floor. He grabbed a glass of water to give to him.

Mugumbi's body was broken down with pain. He tried to stand.

"You need to go to the hospital."

He quickly refused, "No... No hospitals!" he stood up and hopped on one leg. He looked horrible. "Another glass of water." he requested. He tried to step forward and fell to the floor like a log. "Ahhhh!"

Paul stopped what he was doing and ran over to help him. "I got you my brother." he lifted him from the floor.

Mugumbi stabbed him in his chest with the ice pick.

Paul could not believe what had happen. He thought a chest muscle had cramped. He looked down at his chest; He stabbed him three more times. All of his weight pushed Paul back several steps. Paul's grip loosen, eyes watered, he gasp blood from his lungs on to Mugumbi's face."

"Shhh... just take it easy, don't fight It." he held Paul in his arms as if they were lovers, dancing to slow romance tune. They both slowly fell towards the floor. He slowly pulled the ice pick out of his chest. Blood soaked them both. He tried to speak, but struggled to inhale and clinched on Mugumbi's favorite shirt.

"Just relax, it's going to be ok." Mugumbi whispered. They nodded their heads as they looked into each other's eyes. His breathing shallowed as he slowly drowned on his own blood.

"Take care of Kalargo." His fist loosens, and his lifeless hands fell to the floor.

Mugumbi closed his eyes, sighed and painfully picked himself up from the floor. He looked around the house and tried to figure out what he had to do next. He walked over to the window to make sure no one was outside. He knew he had to get rid of his body, but too hurt to do on his own. He nervously pulls out his cell phone and started to call Kalargo. He paused and looks around one more time to see if he could get rid of Paul by himself. He moaned with every move, his injuries were a lot more severe than he first thought. He tried to drag Paul's body across the floor.

"Aaahhh! I can't!" he yelled out. He hobbled over to the front door and quickly thought about cutting him into smaller pieces.

"Yes! That would lighten the dead weight." he shoved the cell phone in his left rear pocket.

The phone rang, "Damn it," he pull it out, "Yuki, not now, baby." But he knew she would call back if he did not answer. He held the phone to his forehead. He just wanted some time to think. It stopped ringing. But it started to ring again.

"Hello honey..." he sighed deeply with frustration, "...ooh nothing, just got in from a long day." he paced the living room, walked over to the table and picked up the chainsaw.

"Of course not, it shouldn't be much longer..." He looked at Paul, sat it back down on the table, "...well, you know how your father is, sometimes he is too busy to answer your calls. I am sure as soon as he sees that he had missed your call. You will get a call from him."

He frowned from the pain that had gotten worse. He was bleeding. "Yuki, Yuki, please don't cry." he tried to soothe her, but running out of patience. But he did not want her to worry about him, so he could never tell her about his situation.

"Yes, Yuki, I told you those letters are old and most likely meaningless." she cried more. "What's in the letters?" he tossed his hands up and frowned from the pain, "you haven't told me anything..." he paused. "Yes I will understand." he stood in the bathroom looking at his facial wounds.

"Ok, but I want to know what the hell is in these letters that got you so upset. I have to tell you, I just don't like this. You have not been the same since these letters." he Pulled his busted lip down to see how bad it was. He examined his ear."Ok, I love you too. I'll be home in a couple of days." they ended the call.

He sighed and thanked the heavens he was able to get off the phone. He made his way to the living room and leaned on the wall and thought how to dismember Paul without making a bigger mess.

His phone rung, "Damn it! Who's calling me now?!" he looked at the screen, "Kalargo!" he pauses. He knew if anyone would help him, he would.

"Yeah, hello," before he could get a word out, "nephew, I got myself in a bit of a pickle," his voice sounded hurt, desperate, "I fucked up nephew." he moaned.

There was silence, a sigh, "What's wrong?"

"Everything is wrong, but I can't talk about it over the phone." he was bleeding and really could not pull this off by himself. He gave him a list of things to pick up from the hardware store.

"Are you going to be alright?" he asked him. I have a doctor friend if you need medical help.

"No, no, I can see a doctor later…" he grunted and moaned, "…for now, just bring those supplies. I am at the plantation house." there was a pause in both of their voices. "And come alone." the line ended.

*   *   *

Three hours later

Kalargo drove up to the plantation house, with Bennett as back up gun man. The sun hovered the horizon as shadows crawled the island slowly. Everything looked normal, but their guns were cocked and ready. He dialed his number.

"Yeah, where are you? I'm outside, turn the porch light on."

Moments later he peeked through the curtain and saw two people in the car. The light came on, "I told you to come alone! Why! Man this is not good." he insisted.

"This is my partner. He is cool.", before he could say another word.

"Please don't tell me you got Bennett with you?" there was silence, "that idiot, if you can't trust him, how the hell can I trust him." he hobbled around the living room, pissed off.

"Hey all that earlier was just a big misunderstanding, I found out what happened to the money." Kalargo was interrupted.

"Oh yeah, tell me what happen!"

Kalargo looked at him, "Well for one the money had been deposited into the bank account by one of the managers," he paused a little, "and they was not keeping good records of the deposits, but..." he sighed. He threw his hands up at him, "...but everything was accounted for, verified and double checked, so actually you owe him an apology." Kalargo frowned and wondered if he was buying this crap.

"Fuck Bennett, I told you how I feel about him. I told you to come alone! I did not want any witnesses! This is not something your best friend can be trusted with. He will have this on you and me..." he realized that he had no choice, "...forever! Do you hear me?" Before he could respond, "Now think long and hard, do you..." Mugumbi struggled to inhale, "...can you trust him with your life. This is not a game for the weak hearted. He will turn on you and me to save his own skin."

"I vouch for him with my life." Kalargo looked at Bennett.

"And time will tell." the line ended.

The car was unloaded. They can hear the dead bolt locks turn; the lights in the living room were shut off. His flash light was in there face as the door cracked open. They can hear that his breathing was in poor shape, and he wobbled on one good leg. He pointed the flash light in Bennett's face, without saying a word, but he had no choice to trust him. He needed all the help he can get. He let them in as he directed them to put the supplies in the corner of the living room.

"Don't the lights work?" Bennett asked.

"Don't worry about the lights, is that all of it?" Mugumbi said with attitude. "Yeah," before he could tell them anything he stumbled and lost his balance. The flashlight fell to the floor. They both grabbed him.

"Damn, what the hell happened. You are in bad shape." they both looked and seen a body on the floor.

"Holly mother of God!" Bennett said. They helped him into a chair and turned the lights on.

"Who the hell is this?" Kalargo wanted to uncover the body.

"Time will tell." Mugumbi said. "Please tell me you got my cigarettes."

Bennett tossed him the pack, "What a damn pickle this idiot is in."

Kalargo pulled the sheet from the body, "No! What the hell did you do?

This is Paul!" he threw his hands up in the air, and formed a fist. He rubbed his hands through his hair. "Why!" he paced the room.

"He came here to kill you! And there is another guy out there somewhere!" he was stopped mid-sentence.

"No, no, no, he was not here to kill me!" Kalargo sighed and kicked over a chair.

He sucked on his cigarette, "Well, he had some bull shit story." he was stopped again.

Kalargo really wanted to get down to the truth. He was pissed and no longer scared. "And what was his story?" he tapped his index finger on his temple. "Is there something that I need to know?"

He looked at Kalargo, his eye were blurry and dry. He spat in his hand and lubricated his eyes to soothe them from the damage of the alcohol. He sighed and took a deeper puff from his cigarette.

"Hey, snap out of it!"

"You know I could not let them kill you!" he tossed his hands in the air. "I was looking out for you." Mugumbi explained.

"So we," he walked over to him, "you and I have been living a lie all these years?"

He looked at him as if he also knew the truth. He scratched his forehead, "Kalargo, this goes way back." He looked at Bennett.

"Keep on talking." he demanded.

"When you were a little boy," He paused, "I need a drink, a stiff one, very stiff."

Bennett rushed to the cabinet to make him a drink. This was getting good and did not want to miss anything.

"I was a servant, who was hand chosen to get you out of Africa by all means. The genocide was so bad, all of your family had been killed, and it just got out of hand. I wanted to tell you that I was not your uncle, but I just could not break your heart. I mean so many years had gone by. But I also knew that there would be a day that I would have to explain all of this." He sipped his drink. His busted lip burned a little. He sat his drink down and grabbed his pack of cigarettes, tapped them against his thumb, and pulled one out.

"So to answer your next question, yes, you are the son of the King." He felt so relieved of this elephant on his chest. He covered his face in shame. He took another a swallow of his drink.

"So that's why the King of the Gambia was looking at me like he knew me from somewhere," he snapped his finger, "it did not dawn on me at the time because it did not make since." he crossed his arms and looked at Bennett. He did not know what to think. He was intrigued by the whole mess.

"I was so focused on the General..." he was stopped.

Mugumbi had to stop him and tell him. "Well that's another story," he took another drink; "he was your uncle, as in the King's brother."

"Oh! No, don't tell me that!" Kalargo yelped out loud.

Bennett gasped and choked off of his drink.

"I wanted to tell you but I did not know that he was the General until after you had left for the Philippines. No one had contact with you for months." he sighed. "If Paul came here seeking for your return, and your father is ill," he put out his cigarette and slowly, painfully got down on his knees, "your majesty, forgive me for killing the servant of the King. I am your servant as he and my life is now yours." he reached out for his hand. It was a moment of truth, sacrifice, and honor.

Bennett was blown away; it was meaningless to see Paul and Akette act this way, but for Mugumbi to beg for forgiveness was mind blowing. To reach out to kiss his hand was unimaginable.

He crawled on his knees like a wounded dog, grabbed Kalargo's right hand and kissed it like he really meant it.

He grabbed him to pick him up from his knees, Bennett ran over to help him. They stood face to face, "Mugumbi, you have done everything you were supposed to do, and with your life if needed. Even though I don't really understand all of this, but we will worry about that later. For now, let's figure out what we will do with Paul. They all agreed.

After a long night, Mugumbi sat on the edge of his car and sighed. The early morning sky had a chill in the win. The heat from the barn fire simmered. It did cross his mind if Bennett was able to keep this a secret, if not he had no problem killing him if need to be. But he trusted that Kalargo trusted him, so it was ok.

"Well, it's all done," Bennett walked over to him, "What are you thinking of?"

He grinned, "Just glad it's over with." he sighed and looked at him from the corner of his eyes.

Kalargo walked over, "Everything is cleaned up, what about the tools, even though we have cleaned them, pretty sure his blood on them."

Mugumbi scratch his face and nose, he spat in the palm of his left hand, and poured his saliva in his left eye to sooth the arid pain. His vision was no longer the same. His saliva slowly rolled down his face like tears, "Damn." He used his shirt to wipe his cheek. He did the same for the other eye.

"Are you able to drive?"

"Oh yeah, once I get some visine, I'll be all right." his phone rung, it was Yuki. He decided not to answer it.

They all said there good bye, shook hands, patted each other on the back and drove away.

The sunrise was beautiful as he drove the two lane highway, he carefully steered the car with one knee, poured a line of heroin on his forehand and vacuumed the line with his bloody nose. The phone rang again. "Hello."

She was happy to hear his voice, "Hey baby, good morning. I hope I didn't wake you."

"Oh no, just going to get some breakfast. How was your sleep?"

"Well, let's just say a lot better if you were here." she moaned.

"I hear that." He said.

"What day are you flying in?"

"I made reservations for tomorrow. I can't wait to see you." They both grinned. "I'll email you the flight info a little later today. Did you talk to your father?"

Her voice came across as sad, "I left a message." she sighed.

"So you never told me what the letters were about."

She became silent, "Not now, we will talk about it when you get here."

"You can't tell me anything." he tried after all this time he never really paid any attention until it started affecting her mood.

"Well, this is not something that I feel comfortable talking about over the phone."

He knew it had to be serious, "I can't wait to see you." he tossed her a kiss and they said their goodbyes.

Chapter 27

Mugumbi's body felt like he had been through a ringer. The flight was crowded, unable to stretch out, wounds were fresh as a reminder, cramped muscles he forgot he had. He walked toward baggage claim with this god awful limp; he decided to see how far away Yuki was.

"Hello darling, I'm here early, just calling to see if you had left the house yet." his message was short; he tossed his phone in his shirt pocket, grabbed his bag and waited by the curb side.

After thirty minutes, he called again, "Well, I guess you did not get my email, but don't worry, I'll go ahead and take a taxi, see you soon." he gave his address to the driver. His Korean surprised the driver like always. The driver admired that he was able speak so well.

"Are you visiting?"

He looked out of the window before putting visine in his eyes, "No, I live here."

"Ex-military, right?" the driver preceded on to the highway.

He didn't have many words for the driver, "No, not military, I have a Korean wife, and I have lived here for more than 15 years."

The driver eyes opened wide, mouth dropped to his chest. He nodded his head, "That's why your Korean is good."

"You look like you had been in a bad car accident." he pushed pass a white van that almost cut him off.

"Yeah…" he moaned as the swerve of the car added pain to his body, the visine missed his right eye, "…pretty bad accident." Not long after the driver pulled up to his home. "Thanks…" he bowed his head and gave him the fare, "…have a nice day."

He was so happy to be home, he could not wait to take a long hot bath. He opened the door, tossed his bags on the floor, kicked his shoes off, and sighed. He staggered in to the bedroom, "Yuki!"

She was on the floor, prompted up against the bed, "Yuki!" This pain was deeper than any he had ever experienced, he dropped to his knees, grabbed his face in disbelief, "No, no, no! Please!" the needle hung from her arm barely beneath her skin, the belt was tight around her upper right arm. He grabbed her cold body and screamed from the top of his lungs. His anger was unfiltered; he slammed his fist to the floor. He begged her to respond. It was too late to do anything. She was gone. He held his midsection to subdue his pain, it was too great, the screams alerted his neighbor. After calling 911, he called Na Min, "She is dead. Ahh no! She is dead!" Mugumbi screamed.

"What the hell happen?!" Na Min frantically asked.

"I came home and she was dead!" He could hear sirens in the distance.

"Just sit tight, I'm on my way!" Na Min grabbed his keys, slithered into a pair of jeans, and headed to the crime scene.

Upon arrival, the house was wrapped in crime scene tape; Mugumbi sat in the back seat of the police car. Just so happen Na Min saw a familiar face, "Well I'll be damn! What the hell you doing down here?" Na Min shook hands with the lead detective.

"Yeah well, I was off duty until someone call in sick." Detective Park patted him on the back.

"He's a good man," he looked at Mugumbi and nodded his head, "What the hell happen?" Na Min asked.

"Come on..." he smiled, "...I can't discuss this with you." Detective Park

He looked up at the house; tears fell as they carried Yuki's body to the van. Mugumbi screamed.

"She's my daughter for God sake! What the hell happened?!"

The detective held him and whispered in his ear, "It appears to be an over dose."

"His tears fell heavy, can I have a word with her husband?" he asked for permission.

"Sure, why not." Detective Park said.

He looked sad, "Hey you hang in there." He saw his bruises to his face. He tapped twice and then once on the roof of the car, "Cage fighting in Hawaii again." He looked at him.

For the first time he looked at him and knew he had something to do with his wife's murder. This could not have been an overdose. There was something that she had on him from those letters. He rested his head back and held his stomach. The pain was overwhelming. His mouth was dry; throat could not swallow the bullshit that he was feeding him. He closed his eyes with frustration, his left knee bounced up and down. He no longer wanted to look at him. He leaned over and threw up on the seat and the floor of the police car.

The detective walked over, "Sorry guys, it's time for him to go to the station for questioning, it shouldn't take long." They shook hands again.

"I am deeply sorry for you guys lost." No one responded. The detective gave the signal for the officer to drive off. The transporting officer was disgusted with him, but empathized.

Na Min sighed and hoped to find those letters Yuki mentioned on his answering machine. He searched the entire house before leaving her lifeless body. He only found the copies that she had printed out, and very pissed that he no longer had access to the house. He returned home.

The sound of Mugumbi's voice and cries echoed the walls of the police station, "Yuki!" he called her name throughout the interview. He just could not believe his wife was dead. He banged his forehead on the table several times. His nose bled, and the police had to place him under suicide watch. The detectives did confirm that he had been out of the country and freed him after he was cleared from suicide watch.

Twenty four hours later, he was released from the jail, lost and confused, not knowing if he was ready to return home to an empty house. He looked at the sky, a tear rolled down his right cheek. His vision was blurred as he walked two blocks and decided to sit on the curb side. His breathing felt restricted as he forced himself to inhale. The light pole prompted him upward; it was like someone pushed an ice pick in his chest. He reached in his right pants pocket for his visine, drenched his eyes, and didn't care about it falling down his face. He pulled out his cell phone and called Kalargo.

The phone rang several times before a voice relieved him of his impatience, "Kalargo!" He paused as he tried to calm himself, "Yuki is dead!" he could not help it, his voice was explosively loud as the traffic and pedestrians passed him.

"Mugumbi, I heard the horrible news. Na Min told me yesterday," he was interrupted.

"Kalargo!" the pain can be felt through the phone; he laid himself on to the sidewalk, "Yuki is gone!" he cried himself into a ball holding his midsection. "They told me she was two months pregnant!"

Kalargo was speechless, stopped whatever he was doing and took a seat. He rubbed his left hand across his forehead, "Mugumbi…" he knew he had no one to lean on, she was everything to him, and devastation was not powerful enough to describe what he was going through.

For the first time, he had ever seen him weaken like this, "What happened? Do you need me to come there?"

The silence was long, but interrupted, "They say she overdosed, but I know she was murdered! Kalargo, she was killed!" He squirted his eyes again covered his face with his shirt as he let out his cry. "I just can't believe that she is gone!"

"Why would anyone want to kill her?" Kalargo asked.

He started to say why, but thought clearly, and told him he would keep in touch. The phone went dead.

Kalargo could not believe what was going on with him. He signed and slowly placed the receiver on the phone, tried to hold back his tears but sadness overwhelmed him. "Oh my God Na Min." He shook his head. She was like a real sister to him. His stomach filled with grief as he tried to stand. He can hear his son crying like he knew something was wrong with his father. He picked him up and kissed him on the cheek, held him high above his head, and thought if something was to ever happen to him, more tears fell. He held him tight, "I love you." He slowly rocked him back to sleep.

After placing son in the crib, he walked out to the living room to call Na Min. He pushed his right hand across his forehead, used his sleeve to wipe his tears, "Hello, I just got off the phone with Mugumbi."

Na Min's voice came across as troubled, but holding it together. "This has to be one of the worst days of my life." The silence was deeper than a wound to his heart. He sobbed; his wife can be heard in the back ground crying.

"What happened?" he wanted to know so badly, before he could ask another question he was interrupted. Kalargo asked.

"She died of an overdose." Na Min can barely get the words out of his mouth.

"What! Overdose of what?" he never knew they both got high, so this was really blowing his mind.

"She had a heroin over dose." Na Min burst out into tears, his voice cracked to a whisper.

Kalargo was numb to the news, heartbroken that she had had this problem and never knew about it. He could not stop crying, tossing the receiver down to the floor. He didn't want to hear any more.

The funeral was sad as Na Min walked Mugumbi towards Yuki's casket. He touched her face, hair and leaned in to kiss her goodbye. Her face was cold to his lips, as he tried to walk away but couldn't. Na Min slowly tugged his elbow and guided him back to his seat. He was torn to pieces, felt like he could never be put back together.

Kalargo was devastated as he walked over to him. He knew Yuki was his foundation, his everything. "If you ever need anything..." before he could finish he hugged him, "...just let me know."

He didn't say a word, with his chin on his chest and fire in his eyes.

*   *   *

Gambia, Africa
Two weeks later

Kalargo and his son had arrived to Gambia to a nation's welcome. The King had told everyone that his son was coming home to take over and lead the country to victory. When the people found out who he was they were extremely happy. He was known as the karate kid. But not everyone embraced him; he did have some upset reminders he had to clear up.

Akette opened the door to the King's bedroom; his father was in bed, ill and barely able to lift his head. "Your majesty, your son and grandson is here to see you." He was down on one knee with his head bowed.

The King slowly opened one eye, and struggled to open the other. He cracked a smile beneath his shallow breathing, reaching for his oxygen mask, he inhaled. He had not been this happy in years, he shook his head, and his tears warmed his face as he reached for his grandson. He forced himself to sit upright; he was just strong enough to hold the prince. "I always had a feeling it was you Kalargo." He looked at him. "From the day I saw you, I had never felt so confident about you being my son." He looked up at him as he rocked his grandson carefully. He struggled to swallow, "It's time for you to take over."

He kissed the prince on the forehead, "I don't have to say how long I have to live, but as you already know, I am dying." He grabbed his mask and fogged it, looking down to his grandson, "What's his name?"

"Kalargo jr."

He smiled, "Excellent choice, one day he will be King, and follow in your footsteps.

Akette pulled a chair for him to sit next to the bed, "Thank you."

The King told Akette to exit the room so they could talk in private. He closed the door behind him. They spoke for hours, eating together, taking small breaks in between. He had to explain the country's situation, who was the new General of the Army. Who he trusted and who he wanted killed.

The following day he was introduced to the General, monetary advisors, national security, all the government agencies. Everyone had questions in the back of their minds, but dared to ask how an ex prisoner will be King one day, but is mostly known to the people as the karate kid who taught their army how to fight.

The next day he will be introduced to the nation through national television as the prince to the throne, paraded through the streets and make a speech in the town square.

"Come..." the King waved his hand as he slowly dragged his oxygen tank across the worn wooden floor like a nervous caterpillar, inch by inch. "...I want to show you something."

He pointed to a dusty shoe box, "There." he looked up, too high for an old man to grab.

Kalargo reached, barely able, but used his finger tips to slowly push it back and forward until the edge hung off, on his tiptoes, he lifted it and slowly dragged it until it fell on to his chest. The King smiled behind his oxygen mask and proceeded to track his way back to his bed. The shoe box was wrapped in cut up pieces of cloth and duck tape. He blew as much dust as he could.

"There is a pocket knife in the drawer, open it." He rested his tired body across the bed. The sound of the box being torn was like an unexplainable excitement to the King. He finally pulled back the last layer of tape and the top was lifted.

"This shoe box is history." The King coughed, "You need to know who you are." The box was filled with pictures and documents that explained so much. "All of these people are your family, all are now dead due to genocide..." he pointed to a photo, "...you see that?"

"This one?" Kalargo pulled from the pile.

"Yes, he was your brother..." he struggled to breathe but managed with a little oxygen.

"You want some water?" Kalargo asked.

"Yes, my throat gets a little dry when I get emotional." His eyes looked glossy of tears just talking about family.

The sound of the ice dangled the bottom of the glass, water filled it half way, with his hands he slowly made sure he held and watched him sip with his tongue as if it was hot, lapped like a cat, as his lips rested on the edge of the rim. He handed it back to him to place it on the night stand.

"Look on the back, what name is on the back of it?" The King said.

"Well that's not you, he was your brother, there is a photo of you when you were just a baby, and when you were three years old, that's the memory I had of you. You see they were trying to eliminate all of the blood line to my throne." He reached for the glass for a sip. "Now let me explain how I saved your life."

"This one, I found it." He showed him the photo; on the back it said Kalargo three years old.

Kalargo began to get emotional, he never knew anything of his passed and now he feels overwhelmed with excitement but sadness at the same time. "Who is this?" He pushed the photo towards his father.

The King closely examined it; he lifted his head, and took a moment, "Your mother?" He sighed with regret, "Understand, I had multiple wives, many children, after they were killed, you and your brother was the last in the blood line, so I had to come up with a way to keep you both alive. He lifted himself from his pillow, and reached for the box, "My closest friend had two sons, which were servants. I made their father a servant just so he would be close to me and I knew he had all good wishes for me. So anyway, his two sons grew up as a part of the family. I asked him as a favor to do the unthinkable. I gave them a choice…" He waved his index finger, "If they could take my only two sons out of Africa. Take you separately to America, separate cities so no one would find you and kill you both. He looked at Kalargo as he wiped a tear that streamed his face. "You survived, your brother did not." He used the bottom of his shirt to wipe his eyes.

"After all these years of living in Miami, they found him and his family, all dead." He took a deep rough breath that gasped his chest. He looked up at him and smiled, but they did not find you." He grabbed his hand to comfort him. But for all these years I never knew where the hell you were." He looked lost in his eyes, "It was like you had just disappeared, and I thought you were dead, but I had so much hope."

He reached for more water, "What city did you and Mugumbi live in?"

"South Korea." Kalargo said.

He spilled his water, and coughed up more water as he leaned forward. He tried to swallow, but reached for his oxygen mask. His eyes opened wide as he gulped as much oxygen as he could. He raised his hands to stop him.

"Are you going to be ok?" he patting him on his back.

"More water?"The King said. He looked at him with an urgent hell no, he cleared his throat and calmed himself down before speaking. "You mean to tell me, all of this time; you and Mugumbi were in South Korea?" He began to smile, giggled; he shook his head in disbelief. He could not stop laughing as his tears fell harder than his saddest. "I would have never guessed to look there. I have been looking for years. All this time you have been living right beneath the nose of the enemy. He leaned back with laughter, his blacken gums and dentures were revealed, the snake like veins protruded his neck, his body shook with laughter. "How in the hell did you guys end up there?"

Kalargo smiled and began his story from the beginning.

*   *   *

South Korea
Three months later

The air that Mugumbi use to breathe when he was in love with Yuki was different. Now no longer in his life, every breath was like inhaling clouds of dust. He sat on the patio listening to the music from inside. He rubbed his forehead and sighed. He could see the squirrels chase one another up and down the tree. He just wanted to be left alone, sober for a month now; it was just too painful to get high.

It reminded him to much of her. Sometimes he asked himself if he could have stop using when she was alive. Even though he had tried, but did not have a true reason to quit. He lowered his head when he thought about her being pregnant. What he could have had to this day rubbed his emotions raw.

He took a sip of his ice tea. The ice cubes floated to his upper lip, it was then that he had realized that he had never actually made the ice tea, she did. He also knew that it did not taste the same as hers. He took in a deep sigh as his eyes watered.

He was startled by a banging at his front door that obviously caught his attention in between songs. He wiped his face and decided to make his way through the maze of moving boxes that cluttered his living room and kitchen. Without a care in the world to who was banging, he pulled the door open.

"I've been calling you for days, are you ok?" Na Min said.

He looked at Na Min with disgust, but greeted him with a smile. "Yes, I know I have been so busy with packing..." he pointed towards the boxes as he welcomed him in. He sighed from the bottom of his chest. "...as you can imagine, it's hectic. You care for anything to drink?"

"Sure why not."

"I hope ice tea will do? I have packed most of the kitchen already."

"Wow, so you are really leaving South Korea?" They both sat on the two remaining chairs that had not been wrapped up.

Na Min looked around at the boxes. "Well, if you ever need anything, and I mean anything, don't hesitate to pick up that phone."

He sipped his ice tea that didn't taste like hers, more like a stranger had made his tea, too much sugar, not enough tea, what the fuck. He looked at his glass and shook his head.

"Good tea." Na Min said.

He looked at him as he looked at his glass. "So what brings you this far across town?"

"Well I have an executive party for you..." before he could finish he pulled a file from his chest, "...are you up for it?"

A moment of silence from them both was awkward, "I could understand if it's too soon..." he was interrupted.

"Mr Choi, I truly can say that I am done." He rubbed his chin and relaxed his body like he had gotten something huge off of his chest. "I no longer feel like hurting anyone, taking lives. I mean since her death..." his sigh of relief was evident that he was done. "...you know she really really made me complete. She was my everything." He frowned as he shook his head, "I have made up my mind. I am going back home." He had sold their three homes and their business and came out with several million.

Na Min knew that he could not change his mind, so he didn't try. "You need me to help you with anything while I'm here?"

They both stood, "Well I'm pretty much done; besides most of this stuff is so sentimental, I prefer to do it myself."

He reached his hand out and they shook hands firmly, their goodbyes ended with a firm bear hug. The door closed their chapter of friendship.

He turned around to the maze of boxes and downed his drink. He slowly turned the music up and went back to the patio.

Moments later a banging at the door just after he sat down. "What the..." he wondered what more could he want now, as he stormed through the maze of boxes, snatched the door open, it was too late, it happened so fast, before he could take his final breath to utter his mind out loud.

"I have a package for a Yuki that has to be signed."

Mugumbi's heart pounded, but slowly returned to normal after he realized the FedEx delivery man was at his door. "Where did it come from?"

"It looks like it went to the wrong address, all the way to a small village in Peru."

They both looked confused, but he signed it anyway and shut the door, tossed the package on the kitchen counter and went back to the patio.

Chapter 28

Na Min kissed his wife on the lips, grabbed her butt and pulled her close to his chest. "No matter what anyone says, you are still beautiful."

She locked her lips on to his, "I love you, but you need to hurry up and pack before we miss our flight." She pushed him away to finish with her makeup. She sighed, happy to be going to Puerto Rico, it's been more than ten years since her last visit. She could hardly contain herself.

"Well my bags are ready to go, just have to make a couple of phone calls. He button up his neatly pressed shirt, cuffs were folded inward above his wrist, lined up his gig line, last look in the mirror, "Damn I am getting old." He plucked a gray hair from his ear. He peeked around the door to make sure she was not coming to his office, quickly went over to the vent where he had tossed the letters he had taken from Yuki's dead hands.

He sighed because he really wanted the originals. Turned on his shredder, fold each letter multiple times before sliding them into the shredder, once that was done, he dumped the basket into the toilet to soak the little pieces, and down the sewer they went. He quickly looked through the crack of the bathroom door. She had passed through the hallway. He quickly placed the basket beneath the shredder, "Honey, waiting on you."

He grabbed his bags and headed towards the car. "How many bags do you have?" he asked.

"Two, well three if you count my shoe bag." She placed two of her bags next the tailpipe of the car. The driver placed them into the trunk, and then opened their door.

"Yes, yes on time, I can't believe we are finally going to Puerto Rico." She rubbed his hands, kissed him on the neck, removed lent from his eye braw.

They passed through security, and gave their tickets to the woman at the gate, with head of the line privileges; it took them no time to find their seats.

"Drink?" she offered him a glass.

"Of course my love..." Na Min smiled. "How long is this flight?"

"Well including the layover, twenty four hours minimum." She smiled.

"Well double up on my drink, I will need as much as possible."They both smiled and tossed to a great vacation.

The first class seats were soft, big and comfortable, "I need one more drink, stiff one." He could barely hold a straight face.

"No, no I think you have had enough." She held his hand down from calling the flight attendant. He rubbed her inner thigh.

He managed to hit the call button, "You know we have to transfer flights, and you won't be up to all of that if you are drunk." She tried to talk him out of a drink, but to no avail.

"Yes how can I help you?" the flight attendant asked.

He cleared his throat, straighten up and spoke like a little sober hamster that leaned to his left. "Yes an orange juice and gin please."

His wife just turned away as her damaged smile was covered by her right hand. "Please let this be the last one."

He looked at her with blood shot eyes, "It will be the last one." He held up his left index finger in her face and brought it back to his lips, "Shhhhh." He giggled.

After a couple hours the alcohol had settled in and totally relaxed him into a hard snore that induced a dream that seemed so real. He clenched his fist at times, gritted his teeth, raised his heart beat and blood pressure had peaked.

He could not stop dreaming about Mugumbi. This one dream in particular curled his toes; when he came home this one evening. The weekend was great, as he entered the house he had a feeling he was not alone. The fear could burst his heart. His damped hairy chest became cold, his legs were noodle like, and, this strange smell that lingered the house was proof that someone had been there or remained.

He tried to control his breathing, he made it to his office, grabbed his pistol, made sure it was loaded, and took cover behind his office desk. He sat there for hours he would not move until that god awful stench was gone. He had heard nothing, saw nothing, and decided to crawl towards the door that led to the hallway. He listened for anything, used his nose to sniff like a blood hound, nothing, but the smell was close. He pulled the hammer back just in case. He rested on his knees and elbows, peaked around and in between the cracks. Just as he looked to his left, the smell rubbed his nose like a bad wet diaper filled with deification. He remained motionless.

From out of nowhere he felt something grab his ankles and pulled him across the floor, twisted him around, and tossed him into the corner of the office desk. He was unconscious.

When he woke up, his hands, legs were ducked taped to his office chair. He tried to scream but his lips were safety pinned together. He tried to move his tongue but the razor blade was down the middle, it cut his upper gum every time he moved it. He could hear a strange noise from his window. He used his toes and momentum to turn the chair around, with all his might he inched just enough to see above his window seal.

Mugumbi was digging a hole and he knew this could not end well. They made eye contact that lasted a minute. He waved his index finger at him and pointed towards the hole. He violently tried to get out of this but only exhausted himself. He wished he could chew his way through the duck tape. Mugumbi had thought of that. He used his toes and momentum to turn the chair around and noticed plastic covered his office, if his heart was a knife he could cut his way out of this mess. He tried to calm himself and breathe shallow, but he let out a desperate painful yelp like a dying dog. His mouth was filled with blood that drooled his shirt. He looked in the corner, neatly laid out were construction tools. His eyes were covered with fear. His legs moved nonstop. Suddenly, Mugumbi appeared at the doorway.

"Mr Choi, Mr. Choi, I am so glad the shoe is on the other foot." He wiped his hands, face, and neck, tossed the towel over his shoulder. "I know you have plenty to say but there is nothing that will get you out of this situation. He walked over to his desk, grabbed a paper weight and wacked Na Min across his mouth.

His eyes opened wide with pain. He couldn't plea if he tried.

"You will suffer like I did. You took my world away from me. If it takes my last breath to keep you alive just so you can feel the maximum pain. I will grant you that breath that will save your life..." he walked over to his tools and picked up a ball hammer, "...but I promise you, you will beg for death and I will not grant you a death. I will feed you and do whatever I need to keep this pain going. Motherfucker, this is so personal." He smashed his left knee cap to pieces, and with full force smashed his pinky toe till it hung to his left.

"Hmmmmmm! Hmmmmmm! Hmmmmm!" Na Min was in shock and wanted to die so bad he closed his eyes and pretended like he had passed out.

Mugumbi lit a cigarette and puffed slowly, inhaled deeply, "I would offer you a cigarette, but it does not look like you would manage."

Na Min was silent, motionless, holding his pain behind his closed eyes, tears fell, really hoping the pain would stop, maybe he would have some type of compassion.

The ball hammer smashed into his left jawbone, his eyes opened wide, "Hmmmmmmmm! Hmmmmm!" he struggled hard enough to make his chair flip over.

He was hit again to the back of his head. He went silent. He fell over onto the dark brown wood floor that pushed against his face from the weight. His rib cage was attacked until his breathing was affected. He gasped for air, the razor blade cut up his gums until they were soft tissue.

Mugumbi lifted the chair to straighten him up. "You want some water?" No response from him, so he walked over and poured him a glass of alcohol.

Na Min was exhausted, thirsty, anything to swallow would do.

"Hold your head back..." he tried to hold his head up and back, opened his lips as far apart as he could.

He could feel the pressure from the safety pins that resisted, "Awwww!"

"Open!" he dangled the glass above his mouth. "Open up!" he could see his lips begin to rip, blood smeared his face and shirt.

He grabbed his jawbone with his left hand tight enough to force his mouth further apart. He quickly poured the alcohol in his mouth, covered his mouth with his right hand so he could not spit it out. He violently tried to wiggle his head away. He sat on top of him to make sure he doesn't swallow.

"Hmmmmmmmmmm! Hmmmmmmmm!" he pissed on his self as he fought like hell to spit the rubbing alcohol out.

Mugumbi never thought he would be exhausted from sharing his pain, but he was feeling hungry and wanted to take a break. He walked behind him and put him in a choke hold until he was close to death. Tears fell; he gagged for air, just before his last breath he was let go.

Mugumbi stepped in front of him with his index finger in his face, "You are going to pay for what you did!" he yelled at the top of his lungs. He wanted to cry but too piss to let one tear fall. He smashed his right knee cap before leaving him to get something to eat.

"Aaaaah!"

The dream felt so real, "Excuse me sir, you have to raise your seat for landing." The flight attendant tried to wake him. His eyes opened with fear. He looked at his wife.

"Are you ok?" she noticed he had a bad dream, but it was not unusual for it to happen. She gave him a napkin to wipe himself of the sweat. He sighed and lifted himself from his seat to look for Mugumbi. He felt like he was on the plane.

"Honey, are you ok?"

He rubbed his clammy chest; he reached for the air vent. Someone had closed it. He opened it, and looked down the aisle and noticed a black guy seating in the rear of the plane. "Shit."

He looked again but it was not Mugumbi. He rubbed his neck, touched his knee caps, touched his tongue, and looked at his wife.

"I'm ok. I'm ok." He smiled at her and kissed her on the lips. It stung from a small cut. He rubbed his tongue across it and sighed. He looked out the window, below was Los Angeles. He caresses his wife hands and kissed the back of it.

She looked at him, "No hang over? I thought for sure that
you would have a hangover?"

He grinned and kissed her on the lips, "Yeah right my love. I am sober as I can be." He looked behind him one more time to make sure Mugumbi was not on the plane.

*   *   *

Seoul, South Korea

The sound of packing tape can be heard throughout the house as he carefully filled her belongings in boxes. He paused and wondered what he would do with it all. He sighed in disbelief, stopped to wipe his mouth and face. He promised to stop crying because he could not bring her back.

He pulled out her favorite teddy bear that he bought her, well one of her favorites out of dozens that he had gotten her over the years. But this one she loved, most touched of them all. He looked around the bedroom and stopped for a brief moment. The thought of being alone was so unimaginable. It was never a thought that one day he could possible live without her. He came to a decision and placed a call.

"Hello, I wanted to know where to donate some house goods?" he spoke to a thrift store as he paced the floor. What could he possibly do with all of her things? It would drive him insane to smell her, see her most loved items around and know he would never see her, touch her again.

"Yes, we have a location, do you have a pen?"

He began to write and noticed his hands were shaking; just knowing that he was going to do this was hard. He gathered all of her boxes and pushed them in one corner of the living room. He went to the kitchen to grab a drink and noticed the FedEx package. He did not give it a second thought, grabbed it, untapped a box and stuffed it along the side between several pairs of shoes. However, he decided to keep the teddy bear. He arranged for the movers to deliver the boxes, poured a hot cup of tea and sat on the patio.

*   *   *

Puerto Rico

The plane landed in Puerto Rico softly after an uneasy ride through a thunder storm. "Welcome home my love, the weather is gorgeous." Their lips locked with a wet kiss. He pointed out of the window, "I have not seen that in a long time."

She looked out the window to see a huge iguana running across the tarmac. He removed the airplane mode from his cell phone and many messages alerted him. The first message, "We need to talk about the situation in Gambia."

He pressed the button for the second message, "I've been trying to get a hold of you, very important." As they departed the plane with their carry on in tow, he still listened to the next message, "Na Min, your son is working against us? Is it true? How are we going to handle this?" he let out a big sigh of frustration, tossed his cell in his pocket. He knew this day would come to light soon. Nothing seems to be going as planned.

"What's wrong?" she rubbed his back and neck briefly, "work again?" they headed towards the baggage claim.

"Yeah, it was a couple of things that I need to take care of."

Her family surprised her with a huge banner, flowers, "Oh my God..." she looked at him, "...did you set this up?"

He smiled, "Anything for the love of my life."

His cell begins to ring, but he decided to silence it.

"Welcome to Puerto Rico!" her uncle rushed over and hugged her, and kissed her on the cheek.

Her grandmother cried as she tried to stand from her wheelchair. "I love, I love you so much." They embraced as the tears flowed.

Later that afternoon he finally had a chance to respond to the North Koreans, "Yes hello."

"Na Min, we have a serious situation," The sound of his sigh can be heard as he walked the small back yard of her grandmother's house.

"We just heard about Kalargo being the prince to the throne of Gambia. What the heck is going on?" before a response can be heard, "Do you have this under control?"

A moment of silence was not a good sign, "This is not looking good. You need to let him know that he need to step down or else." The threat slapped him and let him know that his adopted son's life is in danger.

He leaned over to smell a beautiful flower that bloomed with lavender and yellowish colors. He pulled it from its root and pushed it against his nose. For the first time he had little to say, the North Koreans had him by the balls. He looked at his wife as she passed the kitchen window. They both smiled at each other. He could see the happiness in her face. The voice on the phone is squawking when reality came to, "Yes I know, this does not look good, nothing looks good right now." He was cut short.

"Handle this problem, you have thirty days." The phone went dead. He looked at the cell with disgust.

"Are you going to hang out in the backyard for your entire visit?" her uncle walked towards him with a smile, unaware of his situation.

"Are you kidding, of course, just had to handle some things I forgot to do before departing South Korea."

The sound of Latin music inspired him to perform his version of a two step with salsa that gave away any thought about his dance moves. They begged him to stop with laughter, but he insisted on his ridiculous dance moves that would most likely get him arrested. It was all in fun and the laughter continued. They gave him a strong Gin and juice and the party went on into the night.

The following day he was exhausted with a hangover, his face covered with his pillow. He looked around the room and could not remember where he was for the first two minutes. He smiled when the multi colored wallpaper, old furniture; wall paintings of Puerto Ricans on farmland slowly reminded him. He rubbed his face and looked over and she was not there. He moaned as he buried his face into the pillow. He scratched his head and wish he had an aspirin.

The French doors were open as the breeze pushed the white linen curtains around. The sounds of chickens were in the distant, smell of breakfast danced around his hangover. He forced his hands to push himself up from the bed. He sat up with his feet reaching for the white shaggy rug. He felt like a broken down wagon, pulled by a donkey. The wrinkles in his face had deepened; his muscles across his chest now perform like breast. There was a time when he was able to make them bounce on command, now they jiggle if he breathes too hard. He could not remember the last time he walked around proudly without a shirt. He smiled at the thought.

Just before he was about to stand, his wife cracked the door, "Good morning, breakfast is ready." She waited for him to acknowledge.

He looked over his shoulder, "Hmmm, I'll be right down."

"I guess that blowjob exhausted you last night?" she smiled.

He turned around with a surprising look on his face, crack a smile because he couldn't remember a once in a life time event. "Oh, well I guess..." he looked at himself in the mirror, "...they aren't the same anymore; even blowjobs are going downhill."

They both laughed as she closed the door, "See you down stairs."

After washing up, he tossed a pair of pants and shirt on, "Hello." He answered his cell. He spoke under his breath in secrecy. "Ok, how does it look?" he stood at the door. "Yes that sound great, can you send it to my email?" he stood with his right hand on the door knob.

"Thanks, you have been a great help..." he smiled. "...let you know soon, ok thanks." As soon as he opened the door his wife was just about to enter, "There you are." They both kissed and headed down stairs.

"Oh these pancakes are great." Na Min stuffed a fork with three layers of pancake with dripping warm syrup.

His mother in law smiled at the fact that she still had the skills in the kitchen. "You know I remember how you guys met, and perhaps..."

Her uncle raised his knife, "How did you guys meet?" Silence had blanketed the table. Na Min stopped mid chew of his pancakes and looked around. When he swallowed his throat looked like a python that swallowed a new born calf.

"Well..." he normally doesn't speak on how they met because his family was killed with a bomb that was meant for him. "She worked at a clothing store and I went in looking for a tie." He cut his sausage and tossed it in his mouth, "And there she was just as beautiful as she could be." He smiled and winked his left eye. "She was all over me, everywhere I went; I couldn't get rid of her."

Everyone laughed at how his wife had looked at him, knowing he was telling a tale. "So, after I finally gave in to her begging me for my number and asking me to take her out to dinner. You know in my mind, I thought she was just hungry" He could barely hold a serious look on his face. He sighed and was happy to digress the conversation away from explaining how his first wife and kids were murdered. She stood up and reached for his plate.

"You want more?"

He laughed knowing it was she who played hard to get, "No thanks, I am stuffed. Breakfast was good..." before he said another word he received an email on his cell.

"Tell them the truth." She patted him on his right shoulder; everyone looked at her and laughed. "Ok, but she was still all over me." He stood up and pulled out his cell, "I got to take this call."

After he walked away from the table, stepped into the living room, and out the back door, "Yes I received it, I like 1429, and it will be all cash, five days, right?" the voice on the phone tried to explain how difficult it would be.

"Well, if you can make it happened, an extra ten thousand for a bonus, tax free." He spoke softly into the cell as he paced the back yard nervously looking over his shoulder.

"Well, try your best this is very important." He pushed the end button.

Five days later he woke up early, tiptoed across the ceramic tile, slithered into his denim jeans and white button up shirt. He looked across his shoulder to make sure she was still sleep. He carefully grabbed his rental car keys and like a snake saturated in baby oil, slid through the door. As soon as he got in the car, the time was seven thirty in the morning, "Hello, are you there?" He quickly drove off. "Ok, I'll be there in fifteen minutes."

He return hours later, sat on the porch and watched the chickens, and the goats stare at him. "There you are…" his wife came out of the house, "…you couldn't sleep?"

He sighed and looked at her with a smile, "Well, just one of those nights." They kissed.

"You have tea this morning?"

"Sure why not." He looked her in the eyes.

"Breakfast will be ready soon." She entered the house.

"Well, I thought we could have breakfast at that restaurant that we had gone to the last time we were here, you know…"

"Oh, hmmm, I'll tell my mom…" she was interrupted.

"I have to pick up a friend of mine before we arrive. He has a couple of paintings I wanted to take a look at." It was kind of odd but it did not bother her one bit.

On the way on a narrow road, they spoke of what it looked like many years ok. How much it had changed since the last time they had visited. She held his right hand and kissed it. The gated horses, goats, and cows passed their window. They pulled up to a townhouse on the beach, "I hope he is ready." He dialed his cell.

"Yeah, I am outside." He looked at her as he spoke on the cell. "Ok, will do." He pushed the end button, turned the car off, "He has the paintings inside, come and see if you like something."

She joyfully unbuckled her seatbelt, slid her sandals on to her feet, and exited the car. The wind gust her sun dress, "Oh my lord..." she held it down as she gain entry to the townhouse, "...this is nice, never knew they had built these."

"Surprise, welcome home!" her family had been waiting for her to arrive. He gave the keys to her beach side townhouse, "This is yours, paid for."

She jumped for joy, walked around in awe. "Are you serious?" she covered her face to hide her tears. She hugged her family, one by one. They gave her a tour of the home, it was furnish, modern, just how she had always said she liked. "How did you know I would have like it?"

He looked at her, grabbed her hand, and kissed her lips, "When you love someone, some things you just know."

The three story, three bedroom, three bathrooms, two car garage sat on a private beach. She was just too overwhelmed. The infinity pool and spa with patio set was an invitation. The door bell rang. "Now who in the world could this be?"

She opened the door, "Wow."

The breakfast will be cooked by the hired chef. They enjoyed the rest of the day.

The sky began to fade to dark as the sun set on the horizon. The sand between his toes was fluffy soft as he walked the beach. He threw stones in the ocean, but constantly thought about the original letters that he could not find.

He knew if those letters were to get out, the career that he had so carefully planned will come to a halt. He wondered did Mugumbi have the letters and started to read them. He shook his head and doubted that he would read a slew of letters from years ago. He sighed and threw a stone hard enough to reach the South Korean shore.

*   *   *

Seoul, South Korea

Mugumbi just could not sleep, tossed and turn throughout the night. He had dreams of Yuki playing in the back yard. She teased him about his growing belly that he had promised to exercise away with time. He opened his eyes to a dark room, rubbed his eyes, reached over to hit the switch on the night lamp.

The walls were bare from the removal of wall paintings, knickknacks, and furniture. The floor was hard and wished he had held on to his mattress. He had pillows tucked strategically alongside to help his back. He grunted after trying to lift his leg. The stab wounds hurt occasionally. He rolled himself to his stomach and pushed himself from the floor. "Aaaah."

He stood tall, stretched his arms and walked into the bathroom. He missed her girly things lying around. He used her deodorant and lotions, none of those things were present. He felt totally upside down. Today is his final day in the house. Everything had been shipped out. He had scheduled for a cleaning crew to come in and paint, shampoo the rugs, clean the house. He could not believe he was saying good bye to South Korea.

The sound of the shower knobs squeaked as the flow of hot water fogged the mirror. He crawled into the shower like a wounded kitten, used his manly soap and shampoo. He stood there for awhile as he cried. Somehow he had to get over her death, but how? He asked himself many times. He felt guilty for not being around. He pounded his fist into the wall softly, "Oh God why her?"

He thought he had heard something, but wasn't sure. He turned the water off, listened carefully. He pulled a towel that hung from the rail on the wall. He dried his face, hair, and listened again. His face frowned and brushed it off.

His mind was playing games with him. He walked over to the mirror, wiped the steam away with the towel with his right hand, and wrapped the towel around his midsection. He stopped and listened. He came to the bathroom door, "I thought I heard something."

He walked down the stairs, looked out the window, nothing. Still a little wet, bare foot with just a towel he went toward the kitchen, "Damn, I should have something for me to eat." He closed the door to the refrigerator. He stopped and listened. He heard a soft knock at the door. He walked over and looked through the peep hole. He opened the door and there she was standing shyfully.

"Yes..." she bowed and spoke in Korean, "I am looking for..." she pulled an envelope that had the address, "...Yuki."

"She is not here, how can I help you?"

She was so surprised that he spoke Korean so well. She hesitated and forgot why she had come there in the first place. "I am so sorry, but she had donated some of her clothes to the thrift store and my boss felt like..." she pulled out the letters, "...these letters were not meant to be discarded." She handed the letters to him.

He was surprised and thought he would never see anything to remind him of her. He sighed, "Oh yes, but…" he held them in his hands as he thumb through them quickly. He adjusted his towel, "You know, I really was just trying to get rid of them."

She bowed before leaving but he stopped her.

"Since when does the thrift store return items that are given to them?

She smiled and shy fully walked away. He closed the door and tossed the letters on to the kitchen counter. He had to pack his bags and catch a flight to Hawaii.

As he packed his luggage, a car horn was blowing from the drive way. "Wow…" he looked at his watch, "…he is early." He ran down stairs to let the driver know to give him a moment to pack. He dashed back into the house grabbed a couple of things that remained out, carried his bags to the door, look one last time, and closed the door.

"What airline are you flying?" the driver asked with a lit cigar hanging from the left corner of his mouth. He grabbed his bags and carefully places them in the trunk.

"Hawaiian Airlines." He sighed as he climbed in the back seat.

The driver drove off for a moment and stopped. The door opened and he quickly ran back towards the house, open the door, and went directly towards the kitchen. The last thing he wanted to forget was his food for the flight. He turned around and headed out, but noticed the letters. Grabbed them and put them underneath his armpit and locked the door.

"Now…" he looked at the driver, "…we can go to the airport." He places the food in his carry on and placed the letters in the side pocket. "Well at least I'll have something to read." He leaned his head back and relaxed.

His flight to Hawaii was smooth, slept most of the way. The seven forty seven landed like a butterfly with sore feet. He was able to read the first dated letters that really raise his suspicion about Na Min. As the plane taxied the tarmac, he neatly folded the letters of the first envelope and tucked it among the others. He could not wait to read more. Each envelope contained at least eight pages, and he knew he had to read every one of them to know what Yuki knew, and why would anyone want her dead.

Later that day he arrived to Kalargo's house, found the spare key, exactly where he was told it would be. Tossed his bags and sighed, happy to be on the ground. He opened the blinds, curtains, windows, and dusted the place up so he could breath. He pulled out his visine to lubricate his eyes before he began to read the rest of the letters.

He kicked off his shoes, removed his blue jeans and got into something more comfortable. He carefully placed the envelopes on the kitchen table in the order by the date they were mailed.

He stood there, plucked a nose hair with his thumb and index fingers. He decided to toss on a white Nostalgic Society t-shirt, navy blue shorts, but he paused. He went to the fridge, "Yes..." he grabbed a bottle of wine, the rest of the food needed to be thrown out, and "...I guess I'll have to order out." He frowned at the food in the fridge. He promised to clean the fridge later. He opened the bottle of wine, and poured until the rim had to be sucked to prevent the over flow from spilling. He carefully walked over to the couch, placed his glass, slid over to the dinner table, grabbed the first envelope, and the next dated envelope. He could not wait to finish the first, and start the second.

By the time he got to the second letter he was adding more visine to his eyes, half of the bottle of wine was sipped, and he was shocked at these accusations he was reading. He had learned about the miscarriage Yuki's mother had, and that she had a brother she had never met from an affair that her biological father had with an African woman. He had to stop reading because he had realized what she was going through. His eyes watered, sad, and to find out in this fashion had to be tough; not being by her side during this ordeal, downright painful He sighed and cussed himself for being so stupid. He wiped his face and gritted his teeth. He had to take a break from reading and the wine. It was too much for him to read and he was not related by blood. But he knew somehow Na Min was at the end of the rainbow, and vowed to find out what she wanted to tell him that was so important that she could not tell him over the phone.

He ordered a pizza, took a break from it all, but mentally went over what he had learned so far, and it was disturbing. Na Min was one the most ruthless men on earth, can't be trusted, and a lot of power. A lot more than he had originally thought, his tentacles reached as far as the white house, and that made him dangerous. He took a bite of his pizza, paused for a moment and wondered why he had not killed him yet?

He placed the rest of his slice on the plate in front of him, stood up and carefully walked to peek out the windows, checked the back yard. He had slowly grown paranoid. He checked the entire house to make sure he was alone. All noise alerted him like a dog, so out of fear he decided to call him. He had to get a feeling, some type of sense of relief through his voice, but he is a professional, would he be able to hide his true emotions from him?

He sighed before dialing his number, paced the living room as the phone rang. If he was going to be hunted and killed, he would need to turn the table on his hunter. The voicemail slithered through the ear piece, with no soothing to his nerves. He opened the French doors to the pool and patio set, walked around the beautiful pool and tried again. "Damn." He thought about trying again, but decided to wait.

Kalargo's backyard retreat was well landscaped with beautiful flowers, thick soft grass; coconut trees lined the wall on the perimeter. He plucked a flower that caught his eye, it smelt good. He wished he knew what kind of flower it was. He sighed before trying to call again. His thoughts were interrupted with a phone call, "Hello Mugumbi, how are you doing?"

Na Min spoke with a crowd of noise in the background, laughter, music, "How is everything going?"

Mugumbi sighed when he heard his voice, but that did not mean he was in the clear, "I was just calling..." not knowing what to really say but wanted to analyze his voice, "...thinking about another executive party."

He slapped his palm on his thigh because that was not what he really wanted to bring up.

"Yeah I remember that, how long ago was that?" Na Min spoke to the crowd in the background, but it almost confused him.

"Sorry about that." He returned to the phone conversation. "Well if anything comes up, I'll let you know." He laughed at his wife making funny faces of him while in bed. Her family really thought it was funny. "Hey I'm in Puerto Rico, and I'm the butt of my wife's jokes. I'll have to call you back; she is killing me, making me look horrible over here. The phone went dead.

Mugumbi flopped into the couch, relieved a little but not convinced. He knew he had time to read the rest of these letters, so he started from where he had left off, and it had gotten even more horrific.

*   *   *

San Juan, Puerto Rico

Moments after Mugumbi's first call

"Excuse me..." Na Min got everyone's attention for a brief moment, "...listen I just got a missed call from my boss and I am having too much fun to talk to him." He smiled with his drink in his hand. "He is going to call back but I need you guys to talk load, turn the music up, and sound like everyone is talking over one another. I really need this to work." He pumped up his wife family to help him with his deception and it worked.

He needed more time to find those original letters, and after the dream he had on his way to Puerto Rico, his life seemed to be coming to an end a lot faster than he had planned. However, if he can get rid of him; the letters may disappear forever. He also knew he would not be an easy kill; after all, he trained him to be an assassin.

He raised his glass of Genifer, kissed his wife and danced the night away. Everyone was happy to have helped him.

"Another drink for his boss." someone yelled out loud. The laughter roared like thunder as they tossed shots of Puerto Rican rum down their throats.

"So..." a voice came from the back of the room, "...what kind of faces does he make?"

The room roared of laughter as he tried to switch the conversation, but it did not work, "Hey, hey..." he raised his glass, "...no need to go there."

But he was interrupted by his wife, "Oh don't get me started..." she looked at him with this grin but went ahead anyway, "...he tries to be so romantic, his eyes began to cross, biting his tongue, and he always look like he is one breathe from a fucking heart attack." She kissed him on his lips. "So while he is having the time of his life. I'm scared to death, and ready to resuscitate his ass as he go through convulsions, and what not..." everyone is holding their sides from laughing to death, she fans her face with her hand, "but I love him for..." she paused and look at him, shook her head, "I want a divorce!"

The room roared with laughter as he started shaking, biting his tongue, and creating undesirable faces as if an orgasm was near. She slapped him on his chest, pushed him away, "Stop it, you are scarring me, again asshole, it's not funny."

He could not help himself from spilling his drink, leaned in and planted a big kiss on her neck, "I love you..." with slurred words, pulled her close, raised his right hand as he swallowed a ball of courage, "...I want everyone in this room." he paused as the room was silenced for his speech, "...to always and forever know that I love her to death and no matter what happens..." he looked around the room. He took a deep sigh, "...there is nothing above her, our love, and how I feel about us." He dropped down on one knee with her hand in his right and the glass of Genifer in the other, "Will you marry me, just one more time?"

"Well hell, I don't know who I am marrying, you or the glass of Genifer?" the room of people fell to the floor with laughter. She pulled him up from the floor, "Baby, I will marry you a hundred times. You are the best thing to have ever happened to me." She planted her lips on to his, locked their tongues like French doors overlooking a mountain side.

"More drinks for everyone!" he raised his drunken hand with a smile. He was happy to know that he had lived a life beyond incredible and no one can take that away from him.

Chapter 29

Gambia, Africa

The King walked the back patio of the palace with his oxygen tank in tow in one hand and Kalargo jr. in the other; side by side Kalargo walked with him, making sure he does not drop him.

"Hey little fellow..." he smiled, Eskimo kissed him, and dance a little, "...he is going to be wonderful. I wish I could be around to see him grow and grow. He held him close and tight, "I love, oh yes I do." He spoke with his version of a toddler, "Naa naa, goo ga."

"Father..." it was strange for him to say that word, but it slowly grew on to him, "...please, oh my God he is going to be speaking monkey if you continue to teach him words like that." They both laughed as they walked towards the grassy area. The King slowly took a knee and placed him on the greenest patch of grass he could find.

"Oh look how fast he is." He placed his other knee down and rested on his stomach, "Ga ga... look at him."

He crawled along side of him, smiling the entire way. The King had not been this happy in years. The servants had never seen this side of him, and as they looked from the windows with joy. Some of them cried to see how happy he was. For years he had requested to bring his son home, everyone thought he was going crazy, losing his mind, but only he knew that there was a blood line in the world that he secretly sent away.

"So father, how do you think the nation accepted me as the Prince to the throne?"

He looked up at him, "Kalargo, the country is looking for leadership, someone who they can trust, believe in, all you have to do is be that great leader." he took his time and swallowed a gulp of oxygen.

"I have a question, what would have happened if you had not have found me?" he stood over them as the King laid flat on his back with the baby on his chest.

He stopped bouncing Kalargo jr., "I had a plan for that type of thing..." he placed his lips on the baby's stomach and blew, "ga ga boo boo." They both laughed.

"So, what was the plan?"

"Well I may be an old man, but I can still have kids, well may be not like I use to. You know these days they have these clinics where they freeze your sperm, right?"

Kalargo laughed and before he could say another word.

"You see I had given myself another two years before I was going to find a surrogate mother." They smiled before laughing hard and loud.

"What?"

"It's not like I did not try the natural way..." he tickled Kalargo to tears. "Hey I had this big parade of women, you know wife prospects to see who I wound pick to be my next wife..." he was using his hands to describe the event, "My lord, it was really overwhelming. All these beautiful gals running around..." he took a deep breath, "...hey I pick six, now at my age..." he gestured to his oh so handsome figure, "...what the hell am I going to do with six model type gals."

They laughed throughout the conversation, "But it was one, she was soooo..." he stressed on her beauty with passion, waved his hands in the air of the shape of a bottle, "...big tits, soft lips, ass?" he frowned like he had took a shot of straight tequila and revealing his teeth that was in desperate need of dental work, "fine, I just knew she shit different." They both laughed hard and long. He puckered his lips like she was in front of him.

"So what happend?"

"Well..." he paused and laid back down, grabbed Kalargo jr. and placed him back on to his chest, "...I tell you what, they couldn't handle this old man." He grinned.

Kalargo could not help but to laugh, "What is that supposed to mean?"

"I worked them gals so hard, they all gave up. It wasn't like I didn't let them know that my penis was in bad shape, you know what I mean?" he tried not to laugh. He cleared his throat. "Now that fine one, oh she..." he shook his head and looked heartbroken, "said God damn, I know you old, penis is in bad shape, but I didn't' know it was in this much bad shape." They both laughed hard, long as their tears rolled down their faces. He inhaled from his oxygen mask. Then they gave me this little blue pill, somehow it was supposed to be able to make a limp dick do tricks, curve up and down, spin around, you know all that type of shit, well..." He slowly lifted himself from the ground, looked around, "...that's how I got my nick name."

Kalargo crossed his arms, trying not to cry., "What nick name?"

"Well, that little blue pill really does work, on some people." He looked disappointed, rubbed his face, "Damn she was so fine..." he rolled over to his side, slapped his palm on to the grass.

"They started calling me cotton dick; I was hard on the tip, hard at the back, and soft as a mother fucka in the middle."

His saliva drooled from the corner of his mouth as laughter retarded them both. After gasping for breath, farting uncontrollably, "excuse me, that damn ghost been trying to get out for a week, be careful; he mad as hell."

"They told me, 'Majesty, may be you can get that surgery where they cut the middle out, attach the tip to the back portion." They rolled across the grass in laughter.

"I knew it was over, when I could walk by a fine piece of ass and it makes me nauseas." He crossed his fingers.

"It's no use in thinking about it. I just rather throw up." His saliva rolled down his neck as he tried to contain himself.

He looked up at Kalargo, "I think I have worked up an appetite. You hungry?" they slowly made their way back to the palace with grins, frowns and laughter.

"Can you believe that I use to walk faster than this?"

After laughing, "Father you are doing just fine." He grabbed Kalargo jr. and pulled his tank for him.

"It would take me two minutes to walk out here, now it's a thirty minutes marathon if it's a good day."

"When the last time you had a doctor's appointment?"

He stopped and it took all his strength to look at him, "As old as I am..." he waved his mask in disappointment, "...the last thing I am worried about is my health. I am so old I know that I am dying. Don't need a doctor to tell me that." he stopped and wiped his forehead with his forearm.

He looked up into the sky and thought, "Well, the last physical was about thirty years ago, the doctor told me he wanted to perform a prostate exam." his eyes grew big, lips crimped with anger, "I pulled my rusty pistol out and told him not with those big ass fingers. I slowly crawled off that table, and got the hell out of there."

"So you don't know if you have anything that will kill you?" Kalargo looked worried.

The King smiled at him, "Do I look worried, I am eighty seven years old..." he did his little dance move, "...I use to be able to do that a lot better than that." They laughed.

"When you get around my age, you wonder about everything that might kill you." He looked up at the windows, "Look."

He pointed, "I am surprised my own servants have not killed me yet." He stopped and grabbed his arm. "Now that I have found you, and..." he smiled at his grandson. He wanted to cry just thinking about the words he was about to say, "I have a grandson. I am truly at peace. I just wish that I can be around to see him flourish in to this great King that he will be one day."

"Father, don't cry." They hugged. Tears from Kalargo's eyes fell on his father's forehead.

"I did the best thing for you, please understand that I had to send you away..." he felt bad about what he had gone through, "...but I am so happy I made that choice, look at you now." he smiled with his tears.

"Later on I want to show you some things that I had set up for you many years ago. You know, just in case I had died before I was able to find you."

Later that night they both sat at the dinner table, long oak wood, dressed with table mats, white sheet covered a portion of the table. The food was tasteful, just the three of them, "You know..." his father slowly chewed his rice, pointed his fork towards the opposite end of the table, "...at one point in time all of these seats were full, full of family, the spirit was high and things were so much different."

He smiled and looked at Kalargo, and then at his grandson, "All of that is going to come back."

Kalargo felt like he had swallowed a huge piece of his chicken, because he knew he was H.I.V. positive and kids he would have will likely be positive. He could not see the same vision as his father, "Yes I can't wait to fill this room with family." He looked him in his eyes and nodded his head.

He sighed, "Well father..." before he could tell him his cell phone rang. He was thankful because at that moment he decided it was better that he did not know. He pulled his cell from his back right pocket with his thumb and index fingers. He sat it on the table, wiped his hands with his table cloth, "Sorry, I have to take this."

"Yes hello." He took a small bite of cornbread. "Na Min." He took a sip of his wine. "I'm doing great, just sitting here with my father, having dinner, going over family matters."

He nodded his head as he spoke, carefully listening to how the North Koreans not approving his decision to one day being the King of Gambia. He sighed heavily as he looked at his father.

"Well I don't understand what I am expected to do different..." he took a sip of wine and listened. Now he felt obliged to his biological father, there is no way he would leave him now. He looked at his father, grabbed his left hand, and nodded his head. He looked at his son; this is all the family he truly has. A gust of wind blew out two candles, servants quickly lit them.

"Na Min..." he let out a huge exhale, "...tell them it is not going to happen and I won't do it." He spoke with some authority. "I thank you for everything you have done for me. You gave me the best life a kid could ever have. I love you for that; you did not have to take me in as one of your own. You were my father, you are my father, and forever will be my father."

Knowing what Na Min said about the North Koreans, it could not change his heart about being home. Even though the threat was very real, and he would do anything to protect him, but this was something that he may not be able to control. Their conversation ended with wishing each other well.

"I apologize for that..." he looked at his father as he inhaled through his mask, "..that was my dad who adopted me." he was interrupted.

"You should have introduced me. I would have loved to thank him for such an amazing job of raising you." He placed his mask on the table next to his plate.

"Next time, I will do that."

The fact that the North Koreans wanted him dead had him speechless but not surprised.

After dinner he sat on the edge of his bed, looked up at the ceiling and noticed hairline cracks, chipped paint. The floor had a navy blue Persian rug that covered the center of the room. The old furniture had been there for decades and everything needed to be replaced. The Palace was falling apart and only the bare necessities were being done. The roof had several leaks that required buckets to catch the rain. He always thought that Kings live lavishly, above the rest of the Kingdom's population, but when there is war, uncertainty; there is no adequate time or resources to put into projects that are not a concern.

He walked the hallways to check out the condition of the palace. He looked into several empty bedrooms, bathrooms, but impressed on the size of this place.

"Your majesty, can I help find what you are looking for?" the servant dressed in all black with a white button up shirt, well groomed.

"No, not at this moment."

The servant walked away and Kalargo entered his father's bedroom.

"My favorite son!" he was all smiles as he sat on his bathing stool. His clothes were removed; warm water poured his sagging muscles. The bubbles from the sponge slowly dripped his body. His right hand was above his head as the servant ran the sponge across his under arm, and across his neck.

"You want me to come back? I can just come back at a better time."

Before he could close the door, he waved him over. "Heck naaah, what you thought I bath myself?" he waved him closer, "It's been more than twenty years since I've been able to bath myself, now I had to be convinced that I needed help, but hey..." he raised his eyebrows, "I'm used to it now." He smiled.

"No matter what no one tells you, it does not pay to get this old. Trust me, this is some bullshit. If I would have known, I would have killed myself at fifty years old, maybe sixty, I can't remember when my pecker stop jumping and everything starting falling apart..." The servants lift him to clean his back side, "ooooh, I think you missed a spot." The servants chocked off their own laughter.

"Your majesty, you say that every time." They both were in good spirit, they had to be; he was a hand full.

"Trust me the fun, shit it's gone. For example, when I was a young man, I say around my mid fifties, plus or minus; I could piss straight. Now as the years came and gone, things started changing, no longer pissing straight. The servants got tired of me missing the toilet, hitting the walls, so guess what they had me do?"

Kalargo was tickled to a grin. The servants could no longer hold their laughter.

"They made me sit down like a girl, can you believe that?" the room filled with laughter. "You know a King don't have no business pissing like a girl." he waved his hands across his well developed glossy body that screamed I'm so sexy, He stressed the word, girl.

"So I went back to my old ways, well trying my best to hit the toilet anyway." He chuckled himself to the point of grabbing his oxygen mask; he fogged it before he continued.

"So now they got me pissing on myself in these baby pampers, damn shame. Whatever you do, don't get this old, Kalargo."

The servants wiped him dry, sat him down, one dressed him, while the other corn rolled his toupee.

"You thought all that hair was my hair, huh?" he smiled. "Yep keep on saying good morning, you will see." He waved his hand and frowned, "I know they are not laughing with me..." he looked at him with his head tilted to the side to give him a hint, "...they are laughing at me, ha ha hell. Then they have the nerve to tell me, oh it's a blessing to be this old, how the hell would they know? I'm the eighty seven year old."

Kalargo had to sit down he was laughing and gasping for air. "Stop! You are killing me." He rolled over on the king size bed.

"I told them I bet them a fat bitch against a skinny pussy, they will most likely commit suicide before they hit seventy five."

Kalargo cried out a painful laughter, "Please stop him."

"These long mouth, nappy head motherfuckas..." He grinned as he slipped his feet into his slippers, "...keep on saying good morning."

Later that night, Kalargo could not get a wink of sleep, tossed and turned; the idea of knowing someone wants to kill him just did not sit well with his stomach. He wondered if his uncle "The General" knew that someone wanted to assassinate him; never would have imagined his own nephew would be his assassin.

He tossed the white sheet off of him; it floated to the other side of the bed. He pushed himself up from his right side, sat upward with both hands on the edge of the bed and sighed. He wondered how safe he was, even though the palace had soldiers walking the perimeter, anything could happen. The General had his own security, and that did not stop him. He looked up at the ceiling and had a bad feeling. No one is safe in this world, you can stall it, but eventually a slip up is all it takes.

He walked over to the window and thought how he would kill himself if he was an assassin. He started to notice some things; like not enough sufficient lighting around the palace. He scratched his neck, reached for a pen and paper to write these flaws down.

"Wow, let me see..." he opened the French doors and walked on to the balcony, "what else?"

He pulled his bottom lip with his upper teeth, slowly let it slip away. He noticed that he was bare feet; wearing his boxers, white t-shirt. He looked over the balcony, three floors up, but he could climb down the water drain, using the protruding bricks along the wall. If so, he can also do the same to climb up. He shook his head; he started writing down some things that needed to be repaired, changed or removed for safety reasons.

"This place should be like Fort Knox; no one should be able to penetrate the security of the King's Palace."

He decided to climb down from his balcony, used the protruding bricks as a ladder. He landed softly into a flower bed, tiptoed across the lawn, dodging security, and cameras.

"Wow, what cameras?" he grew more mad that he had not been approached by anyone. So he took his plan even further.

The early morning dew blanketed the grass, the half moon was like a dim lamp that hung above the Palace; it was not long before he felt a cool breeze that made the sweat down his back chill his body. He looked around before making his way through some bushes; the scratches on his thighs, and right arm cause the sweat to burn like red ants had him by their teeth.

He pushed a branch down just enough to see a soldier sleeping, AK-47 was next to a tree, and shoes were off. He quietly tiptoed in front of him, took his weapon, and butted him in the forehead. The soldier was out cold. He took his pants off, used them to tie his feet, and hands like a hog. He stopped and noticed that he had smelt marijuana in the air. He shook his head in disgust. By the end of the night he had captured three soldiers, hog tied all of them without their uniforms. He will make sure that they go to the front line to fight in the war.

Exhausted, dirty, he climbed the protruding bricks along the wall, rolled over on to his balcony, and with anger he finally fell asleep before the sun could rise.

The following morning, the Palace was in frenzy; the King wanted to know who was behind the security breach, and demanded answers. He towed his tank with a tight fist, and a contorted face of anger.

"For God sake..." he pointed his index finger towards his head security captain, "...find out what the hell is going on." He reached for his mask that hung across his left shoulder, inhaled deeply; the mask fogged as his eyes squinted.

Kalargo came down the stairs, yawning, confused, "Father, what is all the ruckus?"

He tossed a green glass vase at the security captain, but it landed short. The security captain knew from passed occasion not to stand within his reach. It landed just short of his boots.

"Bring your ass here, you purposely standing to far from me." The King threw a paper weight that landed a few feet from his target. "If I was ten years younger..."

"Father, calm down..." he came in between the both of them, it was taking too long for him to reach him with his caterpillar footsteps. "...it was me who tied the soldiers up."

Silence kidnapped the noise, the King's face relaxed and waited for an explanation, "You have some explaining to do!"

"Well..." Kalargo looked around the west wing of the Palace, "...where are the three soldiers?" he walked over to his father, placed his right hand on his left shoulder.

"Bring them to me!" The King looked at the captain and wished he was a little closer, arm distance but not quite.

The three soldiers walked in with their heads hanging low, standing next to one another; uniforms disheveled.

Kalargo walked over, "Now explain why you guys were hog tied and stripped of your uniforms?"

They all tried to explain at once, but were silenced by the King, "One at a time!"

"Someone was playing a joke on us your majesty." They looked silly and pitiful.

"Father, these men were sleeping, and smoking marijuana. I wanted to show you how lax the security is around here, it's a joke."

Before he could say another word, his the King spoke bravely and with confidence, "Well, well, well..." he slowly made his approach to the three of them, "...sleeping on the job?"

Kalargo stepped in before the King reached them, "I think they need to go the front line, fight like real men. They have been too safe and unappreciative of their command." He walked around them.

"That sounds like a great idea..." he turned around and headed towards his desk, "...now we will have to replace them."

"Well I have an idea..." he walked over to his desk, "...how about replacing the soldiers with fifty of the soldiers that I had trained..." he tossed his hands up, "...that way we will have well trained fighting security, battle experienced."

Before he could say another word, the King loved his idea, but there was one issue. He had handpicked his security for the Palace and to bring in unknown soldiers that had not been screened, handpicked from known family and friends could be dangerous.

"Do you think you can trust them like I trust my handpicked?" he sat down behind his desk and looked at Kalargo, the soldiers, and wondered.

"Well, you know as old as I am getting. You will eventually have to pick your own security if you want to replace the ones that are here..." he stood up and headed towards the door, "Kalargo." he turned around, "You have total control; I'm going to play with my Largo."

Everyone in the room looked at Kalargo, a little confused, but not surprised.

"So what's next your majesty?" the captain asked.

He sat behind the desk, pulled out his folded paper of notes, and began to be King.

"First, I want security cameras..." he grabbed a pencil and sketched a map of the Palace, pointed where the cameras should be, "...lights." he circled areas where flood lights needed to be for maximum use, "motion sensors on the perimeter to quickly identify all movement." He stood up and walked over to the window, "You see those bricks?"

The captain and the soldiers that were hogged tied approached and looked out the window, "What about them?"

"Well, I used the bricks to climb down and up to my balcony..." they looked amazed, but could see how it can be done, "...and the tree branches cut them if they are within twelve feet of the Palace."

The captain walked over to him, "I want to apologize for letting you down, and my men are the most trust worthy group of soldiers that you will ever meet. They will give their lives for the King and his family, as you have seen one of our most proud was Paul."

"What is your name?" he walked closer as he went down on his right knee.

"My name is Nanembo." He kissed his hand out of respect.

"To your feet Nanembo..." he placed his left hand on his shoulder, "what do you think I should do about these three?" they both looked at the soldiers that had been hogged tied.

"Well your majesty..." he sighed deeply, tapped his finger nails on the desk, "it's no question that they have to be punished..." he rubbed his index across his mustache, "...just to let the others know not to even think of doing anything wrong."

"Tell everyone, the vacation is over, and to be on their toes; things are changing around here, very fast."

He walked over to the three of them, they quickly bent down to one knee, "I will make this punishment so severe. You will be the spokesman for how not to be..." one by one they kissed the top of his hand, "...and to make it fare, you three will be in charge of designated groups, if they fail?" he walked away from them, sat on the corner of the desk, "...you will be punished severely for what they have done wrong."

He waved his left hand to dismiss them, "Report to me tomorrow, 8 am."

The King was on the floor, racing Kalargo jr.; on their hands and knees. The soft shaggy red carpet was like long grass that snuggled between their fingers as they played, "You can't beat me."

They both laughed a like; smiled at each other as they crawled along the floor.

"Father." A knock at the door disrupted their smiles, halted their race. He was out of breath as the toddler was winning.

"You lucky we were interrupted. I was just about to pass you by." He rubbed his index across his chin, Kalargo jr. took off crawling, giggling, and slobbering.

The King rolled over on to his back like a dying turtle, reached for his mask, and inhaled like his life depended on it, "This little rascal working me..." out of breath as he spoke with the mask over his mouth, "...look at him, still crawling; hey you making me look bad." They both grinned.

"Did you figure out the security situation?" the King asked.

"Yes, so far..." he sat on the corner of the bed, "...getting cameras, flood lights, sensors and some other things that I have in mind."

"Well, it's all yours, run it how you see fit, but you can always come to me for advice..." he turned his attention away, "...hey you, get back here." He pulled the toddler by his ankle, "ga ga nu nu you think you fast, huh?"

It was more like two toddlers were on the floor, both had pampers, barely could walk without fear of falling, and needed undivided attention for their safety.

"Can you say grandpa?"

Kalargo left the toddlers to themselves, "Keep an eye on them two." The servant nodded his head as he passed them in the hallway.

Kalargo pulled out his cell phone and dialed Mugumbi's number. He had noticed that he had dropped egg on his light blue dress shirt, "Damn."

The phone went to the voice mail; he tried again. He looked at his watch, the time difference of eleven hours, "Let me see..." he counted on his fingers, "...he most likely sleep." He ended the call and placed the cell phone in his pocket.

*   *   *

Honolulu, Hi

The night sky was clear, full moon followed Mugumbi like an eye in the sky. He was exhausted, breathing heavy, lost in an unknown forest; to make

328

things worse, no cell phone signal. He was on the run, bleeding from bullet wounds that crazed his hip and shoulder. He felt lucky to be alive, but he had to keep moving; no time to celebrate. He stopped to listen.

The sound of movement through the trees, breaking of old fallen branches was in the distance; he laid down underneath a huge rock that hung over a creek. The stream wet his feet as he held himself in place with his hands by pushing his weight against the rock. His arms trembled like he was in shock. His stomach had the jitters, but he had to be motionless; his life depended on it. His sweat stung his eyes until they were blurry, but he could not move.

He felt something crawl on his neck, slowly moved across his throat, it was slimy, long; the length of time that it took to crawl was starting to freak him out. The only thing he could move was his eyes, but he could not see it; he slowed his breathing. He knew it had legs, many of them; not a snake he had determined.

He pissed on himself and waited for the right moment. This creature, whatever it was lingered around his neck for thirty minutes before it decided to slither down his bloody t- shirt. The feet tickled his stomach, but he did not move; not sure what this thing was, he could not take a chance on moving. It slowly crawled down to his thigh, after it wrapped around his ankle is when he had realized how long this creature really was. The tail had not reached his neck yet, so he held his breath for as long as he could; exhaling in small amounts. He began to feel faint just as the tail reaches his ankle.

"Oh my God, that was close. What in the world was that?"

He slowly, carefully slid in to the creek. "Ahhh!" the pain was unbearable, but he had to keep moving. He reached the other side and hid behind a tree. He used his right hand to peak through the huge leaves. He saw a figure but was unable identify who was chasing him.

"Damn..." he laid back, spat in the right palm, and carefully cupped his palm to catch his saliva. He held his head back and poured his saliva in both eyes, rubbed them well.

"Ahhh!" he was bleeding, luckily he had flesh wounds. His eye sight gradually came to as he sighed in relief. He pulled back the branch to peak again. Finally, he could see.

From behind he saw him washing his hands in the creek; the black mask that covered his head was long. He thought about attacking him from behind until he stood up.

"Wow, who is this guy?" he could not believe his vision, as clear as day, no need for lubricating his eyes. The guy stood 6'5, no more than three hundred forty five pounds, long bubble gum pink boots, ruffle collar; the back of his clothes was black, front was multi colored red, blues, and green. He bent down to pick up a bloody ax and walked across the rocks that reminded him of huge turtles that were just high enough to keep his boots dry.

He walked towards him, looked around to see what direction Mugumbi would have gone. He looked up at the moon and sighed. He rested the ax on his left shoulder, reached for the back of his mask with his right hand and slowly pulled it off.

"What the hell?" Mugumbi heart pounded his chest. He felt like the tongue of a lion was licking the side of his face, being motionless was critical. He gulped fear that bulged his throat the size of a sling shot; very hard to swallow. He slowly, carefully let the branch move back in to its original place. He needed time to process who was trying to kill him. "Oh my Lord..." he whispered beneath his breath. He rubbed his wound, "aaah."

It's no way he could take him on, not like this; his legs were weak and losing blood from his hip was starting to affect him. He slowly pulled the branch down, the assassin was dressed like a clown with stitches across his throat, eight inch stitches that started above his left eyebrow that came down to the right side of his chin. It looked as if he had patched himself up in a disgusting, abandon bathroom with thread, needle and a staple gun.

Mugumbi sighed, not knowing what to do, "Damn, I need to do something fast..." he gritted his teeth, clenched his fist. He thought of a brilliant idea. He smiled, "...now if I could."

He slowly pulled the branch down to see what the killer clown was doing. He peaked over the big leaves and the clown was twelve inches from his face. His heart stopped beating, paralyze by fear he felt the clown's hand around his throat.

"Aaaa!" He scratched like a scared cat, but manages to break free from his huge monstrous hand. He fell backwards, took off in to the forest, jumping, diving across anything that would save him. He was smacked in the face with a low hanging branch, but kept going. Finally, he landed on the edge of a huge slippery rock, breaking three finger nail as he tried to hold on to dear life. He reached for a root, but it gave in to his weight. He tumbled down sixty feet, hitting ledge after ledge, cracking his ribs, legs, and neck. He splashed into a shallow river.

Chapter 30

Mugumbi tossed and turned in bed, sheet mysteriously wrapped around his throat; as he gagged and fought to breath. He soaked the bed with sweat, swung his arms wildly; scared to the point of falling off of the bed, knocking the flower vase off the night stand, spilling water on top of him; it shattered as he woke up gasping for air, like he was drowning. The dark room gave him no comfort; he reached for his throat, leaned forward and compressed his chest in attempt to stop the chest pain. His heart felt like it was jumping out of his chest. The broken glass from the vase gouged his hip, rib cage, and shoulder

"Aaah!" he tried to push himself up off of the floor, he hit the switch on the lamp that lay next to him, "Thank God..." his chest was relieved, his breathing subdued, and a sigh of exhaustion, "...what in the world?!"

He knew he had a bad dream, and could not remember what it was about. He shook his head and raised himself up from the floor.

He limped towards the bathroom, "I can't believe I cut myself..." he looked back at the room, "...made a mess in there." He hit the light switch and looked in the mirror, then looked at his foot. He could see the glass in the heel of his right foot, so he carefully plucked it.

"Damn, it look like I've been in a fight or something." He cleaned himself up, made the bed, and removed the broken vase, threw the flowers in the trash. He looked at the clock and could not believe it was three o'clock in the morning. It was no way he would be able to fall back to sleep.

He entered the living room, hit the power button on the remote for the TV, and decided to make a pot of hot tea. On the coffee table was the last two envelopes to read; he now knew for sure that Na Min had all the reasons to kill Yuki; it really blew his mind that he had killed her biological father.

She had never met her half brother, or knew his name. He sighed as the hot tea whistled and took him from his profound thoughts.

He shook his head, "If it takes my last breath..." he turned the stove off, poured the tea into his cup, "...I am going to make sure to use it, and all my strength to kill this dirty, savage..." he sipped his tea, "...damn, forgot to put sugar."

He carefully walked over to the coffee table, "I really want to know who is her half brother?" without spilling a drop of tea, placed it on the table, sat down with an envelope in his right hand and began reading.

After reading, he was in a ball on the floor crying for revenge, pounding his palm and fist on the floor. He wanted to rip Na Min's throat out.

"That bastard killed my wife!" he wanted to call him, but could not keep a calm composer; too angry, it would give away how he felt. He took a deep breath, trying to calm himself. The pain was too deep and he was not there to help her.

Suddenly, he stopped crying and thought, maybe that was the reason to send him to Hawaii. Perhaps to get him out of the country so he could confront her alone. He burst out with anger, grabbed his stomach, and screamed to the top of his lungs, "Baby!"

"I am so sorry! I let you down!" he covered his face with a pillow, gritted his teeth, and screamed into the pillow. "I promise baby! I promise that I am going get him!"

It took him hours to recover, days to plan, and weeks to prepare his mind, if not the anger would have misled his thought process.

"Micheal J. Song Chi ..." he sighed with curiosity, the half brother's name, but he had never heard of him, for all he knew, he could be dead.

The following day, he made arrangements to fly back to South Korea two weeks in advance. He returned Kalargo's phone call, but did not talk for long. He made sure the house was taken care of, but did not tell him about the broken vase. He gave the impression that he would occupy the home until he closed on his own home. He knew not to say anything about getting rid of Na Min because that would be a problem. He used the next couple of weeks to get in shape.

While sitting by the pool one early morning, his cell phone rung, it was Na Min, "Holly crap..." he did not want to answer, but he swallowed his hesitating fear before hitting the talk button, "Na Min. How is everything going?"

Mugumbi sounded cheerful to hear his voice, like old pals, "Well, just taking it easy. I was thinking of going to South America, you know just to get away." He gritted his teeth hard enough to shatter them.

"So where are you these days?" Na Min asked.

The moment of truth, if he lies, will it be good enough to fool a professional, or give away his sinister, evil deception. His tongue felt tied, thinking quickly is important. He asked himself, 'what do I say?'

He made the sound of static, like the phone had a bad connection, some words came out, but none were audible, "Hello." He hung up and quickly texted him, 'In a bad area, call you later.'

Mugumbi promised to never answer his call again; his heart was pumping blood like he had been running. His armpits were wet. He tugged on his white t-shirt to loosen it; he was obviously uncomfortable. He looked at the clock and it was time to go the gym.

Seven days later, he came up with a plan. It was brilliant he thought, snapped his fingers, and pumped his fist. He stood by the bay window, looked at himself in the reflection, "Yes."

When he arrived back to the house; he made a list of items that he will need to carry out his revenge. He gathered the envelopes from the coffee table, noticed that he had not read the back of the last page. He sighed as he read it.

"Ok..." He nodded, "...her half brother lived with his mother in the Philippines, and I wonder did she read this?" It had an address; he thumped the page with his index finger.

"Now that's what I am talking about..." But he also knew that these letters were written years ago. The joy was deflated like needle bursting a balloon, "...now what's the chance of anyone still living at this address?"

His hopes melted away. He pulled his carry-on bag from the floor, put all the envelopes in the side pocket and zipped them away.

The morning of his flight was rain, thunder, and a flash of lightening in the distance, which awaken him before his alarm went off. He opened his eyes, thankful for not having another nightmare, he sighed as he forced himself to plant his feet on the floor as he rolled out of bed. The light from the partially closed door of the bathroom was enough for him to see his way around. He looked at the clock with less than five hours before his flight, plenty of time to spare, but he knew revenge can't be rushed. The last thing he wanted to do is forget, misplace or not be prepared.

After grooming and primping, he called for a car service. He sighed as he began to think about the butterflies that tickled his stomach. He took his cell phone off the charger, eight missed calls from Na Min. He cleared his throat and shoved his cell in his front left pocket. He made sure the house was secured as he had found it, prepared the water for his hot tea and waited.

He was nervous and could not relate to why this was affecting him in this way. He nibbled on his nails, tapped his feet until he stopped himself. He decided to place his luggage at the front door while he waited. The sound of the tea pot whistled like a freight train.

"Nice..." he sipped, "...a little more sugar." He dipped the tea spoon and added sugar, stirred, "Perfect, almost anyway."

Moments later the gate bell rang, he looked at the security monitor and buzzed the gate to open. He made sure not to leave anything behind, double checked the bedroom, bathroom; he was convinced that he had everything.

"I'm coming!" when he opened the door, the trunk was opened, quickly tossing his luggage in, but noticed that the driver was not helping. 'Mental note, do not tip the driver.' He opened the door, slid across the back seat of the four door black Lincoln, "Honolulu Airport please."

The cold metal of the silencer pressed his forehead, "Bang!"

* * *

San Juan, Puerto Rico

The warm sand between their toes were like wet clay, as they walked the beach holding hands with Carmela, tossing stones in the waves; occasionally they had to avoid getting wet. She pulled him close and planted her lips on his, "I am so happy here."

He wrapped his arms around her, sucked on her neck, and nibbled her ear lobe, "I know. That's what I want you to be, happy."

"Just to be here with my family leaves me speechless." She smiled as she broke free from his embrace, held her yellow, lavender sun dress like wings of a butterfly, skipped across the sand, twirling with a smile that glowed.

"Did you see that?" she pointed out towards the ocean.

He looked but missed what she had seen, "What was it?"

"There." She aimed her index at the dolphins that jumped out of the water.

"Wow!" he also pointed, "Never seen so many at one time, one, two, three, four; that's amazing."

She ran towards him, jumped with her legs wrapping around his love handles; with no choice he had to catch and hold her. She French kissed him as he struggled to hold her. They found a tucked away spot behind some palm trees, and low line bushes where they made out.

He ignored his cell phone as his lips pressed against her throat, and down the center of her breast, but the cell phone would not stop.

She sighed, "Maybe you should answer it or turn it off."

"Hello..." He unbuttons his shirt, letting it fall, and dropped his pants to his ankles, "yes."

While he spoke, she undressed, using her dress to lie on, and she was more than ready as her panties were pulled from under her hips, down her tanned legs, and over her ankles.

"Na Min, it's done." They both halted their conversation. He let out a sigh that was bitter sweet; his once incredible hulk erection was now like putty.

"Noooo!" she looked up at him, and pointed, "I knew you should not have answered that damn phone." She looked disgruntled, but not for long, she quickly began to resuscitate it, after he pressed his body against hers; she smiled as they began to make love.

Later that afternoon, they swam side by side, away from the surf, noise of the crashing waves, where the ocean was motionless, with mirror like reflection; they floated on their backs like happy otters.

She felt something brush up against her feet, "Playing footsie?"

She opened her eyes and realized that he had floated around towards the top of her head and it was not his feet that touched hers, not able to see what it was; she was ready to head back to shore. So they did.

The smell of food from the kitchen smeared their face when they walked into the condo. Her mother cooked her special recipe, pork stew, yellow rice, black beans, and a baked apple pie.

"Mother, it smells wonderful." She kissed her on the cheek.

He rubbed her shoulders as he passed through, "Looks yummy."

"How long before its ready?" he opened his mouth for a taste, blew for a moment, "Mmmm."

His cell phone rang from his back pocket, "Hello."

He ducked into the living room, and through the French doors that led to the patio. He stood with his left hand on his hip, looked over his shoulder, "Yes."

"Well I have been busy. I missed your call..." he looked over his shoulder, "I understand the gravity of this..." he slowly walked further away towards the sandy dunes where the seagulls flocked, "...hey, this could work in our favor, just hear me out." He could not get a word in, but forced his voice to be heard.

"You listen. We may have an easier way to do this. The way I see it, we have an inside man who is the King..." he raised his hands to express a no brainer situation, "...just give it time."

He rubbed his left foot into the sand, twirled his toes to create a circular design, "Well nothing is a guarantee, I have not put that option on the table yet."

Zang was upset, and under a lot of pressure to make this problem go away. The dead line was approaching and it will be out of his control. "Listen, I do like the idea of Kalargo being able to work for us from the throne. As King, the war can come to an end, and then we can take it from there." They both paused.

"Na Min, are you willing to put your life on it?"

"Well..." the seagulls circled, the waves crashed the sand, the wind wiped his sweat like a rag, and how can he buy more time he asked himself. "Well, time is running out." He looked out at the ocean as his eyes watered, bent down and grabbed a couple of stones, "My life?" he tossed a stone at the falling waves. The seagulls dove toward it like it was food.

"Are you willing to put your life on the line?" Zang asked.

To buy more time, he looked at his cell phone like he wanted to throw it in the ocean, "Yes, I am willing to put my life on the line." The call ended.

Carmela arms embraced him from behind; he looked over his shoulder and kissed her. She saw tears in his eyes, turned and tightens their embrace.

She reached up and wiped his tear, "What's wrong my dear?"

With his right hand, guiding her towards the patio, "A good friend of mine died."

"Oh no, so sorry to hear that, anyone that I would know?" she stopped and wiped his other eye.

"No, it was a friend of a friend from the agency." He sighed and pushed her up the steps by her buttocks.

"Dinner is ready!"

"Yes, we are starving. We will be in shortly."

*   *   *

Honolulu, Hawaii

The early morning thunder and lightning shook Mugumbi's bed, waking him up with a loud boom. The sound of rain tapped on the window, wind pushed several plants off of their pedestals, crashing on to the patio. He rubbed the corner of his eyes with the back of his thumbs, and noticed that he had overslept.

He jumped up, tossed his clothes on, groomed, and took his bags out to the car; made sure he had everything, skipped hot tea. When he got behind the wheel he could not see from the rain but he thought he had seen a man in a black hooded poncho walk in the rearview mirror. He quickly jumped out of the car, scared but brave. He stood in the rain, searching with his eyes, walked to the rear of the car, he thought about his shoes that was not water proof, so he crawled back in, placed the key in the ignition. The dash board lights did not come on when he turned the key.

"What the hell..." he slammed his palms on the steering wheel in anger; he pushed away and rested his head on the headrest, "...can't believe this crap. Don't do this." He had two hours to get to the airport. He pulled out his cell phone to call for a car service.

"Hello..." he rubbed his eyebrow, squeezed his nose with his index and thumb, "I am going to the airport. Yes..." he wiped his forehead. He tried to crank the car one more time, nothing, "The address is..." he checked to see if the car was in gear, pushed it, and tried again; it turned over. The dash board lit up and he threw kisses to his higher power, ended the call, tossed the cell in his top pocket and drove off.

Flight KE703 experienced turbulence until it reach the outer bands of the storm, flying first class allowed him to stretch out and dose off. No matter how hard he tried to sleep, his plans were methodically playing out in his mind, every move was calculated. After three hours, four glasses of wine, sleep blanketed his body like a tired old man, his eyes drifted to the back of head and he was out cold.

Once in Seoul, he stopped by his storage unit, and picked up supplies from the second hand store, then made his way to Na Min's house. It was dark, the streets were wet, and the rental van was spacious enough to hide himself until he could jump the fence without someone seeing him. He dosed off.

The sunrise woke him, with anger. He could not believe that he had over slept, "What the..." he thumped himself on the forehead for being so stupid, "...no good."

He knew he had to move the van, can't take the chance of someone seeing him. He knew he was the only black guy with in two hundred miles, so he slowly eased out of the neighborhood unnoticed.

*   *   *

San Juan, Puerto Rico

Na Min kissed his wife goodbye at the San Juan international airport, wiped her tears, but she held him tight enough to take his last breath, "Hey, enjoy the condo for awhile, then fly back to South Korea in a couple of months."

It was his turn to pass through the security line, "I got to go."

"Yes I know." she pouted her lips for one more kiss, and then walked away with her hands over her face.

Before his flight took off he tried to call Kalargo. He left a voice mail.

He landed in Seattle just before mid night; his brother met him at the baggage claim. They drove forty minutes before arriving to his mom's home in Everest, Wa.

"I just never can forget this place; it brings calm over me." The barn can be seen through the darkness, sheep cried out, and he took a deep inhale.

"Do you smell that?" his brother wanted to know if he recognizes their mother's favorite stew.

"Now Kwan, you know I..." he was interrupted by the voice of his mother. She stood at the door, cane in her right hand, a smile from ear to ear. He ran up the stairs to hug her, and plotted a kiss on her cheek, both cheeks. She held him tight.

"What took you so long son?" she slapped his arm, "I've been waiting all day." She followed him with her hand on his back.

His brother stood by the car, "You want me to bring your bags?"

He waved his hand indicating to bring them in, "It looks just like it did when I left." He headed straight towards the wall of photos.

He sighed as the memories flashed cross his mind, "Wow, you still have these pictures."

She waved her hand as she walked into the kitchen.

He looked around at the furniture that was covered in plastic. Not once had he ever sat on it, the plastic was old, hard, and breaking apart in pieces. The lime green carpet had never been changed; it had a permanent path from the dirty foot traffic from over the years.

"Oh my God, these bags are heavy; you got little midgets in these things?" they both laughed as Kwan struggled up the stairs.

After dinner, they sat on the porch, smoked, and sipped on wine. The sky had an abundance of stars. The moon had not risen above the mountain, and Got'em, a mix between Labrador and Great Dane sat near their feet, slumped over from a healthy meal. His ears cover his eyes, his rolls were being pushed to their limits; he weighed a whopping eighty pounds, and needed a bath. He couldn't protect himself from diabetes, none the less the farm. He moved like a dinosaur and barked like a sheep. He was in bad shape.

"So what have you been up to little brother?" Na Min cigar glowed red as he inhaled.

"Not much, just trying to make it. I had a job but it went out of business, and going from one job to the next." Kwan sipped his beer.

"You know you can always come to me for help..." he looked at him, "...here."

He tried to give him some cash, but he refused, "Listen, everyone falls on hard times sooner or later. Everyone needs that helping hand to pick them up when they fall. It's no different." He held the cash in his hand.

"I just, I just don't want to look as if I'm begging or..." he stopped him in his tracks before he could go any further.

"Begging, are you kidding me?" He laughed and grabbed his arm, slapped a couple of hundred dollar bills in his hand.

"You are my brother, stop it. You will be back on your feet in no time."

"Thanks." Kwan held it like it was his last breath, shoved it in his back pocket.

"Don't hesitate if you need more." Even though he knew he most likely wouldn't ask. "Well, I don't know about your eyes, but mine are heavy and I am buzzed from this wine." They agreed and decided to end the night.

*   *   *

Gambia, Africa

Kalargo added an additional fifty soldiers to the Palace security detail, three shifts overlapping one another. The annual Palace party was in days and everything had to be perfect. So he wanted to know more about this party and how important is it.

He walked out to the lawn just beyond the patio, "Father, I see you decided to take it easy."

He leaned and rubbed Kalargo jr. on his head, "Hey you..." he picked him up, held him high above his head, "...yeah, what you doing?" He bounced him, "He is getting big, what are you feeding him?" they both laughed.

The King struggled to inhale, but managed, "That's my boy. My baby boy..." he looked up with his mask in his right hand, shook his head and smiled. "Don't know why they feeding him so much."

"Hey I have a question about the annual party. How many people usually show up and does it have to happen?" he placed the little one back in the hands of the King.

"It's very important, it brings unity, a lot of the village elders, chiefs will be here. It bonds us as one. Giving them..." he coughed and wiped his mouth, "...confidence."

He looked at him, "Well, I guess you will walk me through it?"

The King licked his lips, and plucked a hair from his tongue, "The only thing I am doing, showing up and introducing you to everyone. That's it." He waved his mask, tossed it over his shoulder.

"Hey you, your father don't understand English, ginee googoo. Oh yes I am just starting to get to old for all of this..." he squeezed his cheeks, rubbed his nose, "...just not up for it." The King said.

"Father, all you have to do is relax, enjoy; I will handle everything. The last thing I want you to do is stress when you should not have to." He leaned and kissed him on the forehead and walked away.

The night of the party went well, drinks flowed, people generally got along, and security was very tight but not tight enough, after the party Kalargo found himself in the dark, in his closet with a knife to his throat.

"Don't move..." The voice whispered with a raspy voice, not African. The man pushed him from behind with pressure of the blade cutting his skin, "...don't try anything stupid. I just want to talk and..."

Before he could say another word, Kalargo broke free, twisted the knife and reversed it. Kalargo found himself on his back with a boot on his throat. He quickly buckled his knee, kicked him to the floor, but counted his every move. He blocked his punches, and kicks to the head. He tried to side kick his legs, but was kicked in his chest, falling backwards behind the dresser. The commotion drew attention from a servant in the hallway.

"Majesty!" he ran for help.

The assassin blocked the door with an armoire, "Listen..."

They wrestled to the floor; He was lifted up, but wiggled his way out and landed on his feet. He punched the assassin on the left side of his jaw. He fell, but manage to rise up with the dagger in his right hand. Kalargo stood and braced for his attack.

"What do you want?" before he could ask, the assassin was on top of him, losing his balance, they both slid across the floor with the dagger inches from his heart. Kalargo could not push him off, the weight of the assassin pushed the dagger closer. The eyes of the assassin looked in his eyes, and pushed harder.

The banging on the door vibrated the room, and shook the armoire, "Your majesty! We are coming your majesty!"

"Aaaah!" the dagger broke the skin on Kalargo's chest as they fought back and forth for power. He managed to flip the assassin on to his back, now he had the upper strength as he pushed with all his might. They both gritted their teeth for strength.

"Do you give up!" the dagger was six inches as the assassin was losing strength. They both had their hands on the dagger handle; every muscle is used as they fight for their lives. Kalargo's sweat fell on to the assassin's face and mouth.

"You have to die!" he told him but he was on the bottom, pinned to the floor, struggled to gain control of the dagger. He knew if security came in, it would be over, so he had to do the incredible.

Just before security burst through the door, Kalargo hand slipped from the sweat, cut his palm down the middle, and lost his position. He used his knee to pound his inner thigh and pushed away from him. He fell to the floor next to a lamp that shines on to the dagger. He recognized the engraved blade and paused.

The assassin was wounded but his eyes were filled with tenacity and rage. He jumped on top of him and fought like hell, despite the cuts on his arms and legs. He fell to his knees, but did not give up. Just before he launched again, he was stopped.

"Where did you get this dagger from!" he was punched in the midsection, and the jaw. He fell over the bed. The assassin dove after the dagger, stabbed him in the upper thigh, cut his upper arm and went for his heart.

"You must die!"

"Aaaah!" they both fell, but this time Kalargo's wounded hand would not be able to hold up. The dagger slowly inched closer to his heart. They fought like Lions, bloody from their wounds and exhausted from the fight of their lives.

"Where..." he looked in his killer's eyes, "...did you get this dagger!" the dagger was inches from his death, but his strength slowly eased.

"Come on! Talk to me!" they held on as they were face to face, it was obvious that the assassin was not sweating as much as he was. His skin seemed different.

"Listen, you have no chance to survive, once they come in, you will be killed!"

He loosens his grip on the dagger, reaches down into his shirt and pilled his mask off.

The loud sound of an explosive blew the door off, pushed the armoire and the security blazed their way in and found Kalargo shielding his assassin with his own body.

"Don't shoot! Don't shoot!" His hands were up, back pressed against his assassin's chest.

"Your majesty!" they rushed in nonstop to make sure he was ok. They pushed Kalargo aside, grabbed Jenko by the back of his shirt, they separated them like he was contagious, with guns to his face.

"Do not!" Kalargo raised his voice and left hand, pushed his way towards Jenko.

He bent over, "I do not understand." He lifted him to his feet, as they both limped towards the edge of the bed. "You got a lot of explaining to do!"

Jenko reached and touched his rib cage, "Aaaah!" he frowned and leaned forward as he struggled to inhale for air.

"Get a medic up here, now!" The sound of footsteps can be heard running for the medic. The room was full of soldiers, wondering what the hell is going on.

"Kalargo, your life is in danger..." he tried to explain, but his wound to his ribs had punctured his lung, and bleeding. He sighed and tried to explain.

"The North Koreans are trying to kill you. They hired me and got my family hostage until they hear from me." He tried to sit up, but the pain buckled his face. They were given a towel and some ice to apply to their swollen eyes and face.

"I just can't believe this, out of all people..." Kalargo said.

A nurse held the ice for him, cleaned his face.

"Why didn't you just call me?" Kalargo asked.

The soldiers watched him carefully as he crawled to the floor in pain, the blood from his wound required medical attention, "Kalargo, you got to save my family." He began to cry, "What do I do?"

The King finally made his way to the room, "What the heck is going on?!"

Nanembo approached, "Your majesty, an intruder broke through security and tried to assassinate your son."

He looked into the room, and was devastated; blood smeared the walls, the floor, "Where is Kalargo?" He walked in further.

"He is over here your majesty." a voice from the far corner of the room.

His eyes opened wide, as his mask wavered like a leaf, "Is he the assassin..." before a response could be spoken, "why are they..." he swallowed the fear of his son coming so close to death, "...separate them!"

Kalargo painfully jumped up to his aid, "It's ok father, I know him."

"I know his ass too, kill him! No one comes into my home, attempt to assassinate my son!" he pointed to Nanembo, "Kill him, shoot him dead!"

He walked over, cocked his pistol, aimed at his forehead.

"Stop!" he carefully sat his father down in the couch at the foot of the bed.

"No one touches him!" Kalargo said. Jenko was placed on the stretcher and carried out to the ambulance, the sound of his cries and plea for help did not go unnoticed.

"Father, I'll be back." He held his hand, "I will explain everything later."

"Son, I don't understand, but I hope you know what you are doing. I can't lose you." He gripped his hand as his mask fell to the floor.

He looked at Nanembo, "Take a group of fifteen, secure the hospital, keep an eye on that long mouth killer, his blood is tainted with that Asian shit and I don't trust him. If he breathes too hard, kill his ass." His fist was in a ball, lips frowned, and his eyes squinted. He meant business.

"Nanembo..." he grabbed his arm as he headed out of the door, "If anything happen to my son..." he couldn't get the words out of his mouth, but he knew what he wanted to say, so he assured him that his life was in his hands.

He broke free of the King's grip, and headed out of the door.

The ambulance drove through the gates of the Palace with sirens blaring, four security vehicles, two in the front, two in the back; Kalargo sat with Jenko as his condition worsen.

It was unknown at the time, but he was slowly dying from the internal bleeding, "Kalargo, I am so sorry..." his voice can barely be heard. He gripped his hand, "...if I don't make it, tell my wife and kids that I love them."

His breathing became shallow; he fought death bravely as he took his last breath.

"Jenko! Hey you hang in there..." he grabbed his face, shook him.

His eyes opened, gripped his hands and pulled him closer to his face with his ear to his lips, "Save my..." blood oozed from his mouth, "...family."

"Hey!" Kalargo shook him. "Do something!" he yelled at the E.M.T., before they started cpr, he pushed them a side and performed it himself. "One, two, three." He tilted his head back, pinched his nose with his thumb and index and blew into his mouth.

He repeated several times as they pulled up to the emergency, his lifeless body was pushed through the door as the doctors took over.

*   *   *

Everest, Wa

The fog floated just above the sheep, tiptoed the farm like creepy ghost that thought they were invisible. The dew coated the surfaces as the early morning sun danced across the landscape slowly killing the ghost and leaving shadows that slanted.

Na Min's mother sat on the porch, absorbing the fresh air, using her tip of her toes to move her rocking chair, with both hands she held her coffee to smell, like always, and it brought a smile.

She was seventy five, stood 5'5, slim in stature, born in South Korea and migrated to the United States when she was five years old with her parents. She had lived in Seattle most of her life, graduating from the University of Washington State with a Pharmaceutical degree. She was married for fifteen years, which produced Na Min and Kwan. Her husband died trying to save a man's life when the kids were five and eight years old.

"There you are." Na Min appeared at the screened door, the sound of the door creaked as he came outside.

"How was your sleep?" She said.

He smiled and sat down.

Got'em raised his head for a brief moment, sighed and assumed his usual position. He rubbed his ears as he sat down next to his mom.

"Sleep was good, very good." Na Min said.

"What's the matter, you don't drink coffee?" she sipped.

"Yes mother, I found you before I went into the kitchen." He looked out beyond the farm. The tree line was another farm that had horses, cows and a couple of bulls. He could see the farmer plowing in the distance. He inhaled the fresh morning dew that had a pinch of manure.

"How long are you staying?" she looked at him, Got'em looked as if he understood the question.

"Well..." he rested his head, raised his arms above his head and interlocked his fingers behind his upper neck, popping his neck, "...three more days, just three more days, I wish that I could stay longer."

She smiled and held her hand out, "Boy, you always say that." She blew into her cup to cool her coffee, "I still remember when you were a little boy..." she giggled. "...mommy, mommy, can I ride the sheep?" they both laughed.

"You were such a good little boy. You were always trying to help others." She sipped. "Do you remember Mr. Hagman? You know he passed away about six months ago?" she rested her coffee in her lap.

"Yes I do remember him. He had three kids. I wonder how they are doing."

"Well..." she blew into her cup, "...the oldest, passed away not long after their father died."

"No way, did they say how either of them died?"

"I heard from Ms. Camwittle from the other side of the creek... do you remember her? Well anyway, a heart attack, and his son died of a lung infection, something to do with working in the coal mines in Pennsylvania."

He rubbed Got'em with his foot, "Wow, life is a strange journey."

"Yes it is." She took a sip. She came to life with a smiled from ear to ear, tickled her to the point of no return, "Do you remember when you were a boy scout?" before he could respond. "You tried to pitch that tent up, a camp fire, and you had that sheep crying for his mother." They both laughed. "That mother sheep ripped the tent down trying to get her baby. You screamed like you had seen a mummy." She shook her head.

"Mom, that was not funny. I was terrified." They laughed as he stood up, "Fresh cup?"

"Naaah, I'll be in there soon to cook breakfast."

"Well let me help you up." He held out his hand and used his other hand to help. She held on to his elbow as they walked into the house.

His visit is never long enough as he packs his luggage; the room brings so many memories with the framed photos on the wall. The room seemed so much smaller; the twin size bed had seemed to be for someone else now. His trophies were strapped of ribbons that were lined along the dresser, blanketed with dust. He was taller than his mirror that he used to dress himself, it was like yesterday. He opened the top right dresser drawer, old underwear, t shirts, socks, as if he had never left. Beneath the clothing he noticed a folded letter; it was his exception letter to the C.I.A. He thought about taking it, but placed it back underneath his socks. He decided to clean the room up before he leave, never know when the next time it will be done.

He can hear his mom from down stairs calling his name, "Yes mother! I'll be down, bringing my bags down!"

He head down stairs placing his bags on the porch. He sighed as he looked at Got'em, "Hey little fella."

He bent down, rubbed his hand over his ears, rubbed his cold wet nose across his, "Well, I have to leave you and mom here, once again." He buried his face into his neck, hugged him tight.

Got'em looked like he knew the routine, wagged his tail, rolled on to his back and waited for him to rub his belly.

"Mom, you didn't..." he embraced her and kissed her on the cheek.

"You still look handsome..." she grabbed his cheeks, "...you tell that wife of yours to keep in touch, and I miss talking to her." She handed him a zip lock bag of his favorite chocolate cookies.

He turned around and noticed the pictures of Kalargo, Mugumbi, Yuki on the wall. She rubs his back. He picked up the photo and rubbed his finger over Yuki's face. His eyes watered.

"She was such a beautiful girl." She handed him a Kleenex to wipe his tears. "It's a shame how she died."

He carefully places the photo back on the wall, took a deep breath and hugged his mom. His tears soaked her sweater, "It's hard mom, I just can't believe it myself. It hurts really bad." For the first time, he truly was hurt deep down inside. He wiped his face. They said their goodbyes; Kwan tossed his bags in the trunk, and waved as they drove off.

*   *   *

Seoul, South Korea

Mugumbi was three feet deep into digging a hole in Na Min's backyard, sweating in his all black jumpsuit and he had to be very quite due to the neighbors. He found a great place far in the corner, dark from the light of the neighbor's back porch light. The ground was cold, a lot of roots underneath from a huge tree. He had to cut each root with his jig saw. He was breathing hard, almost out of breath, but this had to be done by sunrise. He laid the shovel down, leaned his buttocks against the now four feet wall of dirt that held his weight. Almost out of breath, his cell phone vibrated, but he refused to answer it. He grabbed the shovel and tossed more dirt over his shoulder.

"Oh my God!" he said under his breath, hit ignore with his right index finger, and peaked through the bushes to make sure no one was watching. He sighed, jumped back into the hole, and used his cutters to clear out the shallow grave. He looked at the half moon, wiped his forehead, rubbed his neck and licked his mustache of sweat. The shovel was cheap and coming apart; if need be, he would finish by hand.

"Not again." he finally decided to see who was calling him, "Oh my God." He tossed his hands up to the stars. He did not want to answer due to his voice could carry over to the neighbors. He used his forearm to wipe the side of his face.

Before he could get started, his cell phone vibrated his back pocket, and pissed him off. The screen was bright enough to illuminate the back yard. He changed the brightness and finally answered after twenty missed calls.

"Yes." He whispered with his hands covering his mouth, looking over his shoulders, through the bushes just to make sure that he was not heard.

"I have been trying to get a hold of you!" Kalargo said.

He looked at the cell phone like he was annoyed, "I've been very busy..." he tiptoed to the other side of the yard trying to be as quiet as possible, "how have you been?"

"Not good Mugumbi, I had a knife at my throat, fighting for my life..." Kalargo said.

Words like this perked Mugumbi ears up like an attentive hound. "What the hell do you mean?"

"Mugumbi, I need you to listen to me carefully..." he sighed hard enough to tickle the grey hairs in his ear, run chills down his neck, "The North Koreans sent an assassin to kill me."

"No!" he said in a low disappointed voice, he bent down to listen.

"I need you to stop whatever you are doing, jump on the next plane to Manila, Philippines." he gave him instructions and he listened carefully, "They have Jenko's family held up until they hear that I am dead. We have less than forty eight hours before he needs to report back to them." he paused and let out another painful sigh, "Or they will kill his entire family."

"Wow..." he looked at the hole in the ground, threw the shovel in it, and wiped his forehead with his index finger, "Where is Jenko?"

"He is recovering from surgery, do you have a pen and paper?" he waited as he grabbed something to write on.

"So Jenko tried to kill you?" the sound of paper unfolded in the background. He also tried to think about this hole he just dug, knowing the sun will be up in forty minutes, and this would be a problem, totally screwing up his plan.

"Well, he had a chance to kill me, but he did not, I understand his situation."

"Ok, I am ready." he wrote down the address, a contact will meet him at the airport; a car will be giving to him with weapons, "I booked you a flight that leaves in two hours."

Mugumbi's sigh was hard to ignore, "So what do you want me to do?" He pulled out his specially made scuba diving suit, rolled it, tucked it under his arm, left everything else and hoped to return before Na Min's vacation ended.

"Rescue his family and kill everyone else." They both ended the call.

*   *   *

Manila, Philippines

Mugumbi pushed his way through to the escalator, going down to the baggage claim, he looked for his name on a sign, nothing. He waited as the travelers slowly gathered around like animals at a zoo expecting food, as the luggage began to spit out off the tread mill. He thought the driver would be there, waiting like a professional. His bag tumbled down, and out towards the bottom of the wheel. He reached in behind a woman, "Excuse me."

He walked towards the doors, "You must be Mugumbi?"
A voice came from behind, no sign, "My name is Joshua, your driver."

They shook hands, "How did you know what I looked like?" Joshua laughed, "This is the Philippines, not to many Blacks here that fly for one, tall for two, and so damn ugly for three." They both laughed to shatter the ice.

To be called ugly and knowing that you are ugly, no complaint, "You sure know how to burst a guys bubble, I was feeling handsome, well at least my wife made me feel that way." He closed his eyes, sighed, "So where is your car?"

"You are looking at it." He waved his hand towards his outdated Toyota sedan.

"Ok." Not impressed, but was eager to get on the road, he gave him the address and directed him on the way. The forty minute ride was quite, windows did not work, the heat came from all directions, and traffic was at a turtle's pace; the smell, just awful.

"Have you been to Manila before?"

He looked at the driver via the rearview mirror, the five air fresheners were point less, his nose and mouth was covered with his t-shirt, "Many years ago, many years ago." He looked out the window, kids played in the canal that was also sewer water. How immune do you have to be, the thought shook him.

They arrived to the address and Joshua turned around, "Well, this is as far as I go." He refused his fare money, "It's been paid already." Opened his door and pulled his short chubby body from the driver seat, open the back door, "Everything you need..." he handed a key to him, "...is in that house." He reached in and pulled the key from the ignition, "When you are done, just leave it at the airport."

Mugumbi sighed, holding the set of keys, climbed from the car, looked around, wanted to inhale, but pinched his nose and inhaled through his mouth.

"Don't worry; you will get use to it." He inhaled as deep as he could, smiled, "Fresh air to me." revealing his thrift store ridiculous dentures that was one size to big.

Before he walked away, hit the alarm on his car, "By the way..." he tossed a cell phone, "I was told to give this to you. If you need me, my number is locked in the contacts." He jumped in his Mazda and left a cloud of floating dust behind him.

After an hour on the road, through the hills, passing rice patties, and farms, he grew to like the old Toyota, it did not stand out, ran good enough to get the job done. It just reminded him so much of Africa, well some of it.

He looked at his GPS, five miles from Jenko's house; the butterflies began to tickle his abdomen. He sighed several times to shake them, intervals grew closer, darkness slowly melted day light. The shadows along the road moved as the sun descended. The bells from bovines rang along the road he drove. He was now within minutes from his destination, a small town was not far, he stopped to get a sense of his surrounding, back roads along the hillside, and possible escape routes. He knew that this had to be done tonight, no exceptions.

He drove around the town, learning as much as he could or until he felt ready. He found a gas station, where he could change into his clothes. He looked in the mirror, at his ugly self, he smiled and shook his head, and "You mean to tell me I've been ugly all this time?" he smiled.

He tossed his bags in the front seat, but he wanted to drive by the house at least one time, to get an idea of what he will face. Four minutes from the house, he turned down a two lane unpaved road, speed was slow enough not to raised suspicion. In sight, the living room, and the porch light was on, two cars were parked in front. Just before he passed the house, he checked the mail box to verify the address, his palms sweated like no other time in his life, he almost stopped breathing when he read the name above the numbers, "Micheal J. Song Chi.

Chapter 31

The rain clouds moved in as Mugumbi crawled towards the patio set, covered in dirt, a drop of rain began to fall like snow. The sound of the T.V., and voices could be heard. He pushed on until safely arriving under the kitchen window. He used a nonreflecting mirror, and counted two men.

Jenko's wife sat at the table reading a news paper, the kids played in the living room, the two men spoke Korean to each other and the floating rain felt heavier, one drop at a time. He sighed, twisted his neck and tried to calm himself.

He got down on his hands and knees, made it to the other side, near the living room window he noticed the shorter North Korean had a pistol tucked in the back of his pants. The taller chubby one sat his gun on the table near his brewing coffee.

He looked up at the clouds, running out of time; it was now or never, until the yard dog began to bark.

"Can we bring our dog in?" the little boy asked his mom. "It's going to start raining soon." He held his toy and looked at his mom as she walked into the living room.

"Don't bother these men about that, it is close to bed time." She began snatching the toys from the floor, tossing them towards the toy box.

"I don't see why he can't have his dog." The chubby one struggled to lift himself from the couch, walked over to the door to see what the dog was barking at. The accumulation of rain, and fast moving clouds, the flash of lightning in the distance had the dog behaving differently.

"Yeah I don't see why not; look like some heavy rain is on its way." The shorter one said.

Mugumbi may have dodge a bullet, the dog would have giving him away sooner or later, but he had to take advantage of the small opening that allowed him. The kid walked out on to the porch, he reached for the light switch and wondered what happened to the light bulb. Just before asking his mom, he was distracted by his dog. He whistled his way towards the tree. He stopped, stood there like he was afraid. Mugumbi was bent down with his dog in his arms, index finger on his lips, trying to tell him to be quiet. He waved for him to come closer. The boy looked over his shoulder and hesitated.

"Come." he waved with a sense of urgency. The boy looked up at the weather approaching, scared, nervous, "I'm here to help you. Your father sent me." The boy relaxed a little.

"What's your name?"

"Sam."

"How many people are in the house?"

"Sam!" he was frightened as the voice of the North Korean came closer, "Where are you?" the chubby one danced the mud to avoid ruining his shoes. "There you go." He looked up and knew it was going to be a good storm coming.

Sam stood there with his dog by his collar like he had seen something odd.

"You better get in before it starts to rain." The North Korean fell down with a bullet to the back of his head. Mugumbi dragged his body behind the tree.

"Stay here and wait for your mom." He quickly ran up to the porch, walked in and began shooting. He looked around; she was curled up with her daughter.

"It's over now." Mugumbi said.

"Bang, bang, bang." he was shot in the leg, arm, and back. He fell on the couch and tumbled to the floor. He returned fire, hitting one in the chest. The mother and the daughter ran for the door. He was hurt as he stumbles on to the porch. He leaned on the pole, and could not believe he had been shot, tried to shake it off.

Zang slowly approached from behind, pointing at his head, the sound of the wooden floors gave him away, "Bang, bang."

The bullet crazed Mugumbi's left ear, and the other burned a line across his upper eyebrow. He jumped to the ground and took cover. From where he was he could see the mother and her kids crotched down behind the car. He ran towards them, dodging gun fire that barely missed.

"Here, take my keys, I have a car parked along the road. Take it, get out of here!" He peeked around the car. A bullet hit the tail light, and scratched his face. "Listen, when I start shooting, run that way…" he pointed, but they were afraid, "ready?" He grabbed her arm, looked at her and the kids, reached in his inner pocket and pulled out the letters. "Give these to your husband."

Maria nodded her head, held her two cubs tight, "We are ready."

"On three, One, two, three." He provided enough cover fire for them to vanish into the bushes that line their property and made it to the car.

He ran towards the rear of the house, Zang fired shots, hitting him in the upper shoulder and thigh. He tumbled to the ground, pushed further into the dense tree line. Bullets ripped through the leaves like razors, he hid behind a tree and reloaded. He saw two cars with reinforcement pull into the driveway.

"He is in the tree line!" Zang pointed in his direction.

He took off running, jumping, diving over rocks; the branches slapped him hard enough to bruise him. He fell again and crashed face first in mud, with no time he had to keep moving. "Aaaahh!" he was hit again. He crawled and blended himself on the other side of a creek, breathing hard, bleeding from his head, his vision blurred. He slowly reached in his backpack for his visine. "Damn it!" he gritted his teeth; the entire box was shot to hell. He soaked two of his fingers in his mouth to lubricate his eyes. When that was not enough he filled his palms with saliva, rubbed them until he cleared his vision. He heard a noise and became motionless.

The sound of men trampled across the creek, to far apart to shoot them all without getting killed himself, "What the heck!" he whispered.

He slowly bent a leaf, pulled out an ammo clip, tossed it in the other direction. When it landed, he took off like a jaguar, jumped like a performance horse, crawled like an alligator. The sound of the gun fire exploded, he reached the edge of the mountainous jungle barely hanging on to a branch, hands slipping, no matter what he tried, it was not meant for him to survive this trip. "Aaaah!"

He looked below, it was dark, the sound of running water did not comfort him, and it sounded far from where he dangled.

The branch slid through his hand like warm butter, the jagged rocks broke his fall, but they were crumbling apart due to the heavy rain. His fingers nails were splitting one by one, the skin on the tips of his fingers were to the bone, he slid with every breath.

"No, this can't be it." He slid closer to the edge that dropped more than sixty feet. "I'm not going to make it." He thought about Yuki and his promise, he cried, feeling defeated, broken down to his last breath that he tried to hold it for as long as he could. When he exhaled, he slid off the cliff, tumbled down a steep rocky mountain side, splashed into the canal.

After two days, he floated down the canal; found by kids playing polo, still alive, in severe pain, the sewer water quenched his thirst. He lay among shallow rocks that stop him from going further down the canal.

"Mr! Mr.!" They were afraid to touch him.

He thought he had died, the sun light impaired his vision, both arms were broken, left collar bone protruded his neck, jaw bone was separated, upper lip busted, rib cage broken in three places and could not feel anything below his waist.

He opened his mouth, "Help me."

The boys tried to drag him across the rocks, but couldn't, they ran for help.

He choked up as tears streamed his face, "I, I survived."

*   *   *

Seoul, South Korea

Na Min walked off the plane, thumbing through his phone, eighteen missed calls from Zang, he sighed in disappointment, not knowing what he wanted, but it could not be good. He checked his emails, returned calls, and waited in baggage claim, left a message for his wife, and took a deep breath. He leaned on the pole, exhausted, could not wait to hit the sack.

He arrived home; he smiled as he paid the driver, grabbed his bags, and tried to answer his cell phone, "Yes." He struggled to push his house key in the lock, finally tossing his bags, and stopped to look in the mirror at the bags beneath his eyes, "Getting old, yes I am here."He rubbed his face. "What are you talking about?"

Zang sounded like Charlie Brown as he yelled through the phone.

"Zang, Zang, calm down..." he scratched his forehead and walked around the living room. "Are you sure it was him?" he covered his mouth, balled his fist, shook his head. "You told me I had thirty days." He took an apple from the bowl on the kitchen counter, wiped it clean with his shirt, and took a big bite. "Yes I hear you."

He walked into his office, poured him a glass of Ginifer, "All I needed was time. This could have worked out a lot smoother. Now you have a bigger mess on your hands." He took a smaller bite, and placed the remaining on the desk, sipped his drink and stood by the window. He sighed and leaned his back side on the window sill.

He walked over to the mini and added ice, more Gin and kicked off his loafers, "Listen, listen, let me handle this, you going about this all wrong." Na Min spoke with confidence.

Zang sounded very concerned about this and needed him to get this right.

"Calm down, take in some oxygen, breath a little, who you think run this side of the Pacific?"

"You do." Zang said.

"When you need something done, who do you come to?"

"You." Zang took a deep breath, calms himself down, "So, how do you want to go about this?"

Finally, he calmed him down, took a sip, "First of all..." he walked over to the window, "as soon as I." His eyes opened wide, choked as Ginifer went down his wind pipe, heart dropped to his rectum, coughed and threw his drink in the corner of his office. "What the fuck!"

He pressed his face to the glass, looked carefully, and could not believe what he was looking at. He tossed the phone down, opened his desk drawer, cocked his gun and ran and hid behind the door. He carefully moved throughout the house, ducking, dodging with his index finger on the trigger. He looked around the home, it was clear. He went out to the back yard and stood over the hole in the ground. "Fuck!"

It was just like the dream, he sighed in between his heartbeat, sweated down his back, and dragged his feet like a four year wearing a grown man shoes. His socks were soaked with mud, "When I find this mother fucka!" He looked at the neighbor's windows to see if anyone had been watching him. He heard the cell phone ringing from up stairs, he ran in the house, tracking mud all the way to his office, crawled beneath the coffee table, "Hello."

"Are you ok?" The phone went silent. Before he could say another word Na Min wanted to know, "So, is he dead?"

"Who Kalargo, not yet, we are working on it, if your plan does not work soon."

"No, not talking about Kalargo!, Mugumbi! Is he dead?!" Unless he is Superman, he is dead. He was shot up pretty bad, fell off a cliff about sixty feet, hitting rocks the entire way down, just horrible."

He was relieved to hear that, but still felt the need to verify it. He let out a huge sigh of relief and told him to keep in touch, "Hey, let me try to work something out with my son."

The call ended.

*　　　*　　　*

One month later

Marcelo Hospital, Baliuag, Philippines

The cold sterilized room, cartoons of Tom and Jerry with no volume displayed on the TV., the pain killers slowly wore off as Mugumbi lay in bed, eyes closed, and thankful to be alive. However, he was not himself; he felt weird that he tried to move but could not. He opened his eyes to a foggy room, blurry and in need of visine. His throat hurt when he swallowed, he felt the restraints that held him to the bed.

His heart rate elevated as he tried to crawled out of bed, "Help me!" he wish he had super powers, perhaps he would be able to move things with his eyes, "What is going on here?"

After two hours of him trying to escape his body cast, exhausted and finally a doctor enter his room with a pad in hand, fair skin, straight hair, slanted eyes, short and slender, "Mugumbi, right?"

He looked into his eyes with a mini flash light, pupils worked fine, "I'm Dr. Gonzales. I have been looking after you since you arrived. Do you know where you are?"

"No."

He rubbed the bottom of his feet, "Do you feel anything?"

"No."

He scratched harder, "Anything?"

"No."

He did not want to alarm him in any way, but it was apparent that he was paralyzed. "Today, we remove the body cast, do more test, and take it from there. Do you remember what happened to you?"

"No." His throat had not healed properly leaving him with a raspy, inaudible at times when he speaks.

"Come closer..." the Dr. Leaned in to his lips, "will I be able to walk again?"

"Of course, of course, you will." He grabbed the clip board and sighed after blurting out a lie to his face. He was not for sure. "Listen, you are in good hands, after we take the cast off, take a look at you. Do you have anyone we can call, you will no longer be able to live on your own, you have a severe brain injury and will be incapacitated."

The blur in the room lifted like the sun beamed in on his tears "Can I have visine for my eyes?"

"Of course, Do you understand what I said?" he leaned over him, several nurses entered to help with the cast removal.

One week later, Mugumbi sat in his wheel chair looking out the window, saliva drooled down his gown, and head leaned to his left, recovering from surgery. The screws that were drilled in to his bones had not healed. He cried often when he made any progress that gave him hope. His voice slowly recovered, but his mind had not.

The nurse entered to feed him soft blended food, for the first time he was excited. "Where is Dr. Gonzales?"

"What did you say?"

"Where, is Dr., Gonzales?" He forced his words out from his tongue that had become lazy.

She stirred his beans, rice, and mashed potatoes all in one circle, "He will be here soon, is there something I can do?"

He opened wide, slowly pushed his white tongue out that had marks from his jagged from biting it, closed his mouth with a spoon full, "Later on we will place you back into your bed, ok."

He nodded as he slowly chewed, "Dr. Gonzales?"

"He won't be in for a while. Do you have to use the restroom?" the nurse asked.

There was a tap on the door, Dr. Gonzales entered with a smile and flash light. He has been asking for you all morning. She stepped aside. He placed the x-rays on the monitor. "Well..." he folded his hands in front of him, interlocking his fingers, "...how can I help this morning?"

He mumbled words that drew the Dr. in close enough to feel his breath. He spoke into his ear and whatever he said, it put a smile on his face, chuckled him to tears, "You got to be kidding?"

He leaned in for more; the nurse thought he had told him a joke, but whatever it was, for the first time Mugumbi smiled. The nurse cleaned up his drool, and placed the straw to his lips. He sucked the orange juice down and made a request for him to do him a favor. He told him to tell the nurse to leave the room so they could talk.

"Will I be able to walk again?"

"Well..." he held up the x-rays, "Do you know you were shot fifteen times, if it wasn't for your bullet proof scuba diving suit..." he faced the light to get a better look at the x-rays, "...you would have been found dead." He explains how severe his injuries were.

Mugumbi turned his head away, disappointed. He indicated that he wanted to write something on paper even that was a task, but managed.

"I can't do that." He looked at him like he was crazy. "Why would you..." before he could say another word.

The anger on Mugumbi's face meant business. He rubbed his index finger and thumb together.

"I just, it's unethical, and I would lose my license."

The sound of the pen scratching on the paper as he scribbled, he held it up to his face, with one finger, then two, his eyes widen.

The Doctor could not believe his request. He went over to the door, made sure no one was listening. "Make it three."

Mugumbi had to think about it, "Why three?"

"It has to be worth the risk." He placed his hands in his medical coat and paced the room.

Mugumbi showed him the paper, "Do you have a laptop?"

"Of course, I'll bring it first thing in the morning." They both nodded their heads.

The Dr. walked out of the room, and told the staff to bath him.

*   *   *

Seoul, South Korea
Three weeks later

Na Min curled into his pillow, with his wife on the phone, trying to explain why the South Americans are the same as the Puerto Ricans, not listening to her, telling her she is wrong about the people of South America.

"Well, besides the fact, that you guys are citizens of the United States, you all speak Spanish..." He said.

She interrupted with anger, "You have to be out of your mind, we don't look alike, culture is nowhere close." She was upset.

"Calm down, calm down, don't get your..." he decided not say what was on his mind, "...honey, I am just messing with you." He blew a kiss in to the mouth piece. "Honey, hold on, I have a call coming in." He pressed the buttom, "Hello."

"Yes, this is Dr. Gonzales, calling from Marcelo Hospital, Baliuag, Philippines..." he waited for a response, "Well... I am looking for the next of kin, is this Na Min Choi?"

Silence between them both were like watching a snail crawl, Na Min felt like this would be a great time to identify Mugumbi's body, "Yes, I am Mr. Choi, how can I help you?"

"We have Mugumbi here..."

"Is he..." before he could say another word, he was interrupted.

"Yes, yes, he is doing great, a little banged up but he survived a tragic fall down a mountain side. However, the reason why I am calling..." he paused and took a deep breath, "...we could not get a hold of his wife, and your number was next to call."

"Mugumbi is a live?" he raised his head from his pillow, eyes wide, lips were heavy like weights, "But how is..."

"He has been severely injured, he will need some assistance with every day choirs, and basically he's incapacitated."

"Oh my God, well..." lost for words, "...his wife had passed away." He jumped from beneath his bed sheets, throwing his pillow, and paced the bedroom. "This has to be horrible, oh my God." He covered his mouth, not knowing what to say or do, but desperately wanted to get his hands on him, and the letters. "What kind of injuries?"

"Anything from head drama, broken bones, punctured lung, and the list goes on, very lucky to be alive. He will need around the clock home care. It's unfortunate for such a young man in his prime. He can't brush his teeth, or feed himself."

"What do you need for me today?"

"I just want to make sure that we are able to release him to his family, who will take care of him?"

"What's the name of the hospital?" he grabbed a pen, wrote it down and looked at his calendar, "Let me arrange some things, I say about thirty days from today. I just can't believe this happened to him." he let out a cry in disbelief. "I'll be there." They ended the call.

He held the receiver to his left ear with his right hand, slumped in the recliner and tried to think how he would handle Mugumbi. He needed a place where he can have complete privacy, but the around the clock care, he tossed his hands up.

"I need some where that is far out of the city." He rubbed his hands together with no ideas in mind, stood up to pace and think. His wife was returning and she liked him, so he knew he would not be able to do what he wanted to do with her around. He licked his thumb and pushed his eye brows, looked into the stand up mirror, deep into his eyes, shook his head, "I can't bring him here." He plucked a grey hair that stood out among his dark mustache.

He snapped his fingers to an idea, and took no time to dialed Zang's phone, but no answer. He smiled at his brilliant idea. Not long after Yang returned his call.

"Hey, you won't believe the phone call I just received." He waited.

"Hmmm, the King is dead?"

"What? No Mugumbi is alive."

"How is that so?"

"He floated down a canal and was found clinging to life with severe injuries. He is incapacitated, require in home care, but I need him alive until I can get some vital information from him." They both sighed.

"So why are you telling me this?" Zang asked.

"I'm going to pick him up from the hospital, however I need a location to secure him. Even though he has brain damage from his fall, I need to extract as much from him as possible" he sat down at his desk, looked out his window at the shallow grave.

"Done, I will have a place for you, preferably secluded?"

He was relieved that he did not have to bring Mugumbi to South Korea, his wife would never find out what he was up to, and getting rid of him would not come back to him.

"Excellent, I will call you the day I leave." They both ended their call.

*   *   *

Gambia, Africa

The morning sun danced across the clear blue sky. The ornaments on the desk were enlarged by its shadows as the day went on. Kalargo waited for Jenko's family to arrive from the airport, he had not heard from Mugumbi and hoped they had some answers to what may have happened to him. He reached for his cell to call him, but stopped. What would another call do? After twenty two messages and no response, it has to be bad news. He tapped his nails, wagged his foot, and never stopped looking at the clock. "They should be here by now."

When his cell phone rung, he was quick to see who was calling. "Hello." He frowned, "Yes, I will be down to greet them. Yes, I will bring Jenko down as well."

Recovering from surgery, he was excited to know that his family had arrived safe. The tap on his door, "They will be down stairs in a few minutes. Do you need help?"

Kalargo peaked in and saw him getting dressed. His wounds were bandaged and caused him to move with caution. He took in a deep breath, looked at him, "I just want to say thanks..." he reached his hand out to him, "...I have all the respect in the world for you, and just want you to hear it from my lips that I am so sorry for what I put you through."

"Hey, you did what it takes to save your family." He shook his hand, and pulled him close, patted each other on the back. "Now let's see your family."

The joy among them can be heard throughout the Palace. The true love of family and the embrace was evident that the right thing had been done. He lifted his son and hugged him breathless with kisses across his face. "I love you." One by one he repeated.

"Kalargo..." his wife began to thank him as she cried and hugged him, "...thank you so much."

"Hey, I'm sure if I needed you guys, the same thing would have been done." He hugged them all as their tears streamed their joyful faces.

"Hey, I have breakfast prepared. I know you guys have to be hungry."

"Starving." Maria said.

He pointed in the direction of the dining room, "Take a seat, anywhere."

Jenko's wife pulled out the letters, "That guy who rescued us wanted you to have these."

"You mean Mugumbi?"

She looked as if the name did not register, "He didn't say his name."

"Did he survive, what had happen?"

"Not sure, he ran into the tree line, a lot of shooting, I don't think he made it out alive. More cars pulled up and people ran after him." She looked very sad for him and shook her head, "I don't think he made it out."

The sad look on Kalargo's face had him staring into the table, lost for words. He looked at the letters wrapped in plastic with a rubber band around them.

"He gave you those letters? Did he say anything?"

"Just to give them to my husband."

"Do you mind if I take a look at them?" Jenko opened them and look at them before passing the first envelope to him. He noticed that his father had sent them to Chicago, "Wow, these are old."

"Oh my God." He looked at Jenko as he read the name on it. He remember taking them from the book, "These will be the longest days you will ever do"

"I remember these letters." He took a sip of his orange juice, "I had these in my home. I took them from a woman's house in Chicago and I wanted to find out why that name sounded so familiar. It was just so odd that it had Song Chi written on them, but I could not remember where I had heard the name at the time. Then when I went to look for them, vanish. It was like they had been stolen from the house or something."

"Why did you go to Chicago?" Jenko looked at him for an answer.

"Well, doing a favor for someone." He brushed the question to the side, "I am starving. Let's dig in."

He could not help to think how did Mugumbi get a hold of these letters, and what was in the letters that was so important for him to have them on him at that moment.

The head of security came over and whispered in Kalargo's ear and walked away. The General of the Army had sent some intelligence that had been found in a town that was taken back from the rebels. He thought this new Intel was significant, but did not know what it was for, passing it on for further review was imperative.

Later that afternoon he provided the family a place to stay until things settled down and to find out what was in the letters.

"Kalargo, I can't thank you enough for what you have done for my family. If there is anything that I can do to help you in anyway..." he raised his hands, "...don't hesitate to call."

They both exited the office and walked towards the waiting car, and six days later they returned to the Philippines.

The King danced to the sounds of Michael Jackson, pushed his oxygen tank like a vacuum as he maneuvered the Persian rug with his bare feet, inhaling from mask until he wore himself out. He lasted almost four minutes, not yet able to dance to the end of any song, but is a personal goal. Before he could blame anyone but himself a knock on the door interrupted him.

"Father, I see you listening to your favorite." He slowly entered.

He let out a hard exhale, sat on the edge of the bed, rubbed his thighs and remembered how firm they used to be. "Keep saying good morning." He smiled and inhaled oxygen.

"I wanted to run a couple of thing by you, just to get your opinion." He held a rolled schematic drawing of something he could not quiet make out.

"What you got there, some art of some sort?"

"It looks like the rebels were building something." He unrolled it and examined it. "It looks like a boat. What kind of boat could this be and why would they need a boat?" he pointed at different parts of the drawing.

"This has to be garbage; it would never work according to these specs." They both shook their heads. "It would sink."

"Yeah, I think you are right, this is just something that could never float." They chuckled. The sound of Kalargo jr cries from the other room ended any further thought about the plans of an imminent attack.

"I'll hang on to them for further review." He rolled them up and they both went to check on the fast growing Prince.

Later that evening the King walked in with a folder under his arm. Kalargo sat at his desk wondering what happened to Mugumbi. "What you have there?"

The folders fell on the desk and slid apart from one another. He slowly took a seat and pointed, "I believe you should know your enemy, and what you are against."

Kalargo opened a folder, "So these are the rebels?"

He looked at photos, and looked at his father. He thought about the weapons he had sent to the rebels, and how he had helped the enemy. He cleared his throat, covered his mouth. He truly felt a shamed at his action in the past. All this time he made money off the people his father had been fighting.

"These people..." the King pointed his finger at him, "...are trying to impose Sharia Law."

"What is Sharia Law?" he looked at more horrible photos of decapitations, amputations that made no sense.

"You have a lot of reading to do, everything you want to know are in those folders. Later on I will tell you some personal experiences and a plan that could help you fight these savages." He stood, nodded his head and inched his way out.

He sat back in his chair until he was comfortable, and began reading.

Sharia law is the body of Islamic law. The term means "way" or "path"; it is the legal framework within which the public and some private aspects of life are regulated for those living in a legal system based on Islam.

Sharia deals with all aspects of day-to-day life, including politics, economics, banking, business law, contract law, sexuality, and social issues.

There is not a strictly codified uniform set of laws that can be called Sharia. It is more like a system of several laws, based on the Qur'an, Hadith and centuries of debate, interpretation and precedent.

There are four major schools of Sunni sharia law (Hanafi, Maliki, Shafi'i and Hanbali), and one major Shia sharia law (Jafari). The sharia law between these schools is same for topics covered in Quran, but in matters that is not covered explicitly in Quran, they sometimes differ from each other.

Marriage

- A Muslim man can marry only a Muslim, Christian or Jewish woman. He cannot marry an atheist, agnostic or polytheist.

- A Muslim woman can marry only a Muslim man. She cannot marry a Christian, Jew, atheist, agnostic or polytheist.

- The minimum age of marriage for females is nine, for males is twelve.

- A Muslim minor girl's father or guardian may arrange the marriage of a girl, without her consent, before she reaches adulthood.

- An adult man cannot marry an adult woman without her consent. An adult woman requires her wali's - father or male guardian - consent to marry, in following schools of sharia: Maliki, Shafi'i, Hanbali and Jafari.

- A marriage is a contract that requires the man to pay, or promise to pay some Mahr (property as brideprice) to the woman. The married woman owns this property.

- A man can divorce his wife any time he wants, without reason. A woman cannot divorce her husband without reason. She may file for divorce for reason, such as he is impotent, missing or biologically related to her.

- A Muslim man can marry four Muslim women. A Muslim woman can marry only one Muslim man.

Crime and punishment

Sharia recognizes three categories of crime:

1. Hudud: crimes against God with fixed punishment

2. Qisas: crimes against Muslims where equal retaliation is allowed

3. Tazir: crimes against Muslims or non-Muslims where a Muslim judge uses his discretion in sentencing

Hudud crimes are seven: theft, highway robbery, zina (illicit sex), sexual slander (accusing someone of zina but failing to produce four witnesses), drinking alcohol, publicly disputing Imam, and apostasy (leaving Islam and converting to another religion or becoming an atheist).

Sharia requires that there be four adult male Muslim witnesses to a hudud crime, or a confession repeated four times, before someone can be punished for a Hudud crime.

Murder, bodily injury and property damage - intentional or unintentional - is considered a civil dispute under sharia law. The victim, victim's heir(s) or guardian is given the option to either forgive the murderer, demand Qisas (equal retaliation) or accept a compensation (Diyya) in lieu of the murder, bodily injury or property damage. Under sharia law, the Diyya compensation received by the victim or victim's family is in cash, and the amount depends on the gender and religion of the victim, for an equivalent crime and circumstances. Muslim women receive less compensation than Muslim man, and non-Muslims receive less compensation than Muslims.

The penalty for theft

Theft (stealing) is a hudud crime in sharia, with a fixed punishment. The punishment is amputating (cutting off) the hands or feet. However, before a person is punished, two eyewitnesses must testify that they saw the person stealing.

The penalty for zina

Sharia law states that if either an unmarried man or an unmarried woman has pre-marital sex, the punishment should be 100 lashes. If a married man or a married woman commit adultery, the punishment should be 100 lashes and then stoning to death. There are some requirements that need to be met before this punishment can happen. For example, the punishment cannot happen unless the person confesses, or unless four male eyewitnesses each saw, at the same time, the man and the women in the action of illicit sex. Those who accuse someone of illicit sex but fail to produce four eyewitnesses are guilty of false accusation and their punishment is 80 lashes. Maliki school of sharia considers pregnancy in an unmarried woman as sufficient evidence that she committed the hudud crime of zina. The Hadiths consider homosexuality as zina, to be punished with death.

The penalty for apostasy

Sharia law does not allow Muslims to leave Islam, in order to become atheist or convert to other religions. This is strictly forbidden, and is called apostasy. In Muslim theology, apostasy is a crime against God. The punishment for apostasy is death for Muslim male apostates. The major schools of sharia law differ in their punishment for female apostates: Maliki, Shafi'i and Hanbali sharia requires execution of female apostates, while Hanafi and Jafari sharia requires arrest, solitary confinement and punishment till she recants and returns to Islam.

In many Muslim countries, some people may be accused of apostasy even if they have non-conventional (non-traditional or unusual) interpretations of the Quran. Sunni and Shia Muslims have historically accused each other of apostasy, since the early days of Islam. Similarly Sufi, Ahmadiyya and other minority groups of Muslims have been accused of apostasy by majority Islamic sects.

He closed the folder, wondered how he got himself into this mess, and how to resolve it. He stood up, and dragged his heavy feet over to the bar, poured a stiff drink of Jack Daniels, without thinking about his health, tossed it down his throat, and that was followed by two more. He knew sooner or later he will need treatment, when is the question. He already began to feel weak at times, symptoms of running nose, tired very early, feverish at times and not knowing that the alcohol break down his immune system.

He looked out the window, inhaled with frustration, "I just can't believe this." His life style in Hawaii was drastically different and wished to return. It was simple, nice, predictable, and safe. Now he can count the fingers on his hand of the people that want him dead.

He rubbed his right palm behind his neck, scratched his head and thought about leaving Gambia. He sighed, "I can pack up my things, my son and just leave. I have money." He could not believe what he was thinking, but this is all crazy. He pinched his nose with his index and thumb, walked out of the office to check on Largo. He thought his future and a reason to expose him to this life, "Is it worth it?"

He cracked open the door, and used his shoulder to push the door open. His father held the little Prince by his hands, teaching him to walk to no avail.

Kalargo's eyes watered, he felt like he was in over his head. He wished he had never come, torn between thoughts of running like a coward, and saving his son from the hardship of war.

What man in this world, don't want to be King, born to the throne? That is a dream. He rubbed his eyes dry, and hated the idea of crushing his dad's heart. He wondered how to break the news to him. He sighed hard enough raise his father's head, not intentionally but it did.

"Are you ok?"

"Yeah, just feeling a little tired, didn't get much sleep last couple of days." Deep down inside he now wished he had joined Jenko and his family as they flew back to the Philippines.

He quickly came to a conclusion; only a poor man would want to be King, rich men don't want the headache. He looked at his son and father. Maybe he could bring them both. The thought drew a smile on his face, but he knew his father would have to be dragged from the mother land. He couldn't blame him though. This is what he know, and changed will devastate him more than death itself.

"What are you thinking about?" The King asked.

He was too frustrated to say, and it bothered him that he didn't have the guts to tell him to his face, and wished this was all a dream. "I read some of..." before he could finish he sighed again.

The King knew that this really bothered him to his core, this was a lot to handle, and to pass it down to anyone would be a challenge. "Listen, I know I dropped a lot on your plate, but this is what it is. Hey you are young and the people will stand up and fight these rebels into the dirt. There is nothing nice about this. If you are not a savage, become one. When your uncle was killed the war was almost over. They were about to surrender. So yes we lost ground when he died." He sucked on his oxygen. "Now we have them where we want them. All you have to do, go full speed ahead. Get them to go for a cease fire, surround them with all we got, at the right moment, attack!" he laughed, kissed Largo on the cheek.

"Yeah that may work." He scratched his head. He made a so call hard fist, "Crush them like the warriors we are." He slowly stood up, "This country need a new, young face that will build them up again. I have done everything that I could do."

He looked through his father as his mind wondered far away, telling himself, 'now is not a good idea or time. He may never make it out of the country alive.'

So he listened and he planned for their escape.

Chapter 32

Manila, Philippines

Dr. Gonzalez sat in his office in front of his computer with a pencil between his lips, holding x-rays into the light above his head. He pulled a Kleenex to blow his nose, just before he did the phone rang, "Hello this is Dr. Gonzales."

He stood from his desk, put the x-rays in the folder and slid it between the others on his desk. The look of urgency on his face as he tried to hang the phone up before the conversation was over, "Yes, tell him..." he had to think of something fast to stall Na Min.

"Tell him I will be down in a few minutes." He slammed the receiver down, quickly ran to the fourth floor, grabbed veils of medication, and took the stairs to the eighth floor. Before opening the door he took a deep breath, fixed his hair and calmly walked the hallway towards Mugumbi's room.

"Mugumbi, its time, you are going home today."

He grabbed his left arm, injected him with a medication, reached down into his underwear and tucked a small veil underneath his testicles and quickly left the room.

Moments later, the elevator doors open to the lobby of the hospital, "You must be Mr. Choi?" he held his hand out.

"You can call me Na Min." Their hands greeted with a firm hand shake.

"I did not know you were coming today." He waved him on to the elevator.

"I would have had him ready." The Doctor said.

Na Min stood alongside him as the elevator came to a stop, doors slid open, "Well it's not every day someone have to fly from another country to pick up a love one from the hospital..." they both nodded, "...especially on short notice."

Na Min fixed his well pressed jeans and shirt. He twisted his neck with anticipation, rubbed his palms and swallowed some anxiety, but could not wait to get his hands on him.

The Dr. waved over to the receptionist, "Is Mugumbi ready to be discharged?"

"Just a few more things on the paper work."

He waved him, "He is in room 4121." he knocked before entering, "Well here he is."

The nurse had prepared his belongings, as he sat in the wheel chair.

"Mr. Choi, he will need around the clock care, like I have already explained over the phone, therapy is vital to his recovery."

He walked over to him, "Mugumbi." He waited for him to respond.

"Like I said, he is in pretty bad shape."

"Mugumbi, it's your pal Na Min…" He smiled at him, "…we are going home."

He had a hard time responding, drool hung from his mouth, "Don't worry old buddy I'm here now." He rubbed his head and kissed him on the forehead, massaged his shoulders. He looked up at the Dr. and raised his eyebrows, "Well, we have a long road ahead of us." The nurse began pushing his wheelchair towards the reception desk; Na Min signed the papers and took custody.

The ride through the streets of Manila never changed, bringing back memories of the congestion that never seemed to dissipate. The partly cloudy sky frequently induced sun light through the moon roof. At the traffic light he looked at him with sadness to the condition he has finally come to. His eyes watered but did not change his mission, or the purpose for his trip. He sighed when his cell phone rang.

"Yes." he rubbed his eyes, and nose to relieve some stress. "No not really, I'm in traffic." He looked up and the light was green, as the honking of car horns had indicated. "Ok, calm down!" He looked over at his limped body, "Mugumbi, are you hungry?" he patiently waited for a response.

"Well Zang, it should not take too long. I'll stop for a bite to eat, so you have everything I need in place?" He nodded his head as he pulled into the Burger King parking lot, "Ok, so leave the key under the mat at the door." They ended their call.

He pulled up to the drive through and the voice from the speaker asked for their request. He looked at him to ask what he wanted, but his tongue and drool was disgusting, so he ordered for him. "Two number ones please."

As he waited he also wondered if torturing him will actually work. He twisted his lips as he thought about it and waited in the drive through. He pulled out a small finger nail file and dug into his thigh. He looked at him, no response. He stabbed him in his rib cage, and twisted it, no response. He leaned his head back in disappointment, wiped the blood on to his pants leg. He sighed like his world was coming to an end, looked into the rearview mirror, the parking lot, and punched him in the face, "Mother fucka!"

He pulled up to the window, "That will be..." before she could say the price. "Keep the change."

She passed him the food and made sure everything was there, placed it on Mugumbi's lap and smiled as he drove off. He took out a few fries and tossed them in his mouth.

It was a two hour drive that placed them in the middle of nowhere, a house on a farm used as a North Korean safe house. The drive up the narrow dirt road on the edges of the mountain look weathered, but occupied.

The dust trailed them as they slowly pulled up to the house. He looked at him, and sighed. He was trying to come up with a method to extract what he wanted from him, something that would be affective.

He sat there, crossed his arms, and shook his head. He dragged his feet getting out of the driver seat, almost like he had been defeated, no ideas in a field that he had perfected. He exited the car, stretched and pulled his left wrist across his chest, and repeated it with the right. He walked around the rear of the car and leaned on the trunk with his arm folded, rubbed his face of sweat with his shoulder, placed his face into his palms and sighed with frustration. He spat, and decided to think about it later.

"Ok, Mugumbi." He opened the door, grabbed the bag of food and realized he had to get the wheelchair from the trunk.

He returned, "It's time to get this over with."

He turned his legs around, pulled him from behind with both arms around his back, "On three, one, two, and three." with all his strength, he pulled him up and placed him into the chair.

Once inside he pushed him into the living room, walked around and made sure everything was in place, but he needed an idea that would work. He grabbed the remote to the T.V., flipped through the channels, walked around him, "Mugumbi, why don't you make it easy on both of us?"

He turned the wheelchair around, "I know you can hear me." He walked into the kitchen and leaned against the wooden island, grabbed a fruit, peeled it with a knife, cut it in to slices, and stabbed the tip in one of the slices. "I really don't want to put you through this unnecessary pain."

He slid the slice into his mouth, carefully pulled the tip away from his lips.

His cell phone rang, too pissed off to answer, so he hit ignore. The kitchen was dated back several years, the island had a tan ceramic tile, and the dust can be seen floating in the sun light that beamed through the windows. The living room sofa had stains that had been poorly cleaned. The carpet was burgundy shag and the old smell of something peculiar lingered the house, perhaps mold.

He unbuttons his shirt, pulled it from his pants, took it off and neatly placed it on the edge of the sofa.

"Mugumbi, you have one more chance to tell me where the letters are." He punched him in the mouth, and the stomach. He gasped for air but could not respond. His eyes showed no fear, just stared at him.

"You better..." he pointed his finger at him, "...I got something for you!" he stormed out the back door, return with several empty jugs and began to fill them with water.

He walked over to him, yanked the wheelchair around and threw him to the floor. He searched the bedrooms for pillow cases, returned with two and placed them over his head. He grabbed the jugs of water and sat them next to his head. "Don't make me do this!"

He straddled on top of him like a bull rider on a lifeless goat. Held his throat in one hand, and poured water with the other. Mugumbi's tried to fight off the drowning of this induced water. He coughed and gagged for air.

"Are you going to talk?" he poured more and squeezed his throat. "You better start talking mother fucka!"

Mugumbi hyperventilated for air, heart beat lifted his chest as the water choked him. He beat him in the face and held his neck down hard. He finally let him go. "Are you going to start talking?"

He raised up to refill the jugs, pissed as he talked out loud. "You know, why she didn't just give me the damn letters, why?" he slammed his fist into the cabinet, tossed a glass into the corner.

"All she had to do, just reason with me." He walked into the living room, placing the jugs beside him. "But no, she had to threaten me about her father's death. After all I did for her!" He shook his head, "That fuck'n Slut, is that what it came down to. She had the audacity to blackmail me?" he kicked him in the ribs, jumped on top of him, and slowly poured water across his face.

Blood began to show through the pillow case; "You will talk!" he sat the jug down and punched him several times.

He moaned, "Aaaaaah!" the feeling of drowning was devastating.

Na Min's cell phone rang again, for the fourth time in a row, "What the hell!" he rolled off of him, walked into the kitchen, "Hello."

"Hey honey. I have been trying to call you." She was excited to hear his voice.

He sighed and tried to calm himself down, "Hey." his voice was calm as if he was planting flowers in a garden, "How are you enjoying the beach condo?" he lit a cigarette and let out a stream of smoke, took a seat at the island, looked at Mugumbi, bounced his head around to her voice, "Of course..."

He laughed at her happiness, and sighed for his eagerness to get off the damn cell phone. "No, no honey, you didn't call me at a bad time, so what else happen?"

They both laughed at each other's comments, "Oh so soon?" he took another puff from his cigarette, "I was just starting to enjoy our conversation." They both laughed, "Ok honey, see you when you arrive." He bounced his head to her blah blah blah.

"Well I may not be able to pick you up from the airport, so go ahead and arrange for a limo service." He smashed the butt into the ash tray. "Yes I'm sure; just call me to see where I am."

He stood up, looked at Mugumbi, "Of course, love you also." They said their goodbyes and he placed the cell phone on the counter. He rubbed his eyes, realized none of this is working and a new strategy was needed. He walked out on to the back porch and sat on the concrete wall that had protruded stones. The wind blew across his five o'clock shadow, cooled his sweat down his back. It was peaceful, birds flew free, and the stench of farm was in the air. Then it crossed his mind, if he had not told anyone, perhaps no one will ever know if he had just killed him. He sighed, because everything he had worked so hard for; now it could come back to haunt him, losing everything, even jail time.

He noticed a trail of ants that marched through the cracks of the stones, took a long drag from the butt of his cigarette, tossed it and stepped on it with the corner of his right shoe. He entered the kitchen searching for sugar, placed it on the counter. He passed Mugumbi on the way searching for washing detergent. "Yes."

He returned to the kitchen, pulled a bowl, spoon; poured sugar and the detergent in the bowl. He added a little water to paste it; finally he sighed and looked at him as he walked over to him. "Ok, we going outside, so..." He lifted him by his feet, dragged him along the floor, scratching his back as they passed the door. Mugumbi's index slightly grabbed the bottom of the door in an effort to hold on. The medication was wearing off slowly. He was placed on the ant bed, returned with the bowl and smeared it on his face, underneath his shirt and left him.

Na Min walked back into the house, made couple of phone calls, took his luggage from the trunk, bathed, went to the grocery store, cooked, and returned to see him covered with ants. He lit a cigarette and sat on the concrete wall.

The darkness allowed the stars and the moon to shine bright, the city lights in the distance was a reminder of the peace and quiet of living on a farm high up along the mountain side, depending on the wind direction; there was the smell of ocean or bovine ass. He puffed his butt and put it out into the wall beneath him.

He looked out the window to make sure he had not been noticed by anyone. He cooked dinner, dragged Mugumbi back into the house. His face and body was swollen with thousands of little bumps filled with puss.

"Damn !" Na Min almost burned his food, quickly turning the stove off, removing the food from the hot burners, and placed his food on the table, took a sip of his coffee, "Shit!"

He burned his tongue, frowned at the pain, "Wow, that's hot." He sat down and began to eat. He blew to cool his coffee, but an idea came to him, that maybe his tongue had feeling. He took a bite of his veggies, dipped his toast in his coffee. He just could not finish his dinner without knowing if his tongue was still sensitive.

He placed the cup of coffee in the micro wave, set it for two minutes. He carefully walked without spilling it, leaned over him and poured it towards his mouth.

"Ahhhh!" Mugumbi's eyes opened wide, his lips were burned severely.

Na Min's paused to answer his cell phone, "Yes hello." He walked out to the back porch, lit a cigarette, "Ok. No, it should not take that long." He sat down on the wall, "No more than another two days." He inhaled his smoke, and smoothly let it out of his nose, "I love you. I will see you soon." He walked back into the house with a new plan, grabbed his keys, and drove to the store for pliers and other tools that would make him talk. When he returned it was late and decided to get some rest for a long day with a new torturing idea.

The following morning, before the sun pushed the shadows across the hills, the chickens crowed and woke him up with time to think about how he will get him to talk. He sighed and snuggled with his pillow. The breeze shifted the curtain and for a change the smell of the ocean was in the air. He rubbed his eyes, yawned, and forced himself upward. He sat on the edge of the bed with his feet inches from the dusty bamboo hardwood floor. He clapped his hands together, and was ready to get the day started. He peeped into the living room, Mugumbi was on the floor.

He entered the bathroom to brush his teeth, and noticed the toilet seat was down. He continued to brush his tongue, and wondered had he used the bathroom in the middle of the night. He cracked the bones in his neck, looked in the mirror and plucked several nose hairs. He looked around, grabbed his face towel and dropped it into the hot running water. After lathering it with soap he washed his face. He sighed as he looked at himself in the mirror, shook his head. He was disappointed in himself, but felt no shame. He had a sudden urge to piss.

After lifting the toilet seat, he saw defecation that pushed him backwards; fear struck him, his chest pounded. He ran towards the living room, but before he knew it, Mugumbi had hit him in the head with a paper weight, and stood over him, ready to strike him again if needed.

Hours later, the living room was foggy; Na Min bled from his head, and the headache giving him no choice but to close his eyes in hopes that this was a dream. He let out a huge sigh of relief, and thanked God it was a dream. He opened his eyes and Mugumbi sat in front of him eating breakfast, sipping on a fresh cup of hot coffee, added butter to his toast. He ate like he had not ate in days.

Na Min tried to scream through the taped that wrapped his entire head. He tried to free himself from the wheelchair that secured him. Finally, he had realized that this was no dream and now the shoe was on the other foot.

"Mmmmm!" he fought and struggled to break free and almost turning the wheelchair on its side.

Mugumbi pointed his butter knife towards him, shook his head. "You..." he stabbed his sausage and tossed it in his mouth, "...are in a bad situation." He grinned and took his time to chew his food. "I got a question for you, what would you do to change places?"

Na Min's cell phone has been ringing all morning, "Damn it, I bet it's your wife calling again." He chuckled and sipped his hot coffee. "You know, maybe I should kill her fine ass." He waited for a reaction.

Na Min's eyes beamed an evil threat that bounce off of him like water.

Mugumbi pushed the plate away, grabbed Na Min's pack of cigarettes, and lit one. He let the smoke linger from his lips like a blown out candle. He stood, adjusted his hospital gown, walked across the floor bare foot and ass hanging out the back of the gown, "Now, I know you have never been on the other side of where I am going to take you. So it's going to hurt like hell, but under no circumstance will I allow you to die. You see, killing you is what I had in mind, but that's not good enough. However, pain, suffering; now I can be happy with that."

He snatched the tape from around his head, leaned the wheelchair until it hit the floor. He walked into the Kitchen, dumped the trash out of the plastic bag on to the floor. He let the juices drain and most of the maggots follow the juice as he walked back to him. He slowly slipped the bag over his head, knotted it tight enough to remove the air, and held it tight as Na Min struggled to breath.

"Hey! Don't fight this shit..." he had to put his weight on top of his chest to tame him. "Just breath, that's all you have to do!" He smiled, with his face inches away from the bag that fogged with Na Min's last breath.

Mugumbi stood, popped the bones in his neck, looked at the clock, and lit a cigarette. He refreshed his cup with hot coffee, and kept an eye on the clock. He walked over to the bay window and sat on the cushion, sipped, and puffed.

After smashing his butt in to the wall, sipped a good amount of coffee, he walked over to him with a close eye on the clock. "Now." He began performing CPR, tilted his head back, pinched his nose, and blew several strong breaths into his lungs, "Come on buddy! You bet not die on me now..." he pressed several times on his chest, hard enough to hear the bones crack, pinched his nose and blew. After five minutes, Na Min gasped for air like he had been under water.

Mugumbi smiled, "And you are back motherfucka!" he stood above him and walked around the living room, "Fuck! I thought you weren't coming back!" he went over and kicked him in the ribs. He grabbed the plastic bag and repeated it.

Six hours later, he was exhausted, sweaty, and on the floor next to him, breathing hard, it was getting harder to revive him and the damage to his brain from the lack of oxygen must be done by now. He rolled over to his knees, with his face in his palms, crying with the satisfaction that he could never harm another soul. He cried because no matter what, Yuki is gone and nothing can bring her back.

He pushed his hands through his over grown hair and beard, wiped his tears and forced himself to his feet. The cell phone on the table began to ring and he knew people would start to look for him.

He removed Na Min's clothes, tossed the hospital gown on the floor, stumbled on to the porch, lit a cigarette, and vanished in to hill side until he was able to get somewhere safe.

*   *   *

Honolulu, Hawaii 3am

Bennett was awaken with the ringing of his cell phone, unhappy about it, but quickly reached to see who the heck was calling. He slithered out of bed, trying not to wake up his wife, with a low voice as he entered the living room, "Hello."

The voice on the line put a smile on his face, "Hey man what have you been up to?"

He sounded stressed; the excitement from Bennett slowly came to a halt when he found out that Kalargo had plans on returning to the Pacific.

"Are you serious? You have been searching for your father for years and now you want to just give up? You are or will be King of your own Kingdom." Nothing seemed to convince him to stay.

Bennett walked out on to his backyard patio, heartbroken to know that his friend was unhappy with his situation. He wanted to see him succeed as King, but the voice on the line, doesn't sound like his pal. The sound of an emotional, confused, man that needed his hand held, a side of him that had never been seen.

"Listen, I don't want to leave my dad. It's just too much to handle, I don't know if I'm up to the task. Then the rebels are these Jihadi religous fanatics that want to convert everyone to their beliefs." He paused, took a breath as he rubbed his son on the head. "I don't know if I want my son to grow up in this mess." He walked over to the office window, and wondered if it really can be done.

"Kalargo, are you serious?" Bennette sat in the patio chair, "I can't believe..." he was interrupted.

"Well I am not ready to be King. Trust me this place in deep shambles, from war and poverty, not like I need the money. I have money. My son is going to have to endure these problems that I would have had to face. It's just not a place you want to be." He walked over to the door, cracked it open to make sure no one was listening to his conversation.

"Then again, I really don't want to leave my father. He has grown to love Largo, that's what he calls him. So I have already made plans to escape without anyone knowing. It would devastate my father if he knew. But I will call you once we are safe and out of Africa." They agreed and the line ended.

Kalargo paced the floor, breathing hard, thinking about his decision that may alter the future of not only him, but Largo's also. He pulled out the box of pictures of his mom, and relatives. One by one, he stared at them and shook his head. He sighed, covered his mouth, just could not understand why he felt this way, but knowing that Largo is safe and would not have to go through what he had been through gave him comfort. He pinched the bridge of his nose with his thumb and index; "Wow..." he leaned onto the desk. His nerves bothered him, giving him this sick feeling to his stomach. He looked at Largo as he crawled on the rug. He picked him up and sat him on top of the boat schematics, raised his arms, "...we are going home, where we belong."

He noticed that his bottle was loose and dripping goat milk that spilled onto the drawings. He pushed and wiped it dry, leaving a wet spot. He pushed it further to the corner of the desk.

"There you go." He twisted it tight and put it in his hands. He looked at his watch; it was five minutes till two in the morning. He walked over to the window, watching the perimeter soldiers for the right time, even though he was not leaving until the next morning, but had to plan this carefully. He knew the window of opportunity was between two and three in the morning. He inhaled and sighed, the glass on the French door fogged for a moment, and satisfied with his decision; he prepared Largo for bed, and tried to get a good night sleep.

He tossed and turned throughout the night, the sick feeling in his stomach made him not want to leave his father, to die alone, heartbroken; knowing no family was around would kill him faster than age. He covered his face with his pillow, rubbed his stomach. It had to be something he ate. He quickly ran to the bathroom.

Moments later, not feeling any better, but relieved to see the sun rise and give life to a new day. He grabbed his bed sheet, wrapped himself from the chills, stood at his window and watched the shadows glide across the lawn.

He could smell the breakfast being prepared, feeling hungry from not eating made him desire something just to help get pass his nervous anticipation of what was to come.

The sound of his father's oxygen tank in the hallway alerted him, then a knock at his door.

"Kalargo." He twisted the knob, peaked in, "There you are." He was looking for his grandson, with a smile he walked over to him, "I've been looking all over for you."

"Good morning." He folded the sheet and placed it on the edge of the bed, slid into a pair of blue denim jeans, and quickly pushed his back pack further under the bed so it wouldn't raise questions about an unplanned travel trip.

"Good morning to you." He picked Largo up and made him smile with baby talk. "Are you coming down for breakfast?" The King asked.

"Of course, I think I gain weight since I've been here. I was thinking of having them revise the meals for something healthier." Kalargo pushed his toes into his shoes, sat on the bed and tied them. As he entered the bathroom, "What are they having for breakfast?" he leaned over the sink, not feeling so well but had to push himself. "Father, why are you still in your pajamas?" he began brushing his teeth.

"Man." he placed Largo on his shoulder, "Oh my, you are getting so big." He walked over to the door of the bathroom, "What I wake up in, is what I eat in, I keep telling you, get my age and you will see." He giggled and bounce Largo around, "Are you hungry? We get food, yeah you hungry too?"

Kalargo exited the bathroom, "Now I'm ready." He took Largo from him so he could pull his tank. But he refused.

"No, I got him, pull my tank and I'll carry him." He kissed him on his chubby cheeks.

"Are you sure, he's getting heavier. And you know how your balance is these days." Kalargo reached for him.

He tilted his head, with a crimpled smile that couldn't harm a kitten, "You pull my tank with your right hand, place your left arm around my shoulder to hold me up as we walk and hold the mask in the left hand in case I need it. I don't care if it takes four days to get there." He pushed his chest out like a proud pigeon. "I'm ready when you are." He looked at him.

"Ok, let me see..." he positioned the tank, placed his left arm around them both, and hung the mask from his collar for quick access.

Later that evening, Kalargo packed food and bottles of water for his escape, time slowly ticked away as he helped his father around with Largo. He looked at his watch, realizing that his bath water was being prepared by the servants. Not long after he would be jumping high fences, ducking branches, and hoping Largo don't make a sound. The thought of him crying had just hit him, with his face in his hands, stressed on the idea.

He snapped his fingers, clapped his hands with a great idea. He quickly went into his fathers' bathroom, took the bottle of Nyquil and slid it into his pocket. Even though it would not take much to put Largo to sleep, it was enough to last the entire trip if he needed more. His heart was racing like mustangs under pounding rain, and thunderous bangs; any and everything began to startle him.

He sighed, looked in the mirror, "I can do this." He swallowed the pain and heart ache that his father would yearn. He walked out of the bathroom; Largo was being caress like a mother loves their new born, Eskimo kisses that made Kalargo shed a tear. He wiped his eyes with his shoulder and felt horrible. The King felt a bond between them that was more protective than a lioness felt for her cubs.

There was a soft knock on the door, letting them know it was time for his bath. Deep down inside he was devastated that this may very well be the last time he hold Largo, but he could not say anything, "Well Largo, its bed time." The old man slowly let Kalargo remove him from his embrace, turned away as if he knew he would see him tomorrow.

"See you guys in the morning." The servants walked along side him, pulling his tank for him as they headed to the bathing station.

Kalargo cried in his room, hated his plan but equally ready to implement it. He looked at his wrist watch, "Oh my God." He was getting nervous, wiping his tears, holding his abdomen. He knew in three hours, it would be now or never situation. He placed Largo in bed with him, closed his eyes and rocked himself to sleep.

The sound of his alarm on his wrist watched chirped. He was startled, thinking he had over slept. He had one hour until his journey will start. He grabbed several items, placed them in his back pack, "Damn, before I forget."

He twisted the cap on the Nyquil, poured just enough in his mouth for a child. The strawberry flavor made it easy, and it did not take long to go into effect. He dressed himself in all black, wrapped Largo to his chest, lowered the knotted sheets down from his balcony and carefully, one knot at a time, down he went into the garden below. He sighed and began to make his way across the lawn, climbed a tree, jumped over a fence, and made his way across a field that led to a dirt road behind the Palace.

He reached the paved road and hiked alongside a creek until he felt safe enough to walk the road. Out of nowhere a small fuel truck had just missed him, "Damn idiot!"

The truck raced on, as the dust left him coughing and waving the air. After five minutes, the sound of gun fire irrupted, then a huge explosion that pushed a fire ball that lit the morning sky. He fell to his knees, looking over his shoulder and knowing that it was the Palace. He quickly ran up the road, the sound of people screaming grew louder, the particles fell from the sky; it was confirmed, the Palace had been attacked. He could not believe it.

"No!" He ran as fast as he could, the chaotic mess and destruction that spared few , watered his eyes. He saw that the fuel truck that had passed him was blown to pieces. The sound of fire trucks were in the distance.

"No!" he was speechless, breathing hard; the east wing of the Palace had collapsed. He ran towards it in search for his father, security, and servants that had survived frantically dug through the rubble for him.

Then a voice screamed, "Oh my Lord!" all heads turned in that direction. "We found him!" he was badly hurt, wedged between fallen concrete, bleeding, and dying.

"Father!" he grabbed his right hand, "We are going to get you out of there!"

More people came, tossing blocks of concrete, pushing as hard they could. "Hang in there!"

The King knew he was dying, and felt it was his time to go. He held his hand and asked for Largo. He rubbed his face, coughed up a lot of blood, "I love you guys, but this is how I am going." He can barely say the words; tears fell from his eyes as he struggled to tell him something. Kalargo leaned in closer to his lips.

"The sail boats..." he turned away and tried harder to tell him what he had discovered when he was in his office looking at the drawings, "...they are not sail boats. They are building under water crafts." He gripped his hand tight, "They look like sail boats, and they will attack from the sea..." he coughed. "...be a great King. It's your turn." He said with his last breath, Kalargo shook him.

"Help!" he screamed so loud, waking Largo, the crowd knew that the King had died. People cried like they had lost one of their parents. It was a terrible day in The Gambia.

He yelped this horrible cry for him to come back, resting his head on his chest, gripping his hands together, "Please!" He felt alone and devastated. He stood and turned around to come off of the mound of destruction. The soldiers, servants, people who came to help, one by one dropped to one knee with their heads down in respect for the new King. He was not alone, because he now had the entire country behind him.

The following morning, King Kalargo sobbed into his pillow, couldn't believe his father was dead and now the situation had changed to the worse. He did not want to open his eyes to face reality, wishing he could just vanish into thin air. He cried until he realized his cell phone vibrated. He reached down the side of the bed, looked at the caller id, "Wow." He had ten missed calls. No mood to answer it, but it rung again, "Hello."

"Oh my God! Thank God you are alive!" Na Min was happy to hear his voice. "I heard about the attack on the Palace, so sorry for your loss." His voice sounded like he struggled to speak well, but forced his words.

Kalargo sobbed more, "I can't believe he is gone. Not like this, this is..." he wiped his face, "...this is the worst day of my life!"

"Just calm down, you can do this, I know you can..." before he could say another word.

"But I don't want to… I just want to go home."

"Well…" Na Min looked up at Zang, "…that may not be a good idea."

Zang slowly slid the barrel of his .45 caliber down the side of Na Min's sweaty face. He pulled the hammer back just before he spoke.

"…I need you to listen to me." Na Min said under the gun.

"This is all too much, now all these people are looking for me to lead this country…" Kalargo said.

"And yes, you can, and you will do a great job. All you need is a little help…" Na Min said.

Zang tapped the gun on his forehead with a horrible smile.

"Find out everything you can about the rebels, how many are there? I am going to check on some things from my end, and get you some type of help." Na Min assured him.

"Like NATO…" Kalargo got excited, "Like the Americans?"

"Well let me work my magic, but I don't have much time but hang in there." They said their goodbyes.

"Not bad Na Min." Zang walked around him with his left hand on his shoulder. He sat in the wheelchair with only his boxers, scared. He looked around at the four other North Koreans with black hoods on. He looked up at the IV bag that hung from above his head; it led to his left arm, wrapped with medical tape that allowed it to flow into his vein. "You know, we are looking for Mugumbi. He spoiled our plan that we had in place." Zang said.

"When I get my hands on him…" he changed his mind, "…you know what; I'll introduce him to our program." He pulled out a cigarette, licked the butt and lit it. "You see we have this, program in North Korea and I think he would fit just fine." He smiled, let out a huge cloud of smoke.

"So what happens to Kalargo?" Na Min asked.

"Right now, that all depends on if he cooperates…" before he could finish.

"Just let me work something out…" he tried to stand. Zang assisted him, handed him a pair of pants and shirt. "My boy will come through with flying colors."

"Well I hope so; so far he doesn't sound like it…" He helped him button up his shirt, "You on the other hand, has a lot of work to do." Zang said.

Na Min was taken to the Manila International airport. Zang raised his hands to his ear, indicating to call him.

Na Min barely able to walk, nodded his head and waved good bye.

The End

I want to thank all of you for taking the time to read my first novel. All reviews can be added to Amazon.com and you can email me to be added to my email list for the sequel to NOSTALGIC BLOOD and the next set of books.

Marketmonsterpublishing@gmail.com

Books to look forward to:

"Nostalgic Blood 2" The inherited Kingdom
"Fairway Mistress"
"What Have We Done?"
"Market Monster Analytics" How to minimize your losses.

nostalgicsociety.com

CPSIA information can be obtained
at www.ICGtesting.com
Printed in the USA
FSOW01n0834021117
40668FS